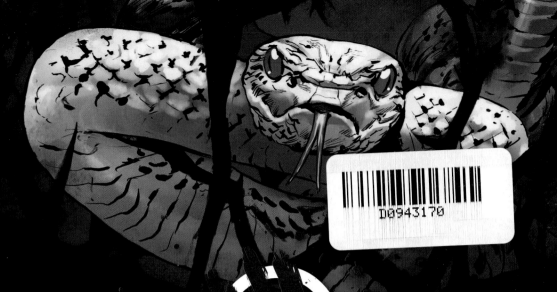

ANIMOSITY™

VOLUME

SOUTHERN GOTHIC

MARGUERITE BENNETT

RAFAEL DE LATORRE

ELTON THOMASI

ROB SCHWAGER

MARCO LESKO

TAYLOR ESPOSITO

MARSHALL DILLON

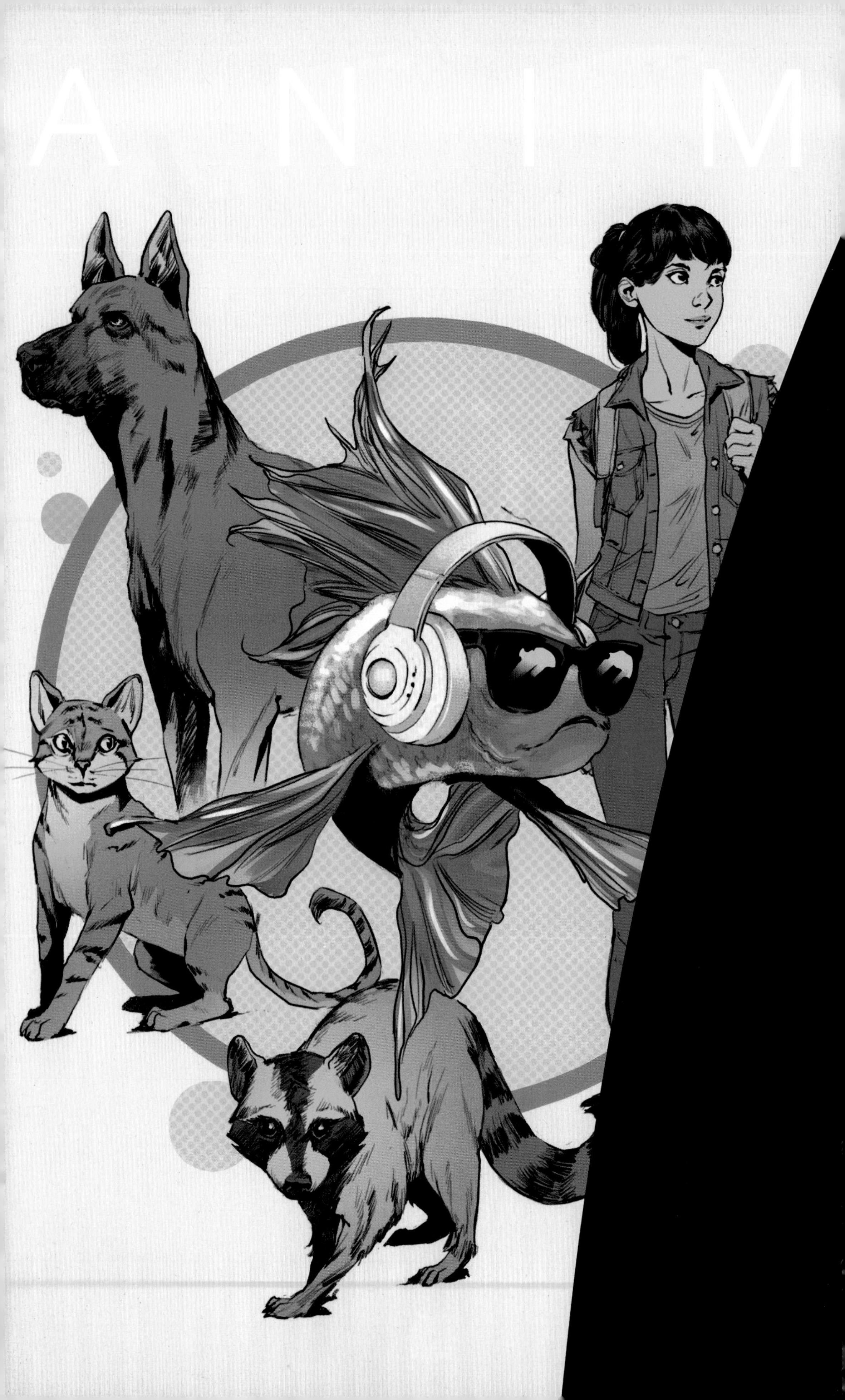
A N I M

OSITY
VOLUME 5
SOUTHERN GOTHIC

MARGUERITE BENNETT creator & writer

RAFAEL DE LATORRE & **ELTON THOMASI** artists

ROB SCHWAGER colorist

MARCO LESKO colorist ANIMOSITY TALES

MARSHALL DILLON, TAYLOR ESPOSITO & **CARLOS M. MANGUAL** letterers

RAFAEL DE LATORRE w/ **MARCELO MAIOLO** front & original series covers

JOHN J. HILL logo designer

COREY BREEN book designer

MIKE MARTS editor

AFTERSHOCK™

MIKE MARTS - Editor-in-Chief • **JOE PRUETT** - Publisher/CCO • **LEE KRAMER** - President • **JON KRAMER** - Chief Executive Officer
STEVE ROTTERDAM - SVP, Sales & Marketing • **DAN SHIRES** - VP, Film & Television UK • **CHRISTINA HARRINGTON** - Managing Editor
MARC HAMMOND - Sr. Retail Sales Development Manager • **RUTHANN THOMPSON** - Sr. Retailer Relations Manager • **KATHERINE JAMISON** - Marketing Manager
BLAKE STOCKER - Director of Finance • **AARON MARION** - Publicist • **LISA MOODY** - Finance • **RYAN CARROLL** - Development Coordinator
JAWAD QURESHI - Technology Advisor/Strategist • **CHARLES PRITCHETT** - Comics Production • **COREY BREEN** - Collections Production
TEDDY LEO - Editorial Assistant • **STEPHANIE CASEBIER** & **SARAH PRUETT** - Publishing Assistants

AfterShock Logo Design by **COMICRAFT**
Publicity: contact **AARON MARION** (aaron@publichausagency.com) & **RYAN CROY** (ryan@publichausagency.com) at **PUBLICHAUS**
Special thanks to: **IRA KURGAN, MARINE KSADZHIKYAN, ANTONIA LIANOS** & **STEPHAN NILSON**

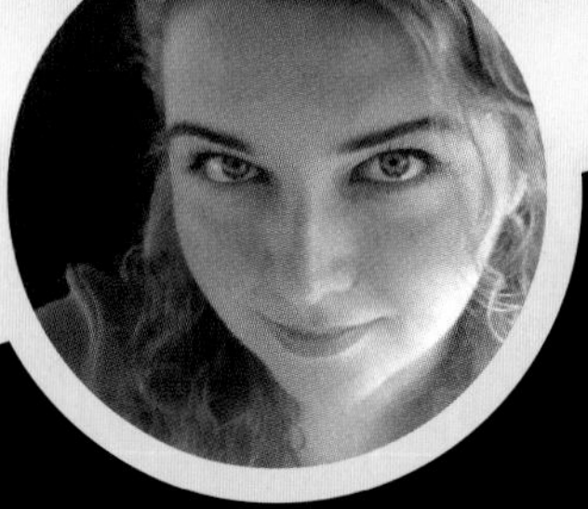

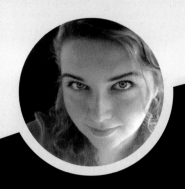

I N T R O D U C T I O N

When did you know you were no longer a child?

Many young animals will remain in their mothers' care for some time. Hairless, blind, horrifying joeys crawl into their mother's pouch and nurse until they transform into the adorable bastards with which we are familiar. Arowanas, slender and knifelike, cradle their fry in their trapdoor mouths, and opossums ferry their brood on their backs. Canid puppies and hatchling birds gorge on the nutrients regurgitated by their mothers and fathers, penguins huddle in the shelter of their parents' wings for months on end, and elephants nurse for six years. Others, like hammerhead sharks, are viviparious, and the pups are on their own from the moment they are born.

As the days and nights go by, the animals begin to change. Fawns lose their spots, and emus and tapirs and wild piglets their stripes. Arthropods molt their carapaces, and snakes shed their skins, growing bigger, larger, stronger with each transformation. Milk fades for meat, or grass, or nectar, or krill. Caterpillars completely dissolve inside of their cocoons and are rewritten from the ground up as moths and butterflies. Flamingos turn pink, and eaglets turn brown. Hormones flux. Hair thickens, feathers sprout, plates meld, organs develop. Scars form.

And when it is time to go, what then?

Surinam toad tadpoles will burrow from the perforated flesh of their mother's back. Matriphagous spiderlings eat their mothers from the inside out. Harp seal pups, abandoned soon after birth, slowly learn to swim, as songbird chicks pushed from their nests learn to fly. Male mammals often exit the pride, or pack, or herd, and seek territory and mates of their own. Females may be gobbled up into the hierarchy of a male, or else form matriarchal families and court or ignore as suits them. Lions who will not leave their father's pride must be driven out, or kill their father to claim his place.

Some parents become rivals to their children. Some parents give their lives for them.

Predators learn to hunt. Prey learn to escape. We all learn to survive—or we don't, and there our story ends. The world goes on, filled with life and death and birth again, and others come after us as we came after those who went before us.

I ask again:

When did you know you were no longer a child?

MARGUERITE BENNETT
December 2019

19

THE MASTER'S HOUSE

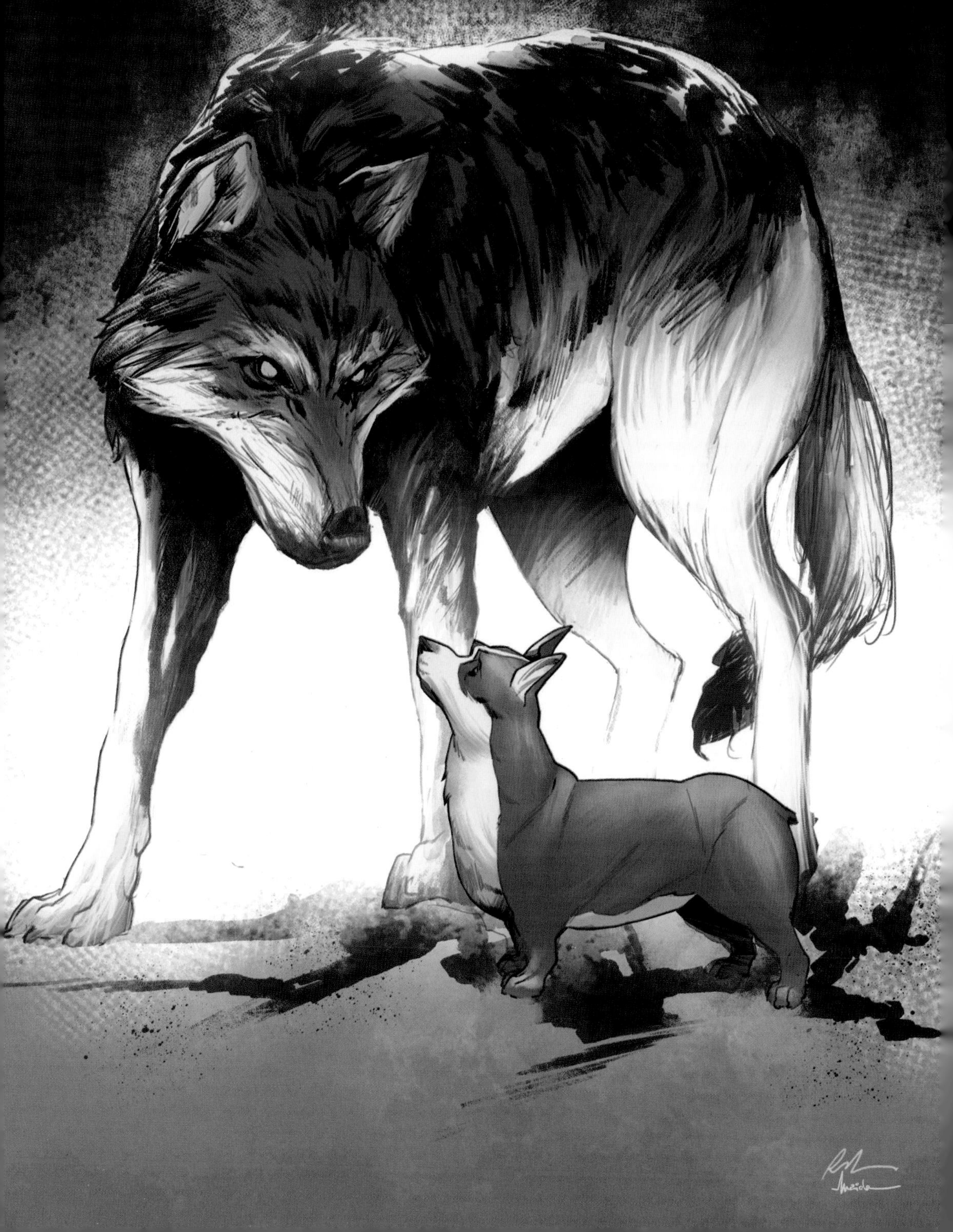

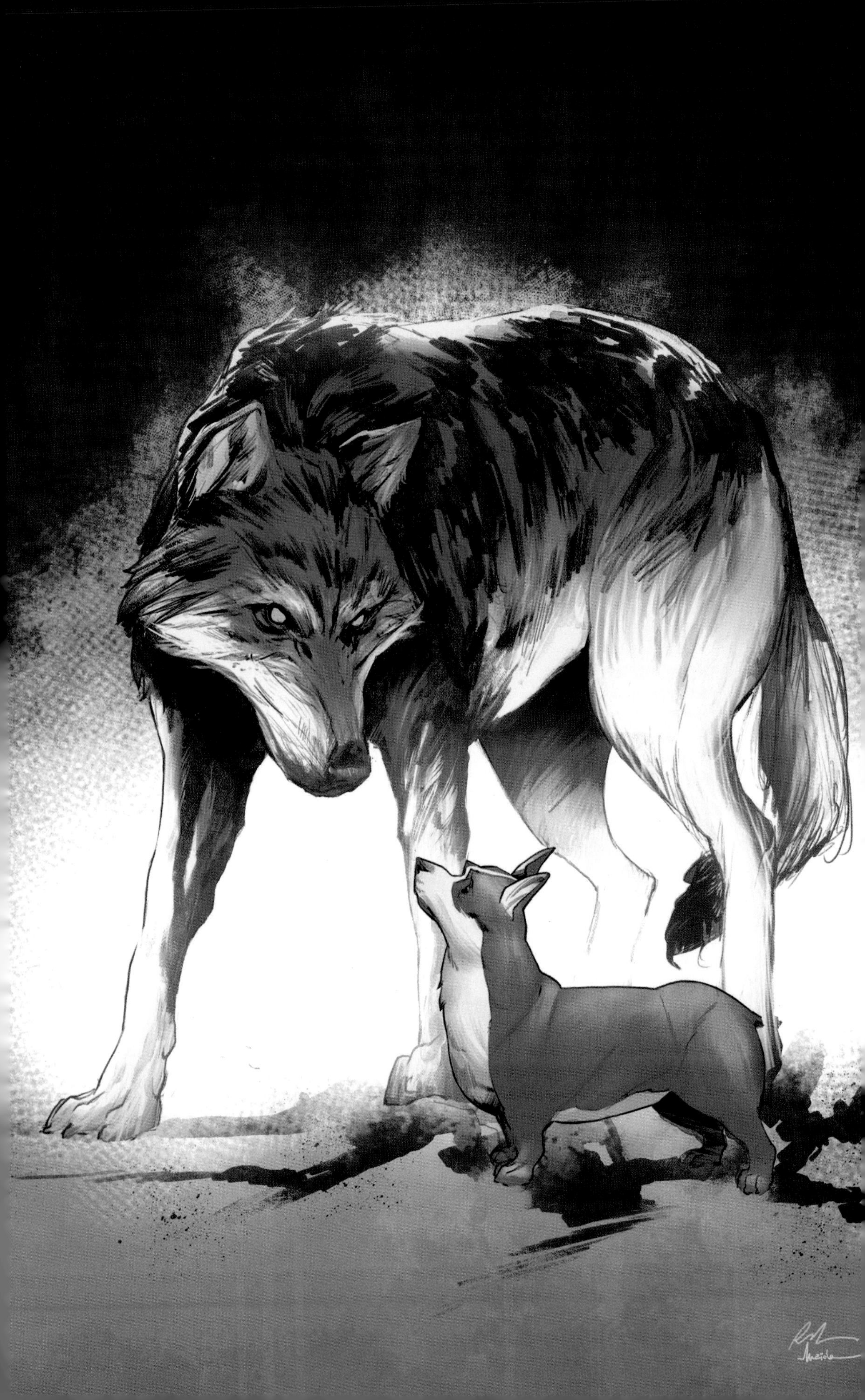

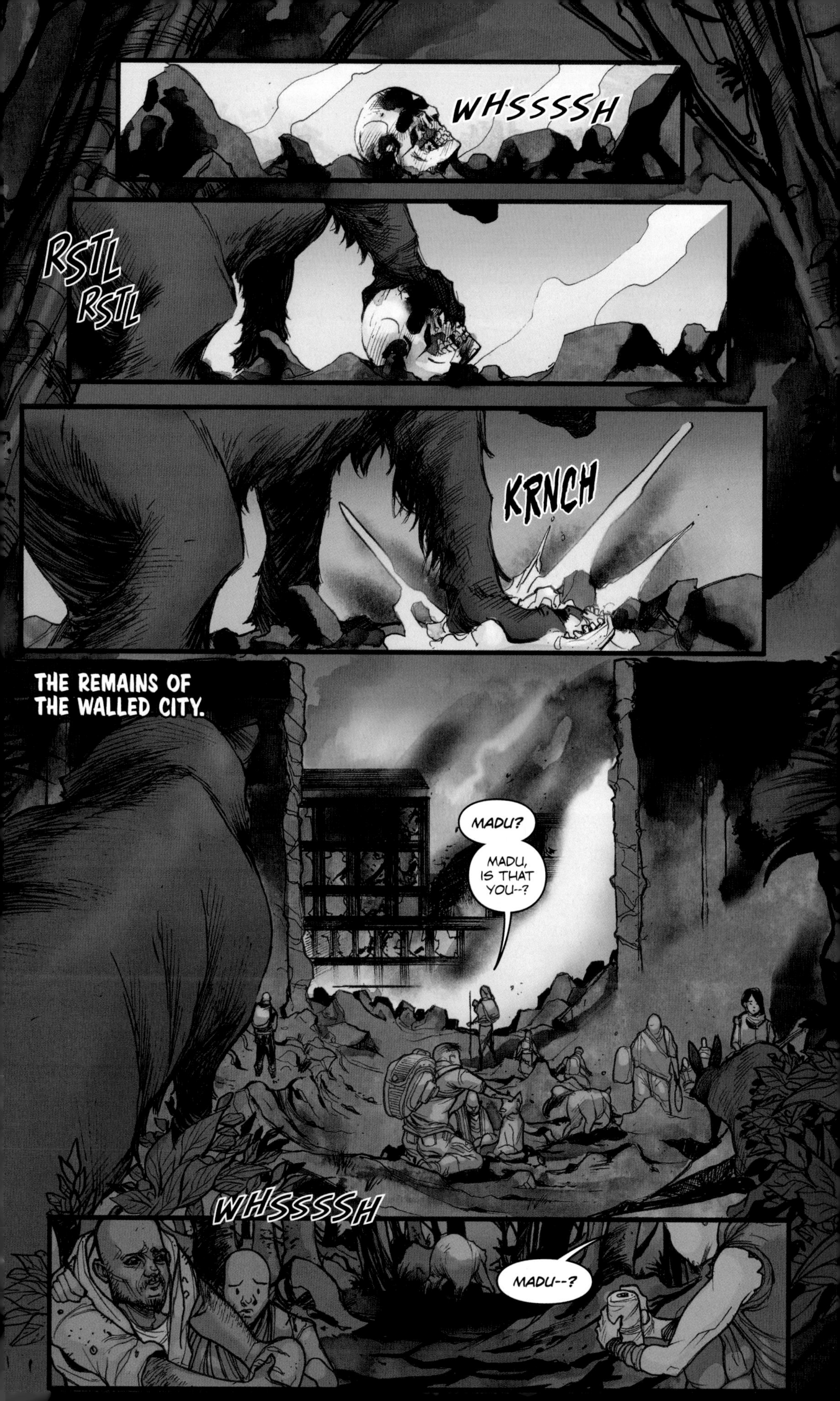
WHSSSSH
RSTL RSTL
KRNCH
THE REMAINS OF THE WALLED CITY.
MADU?
MADU, IS THAT YOU--?
WHSSSSH
MADU--?

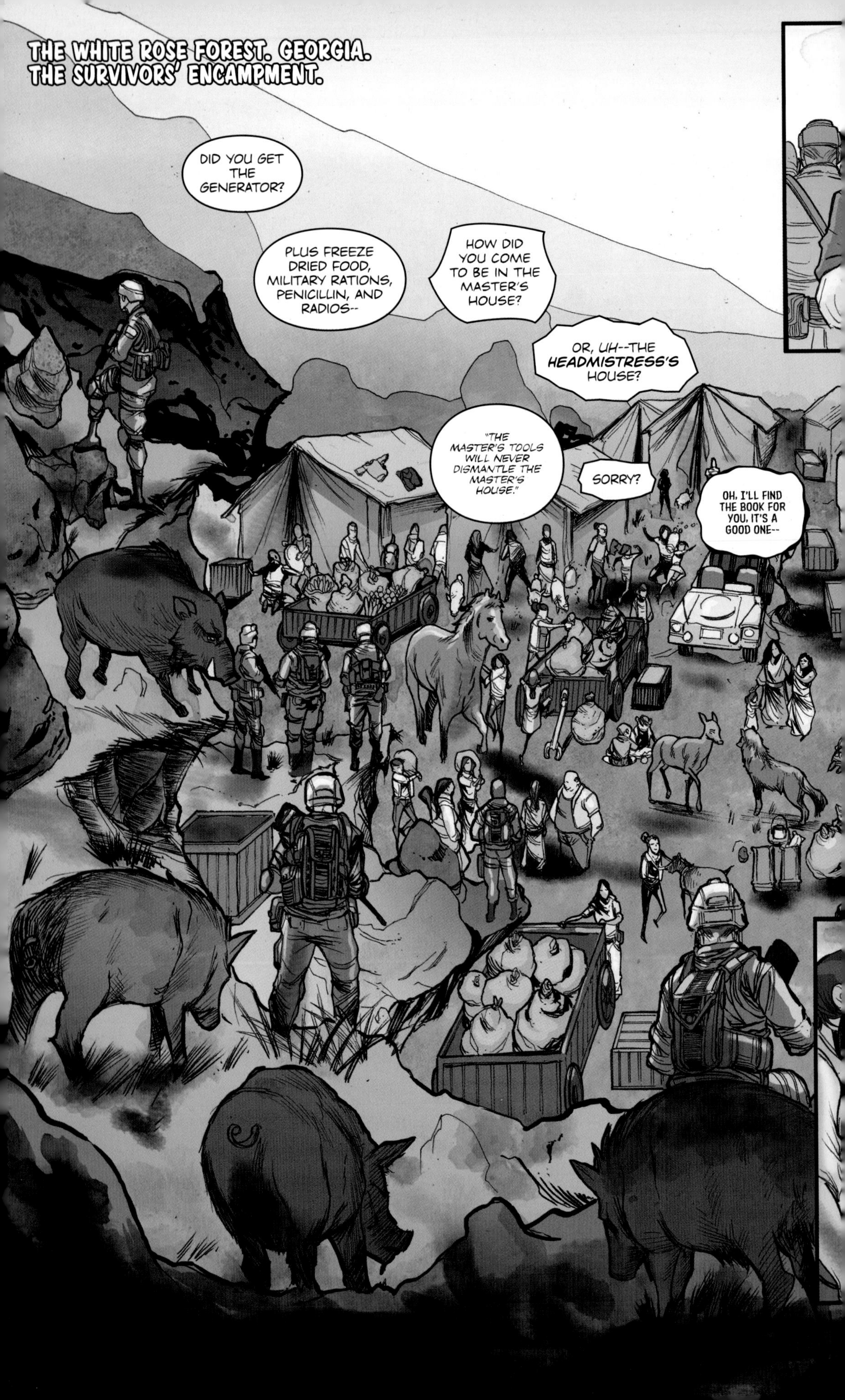
THE WHITE ROSE FOREST. GEORGIA.
THE SURVIVORS' ENCAMPMENT.
DID YOU GET THE GENERATOR?
PLUS FREEZE DRIED FOOD, MILITARY RATIONS, PENICILLIN, AND RADIOS--
HOW DID YOU COME TO BE IN THE MASTER'S HOUSE?
OR, UH--THE HEADMISTRESS'S HOUSE?
"THE MASTER'S TOOLS WILL NEVER DISMANTLE THE MASTER'S HOUSE."
SORRY?
OH, I'LL FIND THE BOOK FOR YOU, IT'S A GOOD ONE--

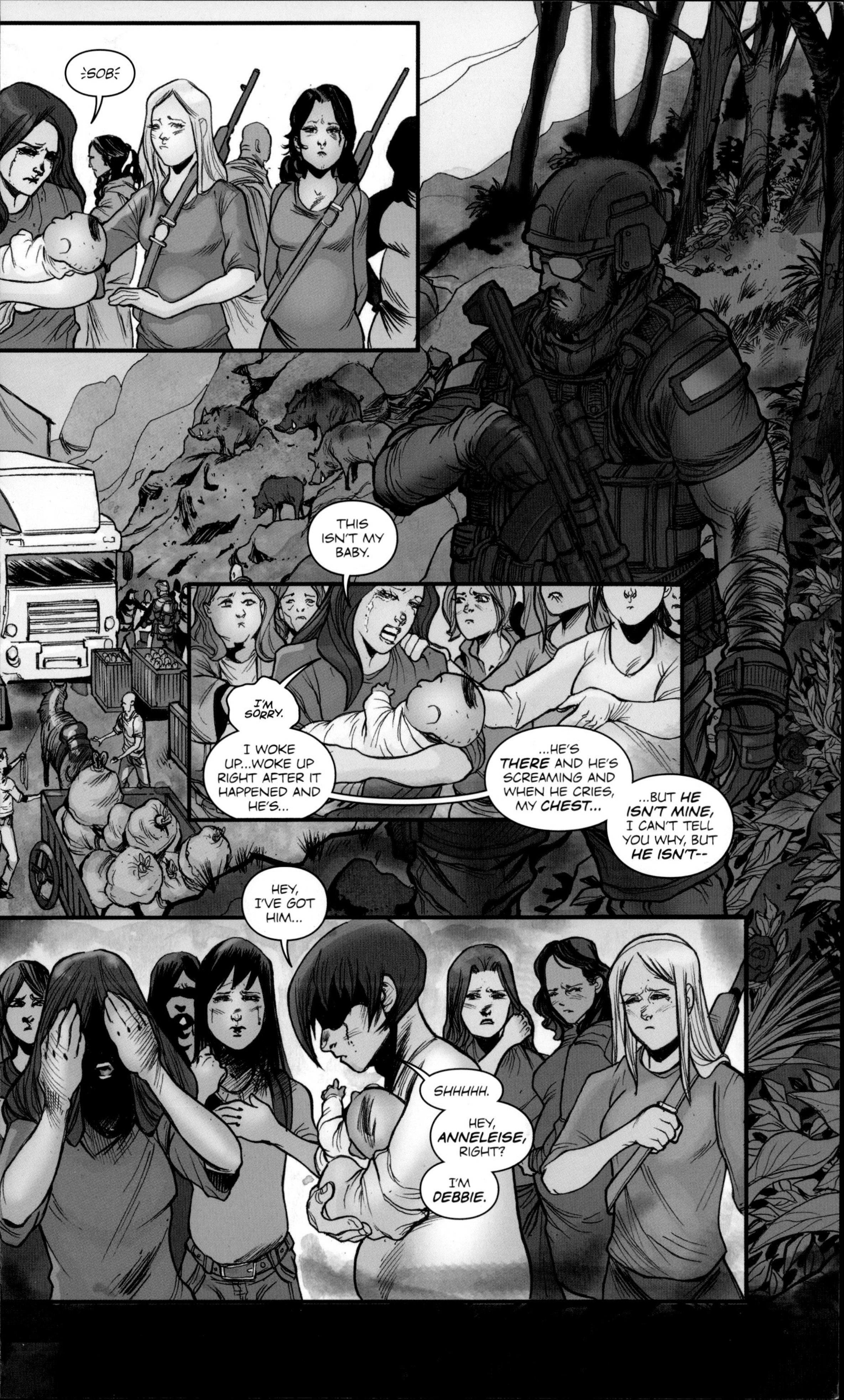

SOB
THIS ISN'T MY BABY.
I'M SORRY.
I WOKE UP...WOKE UP RIGHT AFTER IT HAPPENED AND HE'S...
...HE'S THERE AND HE'S SCREAMING AND WHEN HE CRIES, MY CHEST...
...BUT HE ISN'T MINE, I CAN'T TELL YOU WHY, BUT HE ISN'T--
HEY, I'VE GOT HIM...
SHHHHH.
HEY, ANNELEISE, RIGHT?
I'M DEBBIE.

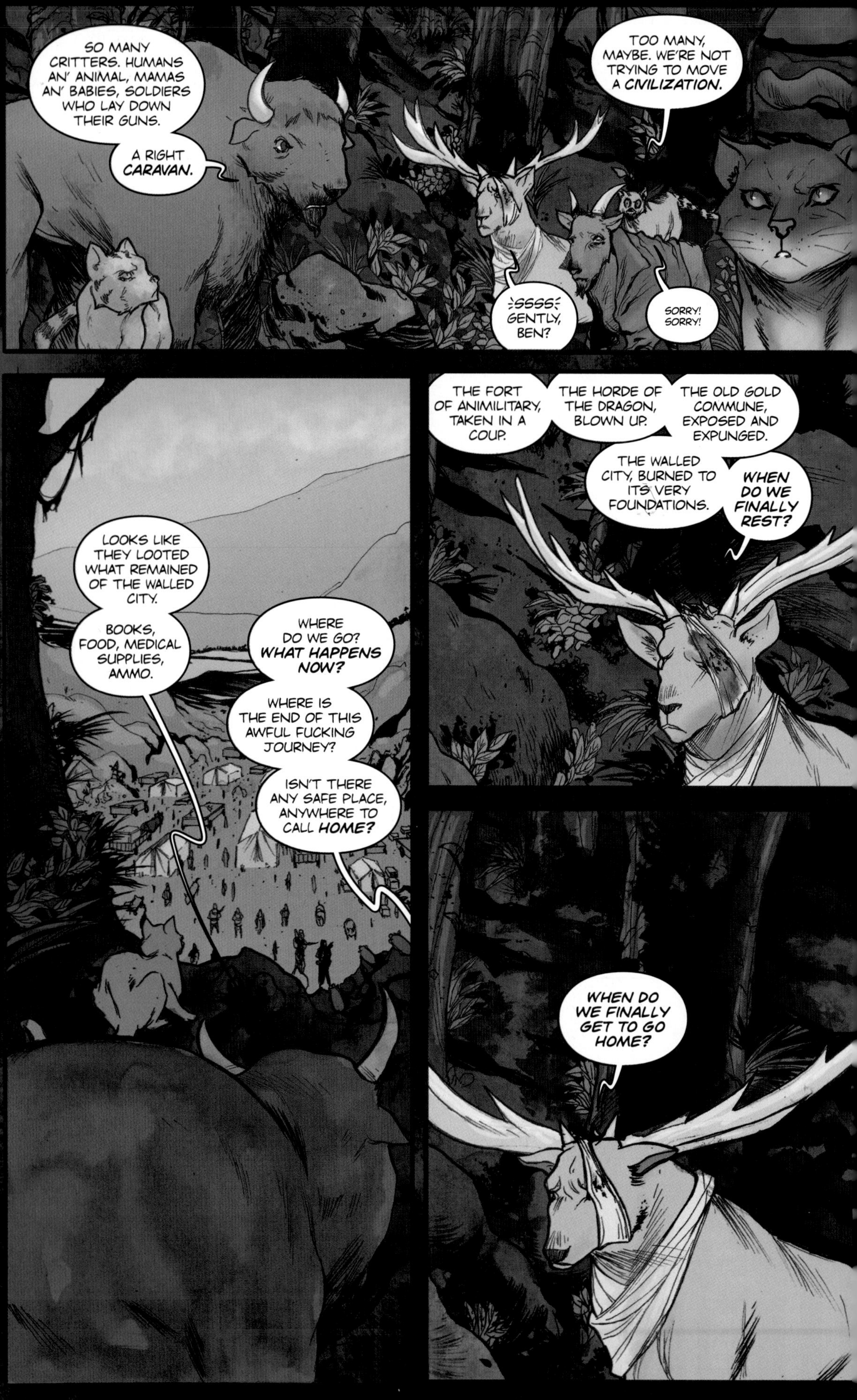
SO MANY CRITTERS. HUMANS AN' ANIMAL, MAMAS AN' BABIES, SOLDIERS WHO LAY DOWN THEIR GUNS.
A RIGHT CARAVAN.
TOO MANY, MAYBE. WE'RE NOT TRYING TO MOVE A CIVILIZATION.
SSSS GENTLY, BEN?
SORRY! SORRY!
LOOKS LIKE THEY LOOTED WHAT REMAINED OF THE WALLED CITY.
BOOKS, FOOD, MEDICAL SUPPLIES, AMMO.
WHERE DO WE GO? WHAT HAPPENS NOW?
WHERE IS THE END OF THIS AWFUL FUCKING JOURNEY?
ISN'T THERE ANY SAFE PLACE, ANYWHERE TO CALL HOME?
THE FORT OF ANIMILITARY, TAKEN IN A COUP.
THE HORDE OF THE DRAGON, BLOWN UP.
THE OLD GOLD COMMUNE, EXPOSED AND EXPUNGED.
THE WALLED CITY, BURNED TO ITS VERY FOUNDATIONS.
WHEN DO WE FINALLY REST?
WHEN DO WE FINALLY GET TO GO HOME?

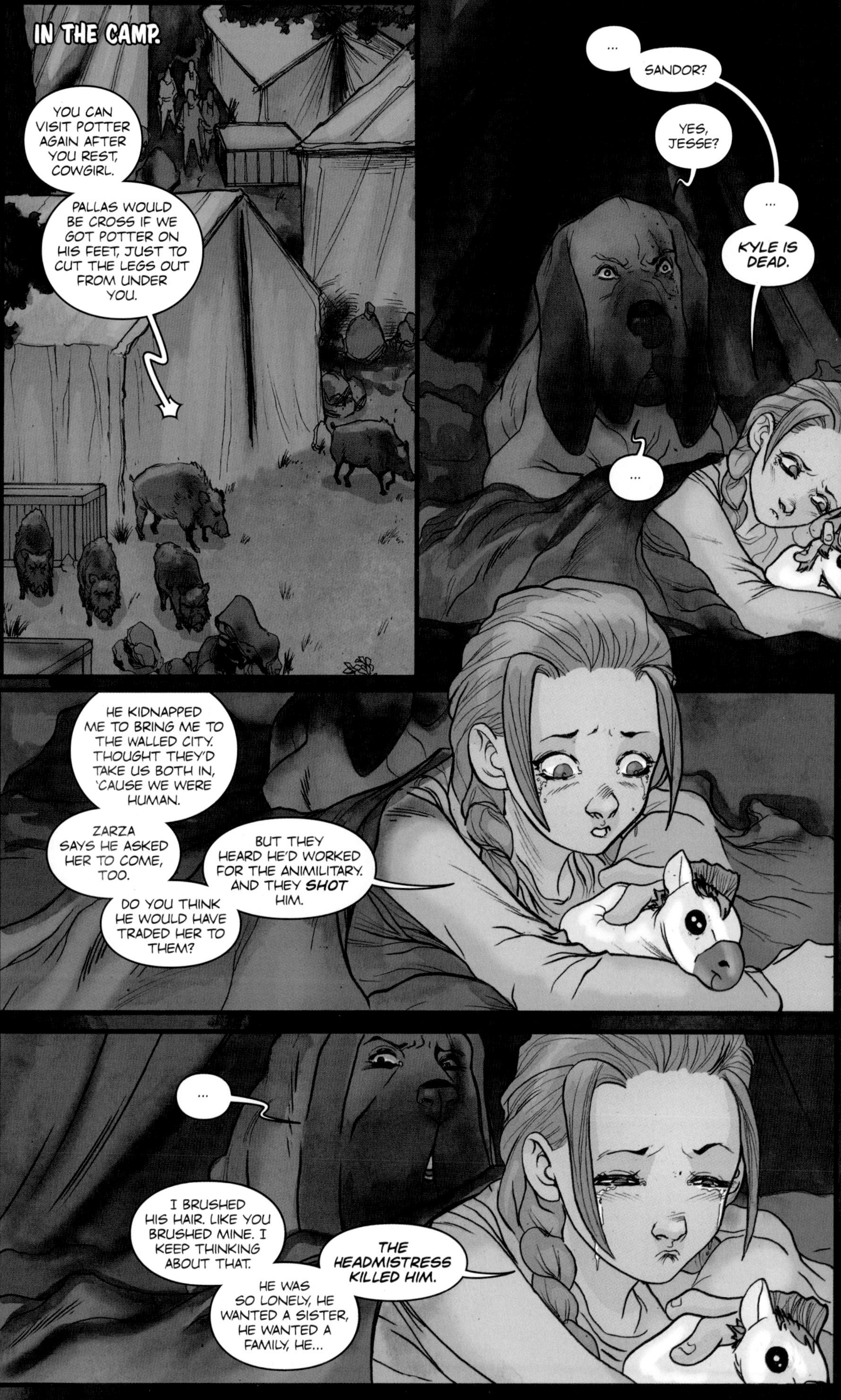
IN THE CAMP.
YOU CAN VISIT POTTER AGAIN AFTER YOU REST, COWGIRL.
PALLAS WOULD BE CROSS IF WE GOT POTTER ON HIS FEET, JUST TO CUT THE LEGS OUT FROM UNDER YOU.
...
SANDOR?
YES, JESSE?
...
KYLE IS DEAD.
...
HE KIDNAPPED ME TO BRING ME TO THE WALLED CITY. THOUGHT THEY'D TAKE US BOTH IN, 'CAUSE WE WERE HUMAN.
BUT THEY HEARD HE'D WORKED FOR THE ANIMILITARY. AND THEY SHOT HIM.
ZARZA SAYS HE ASKED HER TO COME, TOO.
DO YOU THINK HE WOULD HAVE TRADED HER TO THEM?
...
THE HEADMISTRESS KILLED HIM.
I BRUSHED HIS HAIR. LIKE YOU BRUSHED MINE. I KEEP THINKING ABOUT THAT.
HE WAS SO LONELY, HE WANTED A SISTER, HE WANTED A FAMILY, HE...

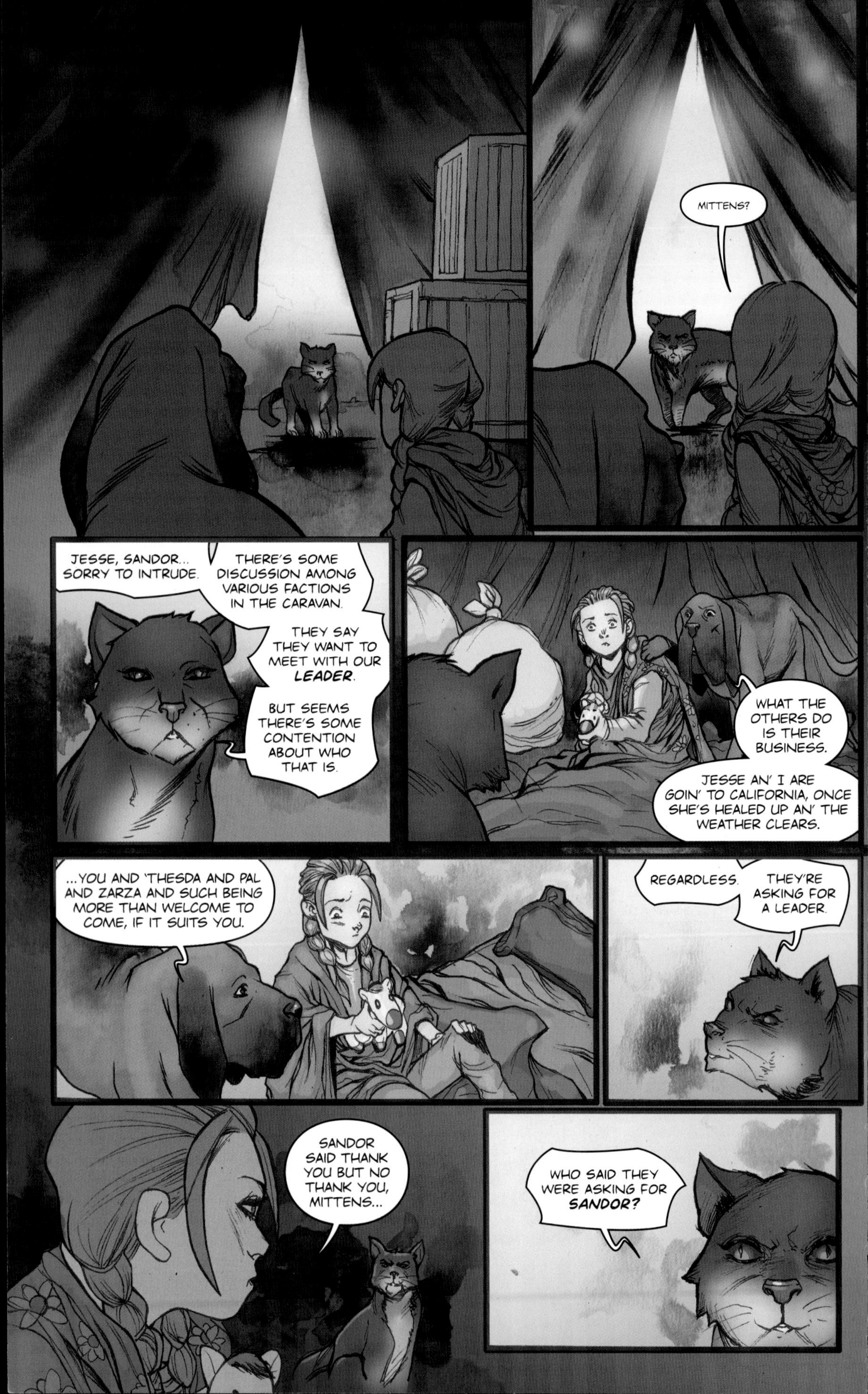
MITTENS?
JESSE, SANDOR... SORRY TO INTRUDE.
THERE'S SOME DISCUSSION AMONG VARIOUS FACTIONS IN THE CARAVAN.
THEY SAY THEY WANT TO MEET WITH OUR LEADER.
BUT SEEMS THERE'S SOME CONTENTION ABOUT WHO THAT IS.
WHAT THE OTHERS DO IS THEIR BUSINESS.
JESSE AN' I ARE GOIN' TO CALIFORNIA, ONCE SHE'S HEALED UP AN' THE WEATHER CLEARS.
...YOU AND 'THESDA AND PAL AND ZARZA AND SUCH BEING MORE THAN WELCOME TO COME, IF IT SUITS YOU.
REGARDLESS.
THEY'RE ASKING FOR A LEADER.
SANDOR SAID THANK YOU BUT NO THANK YOU, MITTENS...
WHO SAID THEY WERE ASKING FOR SANDOR?

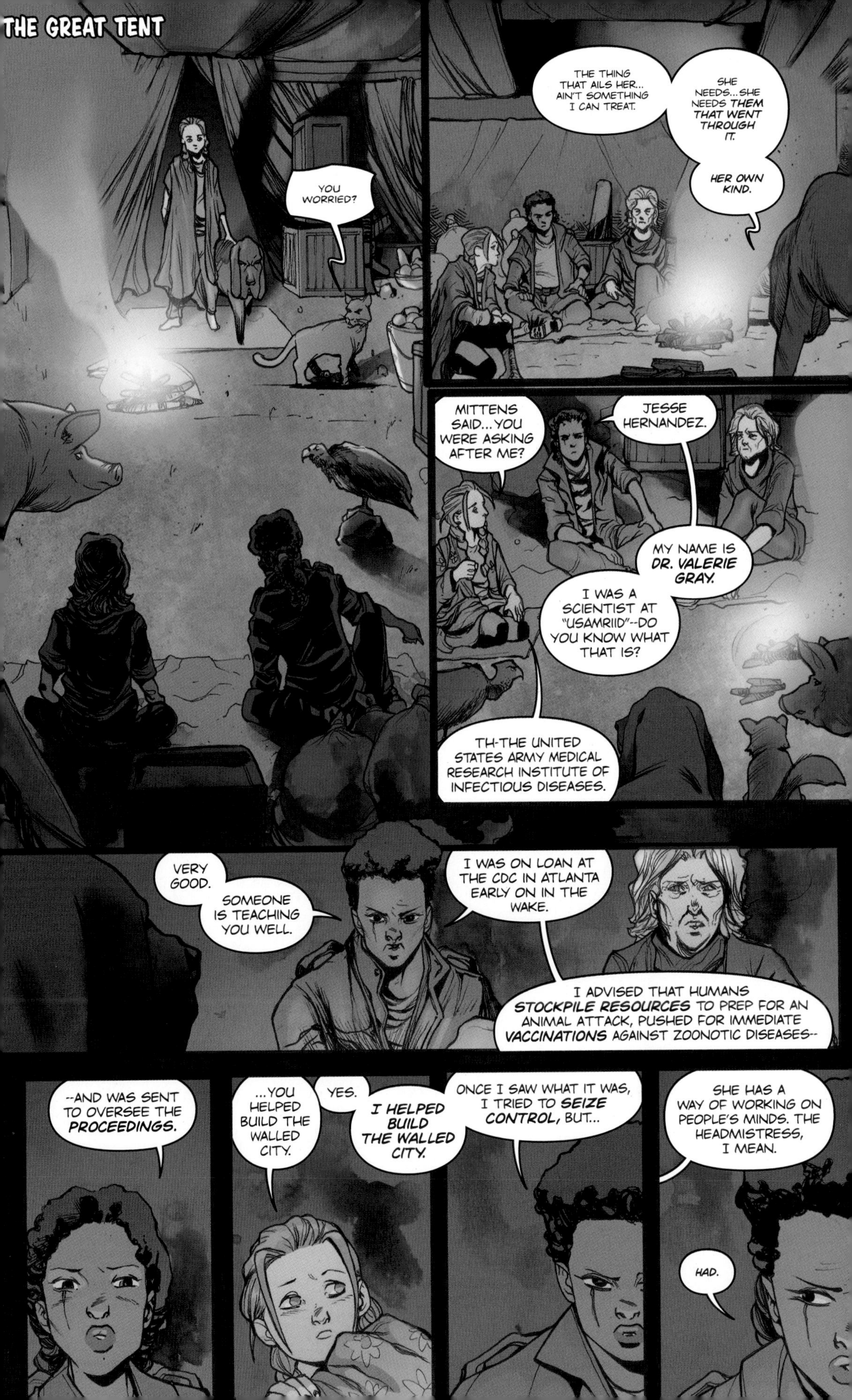
THE GREAT TENT
YOU WORRIED?
THE THING THAT AILS HER... AIN'T SOMETHING I CAN TREAT.
SHE NEEDS...SHE NEEDS THEM THAT WENT THROUGH IT.
HER OWN KIND.
MITTENS SAID...YOU WERE ASKING AFTER ME?
JESSE HERNANDEZ.
MY NAME IS DR. VALERIE GRAY.
I WAS A SCIENTIST AT "USAMRIID"--DO YOU KNOW WHAT THAT IS?
TH-THE UNITED STATES ARMY MEDICAL RESEARCH INSTITUTE OF INFECTIOUS DISEASES.
VERY GOOD.
SOMEONE IS TEACHING YOU WELL.
I WAS ON LOAN AT THE CDC IN ATLANTA EARLY ON IN THE WAKE.
I ADVISED THAT HUMANS STOCKPILE RESOURCES TO PREP FOR AN ANIMAL ATTACK, PUSHED FOR IMMEDIATE VACCINATIONS AGAINST ZOONOTIC DISEASES--
--AND WAS SENT TO OVERSEE THE PROCEEDINGS.
...YOU HELPED BUILD THE WALLED CITY.
YES.
I HELPED BUILD THE WALLED CITY.
ONCE I SAW WHAT IT WAS, I TRIED TO SEIZE CONTROL, BUT...
SHE HAS A WAY OF WORKING ON PEOPLE'S MINDS. THE HEADMISTRESS, I MEAN.
HAD.

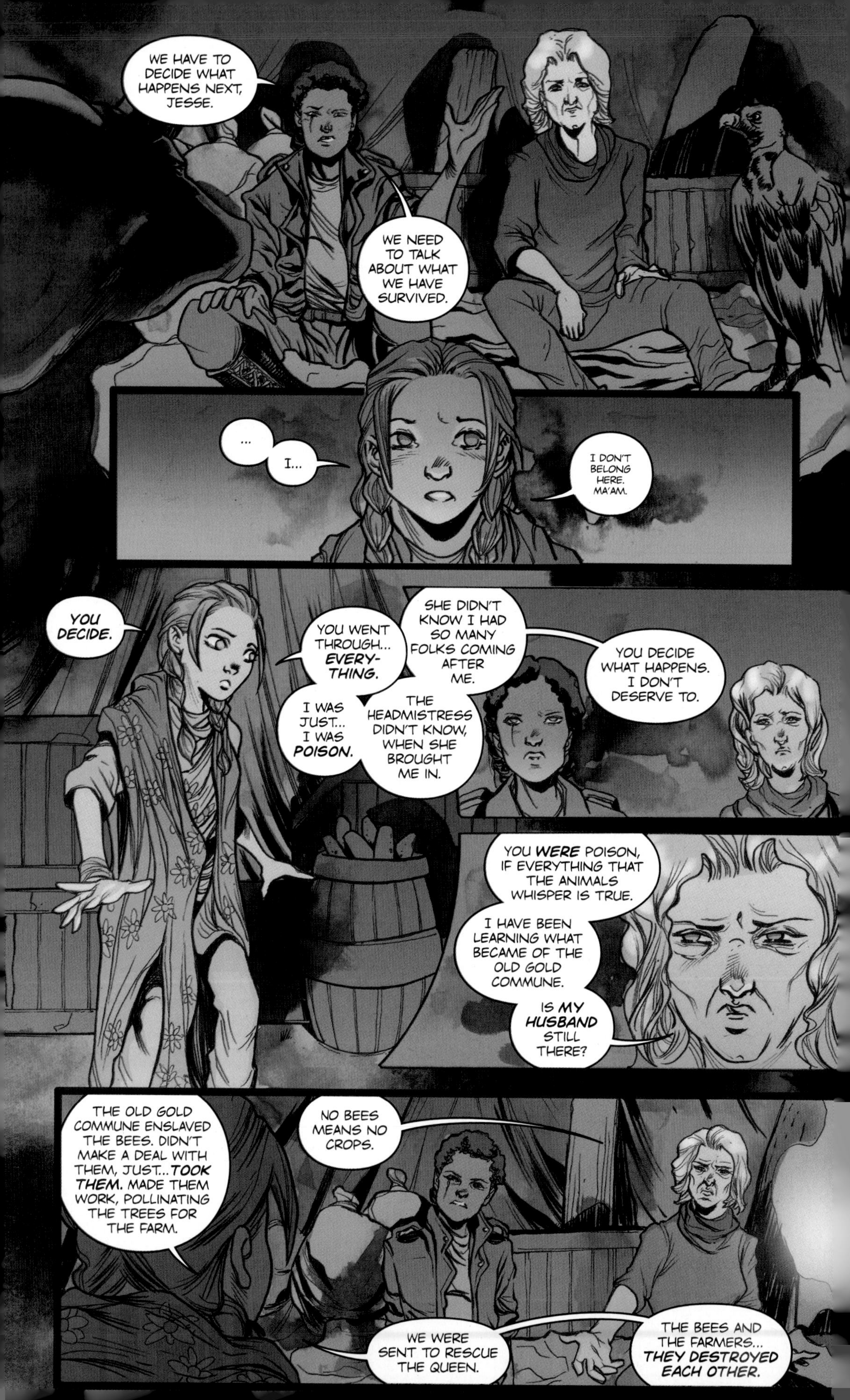
WE HAVE TO DECIDE WHAT HAPPENS NEXT, JESSE.
WE NEED TO TALK ABOUT WHAT WE HAVE SURVIVED.
...
I...
I DON'T BELONG HERE. MA'AM.
YOU DECIDE.
YOU WENT THROUGH... EVERY-THING.
I WAS JUST... I WAS POISON.
SHE DIDN'T KNOW I HAD SO MANY FOLKS COMING AFTER ME.
THE HEADMISTRESS DIDN'T KNOW, WHEN SHE BROUGHT ME IN.
YOU DECIDE WHAT HAPPENS. I DON'T DESERVE TO.
YOU WERE POISON, IF EVERYTHING THAT THE ANIMALS WHISPER IS TRUE.
I HAVE BEEN LEARNING WHAT BECAME OF THE OLD GOLD COMMUNE.
IS MY HUSBAND STILL THERE?
THE OLD GOLD COMMUNE ENSLAVED THE BEES. DIDN'T MAKE A DEAL WITH THEM, JUST...TOOK THEM. MADE THEM WORK, POLLINATING THE TREES FOR THE FARM.
NO BEES MEANS NO CROPS.
WE WERE SENT TO RESCUE THE QUEEN.
THE BEES AND THE FARMERS... THEY DESTROYED EACH OTHER.

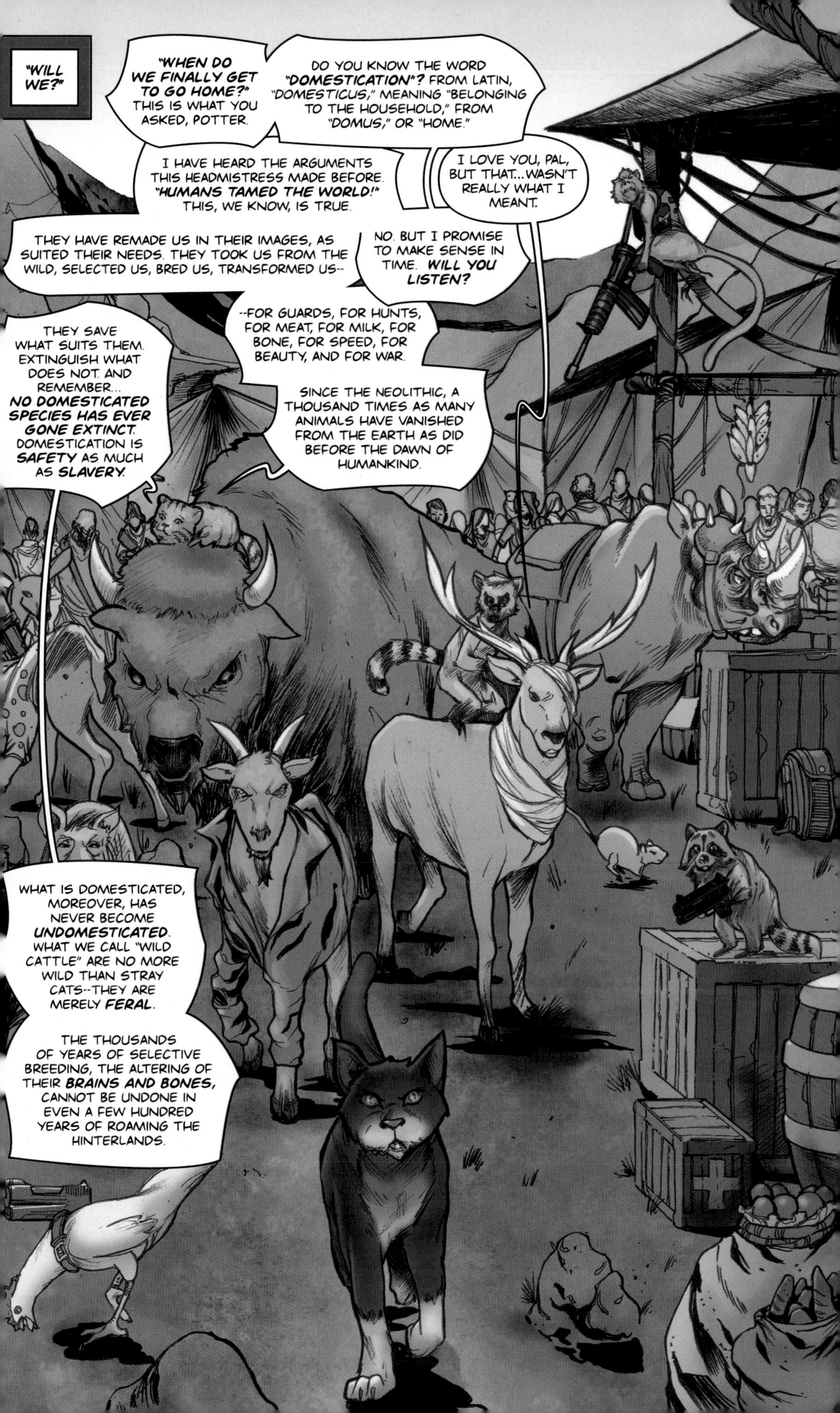
"WILL WE?"
"WHEN DO WE FINALLY GET TO GO HOME?" THIS IS WHAT YOU ASKED, POTTER.
DO YOU KNOW THE WORD "DOMESTICATION"? FROM LATIN, "DOMESTICUS," MEANING "BELONGING TO THE HOUSEHOLD," FROM "DOMUS," OR "HOME."
I LOVE YOU, PAL, BUT THAT...WASN'T REALLY WHAT I MEANT.
NO. BUT I PROMISE TO MAKE SENSE IN TIME. WILL YOU LISTEN?
I HAVE HEARD THE ARGUMENTS THIS HEADMISTRESS MADE BEFORE. "HUMANS TAMED THE WORLD!" THIS, WE KNOW, IS TRUE.
THEY HAVE REMADE US IN THEIR IMAGES, AS SUITED THEIR NEEDS. THEY TOOK US FROM THE WILD, SELECTED US, BRED US, TRANSFORMED US--
--FOR GUARDS, FOR HUNTS, FOR MEAT, FOR MILK, FOR BONE, FOR SPEED, FOR BEAUTY, AND FOR WAR.
THEY SAVE WHAT SUITS THEM. EXTINGUISH WHAT DOES NOT. AND REMEMBER... NO DOMESTICATED SPECIES HAS EVER GONE EXTINCT. DOMESTICATION IS SAFETY AS MUCH AS SLAVERY.
SINCE THE NEOLITHIC, A THOUSAND TIMES AS MANY ANIMALS HAVE VANISHED FROM THE EARTH AS DID BEFORE THE DAWN OF HUMANKIND.
WHAT IS DOMESTICATED, MOREOVER, HAS NEVER BECOME UNDOMESTICATED. WHAT WE CALL "WILD CATTLE" ARE NO MORE WILD THAN STRAY CATS--THEY ARE MERELY FERAL.
THE THOUSANDS OF YEARS OF SELECTIVE BREEDING, THE ALTERING OF THEIR BRAINS AND BONES, CANNOT BE UNDONE IN EVEN A FEW HUNDRED YEARS OF ROAMING THE HINTERLANDS.

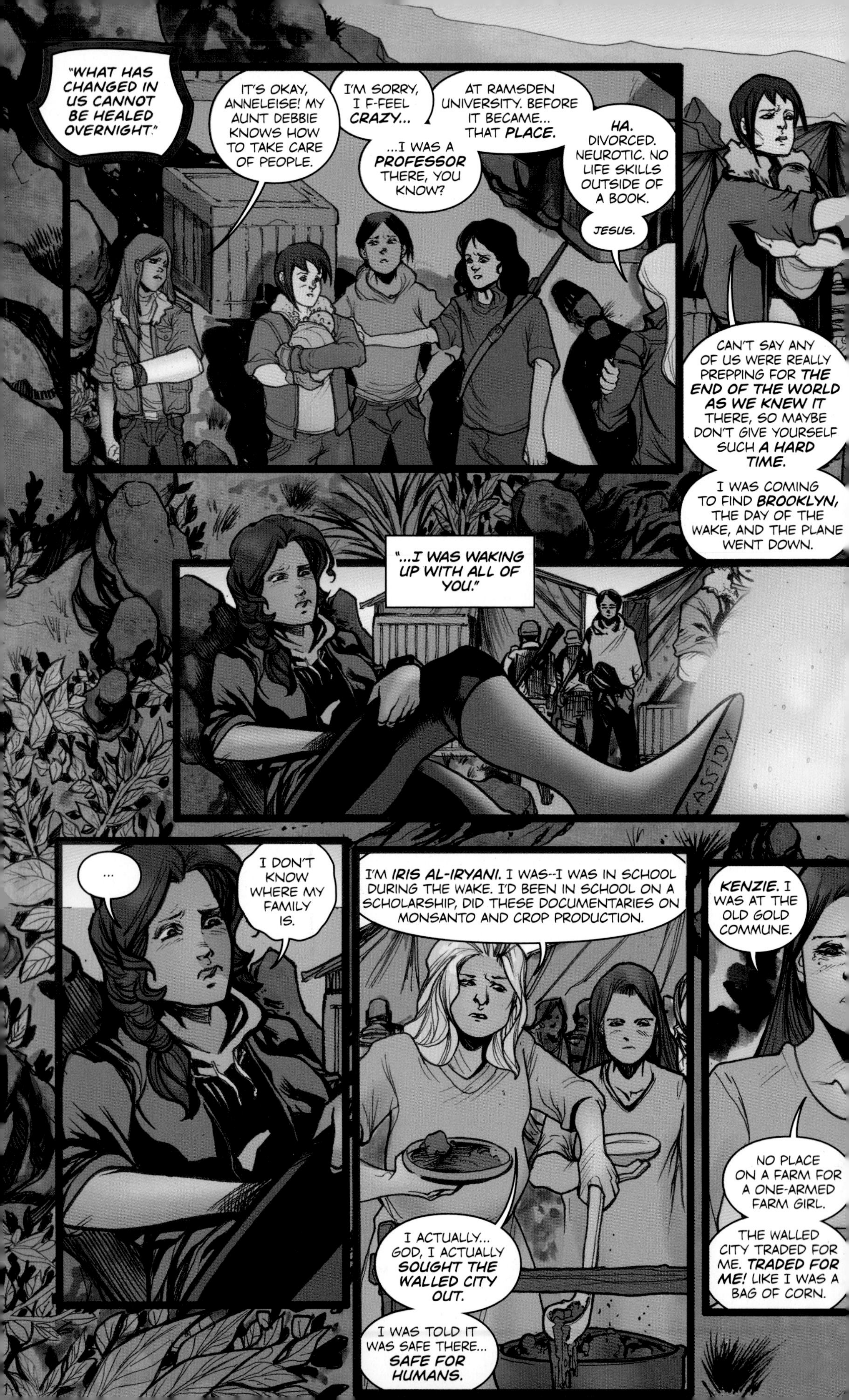
"WHAT HAS CHANGED IN US CANNOT BE HEALED OVERNIGHT."
IT'S OKAY, ANNELEISE! MY AUNT DEBBIE KNOWS HOW TO TAKE CARE OF PEOPLE.
I'M SORRY, I F-FEEL CRAZY...
...I WAS A PROFESSOR THERE, YOU KNOW?
AT RAMSDEN UNIVERSITY. BEFORE IT BECAME... THAT PLACE.
HA. DIVORCED. NEUROTIC. NO LIFE SKILLS OUTSIDE OF A BOOK.
JESUS.
CAN'T SAY ANY OF US WERE REALLY PREPPING FOR THE END OF THE WORLD AS WE KNEW IT THERE, SO MAYBE DON'T GIVE YOURSELF SUCH A HARD TIME.
I WAS COMING TO FIND BROOKLYN, THE DAY OF THE WAKE, AND THE PLANE WENT DOWN.
"...I WAS WAKING UP WITH ALL OF YOU."
CASSIDY
...
I DON'T KNOW WHERE MY FAMILY IS.
I'M IRIS AL-IRYANI. I WAS--I WAS IN SCHOOL DURING THE WAKE. I'D BEEN IN SCHOOL ON A SCHOLARSHIP, DID THESE DOCUMENTARIES ON MONSANTO AND CROP PRODUCTION.
I ACTUALLY... GOD, I ACTUALLY SOUGHT THE WALLED CITY OUT.
I WAS TOLD IT WAS SAFE THERE... SAFE FOR HUMANS.
KENZIE. I WAS AT THE OLD GOLD COMMUNE.
NO PLACE ON A FARM FOR A ONE-ARMED FARM GIRL.
THE WALLED CITY TRADED FOR ME. TRADED FOR ME! LIKE I WAS A BAG OF CORN.

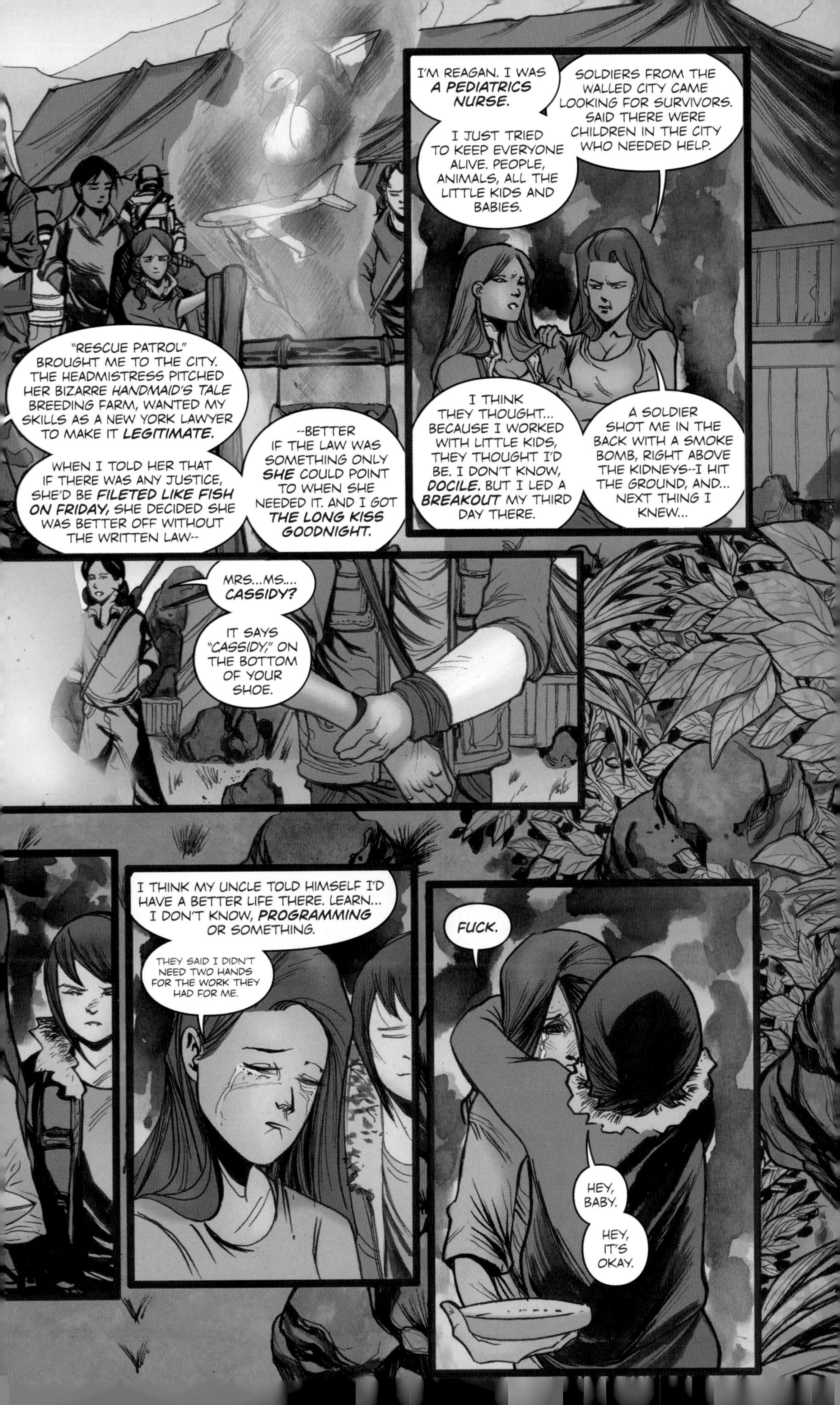

I'M REAGAN. I WAS A PEDIATRICS NURSE.
I JUST TRIED TO KEEP EVERYONE ALIVE. PEOPLE, ANIMALS, ALL THE LITTLE KIDS AND BABIES.
SOLDIERS FROM THE WALLED CITY CAME LOOKING FOR SURVIVORS. SAID THERE WERE CHILDREN IN THE CITY WHO NEEDED HELP.
"RESCUE PATROL" BROUGHT ME TO THE CITY. THE HEADMISTRESS PITCHED HER BIZARRE HANDMAID'S TALE BREEDING FARM, WANTED MY SKILLS AS A NEW YORK LAWYER TO MAKE IT LEGITIMATE.
WHEN I TOLD HER THAT IF THERE WAS ANY JUSTICE, SHE'D BE FILETED LIKE FISH ON FRIDAY, SHE DECIDED SHE WAS BETTER OFF WITHOUT THE WRITTEN LAW--
--BETTER IF THE LAW WAS SOMETHING ONLY SHE COULD POINT TO WHEN SHE NEEDED IT. AND I GOT THE LONG KISS GOODNIGHT.
I THINK THEY THOUGHT... BECAUSE I WORKED WITH LITTLE KIDS, THEY THOUGHT I'D BE. I DON'T KNOW, DOCILE. BUT I LED A BREAKOUT MY THIRD DAY THERE.
A SOLDIER SHOT ME IN THE BACK WITH A SMOKE BOMB, RIGHT ABOVE THE KIDNEYS--I HIT THE GROUND, AND... NEXT THING I KNEW...
MRS...MS... CASSIDY?
IT SAYS "CASSIDY," ON THE BOTTOM OF YOUR SHOE.
I THINK MY UNCLE TOLD HIMSELF I'D HAVE A BETTER LIFE THERE. LEARN... I DON'T KNOW, PROGRAMMING OR SOMETHING.
THEY SAID I DIDN'T NEED TWO HANDS FOR THE WORK THEY HAD FOR ME.
FUCK.
HEY, BABY.
HEY, IT'S OKAY.

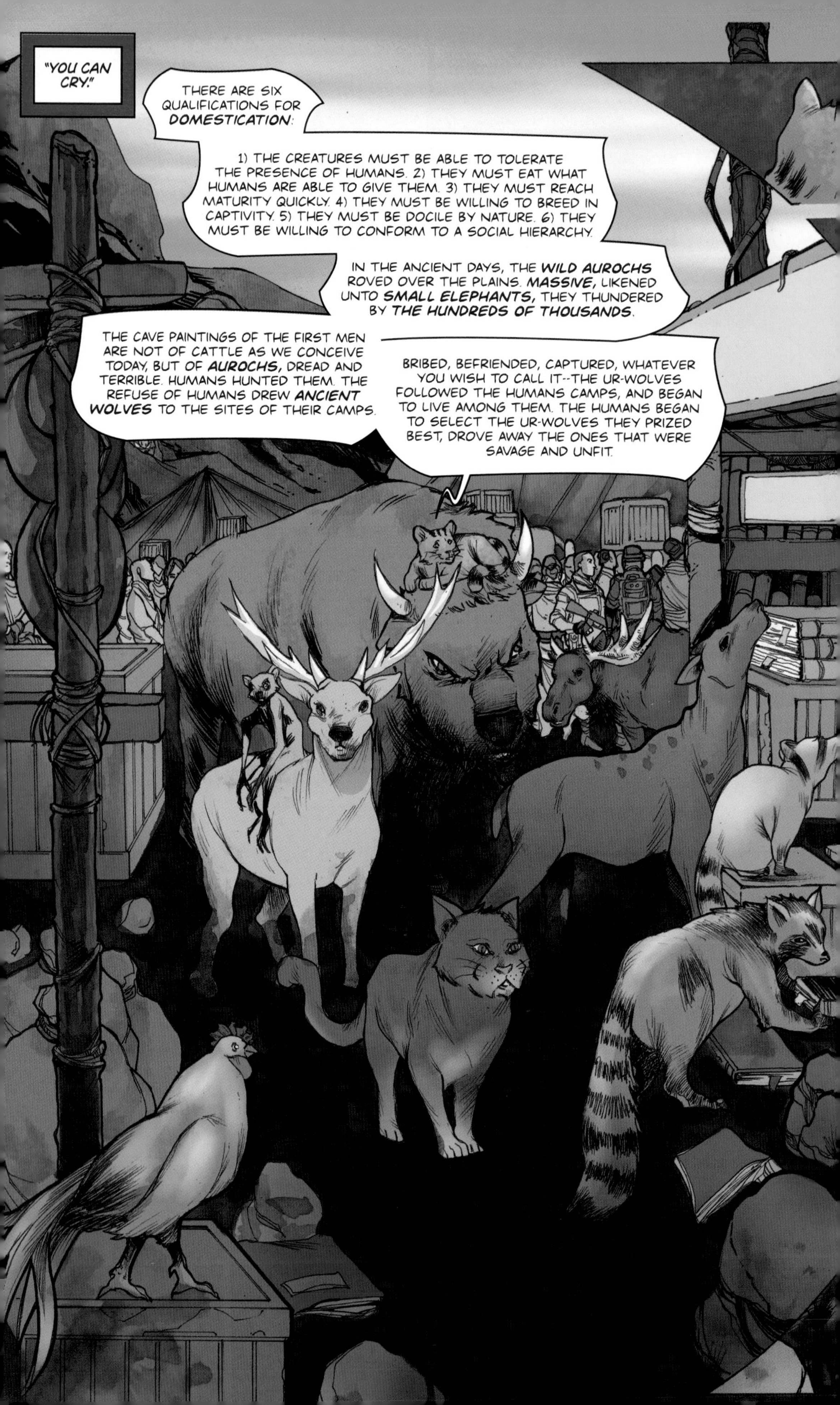
"YOU CAN CRY."
THERE ARE SIX QUALIFICATIONS FOR **DOMESTICATION**:
1) THE CREATURES MUST BE ABLE TO TOLERATE THE PRESENCE OF HUMANS. 2) THEY MUST EAT WHAT HUMANS ARE ABLE TO GIVE THEM. 3) THEY MUST REACH MATURITY QUICKLY. 4) THEY MUST BE WILLING TO BREED IN CAPTIVITY. 5) THEY MUST BE DOCILE BY NATURE. 6) THEY MUST BE WILLING TO CONFORM TO A SOCIAL HIERARCHY.
IN THE ANCIENT DAYS, THE **WILD AUROCHS** ROVED OVER THE PLAINS. **MASSIVE,** LIKENED UNTO **SMALL ELEPHANTS,** THEY THUNDERED BY **THE HUNDREDS OF THOUSANDS**.
THE CAVE PAINTINGS OF THE FIRST MEN ARE NOT OF CATTLE AS WE CONCEIVE TODAY, BUT OF **AUROCHS,** DREAD AND TERRIBLE. HUMANS HUNTED THEM. THE REFUSE OF HUMANS DREW **ANCIENT WOLVES** TO THE SITES OF THEIR CAMPS.
BRIBED, BEFRIENDED, CAPTURED, WHATEVER YOU WISH TO CALL IT--THE UR-WOLVES FOLLOWED THE HUMANS CAMPS, AND BEGAN TO LIVE AMONG THEM. THE HUMANS BEGAN TO SELECT THE UR-WOLVES THEY PRIZED BEST, DROVE AWAY THE ONES THAT WERE SAVAGE AND UNFIT.

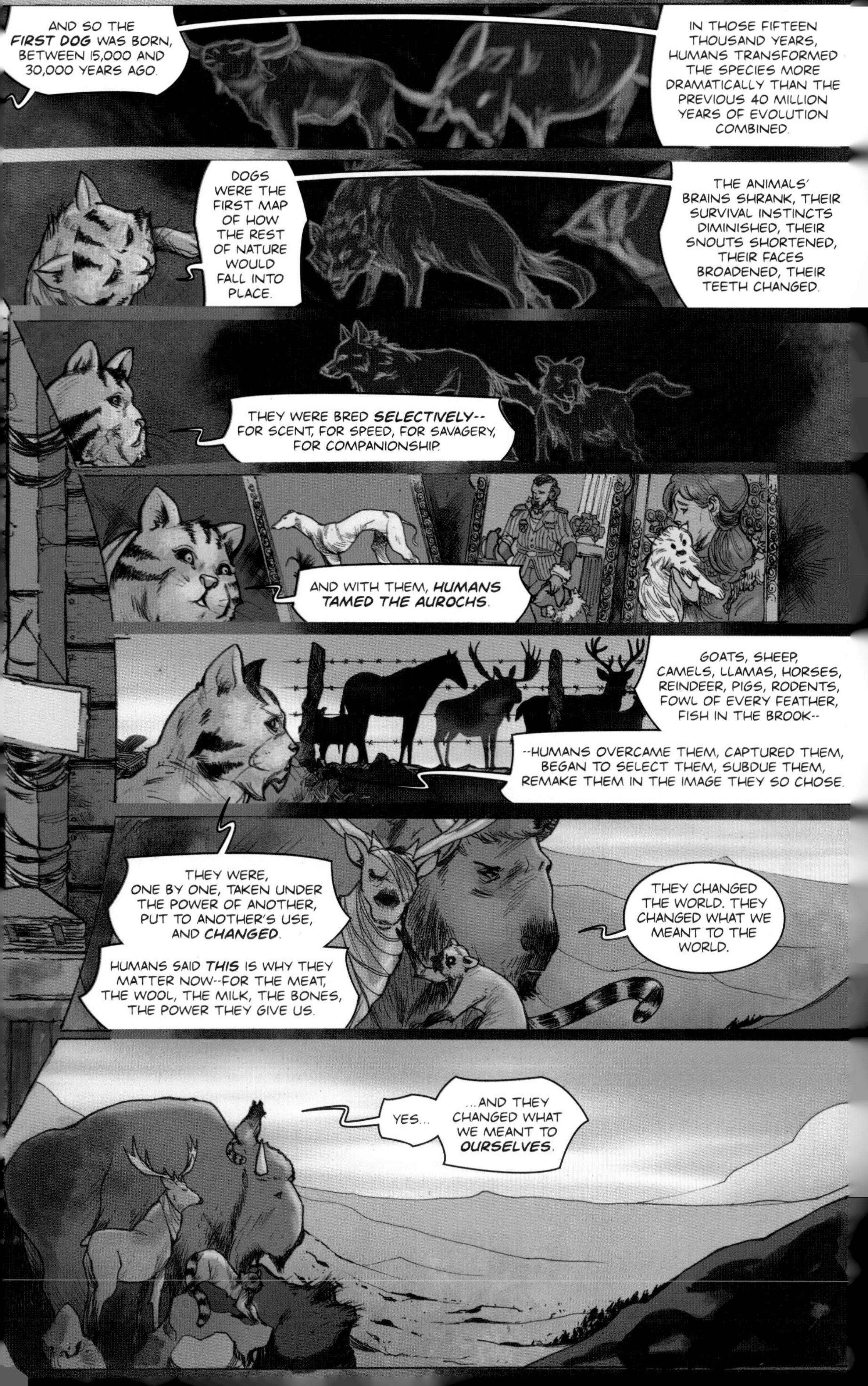
AND SO THE FIRST DOG WAS BORN, BETWEEN 15,000 AND 30,000 YEARS AGO.
IN THOSE FIFTEEN THOUSAND YEARS, HUMANS TRANSFORMED THE SPECIES MORE DRAMATICALLY THAN THE PREVIOUS 40 MILLION YEARS OF EVOLUTION COMBINED.
DOGS WERE THE FIRST MAP OF HOW THE REST OF NATURE WOULD FALL INTO PLACE.
THE ANIMALS' BRAINS SHRANK, THEIR SURVIVAL INSTINCTS DIMINISHED, THEIR SNOUTS SHORTENED, THEIR FACES BROADENED, THEIR TEETH CHANGED.
THEY WERE BRED SELECTIVELY-- FOR SCENT, FOR SPEED, FOR SAVAGERY, FOR COMPANIONSHIP.
AND WITH THEM, HUMANS TAMED THE AUROCHS.
GOATS, SHEEP, CAMELS, LLAMAS, HORSES, REINDEER, PIGS, RODENTS, FOWL OF EVERY FEATHER, FISH IN THE BROOK--
--HUMANS OVERCAME THEM, CAPTURED THEM, BEGAN TO SELECT THEM, SUBDUE THEM, REMAKE THEM IN THE IMAGE THEY SO CHOSE.
THEY WERE, ONE BY ONE, TAKEN UNDER THE POWER OF ANOTHER, PUT TO ANOTHER'S USE, AND CHANGED.
HUMANS SAID THIS IS WHY THEY MATTER NOW--FOR THE MEAT, THE WOOL, THE MILK, THE BONES, THE POWER THEY GIVE US.
THEY CHANGED THE WORLD. THEY CHANGED WHAT WE MEANT TO THE WORLD.
YES...
...AND THEY CHANGED WHAT WE MEANT TO OURSELVES.

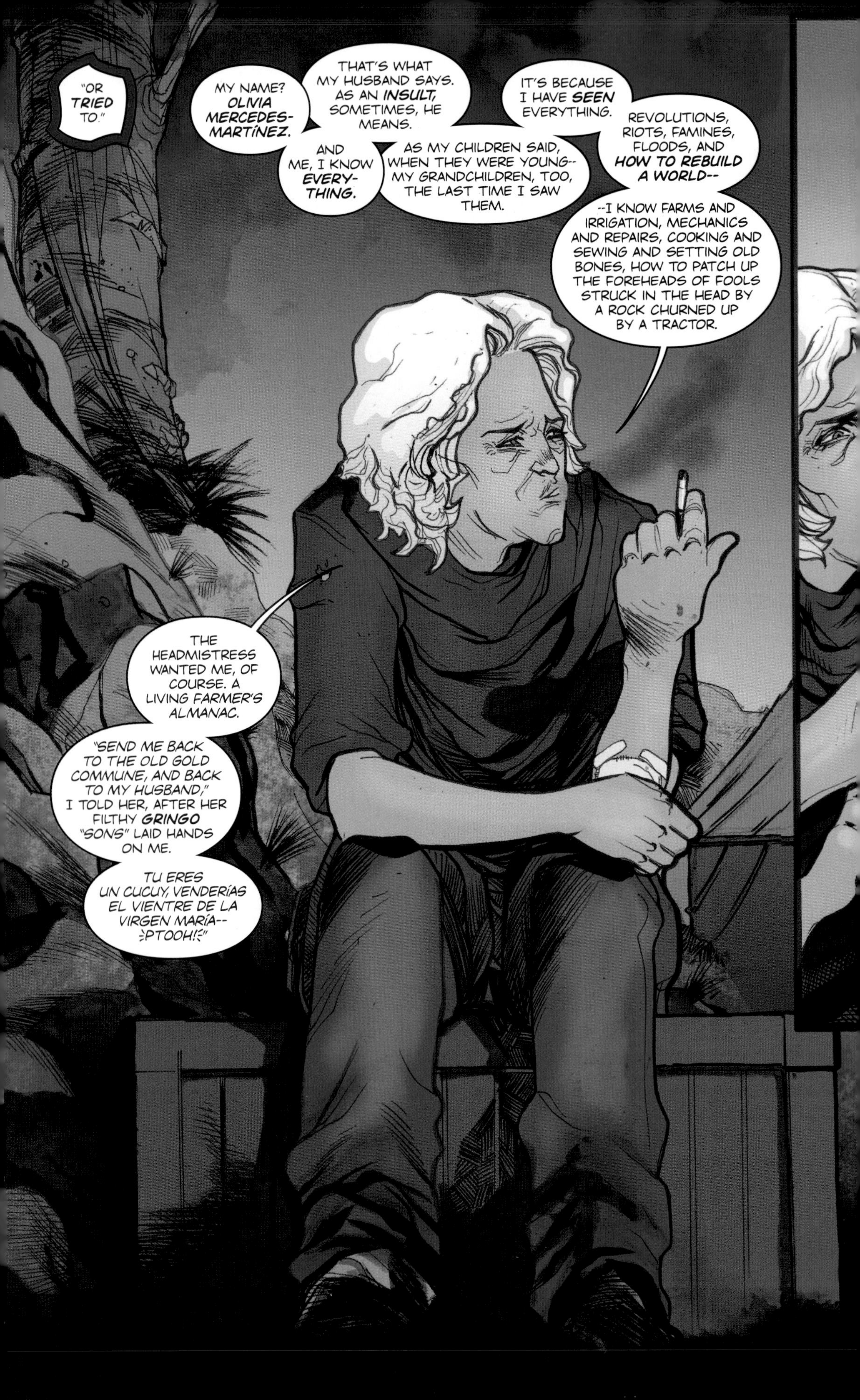
"OR TRIED TO."
MY NAME? OLIVIA MERCEDES-MARTÍNEZ.
THAT'S WHAT MY HUSBAND SAYS. AS AN INSULT, SOMETIMES, HE MEANS.
AND ME, I KNOW EVERYTHING.
AS MY CHILDREN SAID, WHEN THEY WERE YOUNG-- MY GRANDCHILDREN, TOO, THE LAST TIME I SAW THEM.
IT'S BECAUSE I HAVE SEEN EVERYTHING.
REVOLUTIONS, RIOTS, FAMINES, FLOODS, AND HOW TO REBUILD A WORLD--
--I KNOW FARMS AND IRRIGATION, MECHANICS AND REPAIRS, COOKING AND SEWING AND SETTING OLD BONES, HOW TO PATCH UP THE FOREHEADS OF FOOLS STRUCK IN THE HEAD BY A ROCK CHURNED UP BY A TRACTOR.
THE HEADMISTRESS WANTED ME, OF COURSE. A LIVING FARMER'S ALMANAC.
"SEND ME BACK TO THE OLD GOLD COMMUNE, AND BACK TO MY HUSBAND," I TOLD HER, AFTER HER FILTHY GRINGO "SONS" LAID HANDS ON ME.
TU ERES UN CUCUY, VENDERÍAS EL VIENTRE DE LA VIRGEN MARÍA-- PTOOH!"

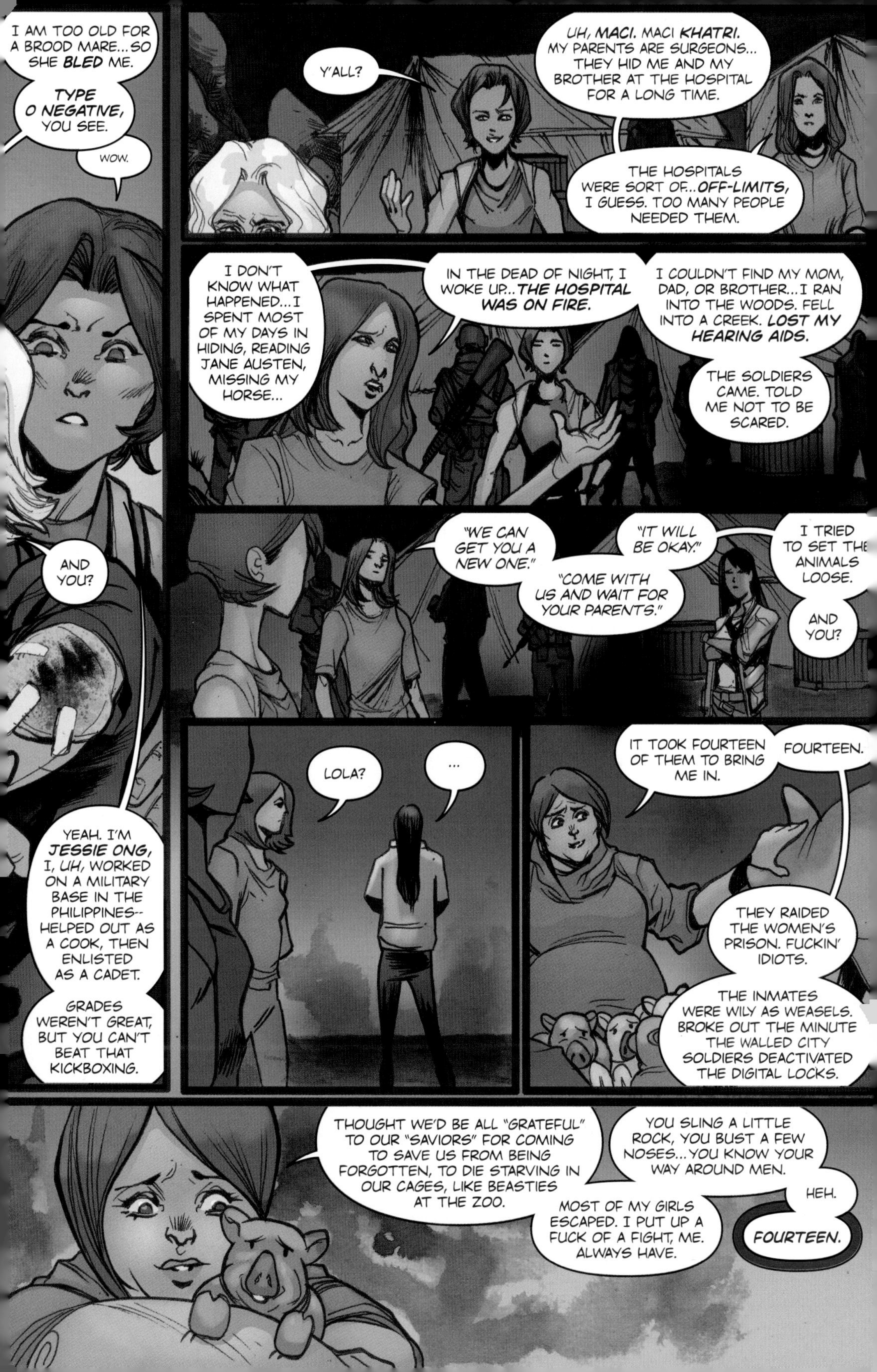

I AM TOO OLD FOR A BROOD MARE...SO SHE **BLED** ME.
TYPE O NEGATIVE, YOU SEE.
WOW.
Y'ALL?
UH, **MACI.** MACI **KHATRI.** MY PARENTS ARE SURGEONS... THEY HID ME AND MY BROTHER AT THE HOSPITAL FOR A LONG TIME.
THE HOSPITALS WERE SORT OF...**OFF-LIMITS,** I GUESS. TOO MANY PEOPLE NEEDED THEM.
I DON'T KNOW WHAT HAPPENED...I SPENT MOST OF MY DAYS IN HIDING, READING JANE AUSTEN, MISSING MY HORSE...
IN THE DEAD OF NIGHT, I WOKE UP...***THE HOSPITAL WAS ON FIRE.***
I COULDN'T FIND MY MOM, DAD, OR BROTHER...I RAN INTO THE WOODS. FELL INTO A CREEK. ***LOST MY HEARING AIDS.***
THE SOLDIERS CAME. TOLD ME NOT TO BE SCARED.
"WE CAN GET YOU A NEW ONE."
"IT WILL BE OKAY."
"COME WITH US AND WAIT FOR YOUR PARENTS."
I TRIED TO SET THE ANIMALS LOOSE.
AND YOU?
AND YOU?
YEAH. I'M ***JESSIE ONG,*** I, *UH,* WORKED ON A MILITARY BASE IN THE PHILIPPINES-- HELPED OUT AS A COOK, THEN ENLISTED AS A CADET.
GRADES WEREN'T GREAT, BUT YOU CAN'T BEAT THAT KICKBOXING.
LOLA?
...
IT TOOK FOURTEEN OF THEM TO BRING ME IN.
FOURTEEN.
THEY RAIDED THE WOMEN'S PRISON. FUCKIN' IDIOTS.
THE INMATES WERE WILY AS WEASELS. BROKE OUT THE MINUTE THE WALLED CITY SOLDIERS DEACTIVATED THE DIGITAL LOCKS.
THOUGHT WE'D BE ALL "GRATEFUL" TO OUR "SAVIORS" FOR COMING TO SAVE US FROM BEING FORGOTTEN, TO DIE STARVING IN OUR CAGES, LIKE BEASTIES AT THE ZOO.
MOST OF MY GIRLS ESCAPED. I PUT UP A FUCK OF A FIGHT, ME. ALWAYS HAVE.
YOU SLING A LITTLE ROCK, YOU BUST A FEW NOSES...YOU KNOW YOUR WAY AROUND MEN.
HEH.
FOURTEEN.

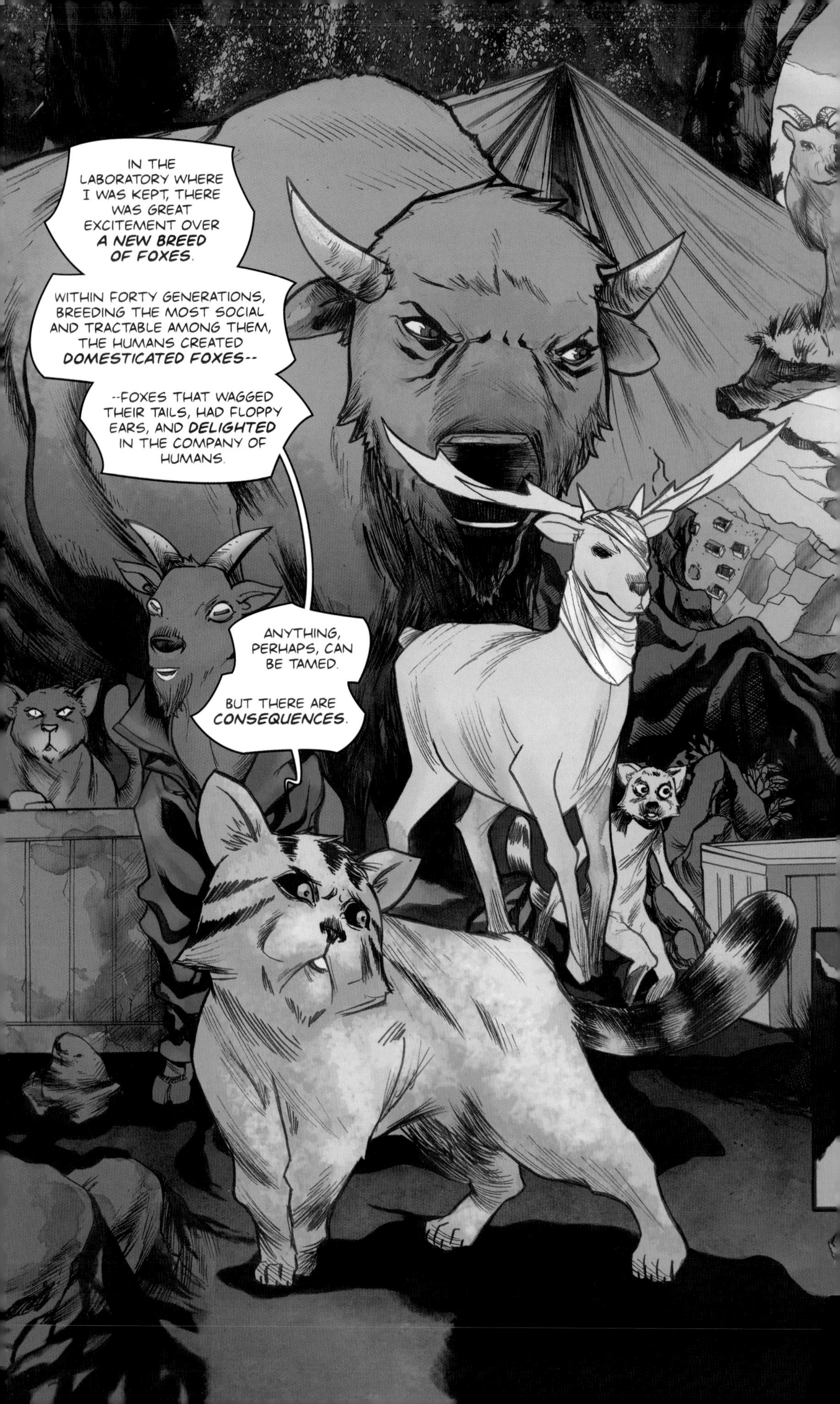
IN THE LABORATORY WHERE I WAS KEPT, THERE WAS GREAT EXCITEMENT OVER **A NEW BREED OF FOXES**.
WITHIN FORTY GENERATIONS, BREEDING THE MOST SOCIAL AND TRACTABLE AMONG THEM, THE HUMANS CREATED **DOMESTICATED FOXES**--
--FOXES THAT WAGGED THEIR TAILS, HAD FLOPPY EARS, AND **DELIGHTED** IN THE COMPANY OF HUMANS.
ANYTHING, PERHAPS, CAN BE TAMED.
BUT THERE ARE **CONSEQUENCES**.

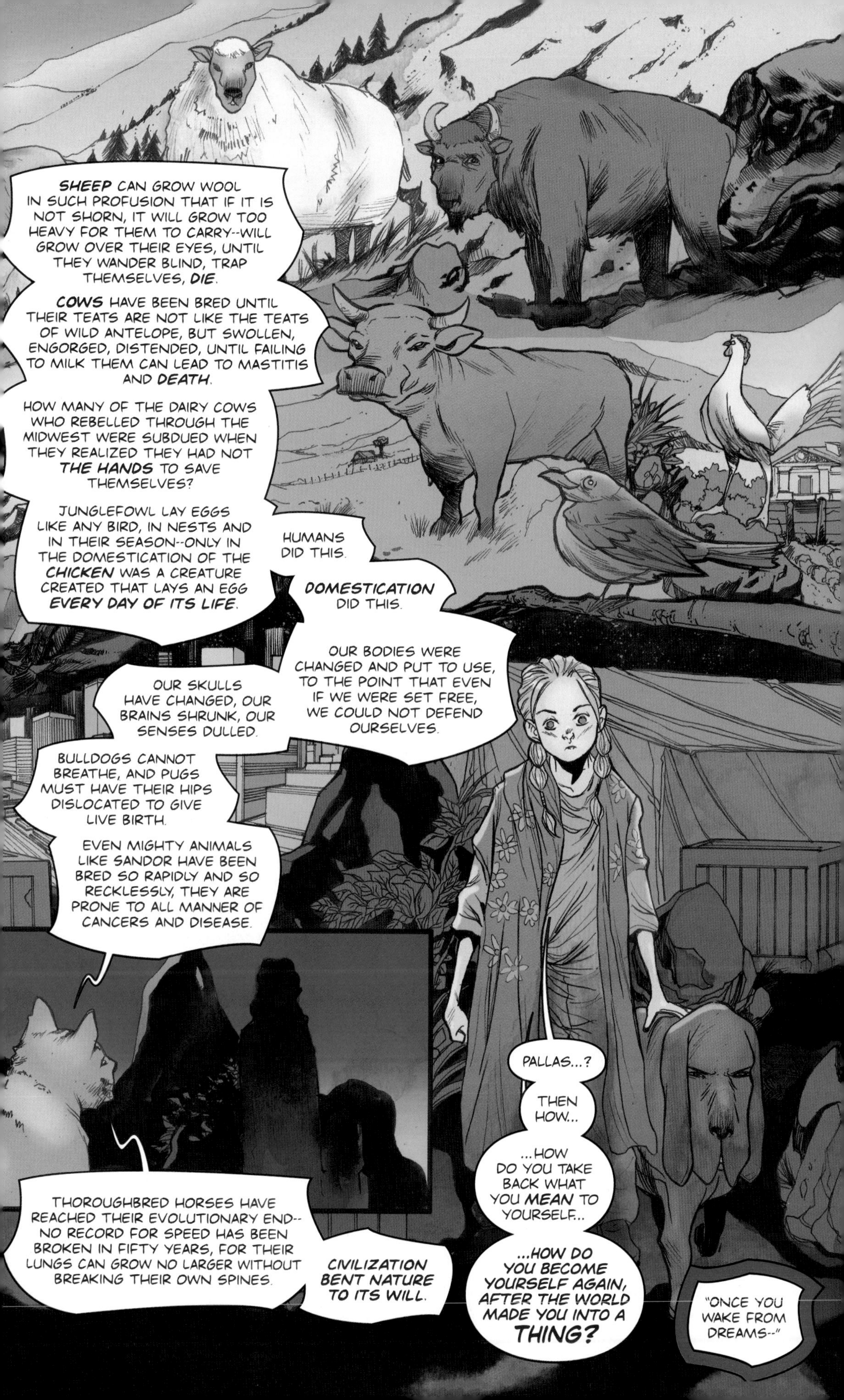
SHEEP CAN GROW WOOL IN SUCH PROFUSION THAT IF IT IS NOT SHORN, IT WILL GROW TOO HEAVY FOR THEM TO CARRY--WILL GROW OVER THEIR EYES, UNTIL THEY WANDER BLIND, TRAP THEMSELVES, DIE.
COWS HAVE BEEN BRED UNTIL THEIR TEATS ARE NOT LIKE THE TEATS OF WILD ANTELOPE, BUT SWOLLEN, ENGORGED, DISTENDED, UNTIL FAILING TO MILK THEM CAN LEAD TO MASTITIS AND DEATH.
HOW MANY OF THE DAIRY COWS WHO REBELLED THROUGH THE MIDWEST WERE SUBDUED WHEN THEY REALIZED THEY HAD NOT THE HANDS TO SAVE THEMSELVES?
JUNGLEFOWL LAY EGGS LIKE ANY BIRD, IN NESTS AND IN THEIR SEASON--ONLY IN THE DOMESTICATION OF THE CHICKEN WAS A CREATURE CREATED THAT LAYS AN EGG EVERY DAY OF ITS LIFE.
HUMANS DID THIS.
DOMESTICATION DID THIS.
OUR BODIES WERE CHANGED AND PUT TO USE, TO THE POINT THAT EVEN IF WE WERE SET FREE, WE COULD NOT DEFEND OURSELVES.
OUR SKULLS HAVE CHANGED, OUR BRAINS SHRUNK, OUR SENSES DULLED.
BULLDOGS CANNOT BREATHE, AND PUGS MUST HAVE THEIR HIPS DISLOCATED TO GIVE LIVE BIRTH.
EVEN MIGHTY ANIMALS LIKE SANDOR HAVE BEEN BRED SO RAPIDLY AND SO RECKLESSLY, THEY ARE PRONE TO ALL MANNER OF CANCERS AND DISEASE.
THOROUGHBRED HORSES HAVE REACHED THEIR EVOLUTIONARY END-- NO RECORD FOR SPEED HAS BEEN BROKEN IN FIFTY YEARS, FOR THEIR LUNGS CAN GROW NO LARGER WITHOUT BREAKING THEIR OWN SPINES.
CIVILIZATION BENT NATURE TO ITS WILL.
PALLAS...?
THEN HOW...
...HOW DO YOU TAKE BACK WHAT YOU MEAN TO YOURSELF...
...HOW DO YOU BECOME YOURSELF AGAIN, AFTER THE WORLD MADE YOU INTO A THING?
"ONCE YOU WAKE FROM DREAMS--"

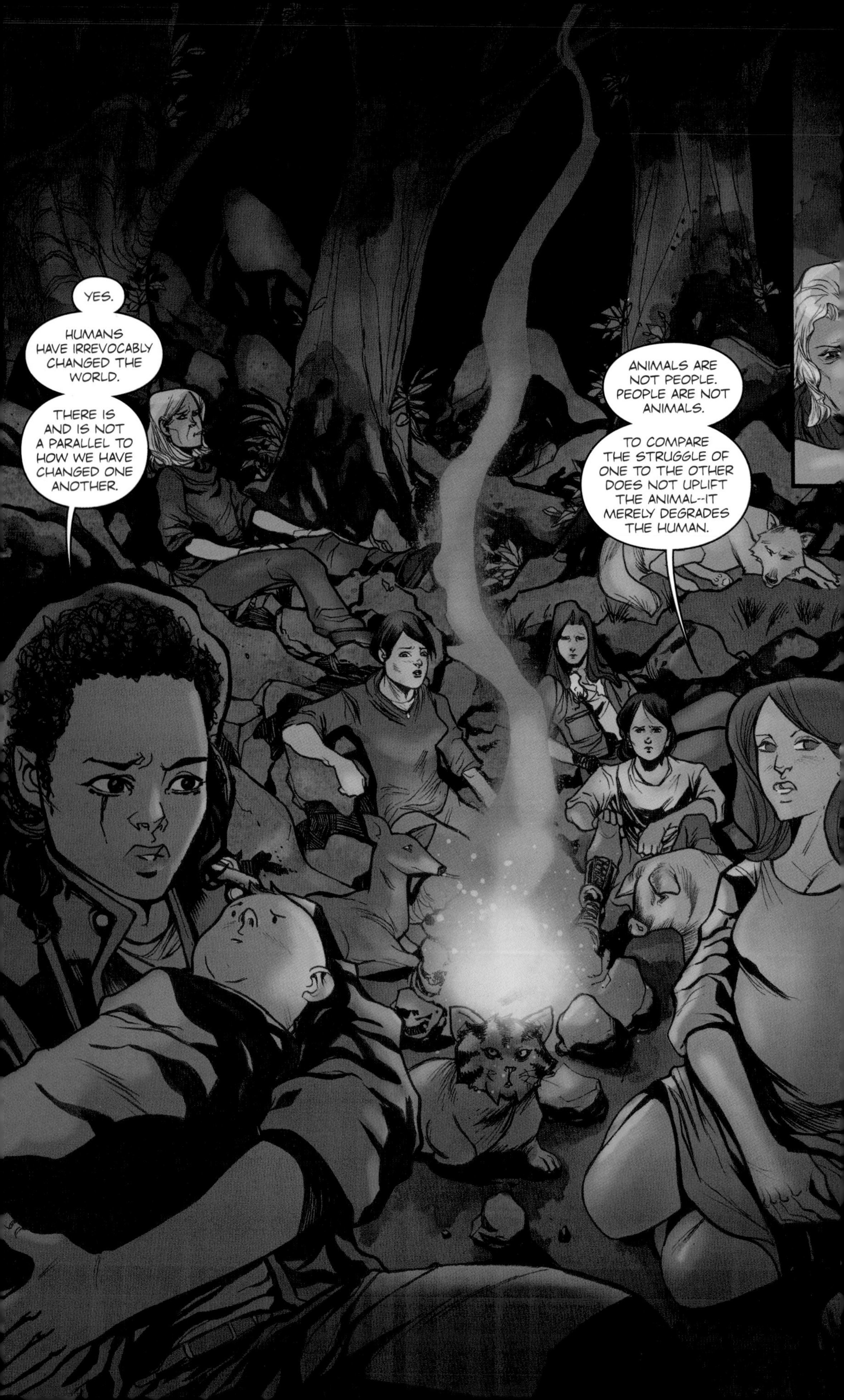
YES.
HUMANS HAVE IRREVOCABLY CHANGED THE WORLD.
THERE IS AND IS NOT A PARALLEL TO HOW WE HAVE CHANGED ONE ANOTHER.
ANIMALS ARE NOT PEOPLE. PEOPLE ARE NOT ANIMALS.
TO COMPARE THE STRUGGLE OF ONE TO THE OTHER DOES NOT UPLIFT THE ANIMAL--IT MERELY DEGRADES THE HUMAN.

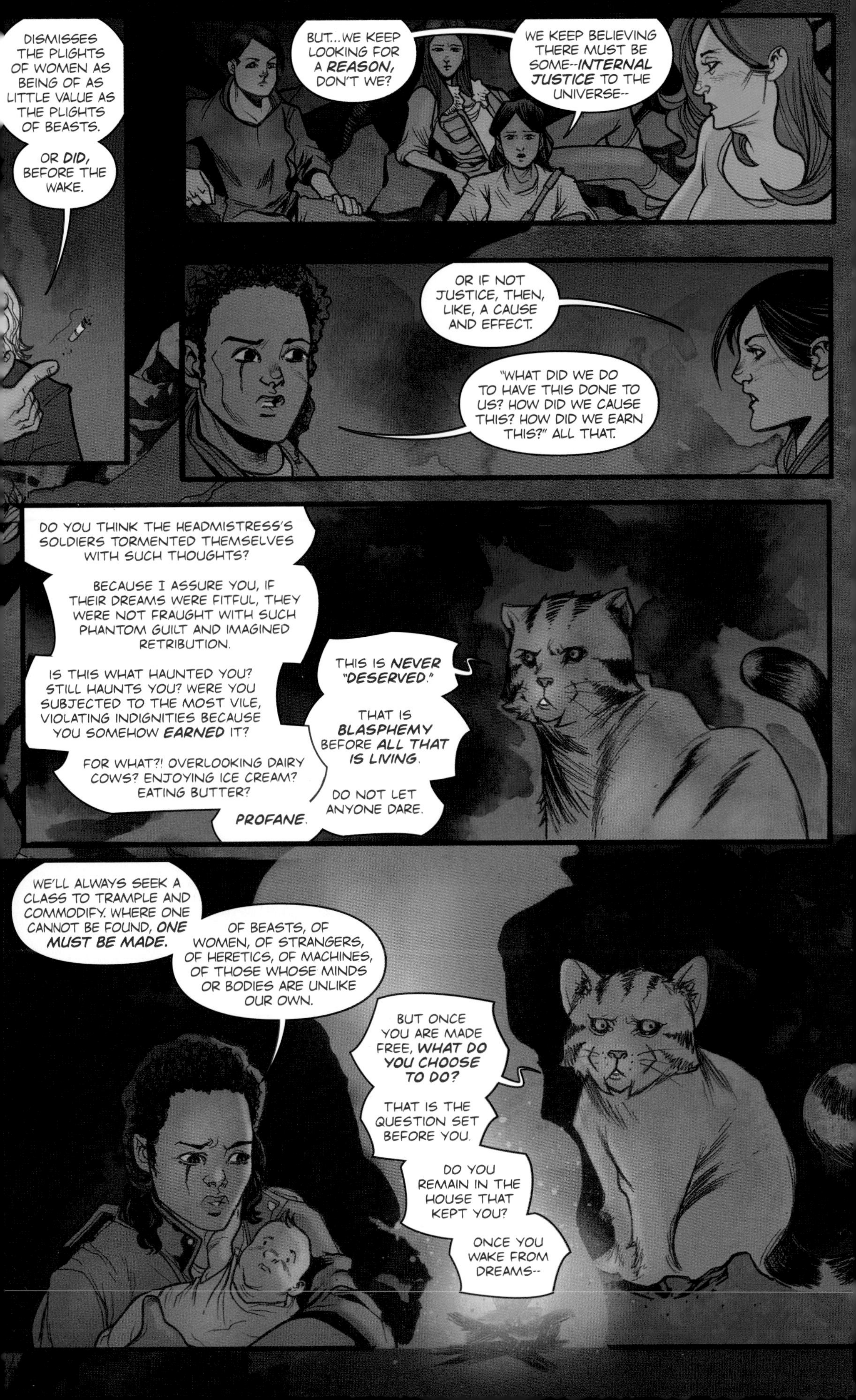
DISMISSES THE PLIGHTS OF WOMEN AS BEING OF AS LITTLE VALUE AS THE PLIGHTS OF BEASTS.
OR **DID,** BEFORE THE WAKE.
BUT...WE KEEP LOOKING FOR A **REASON,** DON'T WE?
WE KEEP BELIEVING THERE MUST BE SOME--**INTERNAL JUSTICE** TO THE UNIVERSE--
OR IF NOT JUSTICE, THEN, LIKE, A CAUSE AND EFFECT.
"WHAT DID WE DO TO HAVE THIS DONE TO US? HOW DID WE CAUSE THIS? HOW DID WE EARN THIS?" ALL THAT.
DO YOU THINK THE HEADMISTRESS'S SOLDIERS TORMENTED THEMSELVES WITH SUCH THOUGHTS?
BECAUSE I ASSURE YOU, IF THEIR DREAMS WERE FITFUL, THEY WERE NOT FRAUGHT WITH SUCH PHANTOM GUILT AND IMAGINED RETRIBUTION.
IS THIS WHAT HAUNTED YOU? STILL HAUNTS YOU? WERE YOU SUBJECTED TO THE MOST VILE, VIOLATING INDIGNITIES BECAUSE YOU SOMEHOW **EARNED** IT?
FOR WHAT?! OVERLOOKING DAIRY COWS? ENJOYING ICE CREAM? EATING BUTTER?
PROFANE.
THIS IS **NEVER "DESERVED."**
THAT IS **BLASPHEMY** BEFORE **ALL THAT IS LIVING.**
DO NOT LET ANYONE DARE.
WE'LL ALWAYS SEEK A CLASS TO TRAMPLE AND COMMODIFY. WHERE ONE CANNOT BE FOUND, **ONE MUST BE MADE.**
OF BEASTS, OF WOMEN, OF STRANGERS, OF HERETICS, OF MACHINES, OF THOSE WHOSE MINDS OR BODIES ARE UNLIKE OUR OWN.
BUT ONCE YOU ARE MADE FREE, **WHAT DO YOU CHOOSE TO DO?**
THAT IS THE QUESTION SET BEFORE YOU.
DO YOU REMAIN IN THE HOUSE THAT KEPT YOU?
ONCE YOU WAKE FROM DREAMS--

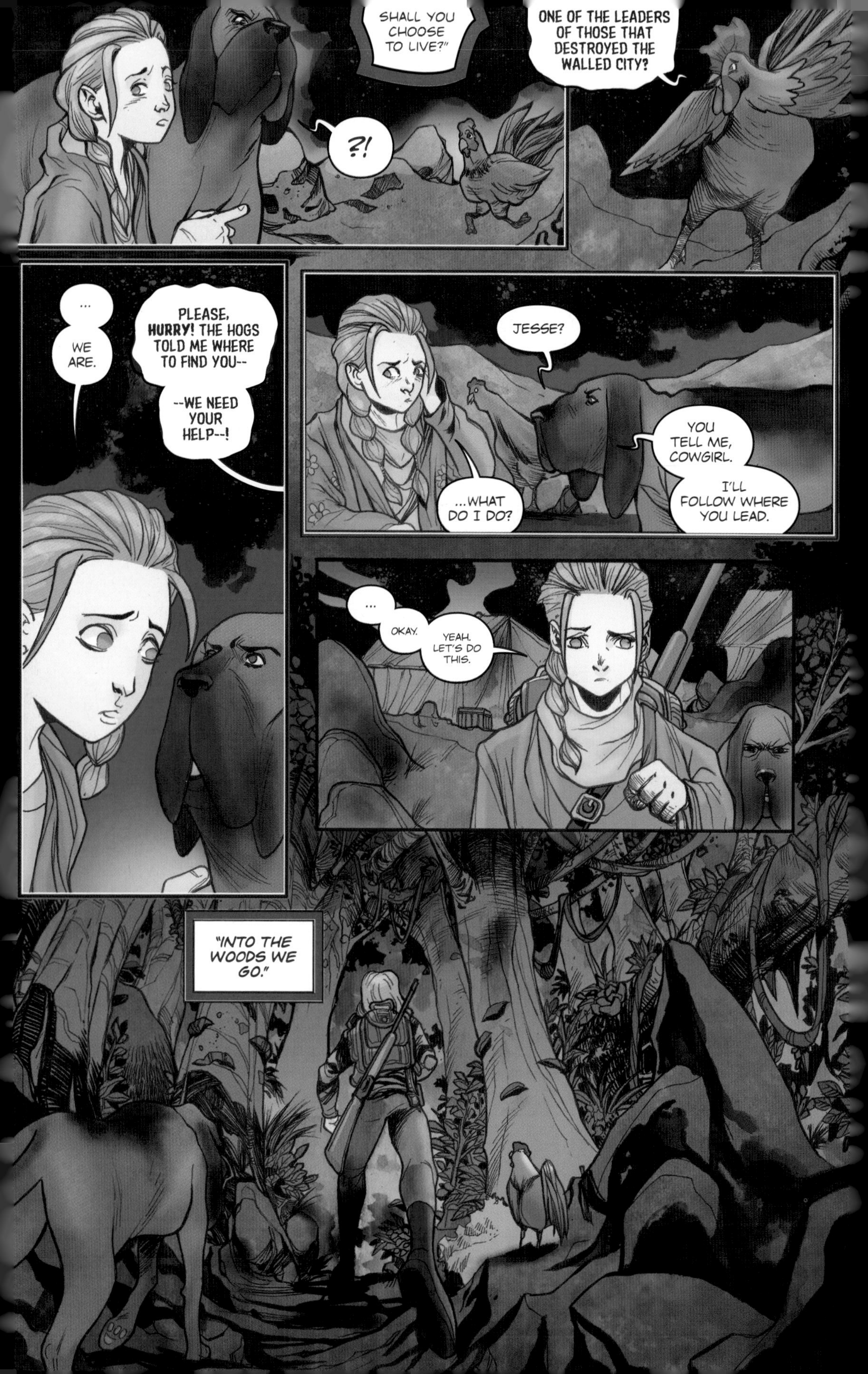
SHALL YOU CHOOSE TO LIVE?"
?!
ONE OF THE LEADERS OF THOSE THAT DESTROYED THE WALLED CITY?
...
WE ARE.
PLEASE, **HURRY!** THE HOGS TOLD ME WHERE TO FIND YOU--
--WE NEED YOUR HELP--!
JESSE?
...WHAT DO I DO?
YOU TELL ME, COWGIRL.
I'LL FOLLOW WHERE YOU LEAD.
...
OKAY.
YEAH. LET'S DO THIS.
"INTO THE WOODS WE GO."

20
SOUTHERN GOTHIC

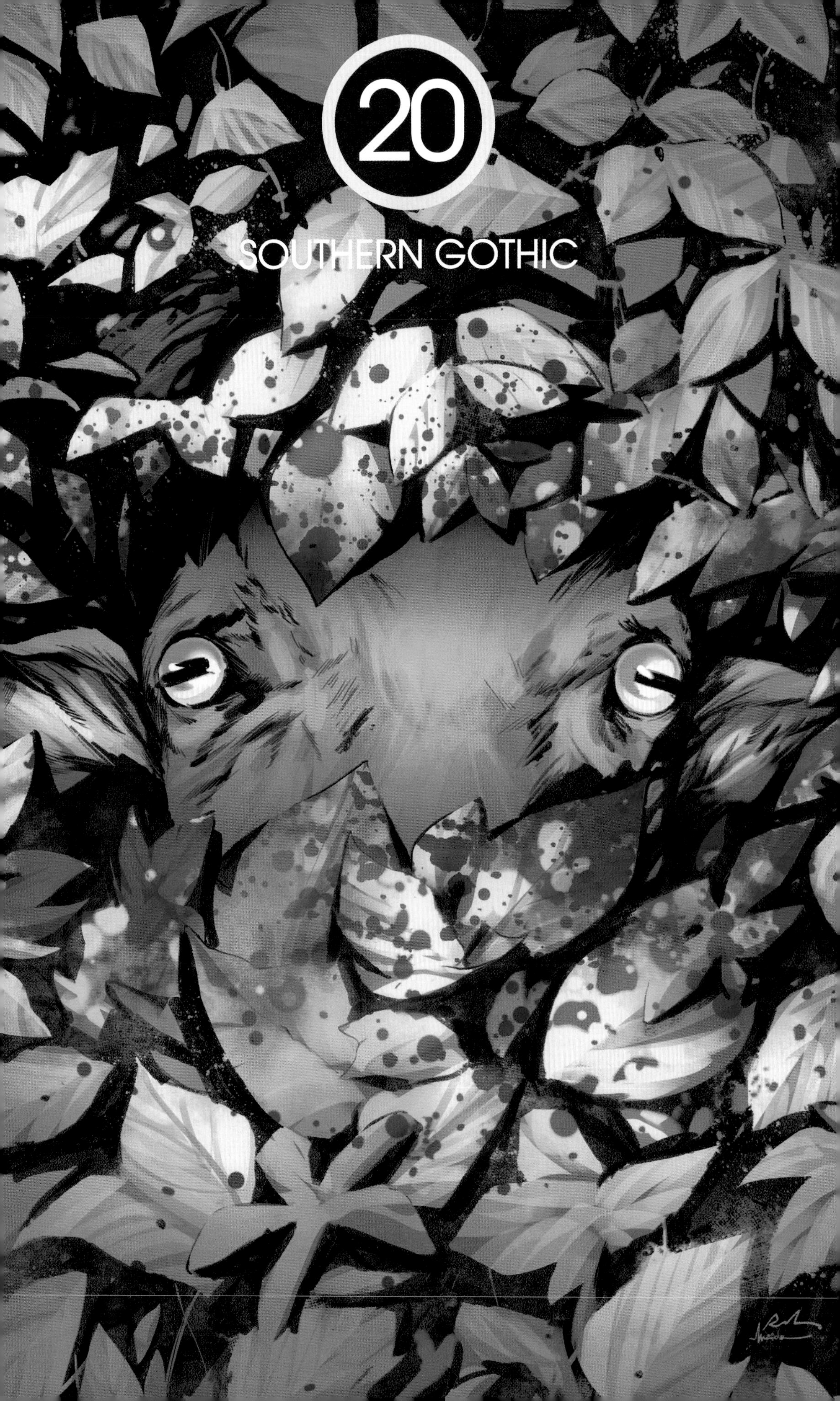

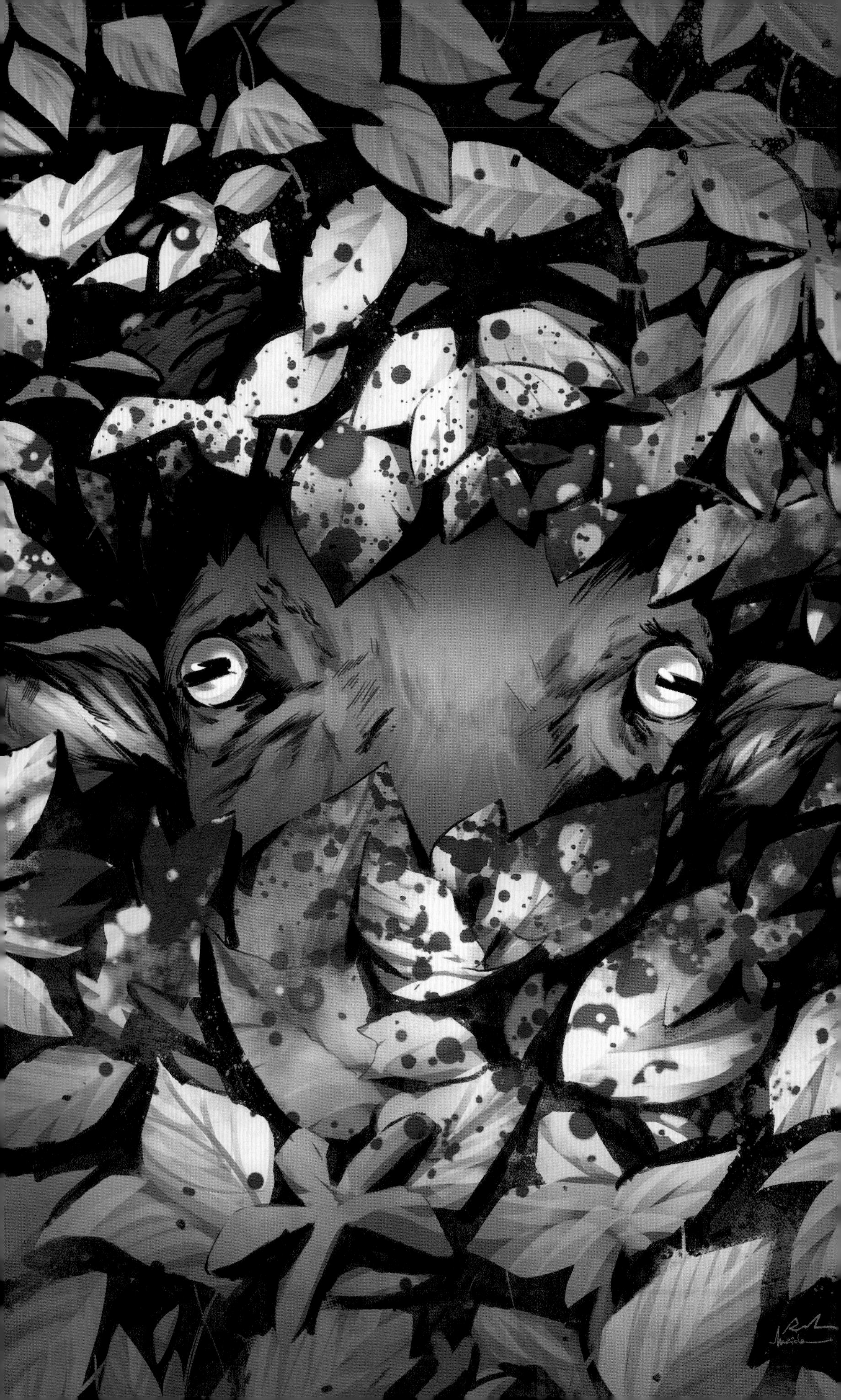

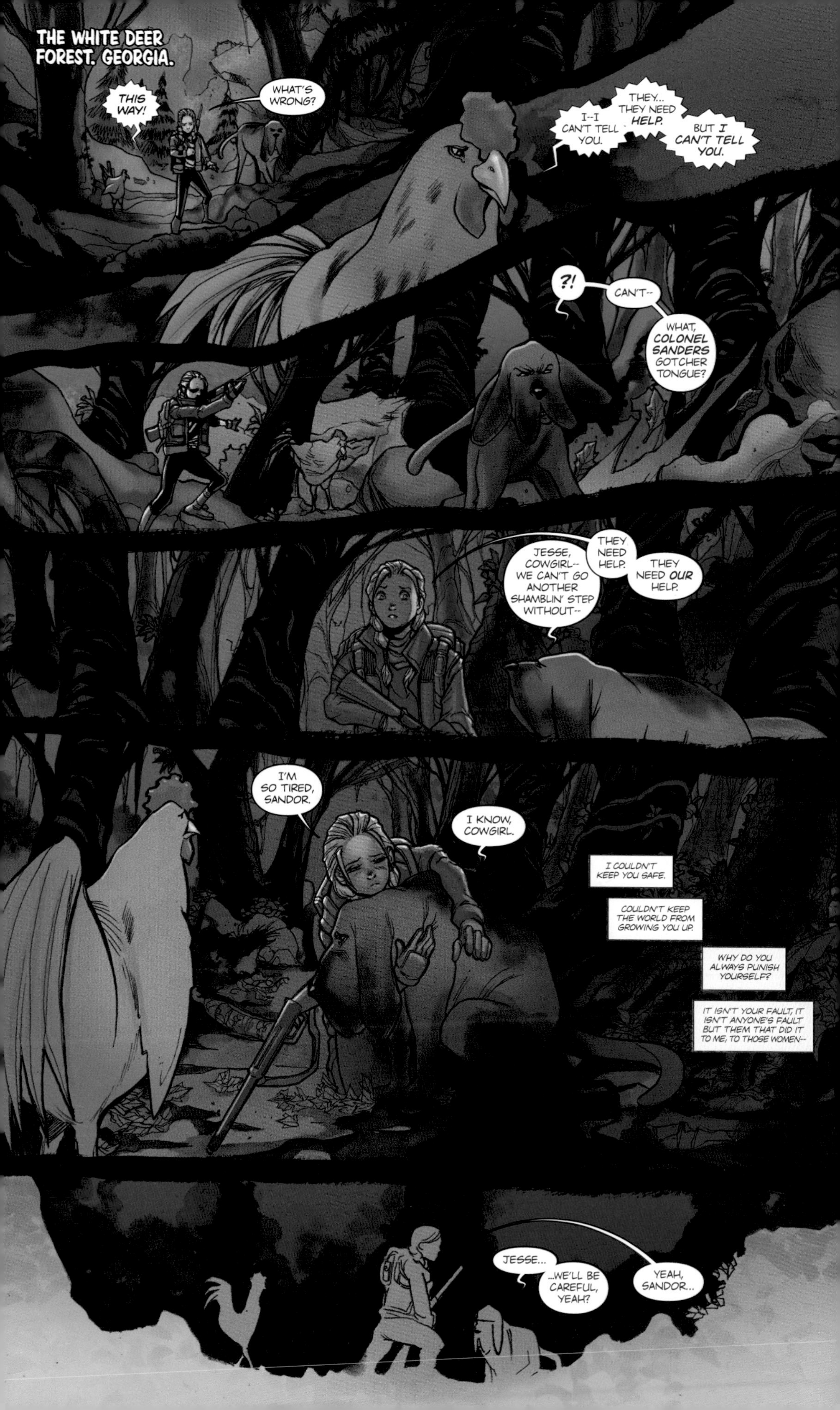

THE WHITE DEER FOREST. GEORGIA.
THIS WAY!
WHAT'S WRONG?
I--I CAN'T TELL YOU.
THEY... THEY NEED HELP.
BUT I CAN'T TELL YOU.
?!
CAN'T--
WHAT, COLONEL SANDERS GOTCHER TONGUE?
JESSE, COWGIRL-- WE CAN'T GO ANOTHER SHAMBLIN' STEP WITHOUT--
THEY NEED HELP.
THEY NEED OUR HELP.
I'M SO TIRED, SANDOR.
I KNOW, COWGIRL.
I COULDN'T KEEP YOU SAFE.
COULDN'T KEEP THE WORLD FROM GROWING YOU UP.
WHY DO YOU ALWAYS PUNISH YOURSELF?
IT ISN'T YOUR FAULT, IT ISN'T ANYONE'S FAULT BUT THEM THAT DID IT TO ME, TO THOSE WOMEN--
JESSE...
...WE'LL BE CAREFUL, YEAH?
YEAH, SANDOR...

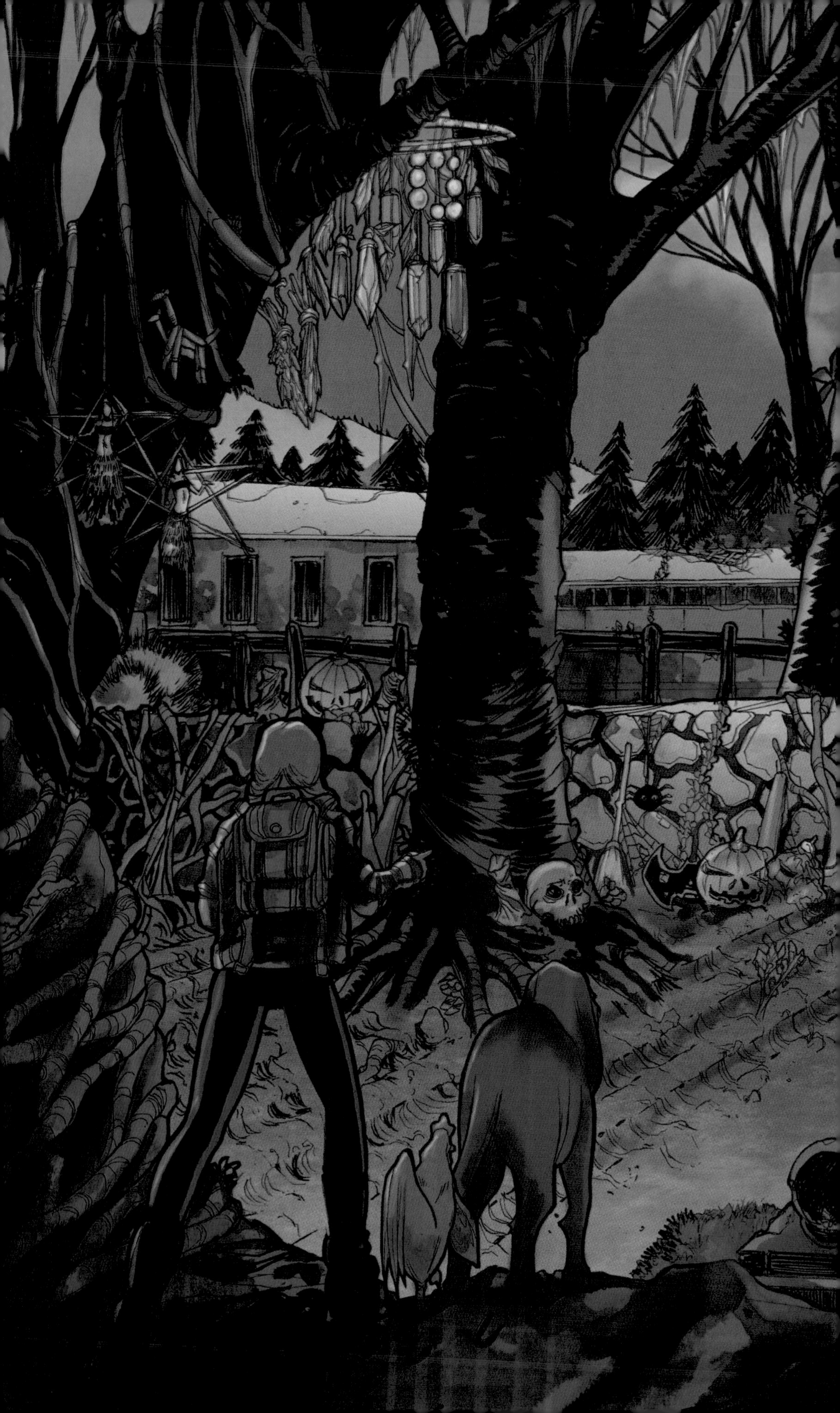

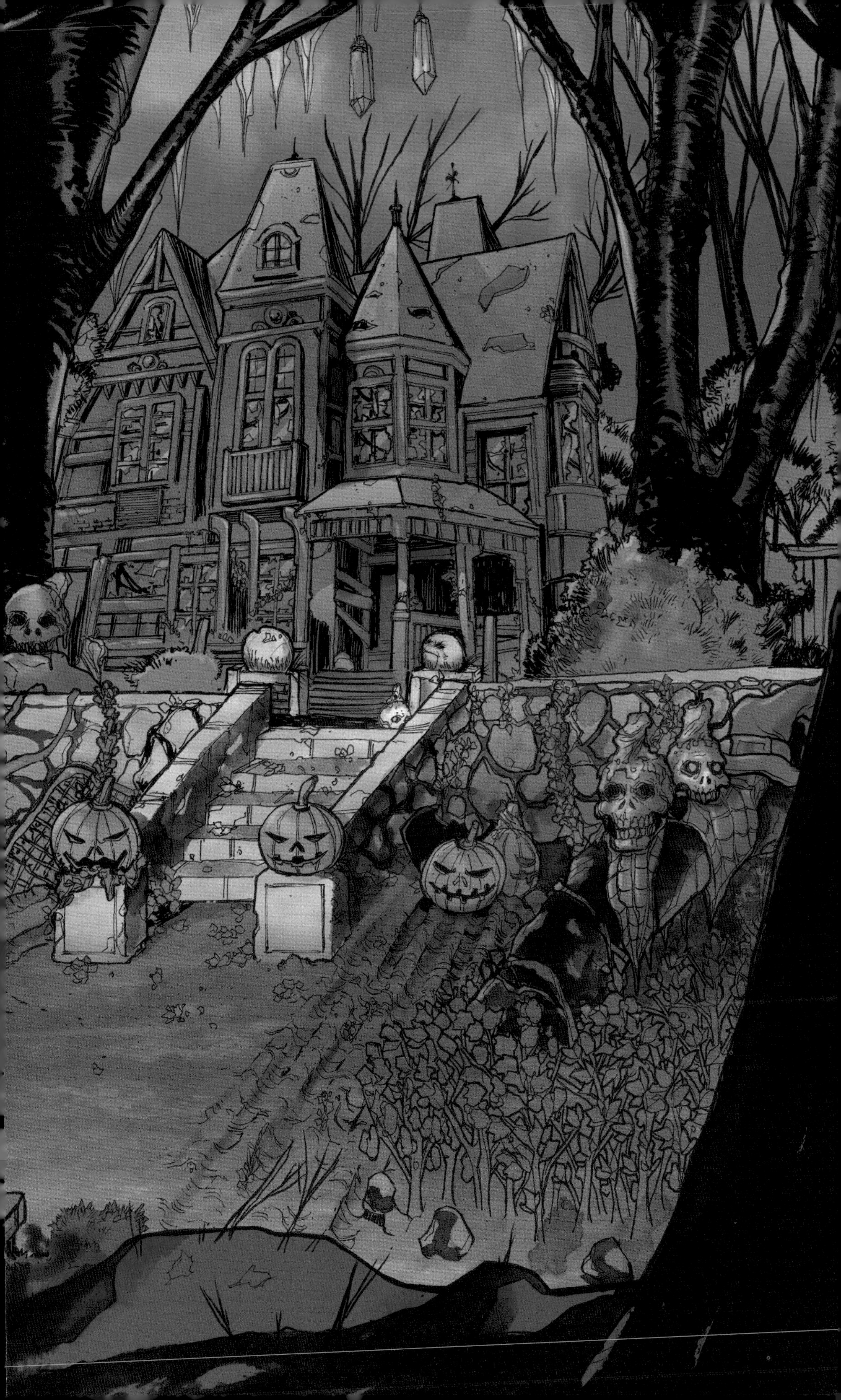

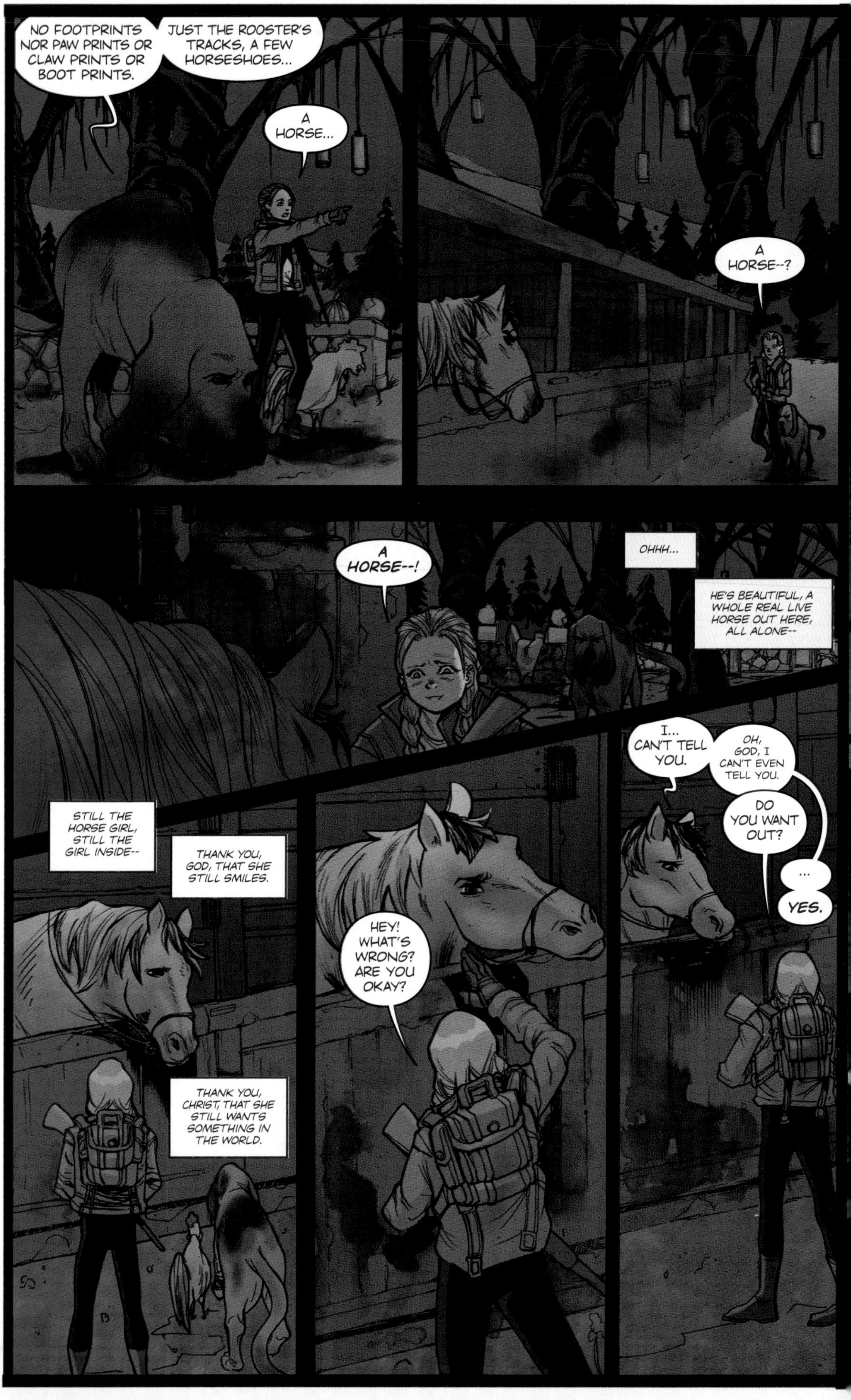
NO FOOTPRINTS NOR PAW PRINTS OR CLAW PRINTS OR BOOT PRINTS.
JUST THE ROOSTER'S TRACKS, A FEW HORSESHOES...
A HORSE...
A HORSE--?
A HORSE--!
OHHH...
HE'S BEAUTIFUL, A WHOLE REAL LIVE HORSE OUT HERE, ALL ALONE--
STILL THE HORSE GIRL, STILL THE GIRL INSIDE--
THANK YOU, GOD, THAT SHE STILL SMILES.
THANK YOU, CHRIST, THAT SHE STILL WANTS SOMETHING IN THE WORLD.
HEY! WHAT'S WRONG? ARE YOU OKAY?
I... CAN'T TELL YOU.
OH, GOD, I CAN'T EVEN TELL YOU.
DO YOU WANT OUT?
...
YES.

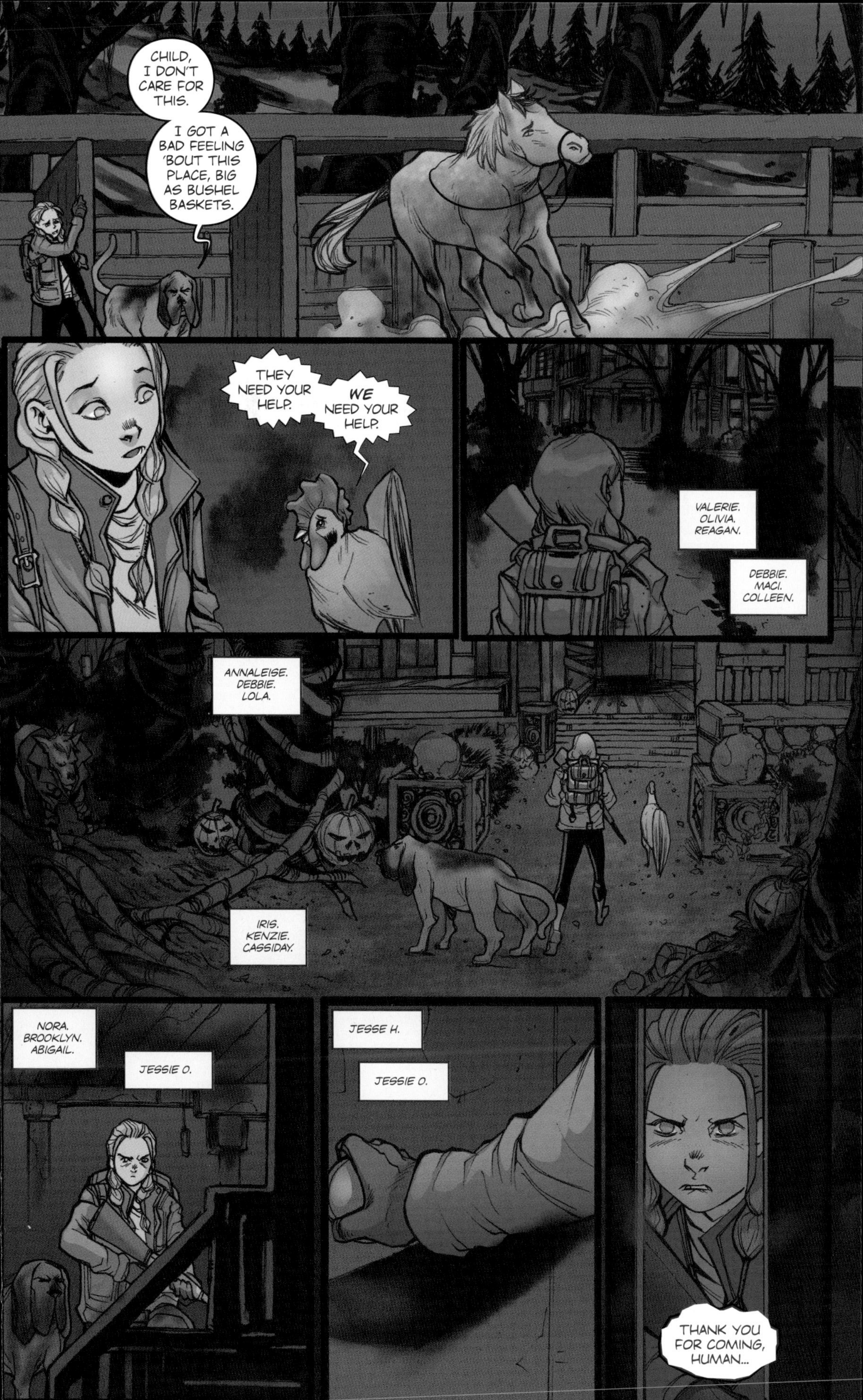
CHILD, I DON'T CARE FOR THIS.
I GOT A BAD FEELING 'BOUT THIS PLACE, BIG AS BUSHEL BASKETS.
THEY NEED YOUR HELP.
WE NEED YOUR HELP.
VALERIE. OLIVIA. REAGAN.
DEBBIE. MACI. COLLEEN.
ANNALEISE. DEBBIE. LOLA.
IRIS. KENZIE. CASSIDAY.
NORA. BROOKLYN. ABIGAIL.
JESSIE O.
JESSE H.
JESSIE O.
THANK YOU FOR COMING, HUMAN...

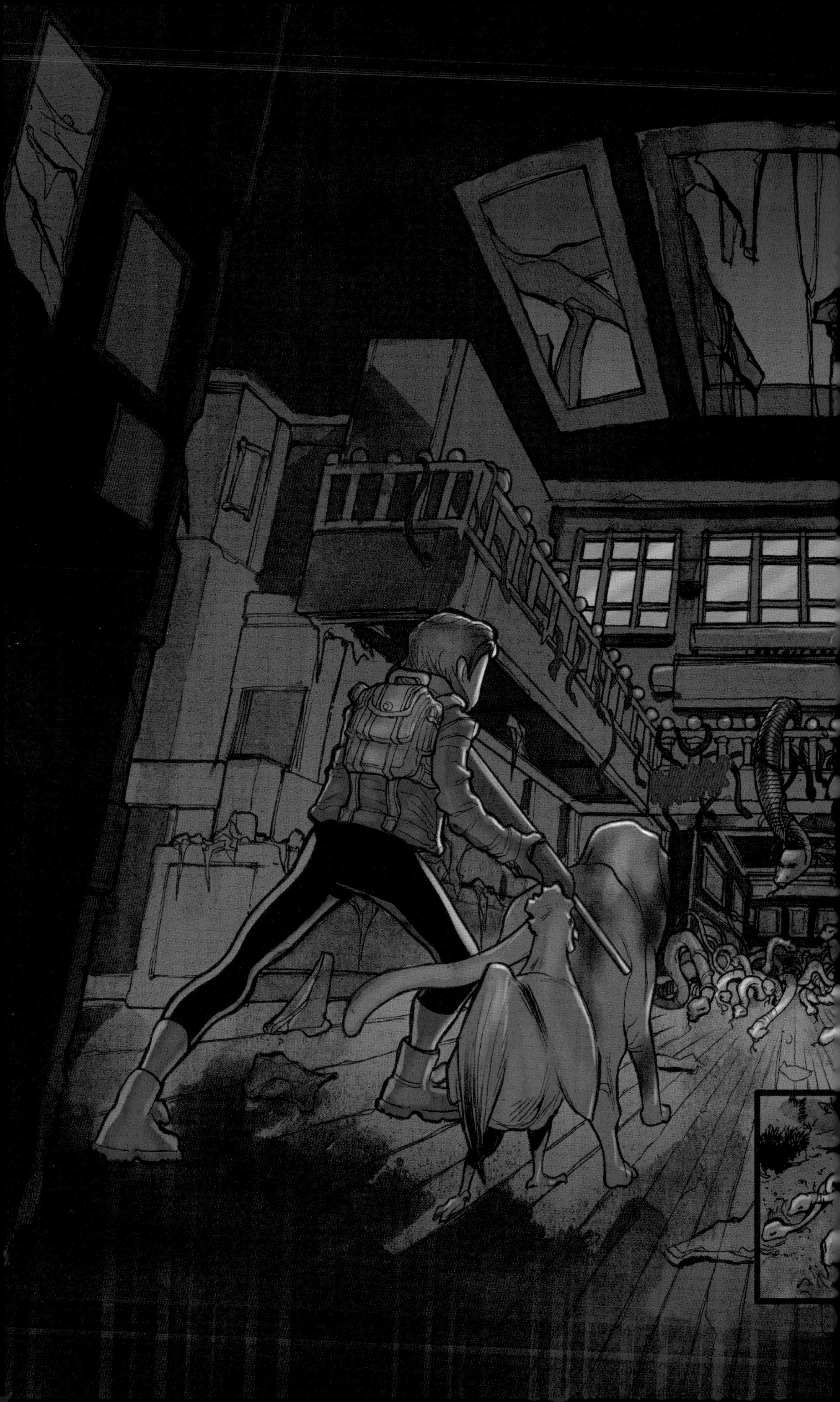

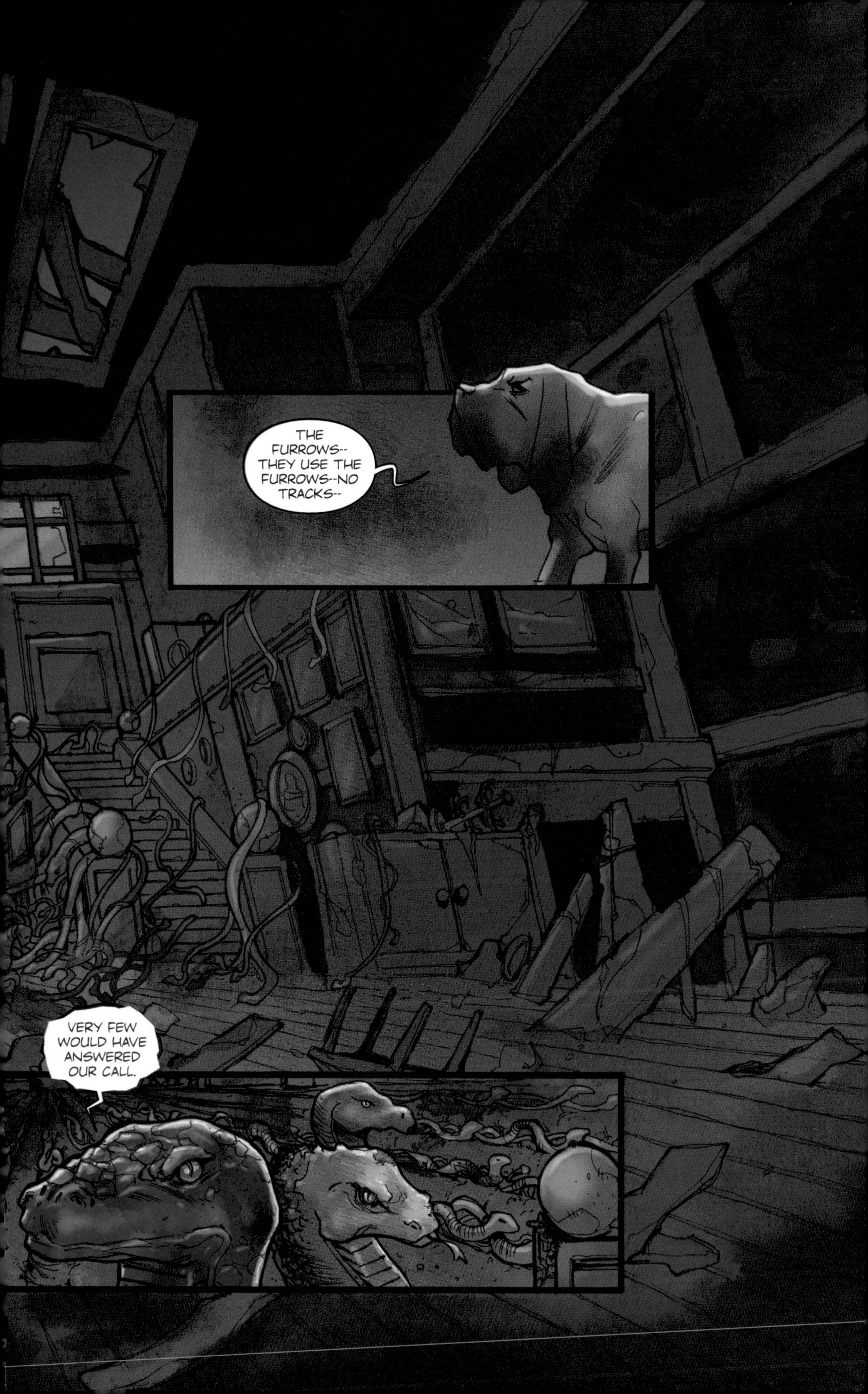
THE FURROWS-- THEY USE THE FURROWS--NO TRACKS--
VERY FEW WOULD HAVE ANSWERED OUR CALL.

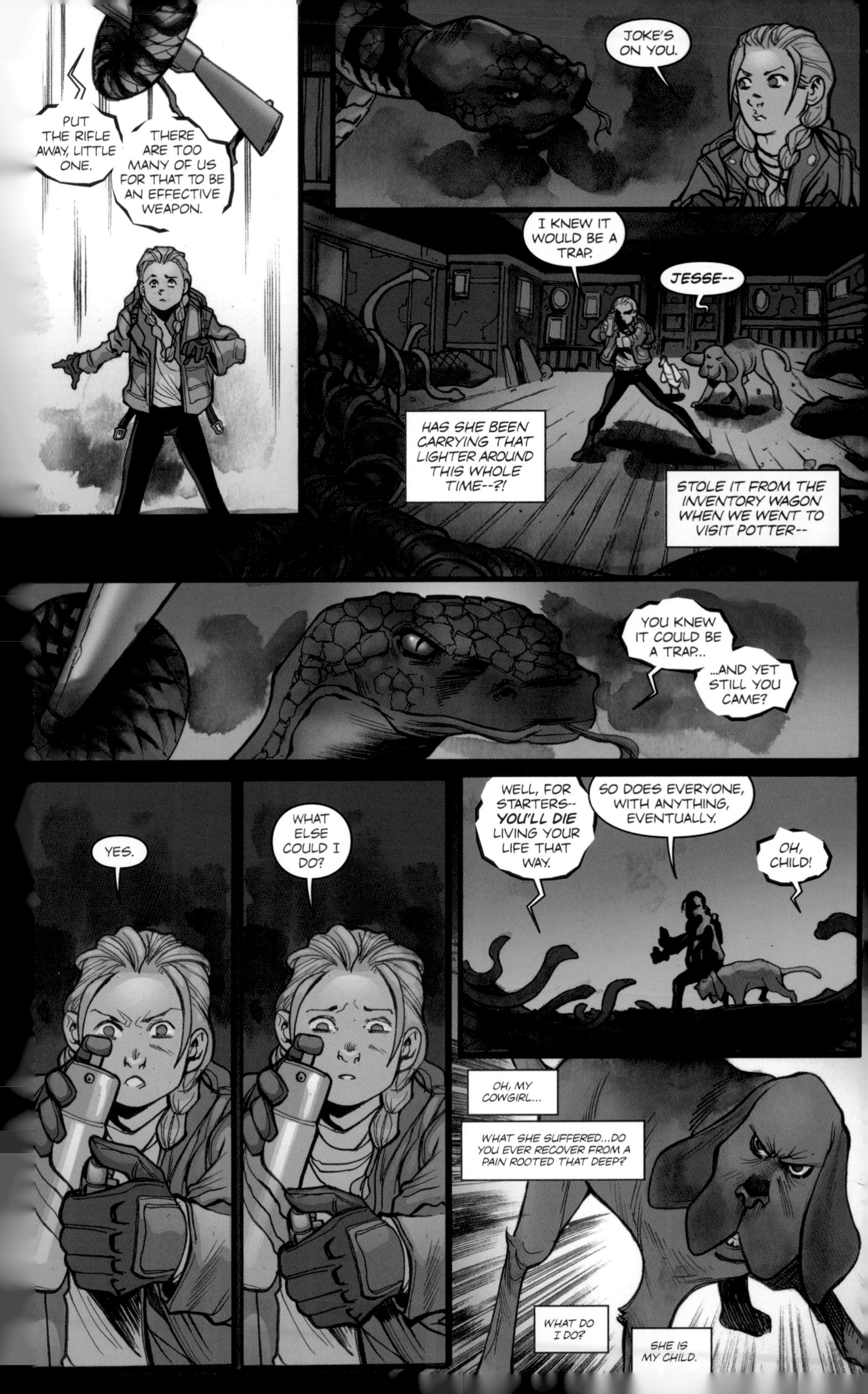
PUT THE RIFLE AWAY, LITTLE ONE.
THERE ARE TOO MANY OF US FOR THAT TO BE AN EFFECTIVE WEAPON.
JOKE'S ON YOU.
I KNEW IT WOULD BE A TRAP.
JESSE--
HAS SHE BEEN CARRYING THAT LIGHTER AROUND THIS WHOLE TIME--?!
STOLE IT FROM THE INVENTORY WAGON WHEN WE WENT TO VISIT POTTER--
YOU KNEW IT COULD BE A TRAP...
...AND YET STILL YOU CAME?
YES.
WHAT ELSE COULD I DO?
WELL, FOR STARTERS-- YOU'LL DIE LIVING YOUR LIFE THAT WAY.
SO DOES EVERYONE, WITH ANYTHING, EVENTUALLY.
OH, CHILD!
OH, MY COWGIRL...
WHAT SHE SUFFERED...DO YOU EVER RECOVER FROM A PAIN ROOTED THAT DEEP?
WHAT DO I DO?
SHE IS MY CHILD.

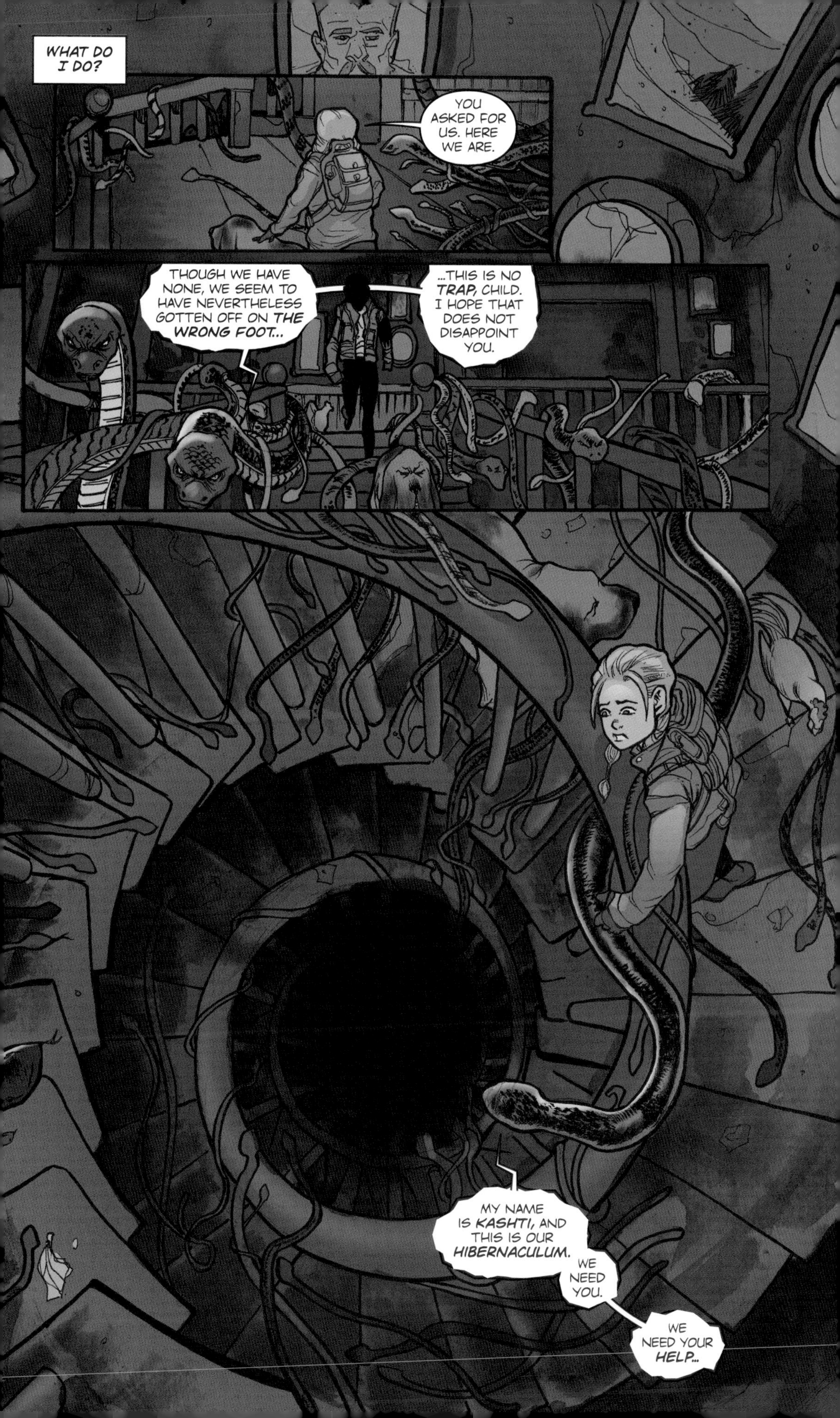
WHAT DO I DO?
YOU ASKED FOR US. HERE WE ARE.
THOUGH WE HAVE NONE, WE SEEM TO HAVE NEVERTHELESS GOTTEN OFF ON **THE WRONG FOOT...**
...THIS IS NO ***TRAP,*** CHILD. I HOPE THAT DOES NOT DISAPPOINT YOU.
MY NAME IS ***KASHTI,*** AND THIS IS OUR ***HIBERNACULUM.***
WE NEED YOU.
WE NEED YOUR ***HELP...***

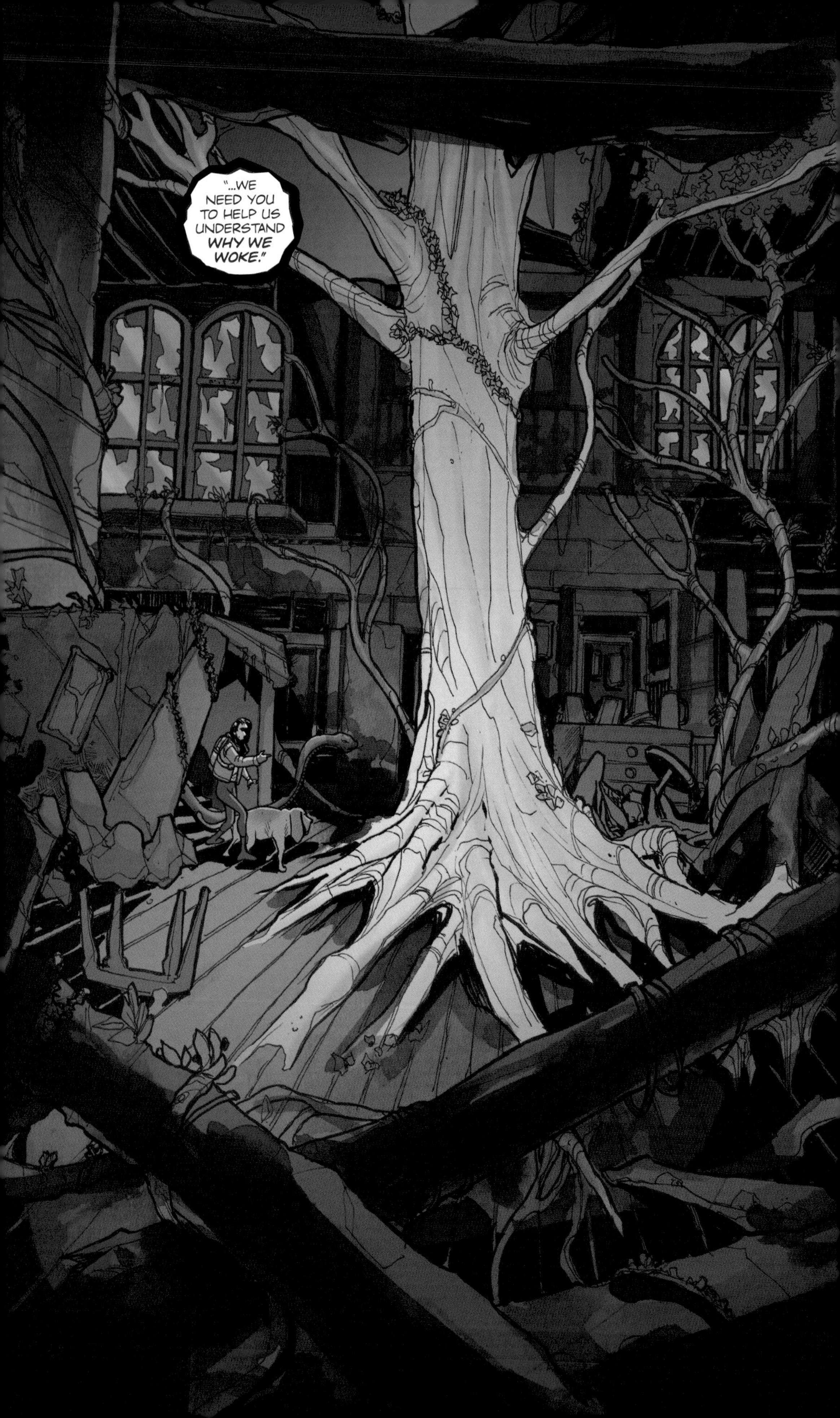
"...WE NEED YOU TO HELP US UNDERSTAND WHY WE WOKE."

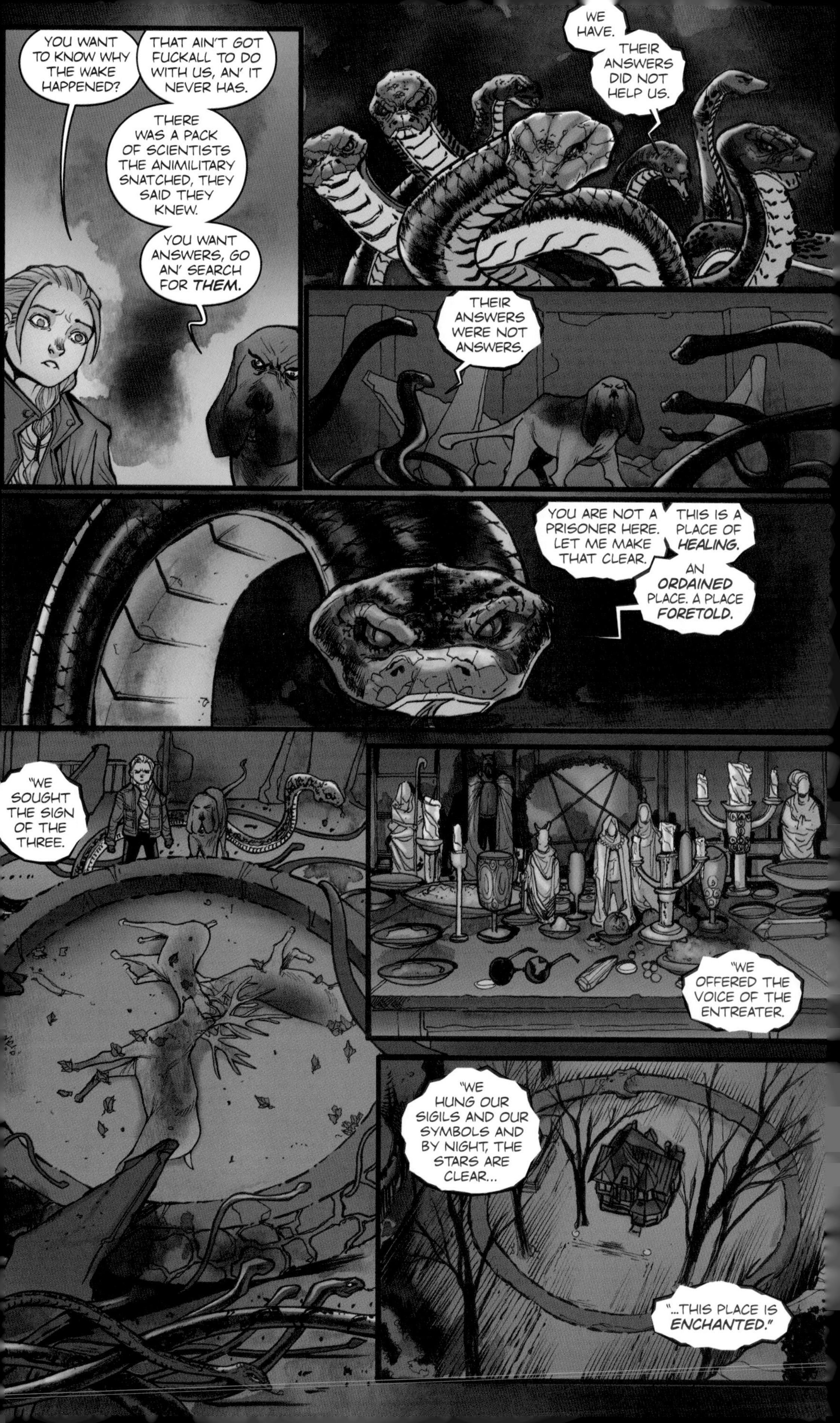
YOU WANT TO KNOW WHY THE WAKE HAPPENED?
THAT AIN'T GOT FUCKALL TO DO WITH US, AN' IT NEVER HAS.
THERE WAS A PACK OF SCIENTISTS THE ANIMILITARY SNATCHED, THEY SAID THEY KNEW.
YOU WANT ANSWERS, GO AN' SEARCH FOR *THEM.*
WE HAVE.
THEIR ANSWERS DID NOT HELP US.
THEIR ANSWERS WERE NOT ANSWERS.
YOU ARE NOT A PRISONER HERE. LET ME MAKE THAT CLEAR.
THIS IS A PLACE OF *HEALING.*
AN *ORDAINED* PLACE. A PLACE *FORETOLD.*
"WE SOUGHT THE SIGN OF THE THREE.
"WE OFFERED THE VOICE OF THE ENTREATER.
"WE HUNG OUR SIGILS AND OUR SYMBOLS AND BY NIGHT, THE STARS ARE CLEAR...
"...THIS PLACE IS *ENCHANTED.*"

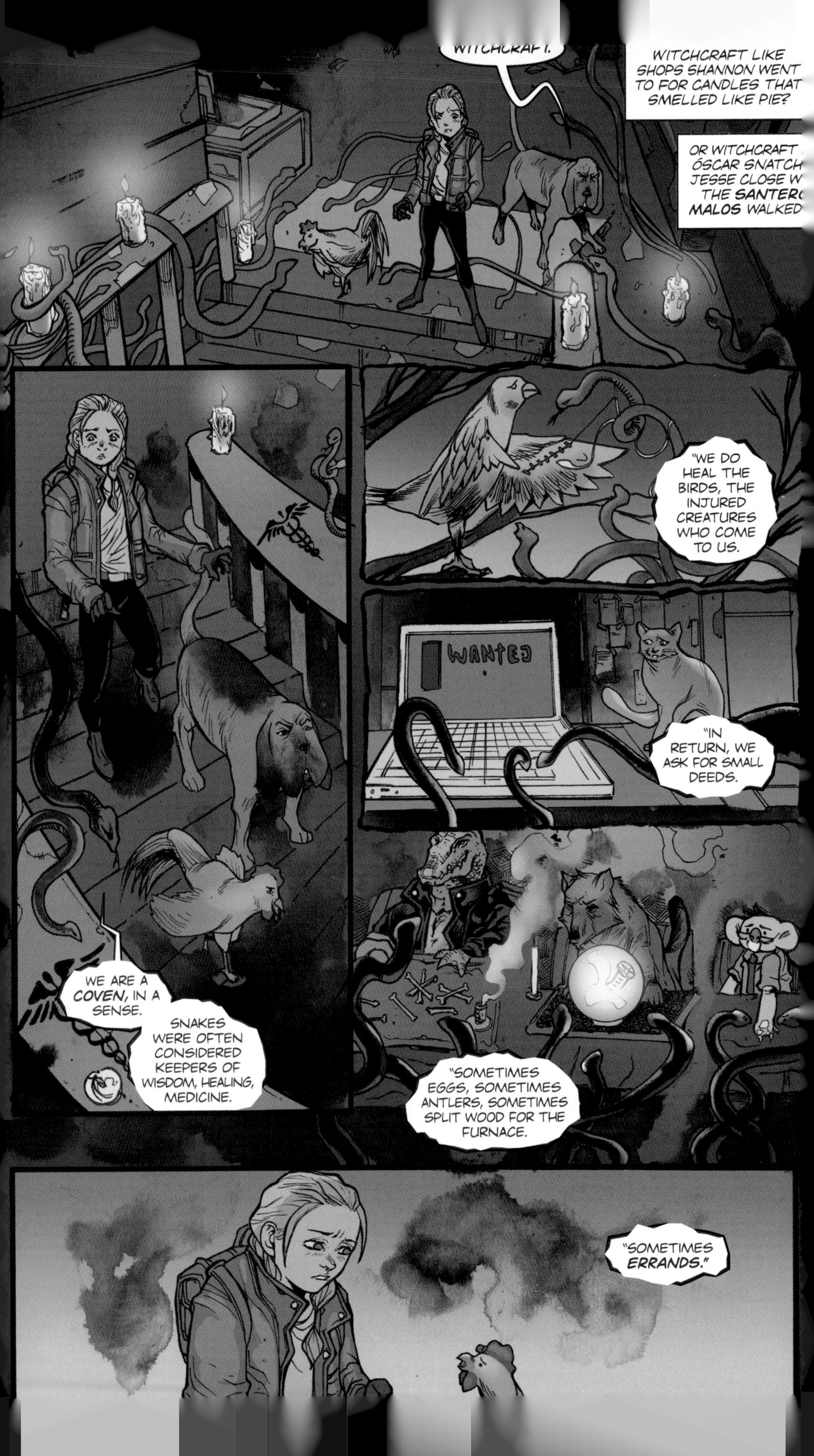

WITCHCRAFT.
WITCHCRAFT LIKE SHOPS SHANNON WENT TO FOR CANDLES THAT SMELLED LIKE PIE?
OR WITCHCRAFT ÓSCAR SNATCH JESSE CLOSE W THE SANTERO MALOS WALKED
"WE DO HEAL THE BIRDS, THE INJURED CREATURES WHO COME TO US.
WANTED
"IN RETURN, WE ASK FOR SMALL DEEDS.
WE ARE A COVEN, IN A SENSE.
SNAKES WERE OFTEN CONSIDERED KEEPERS OF WISDOM, HEALING, MEDICINE.
"SOMETIMES EGGS, SOMETIMES ANTLERS, SOMETIMES SPLIT WOOD FOR THE FURNACE.
"SOMETIMES ERRANDS."

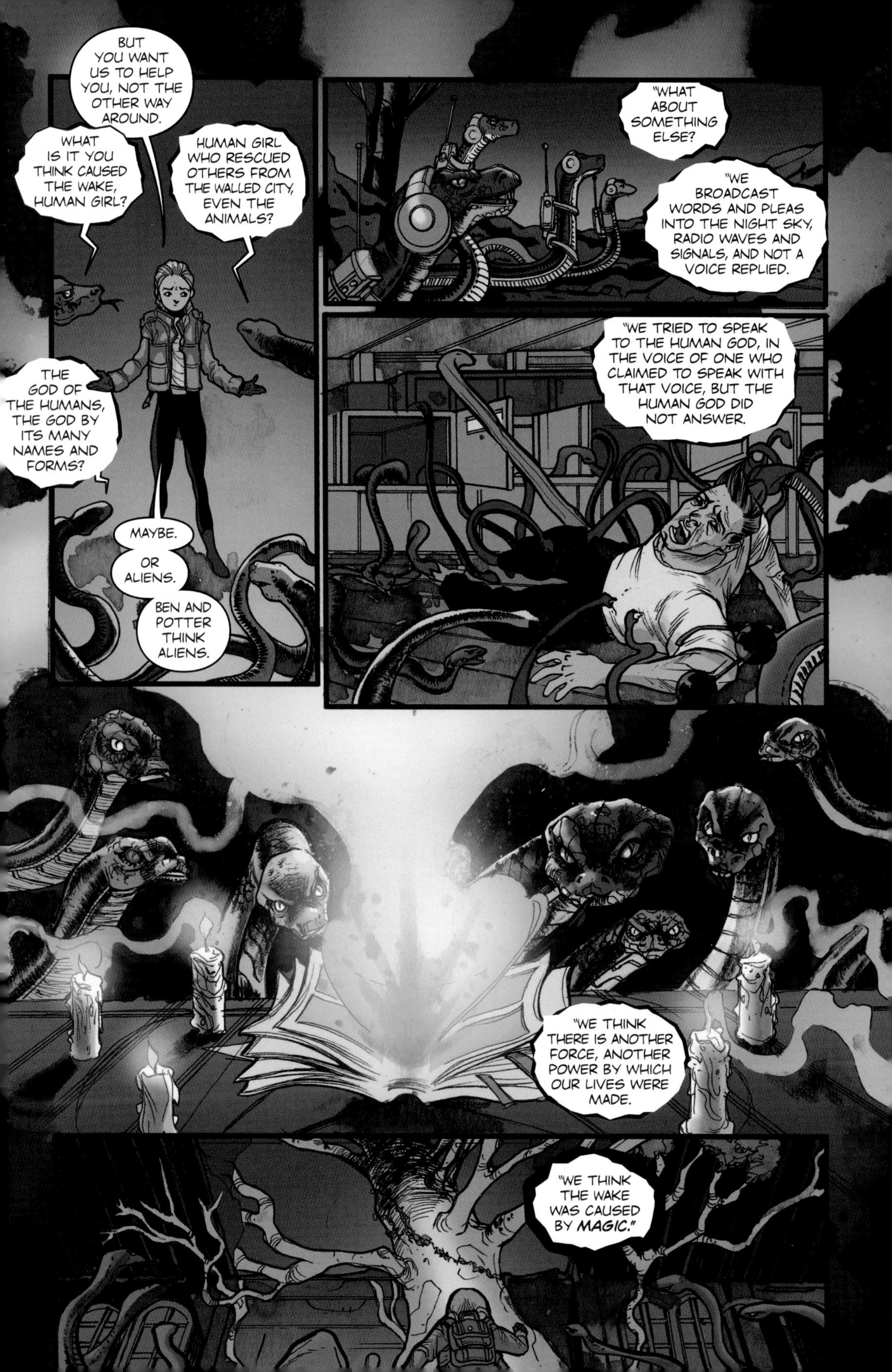
BUT YOU WANT US TO HELP YOU, NOT THE OTHER WAY AROUND.
WHAT IS IT YOU THINK CAUSED THE WAKE, HUMAN GIRL?
HUMAN GIRL WHO RESCUED OTHERS FROM THE WALLED CITY, EVEN THE ANIMALS?
THE GOD OF THE HUMANS, THE GOD BY ITS MANY NAMES AND FORMS?
MAYBE.
OR ALIENS.
BEN AND POTTER THINK ALIENS.
"WHAT ABOUT SOMETHING ELSE?
"WE BROADCAST WORDS AND PLEAS INTO THE NIGHT SKY, RADIO WAVES AND SIGNALS, AND NOT A VOICE REPLIED.
"WE TRIED TO SPEAK TO THE HUMAN GOD, IN THE VOICE OF ONE WHO CLAIMED TO SPEAK WITH THAT VOICE, BUT THE HUMAN GOD DID NOT ANSWER.
"WE THINK THERE IS ANOTHER FORCE, ANOTHER POWER BY WHICH OUR LIVES WERE MADE.
"WE THINK THE WAKE WAS CAUSED BY MAGIC."

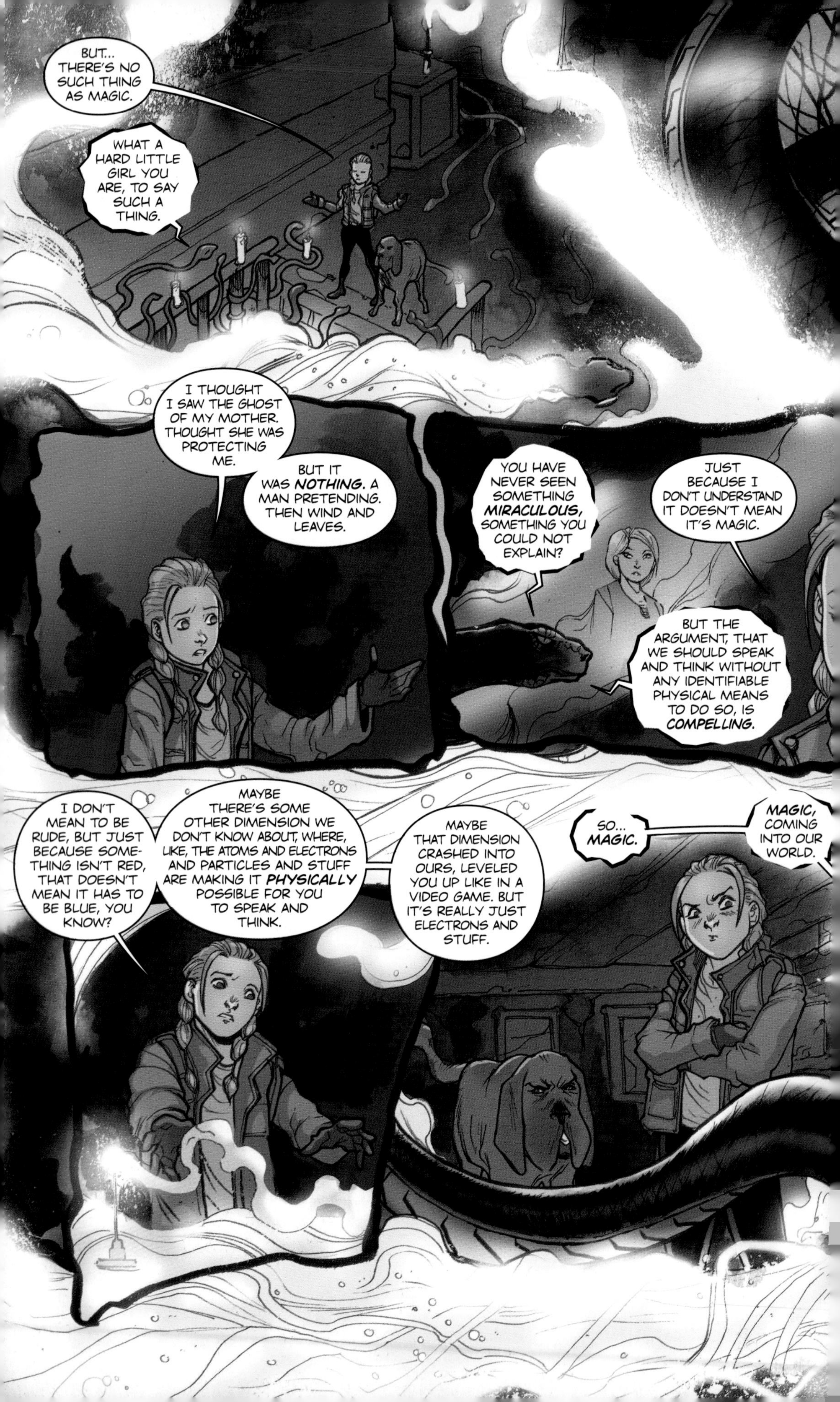
BUT... THERE'S NO SUCH THING AS MAGIC.
WHAT A HARD LITTLE GIRL YOU ARE, TO SAY SUCH A THING.
I THOUGHT I SAW THE GHOST OF MY MOTHER. THOUGHT SHE WAS PROTECTING ME.
BUT IT WAS NOTHING. A MAN PRETENDING. THEN WIND AND LEAVES.
YOU HAVE NEVER SEEN SOMETHING MIRACULOUS, SOMETHING YOU COULD NOT EXPLAIN?
JUST BECAUSE I DON'T UNDERSTAND IT DOESN'T MEAN IT'S MAGIC.
BUT THE ARGUMENT, THAT WE SHOULD SPEAK AND THINK WITHOUT ANY IDENTIFIABLE PHYSICAL MEANS TO DO SO, IS COMPELLING.
I DON'T MEAN TO BE RUDE, BUT JUST BECAUSE SOMETHING ISN'T RED, THAT DOESN'T MEAN IT HAS TO BE BLUE, YOU KNOW?
MAYBE THERE'S SOME OTHER DIMENSION WE DON'T KNOW ABOUT, WHERE, LIKE, THE ATOMS AND ELECTRONS AND PARTICLES AND STUFF ARE MAKING IT PHYSICALLY POSSIBLE FOR YOU TO SPEAK AND THINK.
MAYBE THAT DIMENSION CRASHED INTO OURS, LEVELED YOU UP LIKE IN A VIDEO GAME. BUT IT'S REALLY JUST ELECTRONS AND STUFF.
SO... MAGIC.
MAGIC, COMING INTO OUR WORLD.

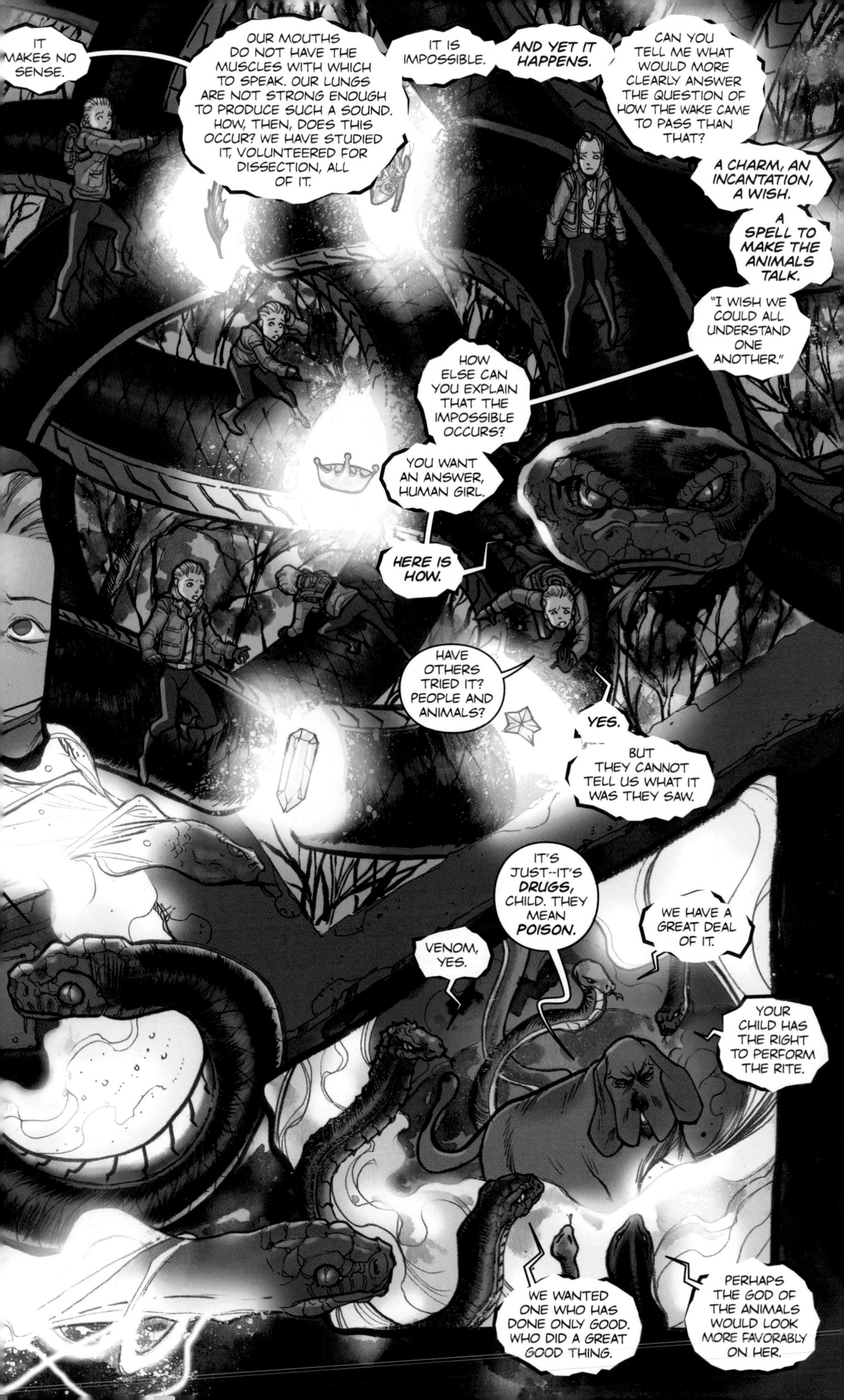

IT MAKES NO SENSE.
OUR MOUTHS DO NOT HAVE THE MUSCLES WITH WHICH TO SPEAK. OUR LUNGS ARE NOT STRONG ENOUGH TO PRODUCE SUCH A SOUND. HOW, THEN, DOES THIS OCCUR? WE HAVE STUDIED IT, VOLUNTEERED FOR DISSECTION, ALL OF IT.
IT IS IMPOSSIBLE.
AND YET IT HAPPENS.
CAN YOU TELL ME WHAT WOULD MORE CLEARLY ANSWER THE QUESTION OF HOW THE WAKE CAME TO PASS THAN THAT?
A CHARM, AN INCANTATION, A WISH.
A SPELL TO MAKE THE ANIMALS TALK.
"I WISH WE COULD ALL UNDERSTAND ONE ANOTHER."
HOW ELSE CAN YOU EXPLAIN THAT THE IMPOSSIBLE OCCURS?
YOU WANT AN ANSWER, HUMAN GIRL.
HERE IS HOW.
HAVE OTHERS TRIED IT? PEOPLE AND ANIMALS?
YES.
BUT THEY CANNOT TELL US WHAT IT WAS THEY SAW.
IT'S JUST--IT'S DRUGS, CHILD. THEY MEAN POISON.
VENOM, YES.
WE HAVE A GREAT DEAL OF IT.
YOUR CHILD HAS THE RIGHT TO PERFORM THE RITE.
WE WANTED ONE WHO HAS DONE ONLY GOOD. WHO DID A GREAT GOOD THING.
PERHAPS THE GOD OF THE ANIMALS WOULD LOOK MORE FAVORABLY ON HER.

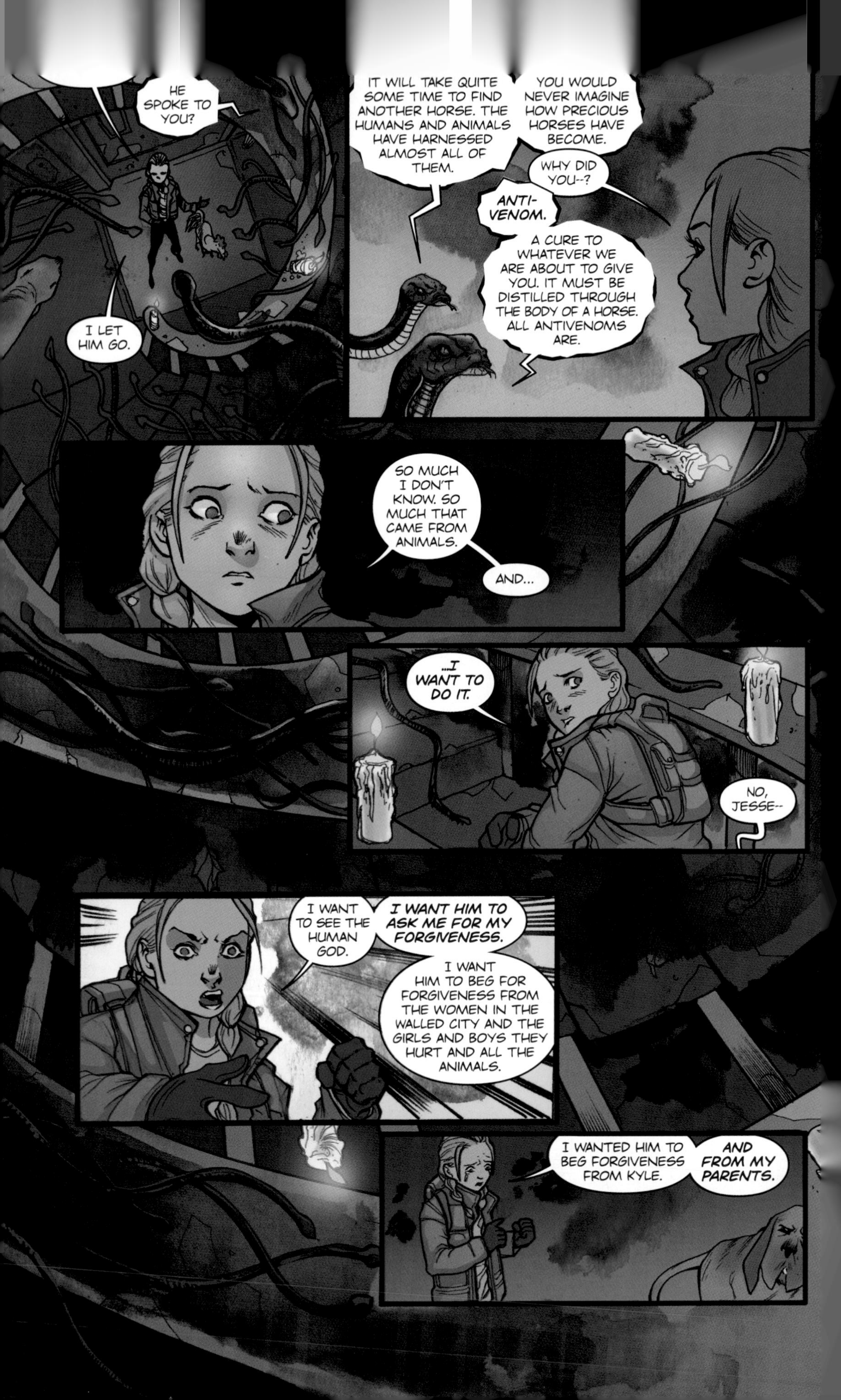
HE SPOKE TO YOU?
I LET HIM GO.
IT WILL TAKE QUITE SOME TIME TO FIND ANOTHER HORSE. THE HUMANS AND ANIMALS HAVE HARNESSED ALMOST ALL OF THEM.
YOU WOULD NEVER IMAGINE HOW PRECIOUS HORSES HAVE BECOME.
WHY DID YOU--?
ANTI-VENOM.
A CURE TO WHATEVER WE ARE ABOUT TO GIVE YOU. IT MUST BE DISTILLED THROUGH THE BODY OF A HORSE. ALL ANTIVENOMS ARE.
SO MUCH I DON'T KNOW. SO MUCH THAT CAME FROM ANIMALS.
AND...
...I WANT TO DO IT.
NO, JESSE--
I WANT TO SEE THE HUMAN GOD.
I WANT HIM TO ASK ME FOR MY FORGIVENESS.
I WANT HIM TO BEG FOR FORGIVENESS FROM THE WOMEN IN THE WALLED CITY AND THE GIRLS AND BOYS THEY HURT AND ALL THE ANIMALS.
I WANTED HIM TO BEG FORGIVENESS FROM KYLE.
AND FROM MY PARENTS.

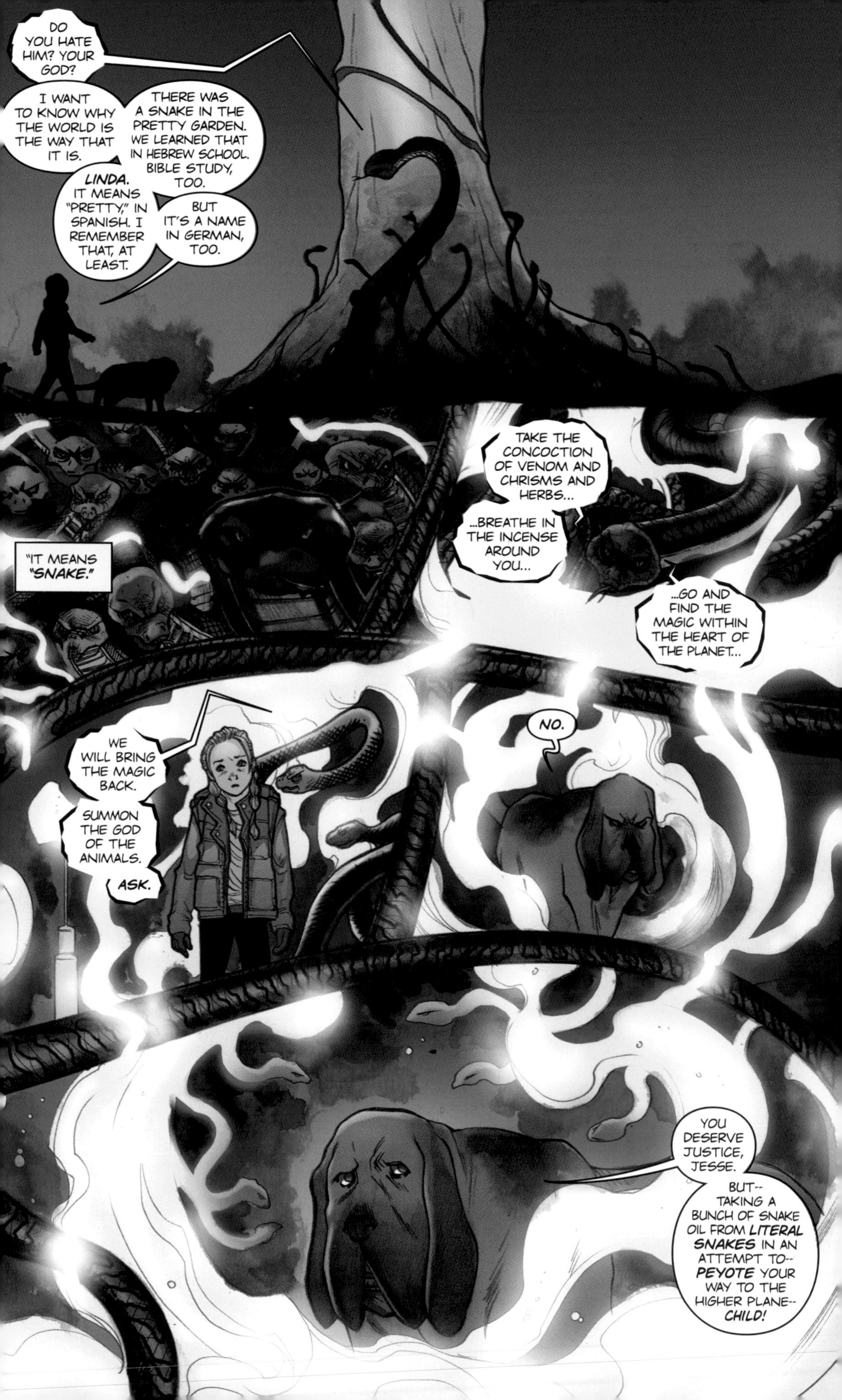
DO YOU HATE HIM? YOUR GOD?
I WANT TO KNOW WHY THE WORLD IS THE WAY THAT IT IS.
THERE WAS A SNAKE IN THE PRETTY GARDEN. WE LEARNED THAT IN HEBREW SCHOOL. BIBLE STUDY, TOO.
LINDA. IT MEANS "PRETTY," IN SPANISH. I REMEMBER THAT, AT LEAST.
BUT IT'S A NAME IN GERMAN, TOO.
"IT MEANS "SNAKE."
TAKE THE CONCOCTION OF VENOM AND CHRISMS AND HERBS...
...BREATHE IN THE INCENSE AROUND YOU...
...GO AND FIND THE MAGIC WITHIN THE HEART OF THE PLANET...
WE WILL BRING THE MAGIC BACK.
SUMMON THE GOD OF THE ANIMALS.
ASK.
NO.
YOU DESERVE JUSTICE, JESSE.
BUT-- TAKING A BUNCH OF SNAKE OIL FROM LITERAL SNAKES IN AN ATTEMPT TO-- PEYOTE YOUR WAY TO THE HIGHER PLANE-- CHILD!

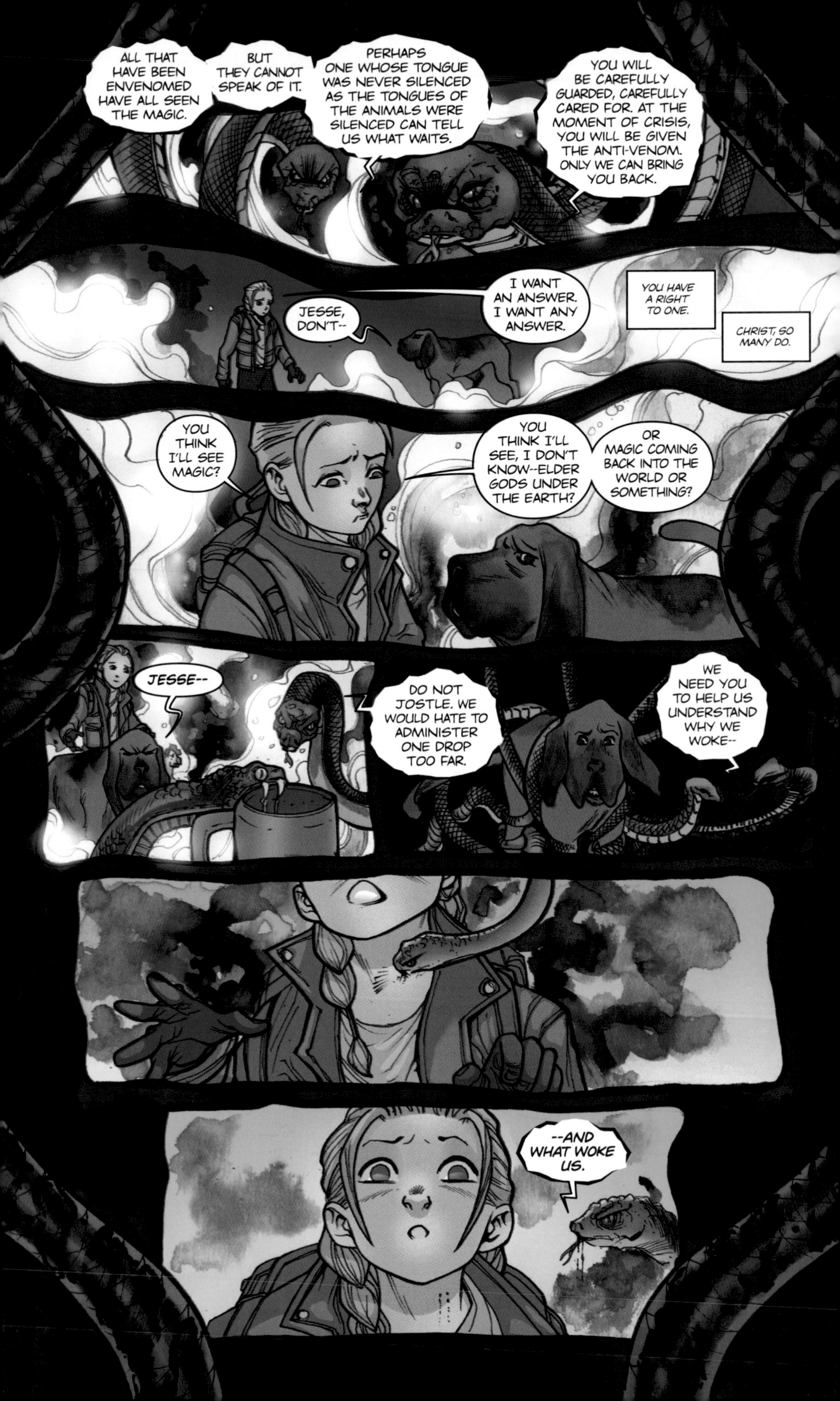
ALL THAT HAVE BEEN ENVENOMED HAVE ALL SEEN THE MAGIC.
BUT THEY CANNOT SPEAK OF IT.
PERHAPS ONE WHOSE TONGUE WAS NEVER SILENCED AS THE TONGUES OF THE ANIMALS WERE SILENCED CAN TELL US WHAT WAITS.
YOU WILL BE CAREFULLY GUARDED, CAREFULLY CARED FOR. AT THE MOMENT OF CRISIS, YOU WILL BE GIVEN THE ANTI-VENOM. ONLY WE CAN BRING YOU BACK.
JESSE, DON'T--
I WANT AN ANSWER. I WANT ANY ANSWER.
YOU HAVE A RIGHT TO ONE.
CHRIST, SO MANY DO.
YOU THINK I'LL SEE MAGIC?
YOU THINK I'LL SEE, I DON'T KNOW--ELDER GODS UNDER THE EARTH?
OR MAGIC COMING BACK INTO THE WORLD OR SOMETHING?
JESSE--
DO NOT JOSTLE. WE WOULD HATE TO ADMINISTER ONE DROP TOO FAR.
WE NEED YOU TO HELP US UNDERSTAND WHY WE WOKE--
--AND WHAT WOKE US.

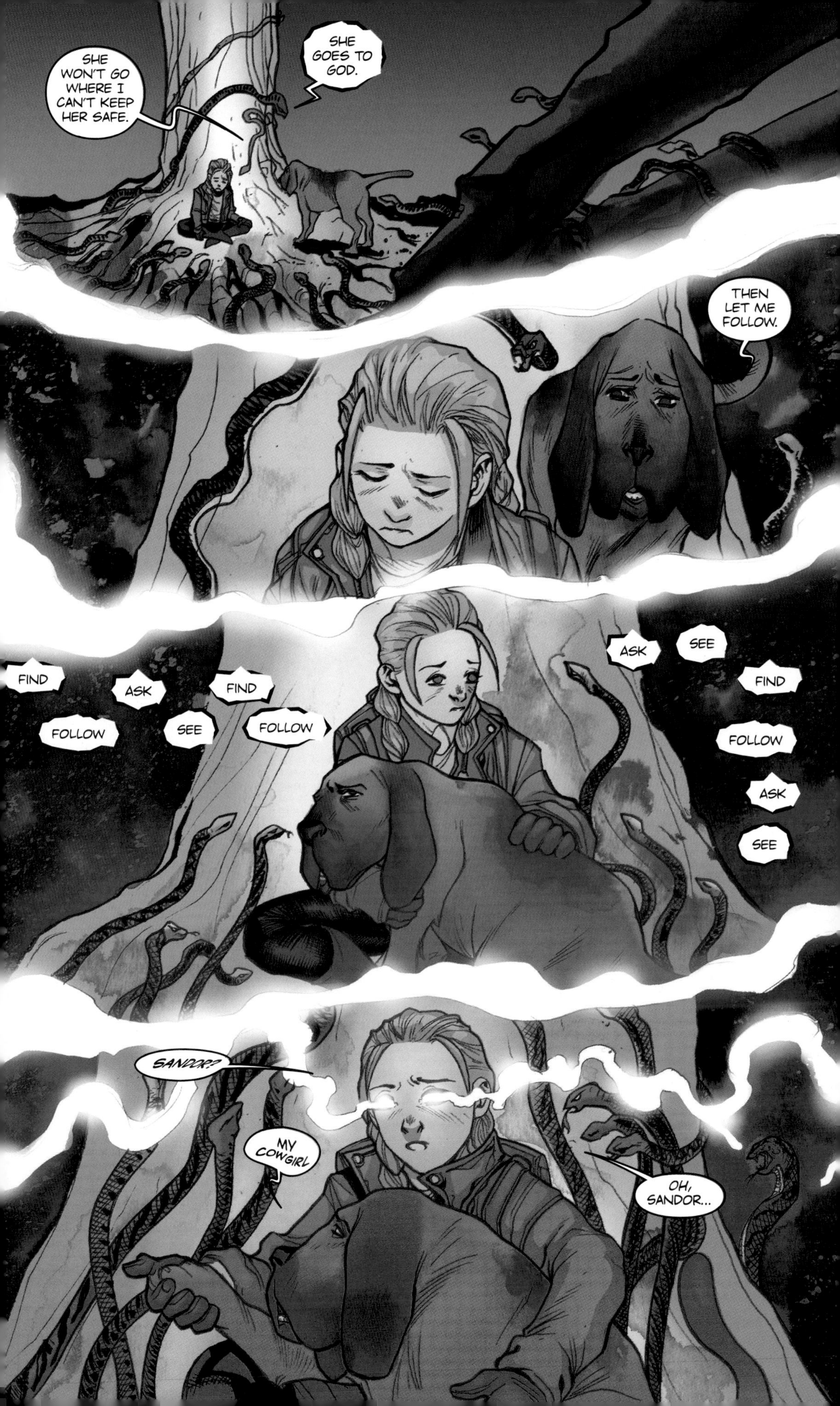
SHE WON'T GO WHERE I CAN'T KEEP HER SAFE.
SHE GOES TO GOD.
THEN LET ME FOLLOW.
FIND
ASK
FIND
FOLLOW
SEE
FOLLOW
ASK
SEE
FIND
FOLLOW
ASK
SEE
SANDOR?
MY COWGIRL
OH, SANDOR...

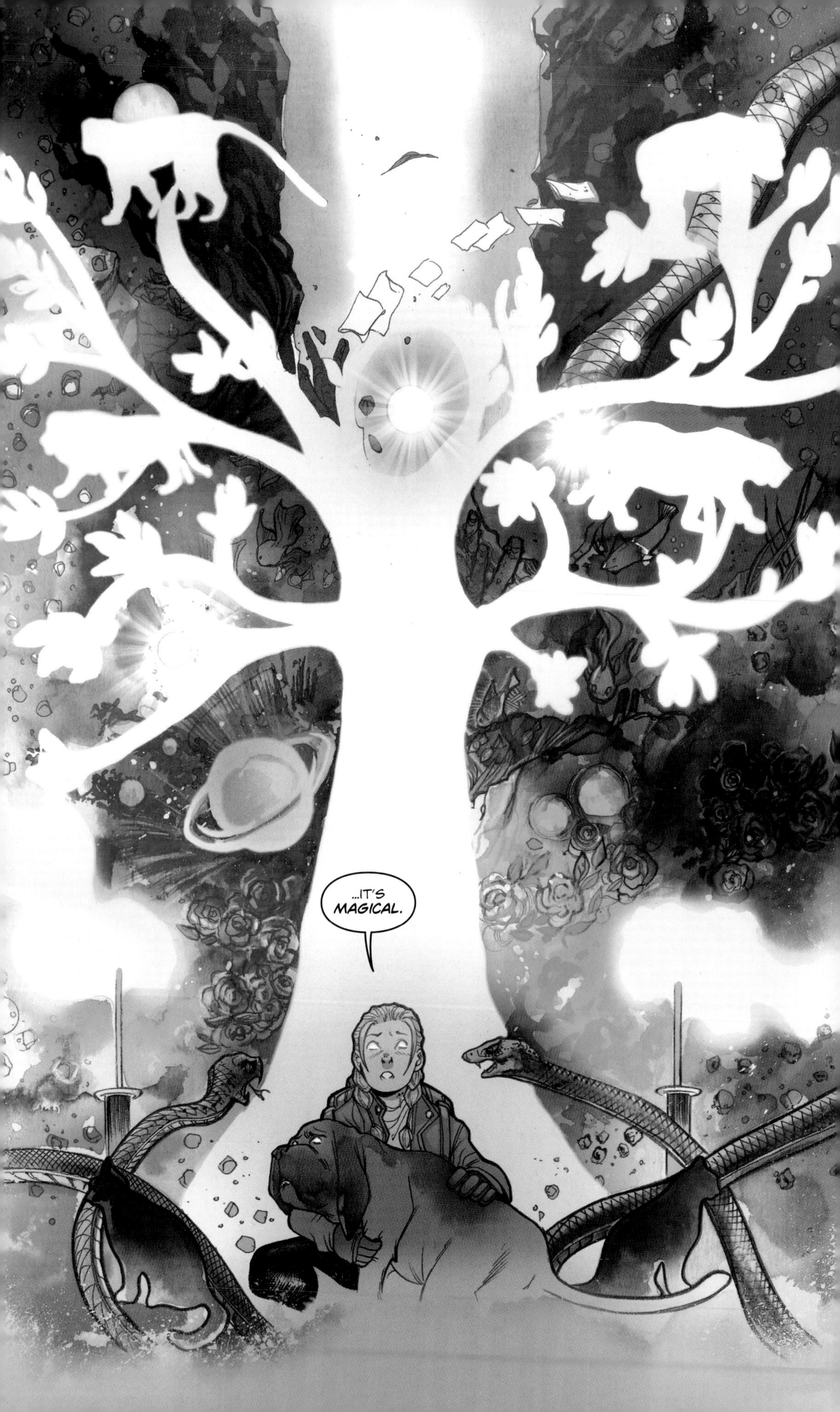
...IT'S MAGICAL.

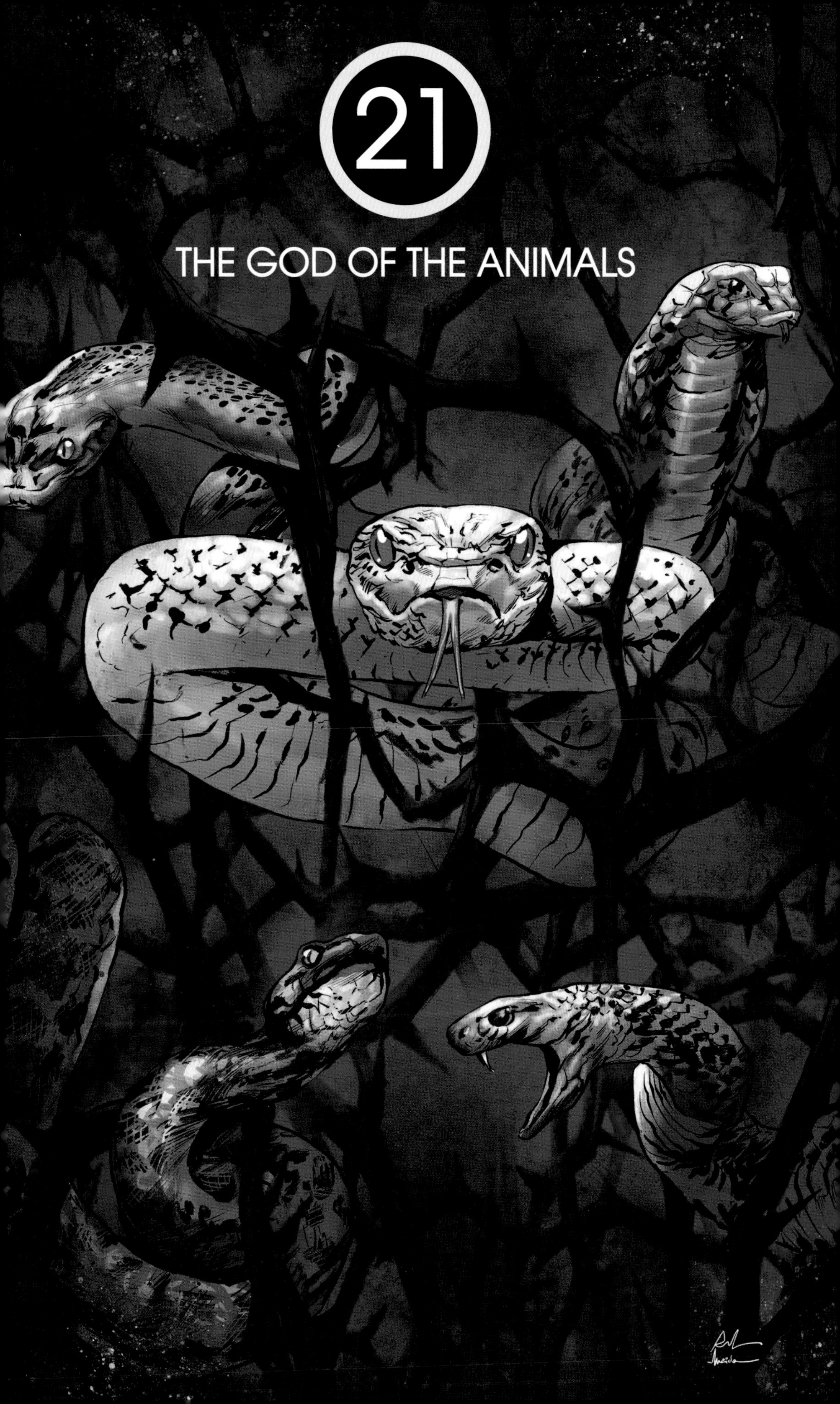
21
THE GOD OF THE ANIMALS

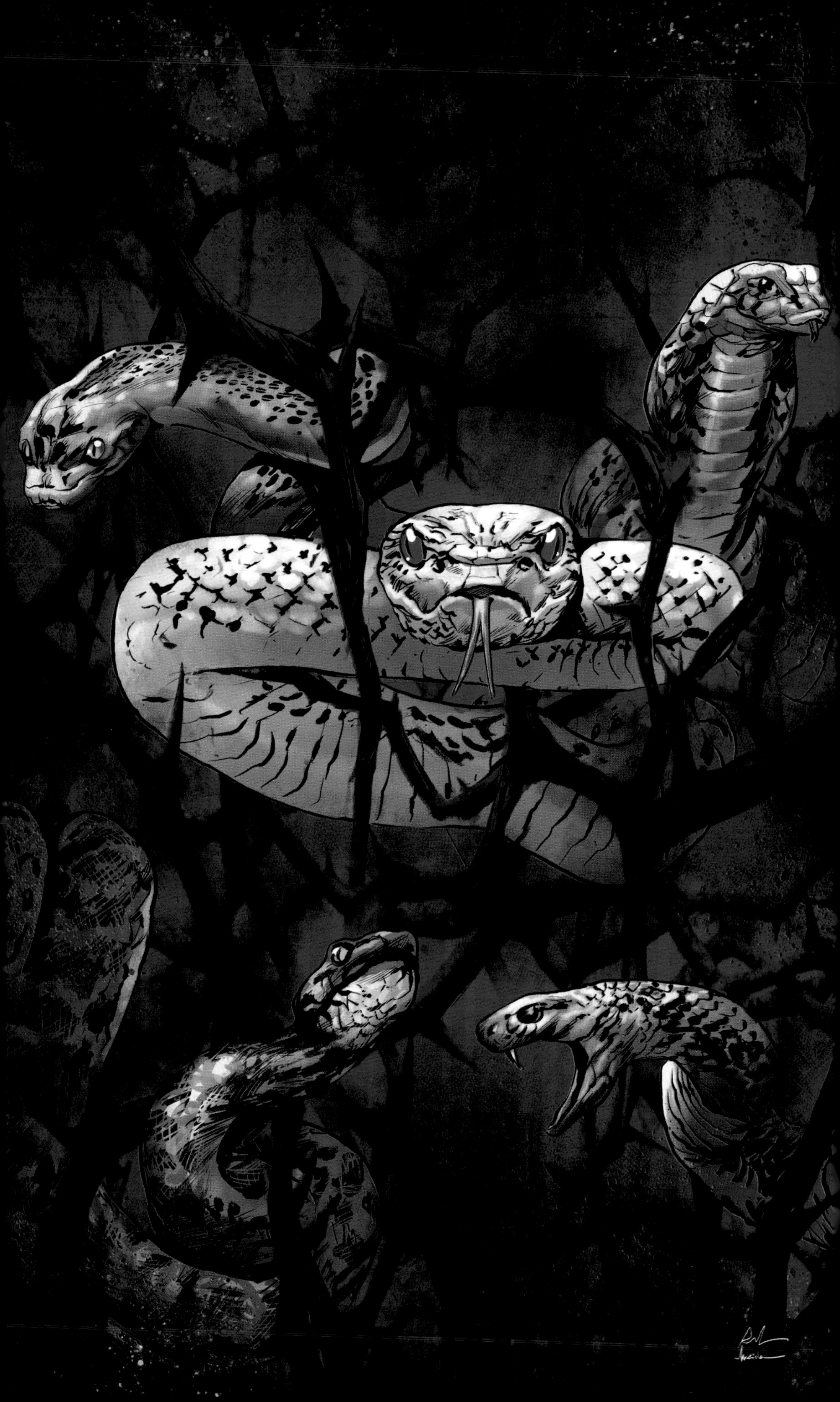

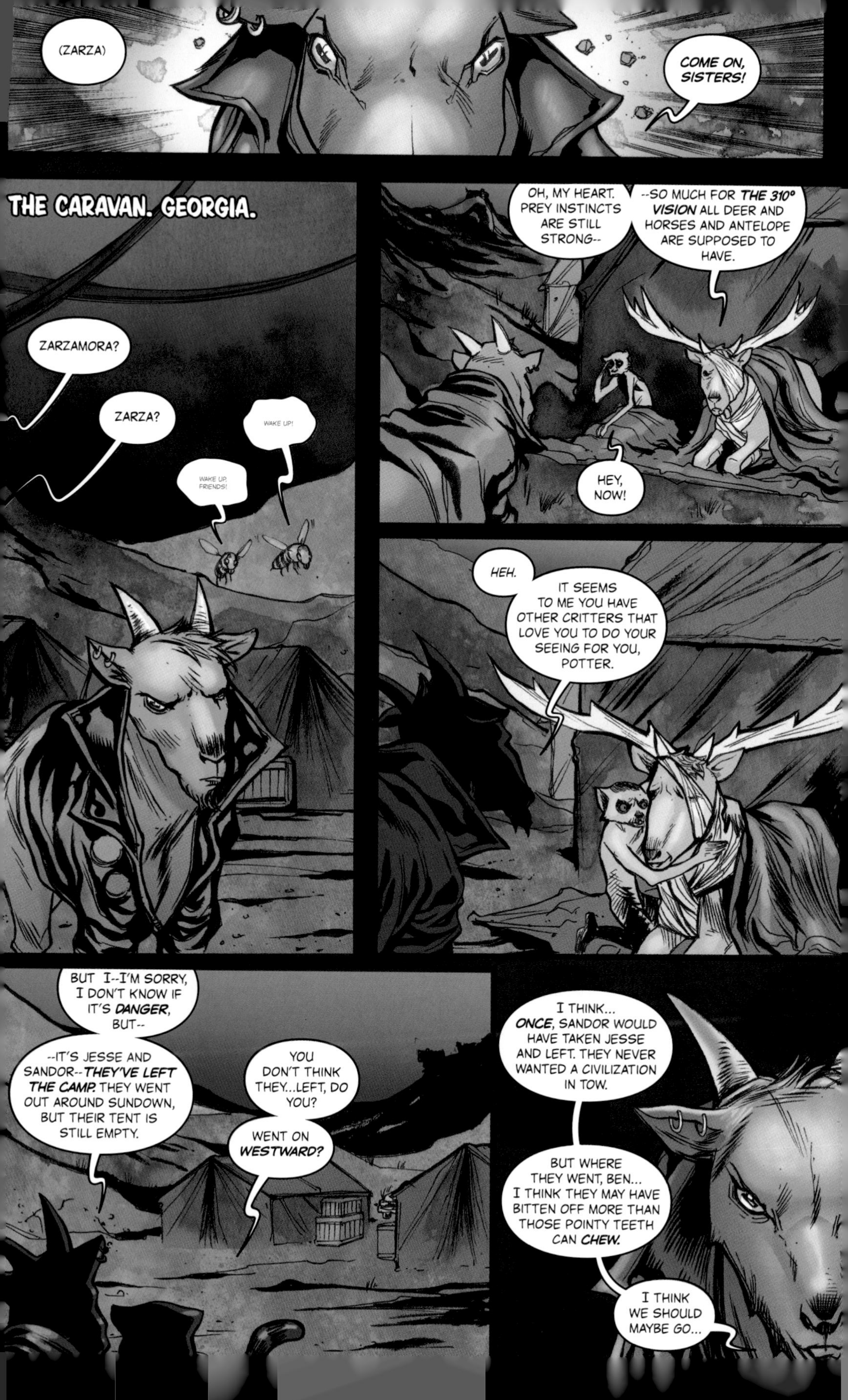
(ZARZA)
COME ON, SISTERS!
THE CARAVAN. GEORGIA.
ZARZAMORA?
ZARZA?
WAKE UP!
WAKE UP, FRIENDS!
OH, MY HEART. PREY INSTINCTS ARE STILL STRONG--
--SO MUCH FOR THE 310° VISION ALL DEER AND HORSES AND ANTELOPE ARE SUPPOSED TO HAVE.
HEY, NOW!
HEH.
IT SEEMS TO ME YOU HAVE OTHER CRITTERS THAT LOVE YOU TO DO YOUR SEEING FOR YOU, POTTER.
BUT I--I'M SORRY, I DON'T KNOW IF IT'S DANGER, BUT--
--IT'S JESSE AND SANDOR--THEY'VE LEFT THE CAMP. THEY WENT OUT AROUND SUNDOWN, BUT THEIR TENT IS STILL EMPTY.
YOU DON'T THINK THEY...LEFT, DO YOU?
WENT ON WESTWARD?
I THINK... ONCE, SANDOR WOULD HAVE TAKEN JESSE AND LEFT. THEY NEVER WANTED A CIVILIZATION IN TOW.
BUT WHERE THEY WENT, BEN... I THINK THEY MAY HAVE BITTEN OFF MORE THAN THOSE POINTY TEETH CAN CHEW.
I THINK WE SHOULD MAYBE GO...

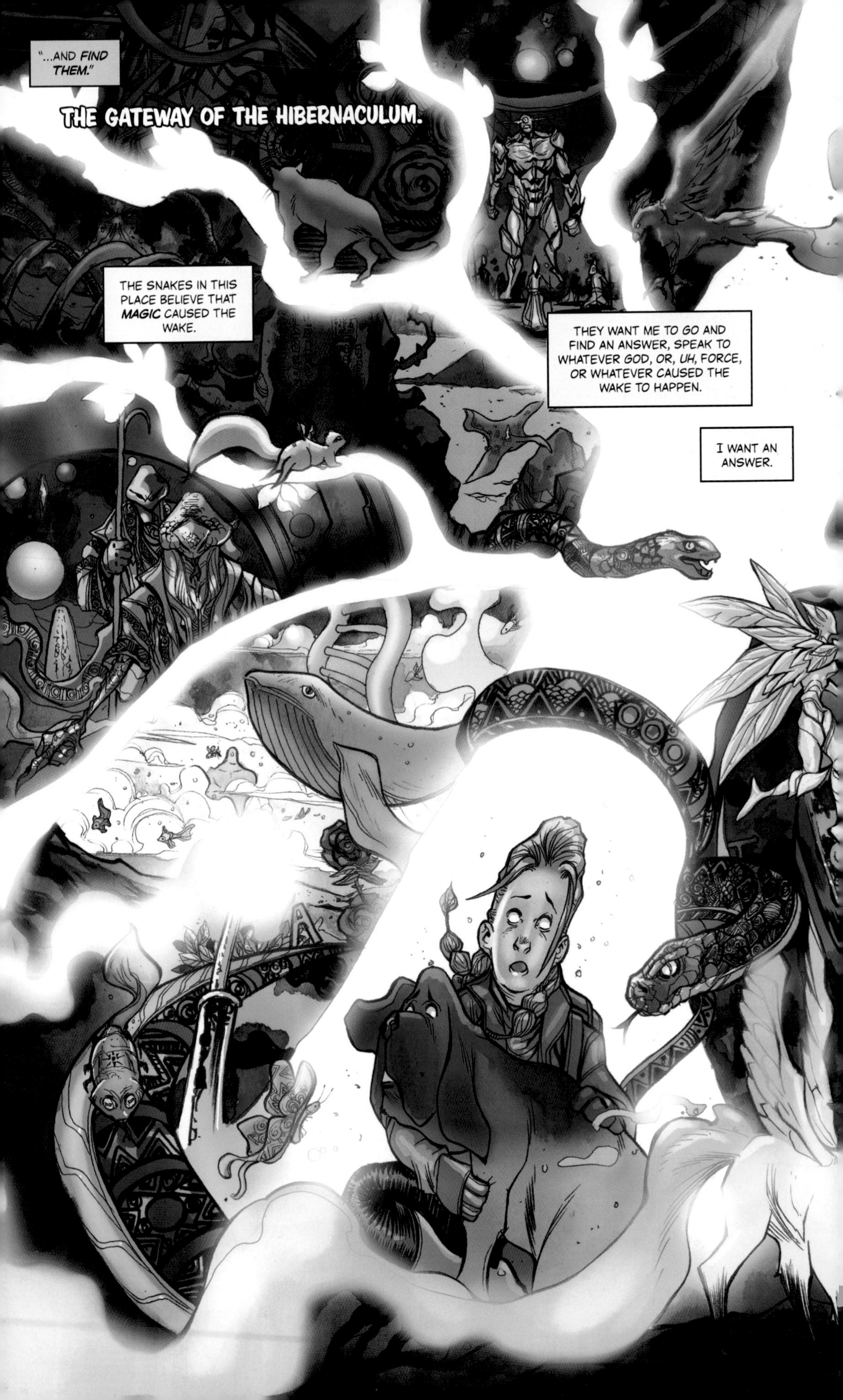
"...AND FIND THEM."
THE GATEWAY OF THE HIBERNACULUM.
THE SNAKES IN THIS PLACE BELIEVE THAT MAGIC CAUSED THE WAKE.
THEY WANT ME TO GO AND FIND AN ANSWER, SPEAK TO WHATEVER GOD, OR, UH, FORCE, OR WHATEVER CAUSED THE WAKE TO HAPPEN.
I WANT AN ANSWER.

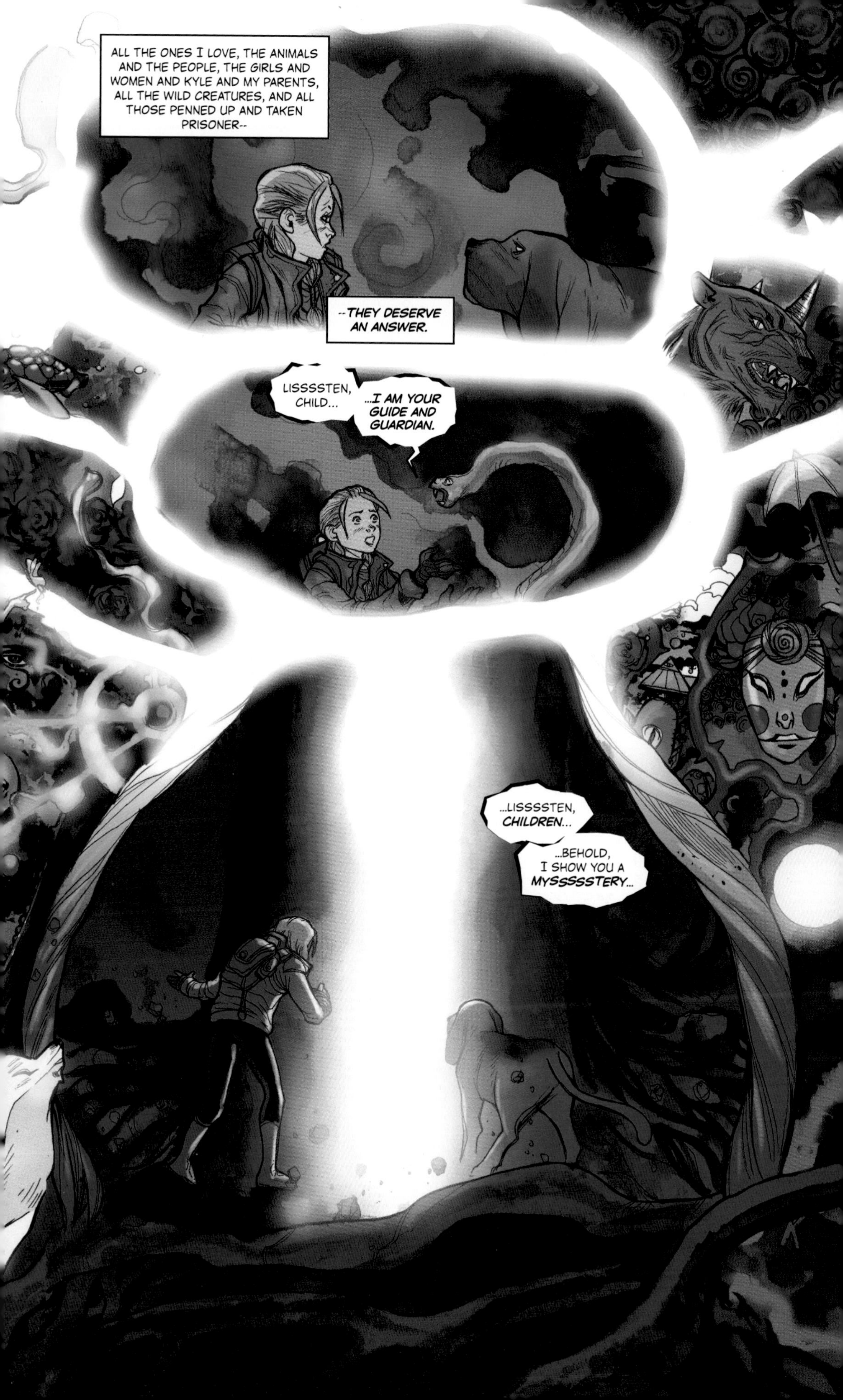
ALL THE ONES I LOVE, THE ANIMALS AND THE PEOPLE, THE GIRLS AND WOMEN AND KYLE AND MY PARENTS, ALL THE WILD CREATURES, AND ALL THOSE PENNED UP AND TAKEN PRISONER--
--THEY DESERVE AN ANSWER.
LISSSSTEN, CHILD...
...I AM YOUR GUIDE AND GUARDIAN.
...LISSSSTEN, CHILDREN...
...BEHOLD, I SHOW YOU A MYSSSSSTERY...

FOR JESSE.

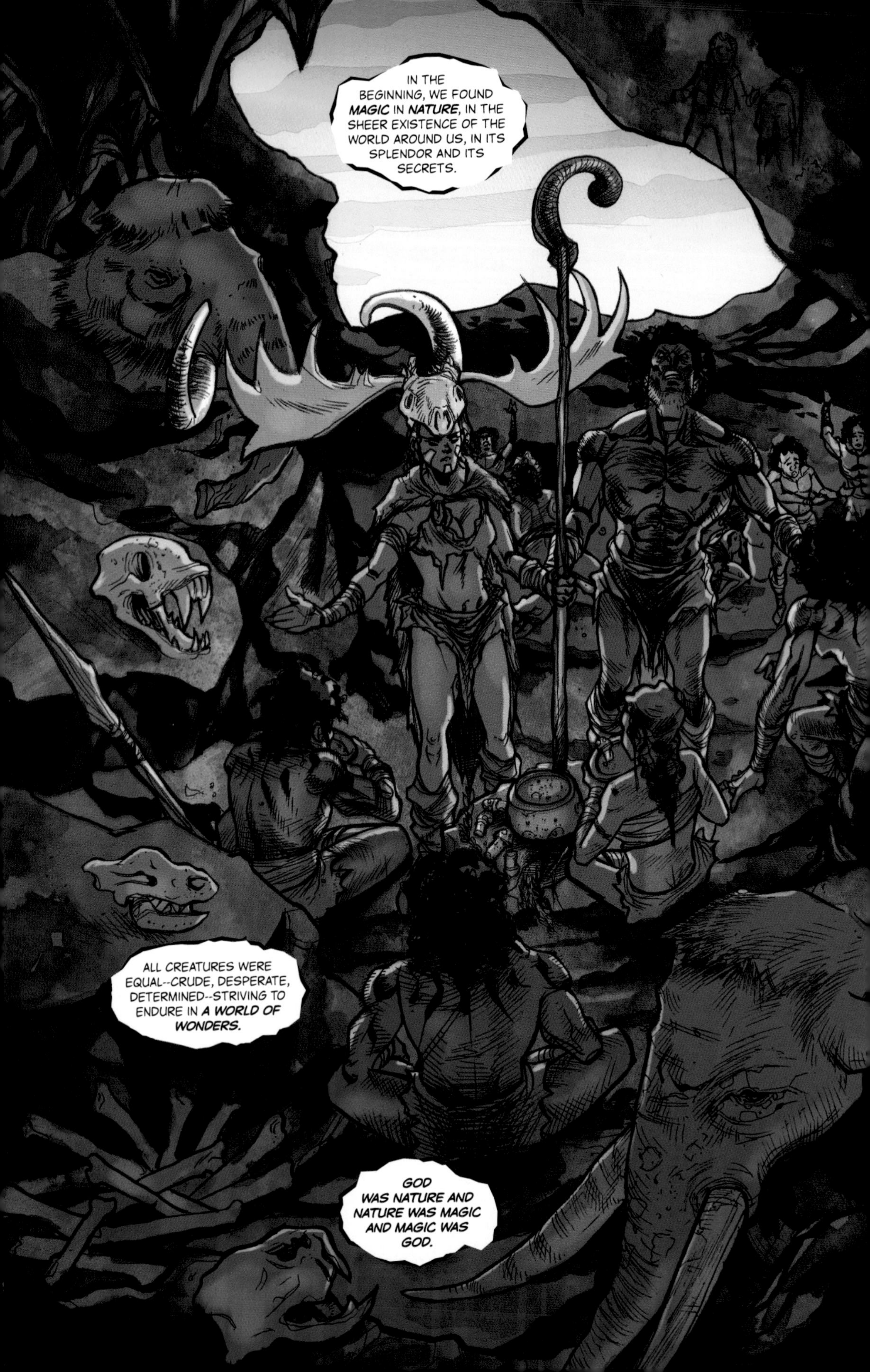

IN THE BEGINNING, WE FOUND MAGIC IN NATURE, IN THE SHEER EXISTENCE OF THE WORLD AROUND US, IN ITS SPLENDOR AND ITS SECRETS.
ALL CREATURES WERE EQUAL--CRUDE, DESPERATE, DETERMINED--STRIVING TO ENDURE IN A WORLD OF WONDERS.
GOD WAS NATURE AND NATURE WAS MAGIC AND MAGIC WAS GOD.

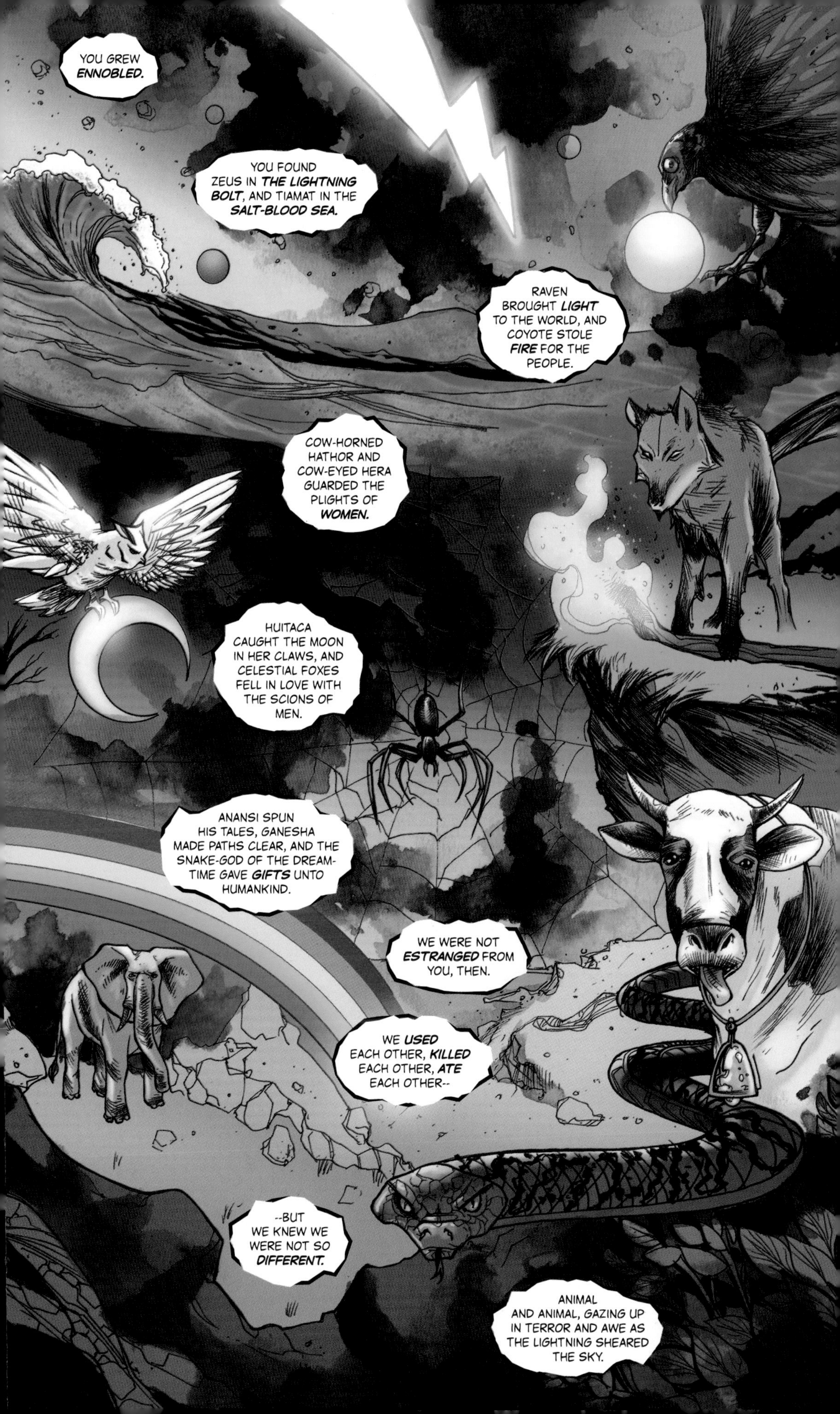
YOU GREW ENNOBLED.
YOU FOUND ZEUS IN THE LIGHTNING BOLT, AND TIAMAT IN THE SALT-BLOOD SEA.
RAVEN BROUGHT LIGHT TO THE WORLD, AND COYOTE STOLE FIRE FOR THE PEOPLE.
COW-HORNED HATHOR AND COW-EYED HERA GUARDED THE PLIGHTS OF WOMEN.
HUITACA CAUGHT THE MOON IN HER CLAWS, AND CELESTIAL FOXES FELL IN LOVE WITH THE SCIONS OF MEN.
ANANSI SPUN HIS TALES, GANESHA MADE PATHS CLEAR, AND THE SNAKE-GOD OF THE DREAM-TIME GAVE GIFTS UNTO HUMANKIND.
WE WERE NOT ESTRANGED FROM YOU, THEN.
WE USED EACH OTHER, KILLED EACH OTHER, ATE EACH OTHER--
--BUT WE KNEW WE WERE NOT SO DIFFERENT.
ANIMAL AND ANIMAL, GAZING UP IN TERROR AND AWE AS THE LIGHTNING SHEARED THE SKY.

So it was, even in the story of **the snake and the garden.**

Every herb-bearing seed and every fruit-bearing tree was given to the first humans, for in paradise, no blood was shed.

Paradise was **harmony.**

Paradise was no more than **a tale.**

Grew so great, that the god to whom you gave us as sacrifice grew in turn **disgusted** with the world that he had made.

Can animals **sin**, as humans can? Did we call down as much of the annihilation as you did?

Is it the prerogative of a disappointed father to amend his unruly children?

What chance have children against a vengeful father?

God sent the flood, and swept life and all flesh from the earth.

And when the flood receded, Noah sacrificed chosen animals to God.

And God, who had given mankind only fruit and bread and the herb of the field for food, now told mankind that the animals should be their sustenance, that mankind might grow many in number, and strong.

The division grew between us.

We grew farther and farther from one another.

After the eviction from Eden, blood was shed in the bearing of children.

Cain and Abel arose. One sacrificed plants to God. The other sacrificed animals.
God was pleased by Abel's offering.

Why?

Did you know there was power in us, more than in the other living things around us?

Was there more in a ram than in a rose?

You saw something **greater** in us, and because of that greatness,
you gave us to your god.

Cain grew jealous.

Once the blood of animals was shed, the way was open for the blood of humans.

A cruel sort of joke--four humans in the whole wide world,
and one of them is a **murderer.**

With your cruelty to us, your cruelty to your own kind grew.

You no longer saw God in nature and nature in magic and magic in God.
You saw yourselves in **everything.**

Once you shed our blood, you understood how easily you might shed
the blood of others.

We were the first to die.
But you...
...you were the first to follow.

What **hope** have children against a **misled** father?

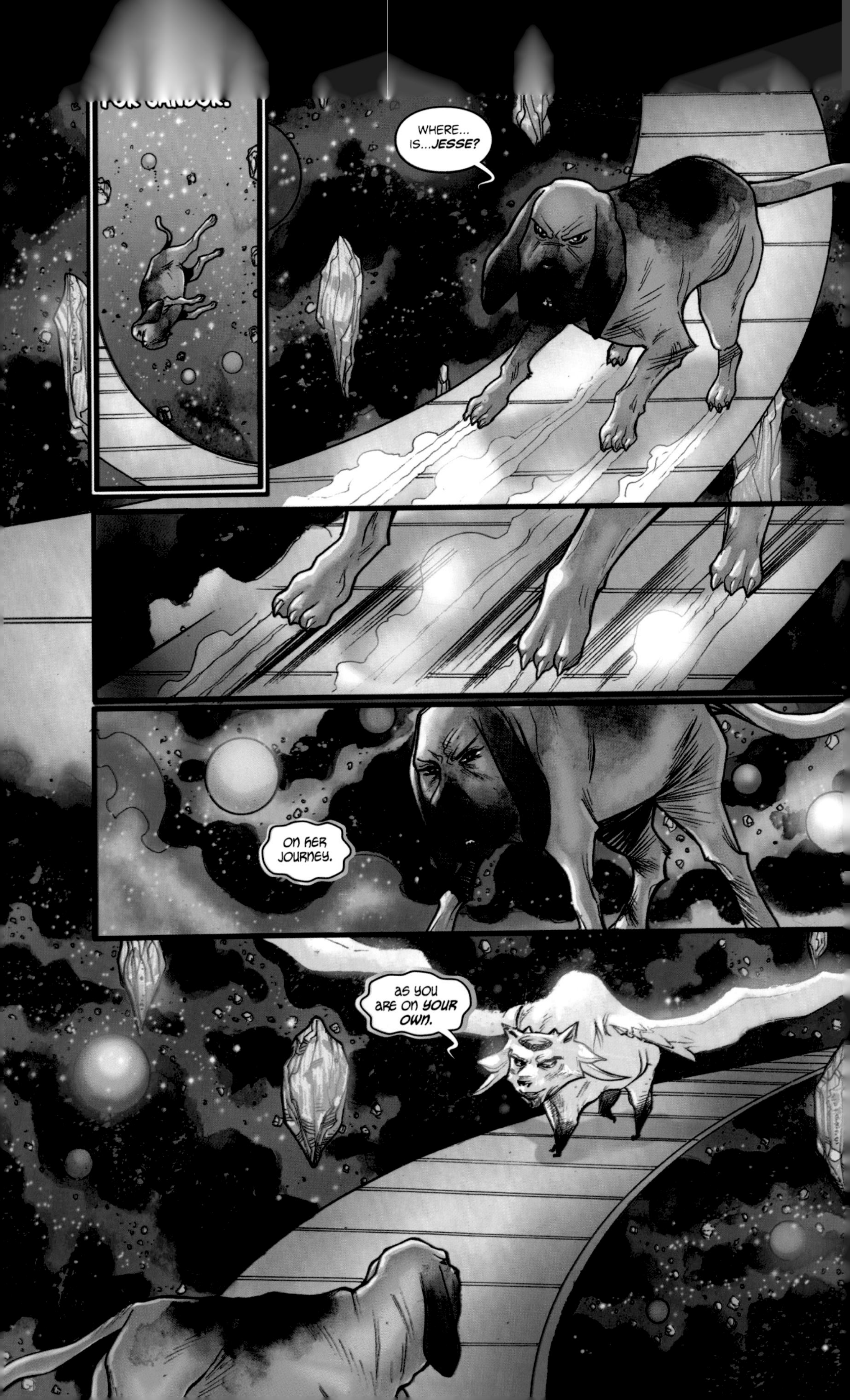
WHERE... IS...JESSE?
ON HER JOURNEY.
AS YOU ARE ON YOUR OWN.

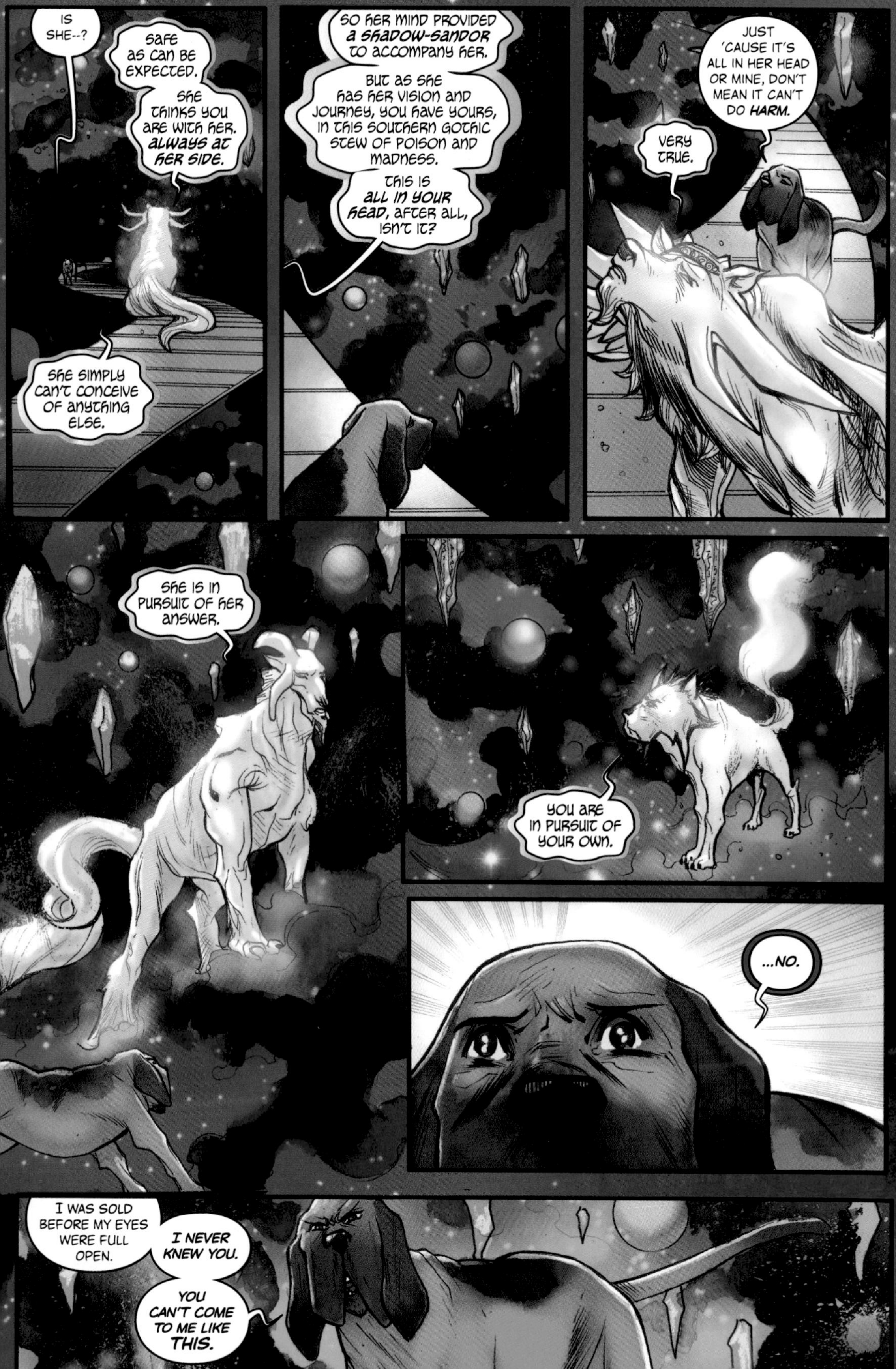
IS SHE--?
SAFE AS CAN BE EXPECTED.
SHE THINKS YOU ARE WITH HER. ALWAYS AT HER SIDE.
SHE SIMPLY CAN'T CONCEIVE OF ANYTHING ELSE.
SO HER MIND PROVIDED A SHADOW-SANDOR TO ACCOMPANY HER.
BUT AS SHE HAS HER VISION AND JOURNEY, YOU HAVE YOURS, IN THIS SOUTHERN GOTHIC STEW OF POISON AND MADNESS.
THIS IS ALL IN YOUR HEAD, AFTER ALL, ISN'T IT?
JUST 'CAUSE IT'S ALL IN HER HEAD OR MINE, DON'T MEAN IT CAN'T DO HARM.
VERY TRUE.
SHE IS IN PURSUIT OF HER ANSWER.
YOU ARE IN PURSUIT OF YOUR OWN.
...NO.
I WAS SOLD BEFORE MY EYES WERE FULL OPEN.
I NEVER KNEW YOU.
YOU CAN'T COME TO ME LIKE THIS.

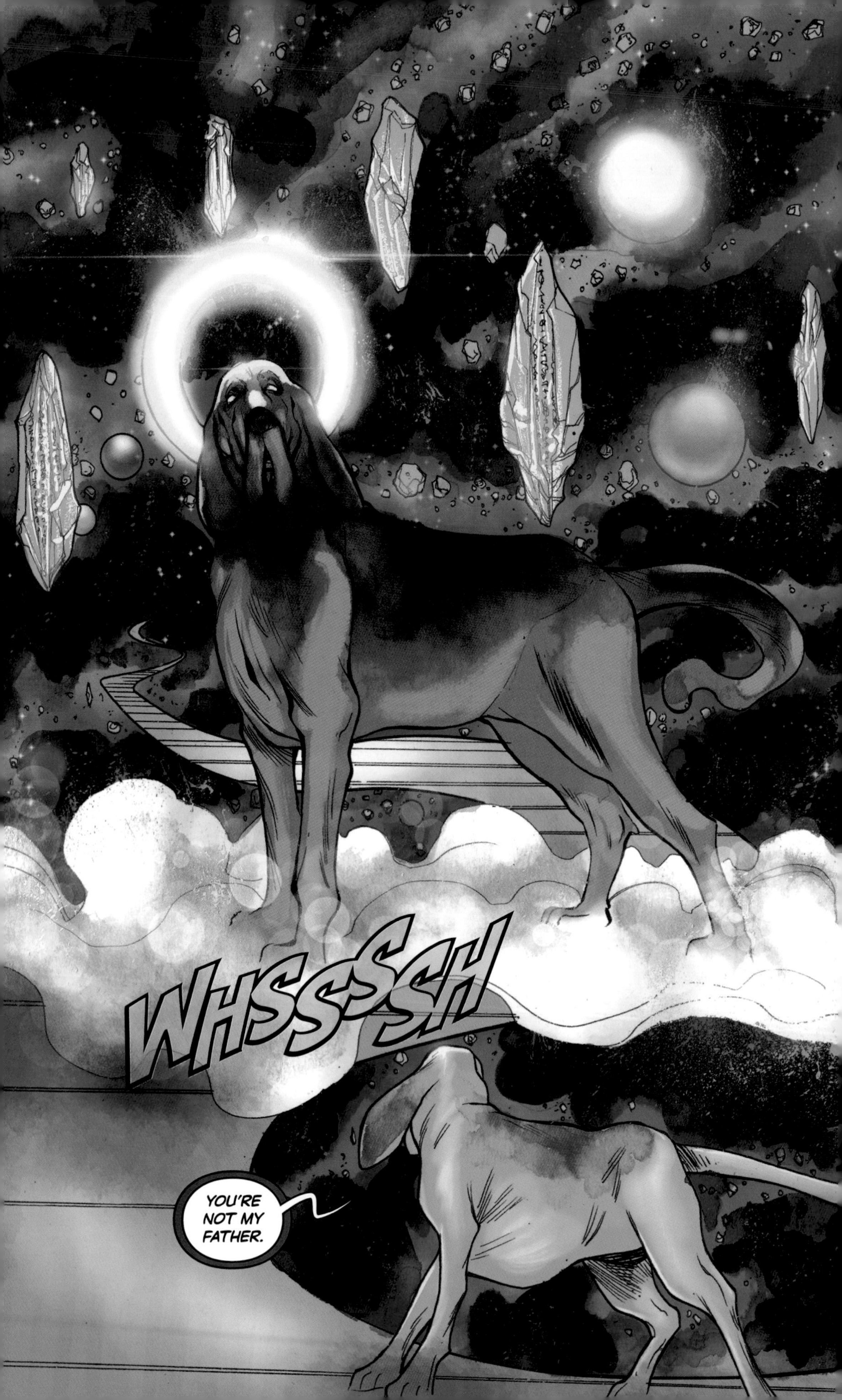
WHSSSH
YOU'RE NOT MY FATHER.

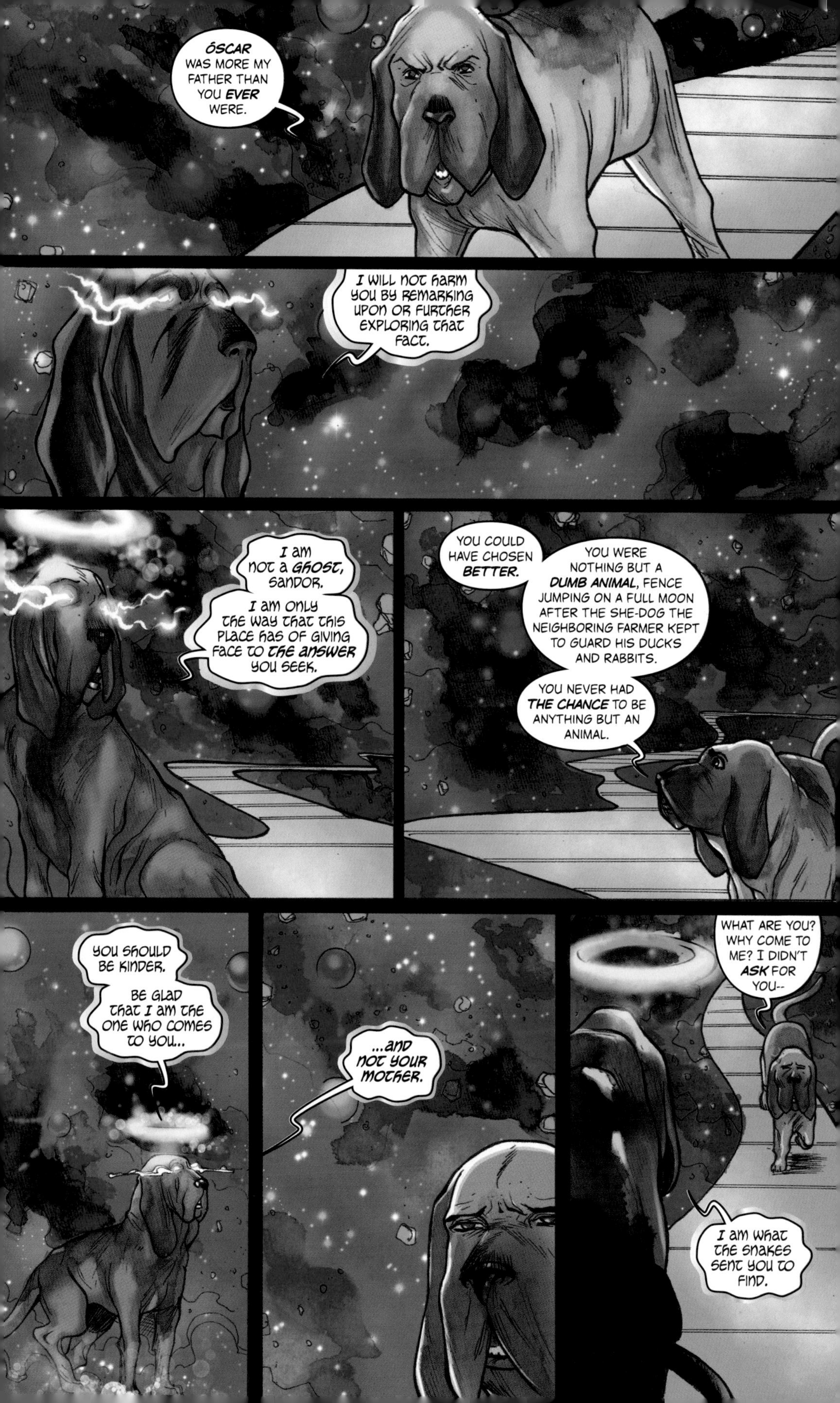

ÓSCAR WAS MORE MY FATHER THAN YOU EVER WERE.
I WILL NOT HARM YOU BY REMARKING UPON OR FURTHER EXPLORING THAT FACT.
I AM NOT A GHOST, SANDOR.
I AM ONLY THE WAY THAT THIS PLACE HAS OF GIVING FACE TO THE ANSWER YOU SEEK.
YOU COULD HAVE CHOSEN BETTER.
YOU WERE NOTHING BUT A DUMB ANIMAL, FENCE JUMPING ON A FULL MOON AFTER THE SHE-DOG THE NEIGHBORING FARMER KEPT TO GUARD HIS DUCKS AND RABBITS.
YOU NEVER HAD THE CHANCE TO BE ANYTHING BUT AN ANIMAL.
YOU SHOULD BE KINDER.
BE GLAD THAT I AM THE ONE WHO COMES TO YOU...
...AND NOT YOUR MOTHER.
WHAT ARE YOU? WHY COME TO ME? I DIDN'T ASK FOR YOU--
I AM WHAT THE SNAKES SENT YOU TO FIND.

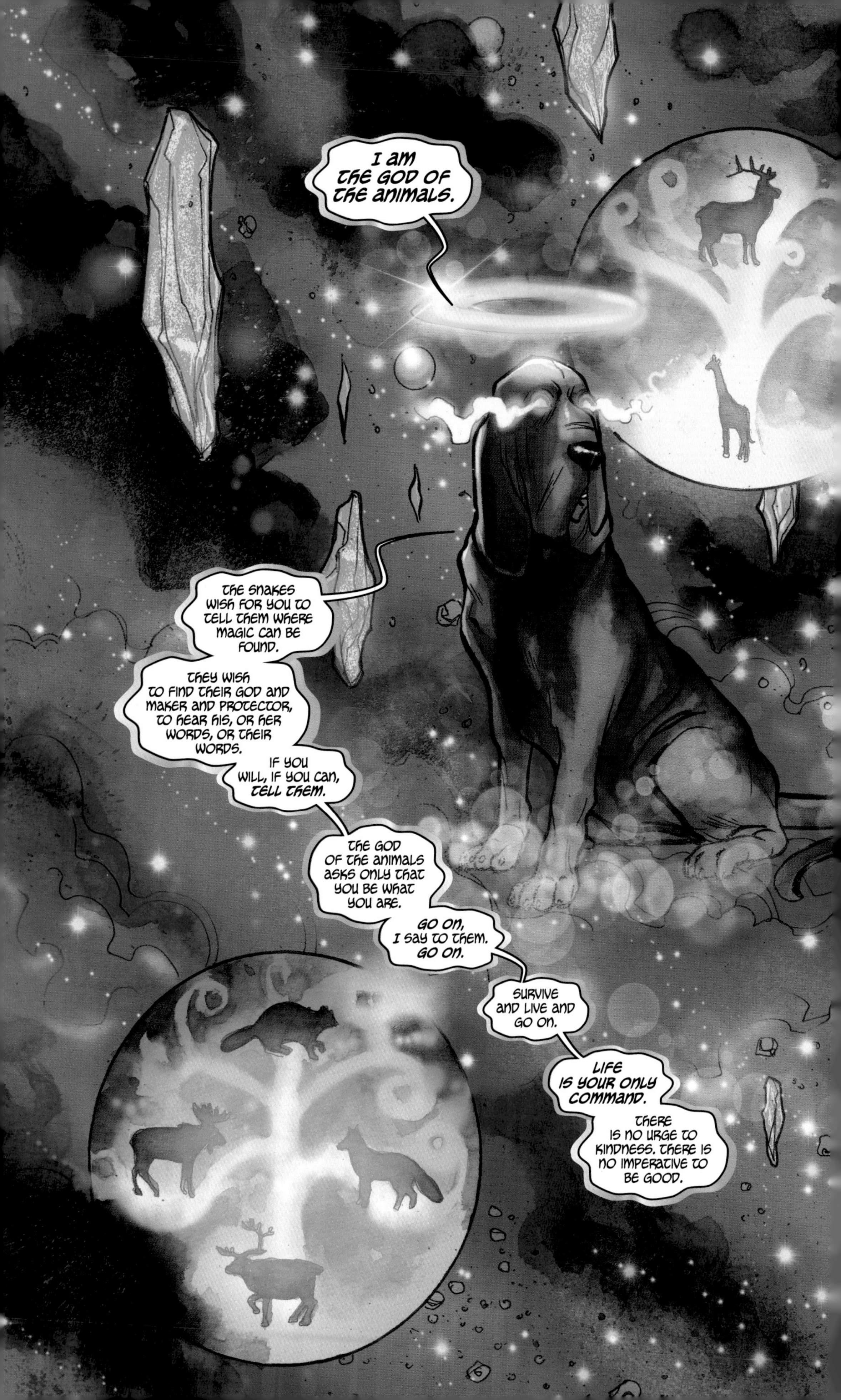
I AM THE GOD OF THE ANIMALS.
THE SNAKES WISH FOR YOU TO TELL THEM WHERE MAGIC CAN BE FOUND.
THEY WISH TO FIND THEIR GOD AND MAKER AND PROTECTOR, TO HEAR HIS, OR HER WORDS, OR THEIR WORDS.
IF YOU WILL, IF YOU CAN, TELL THEM.
THE GOD OF THE ANIMALS ASKS ONLY THAT YOU BE WHAT YOU ARE.
GO ON, I SAY TO THEM. GO ON.
SURVIVE AND LIVE AND GO ON.
LIFE IS YOUR ONLY COMMAND.
THERE IS NO URGE TO KINDNESS. THERE IS NO IMPERATIVE TO BE GOOD.

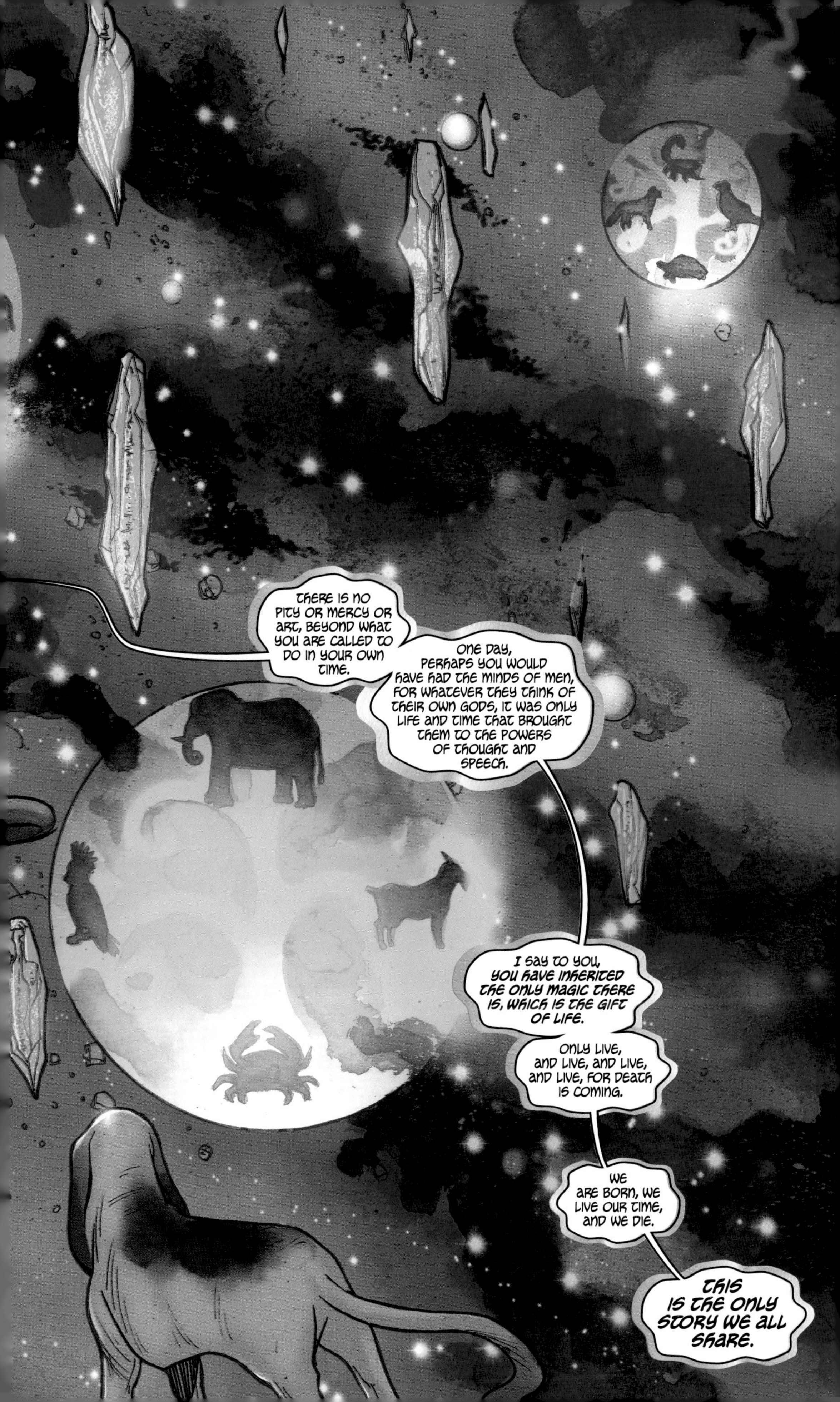
THERE IS NO PITY OR MERCY OR ART, BEYOND WHAT YOU ARE CALLED TO DO IN YOUR OWN TIME.
ONE DAY, PERHAPS YOU WOULD HAVE HAD THE MINDS OF MEN, FOR WHATEVER THEY THINK OF THEIR OWN GODS, IT WAS ONLY LIFE AND TIME THAT BROUGHT THEM TO THE POWERS OF THOUGHT AND SPEECH.
I SAY TO YOU, YOU HAVE INHERITED THE ONLY MAGIC THERE IS, WHICH IS THE GIFT OF LIFE.
ONLY LIVE, AND LIVE, AND LIVE, AND LIVE, FOR DEATH IS COMING.
WE ARE BORN, WE LIVE OUR TIME, AND WE DIE.
THIS IS THE ONLY STORY WE ALL SHARE.

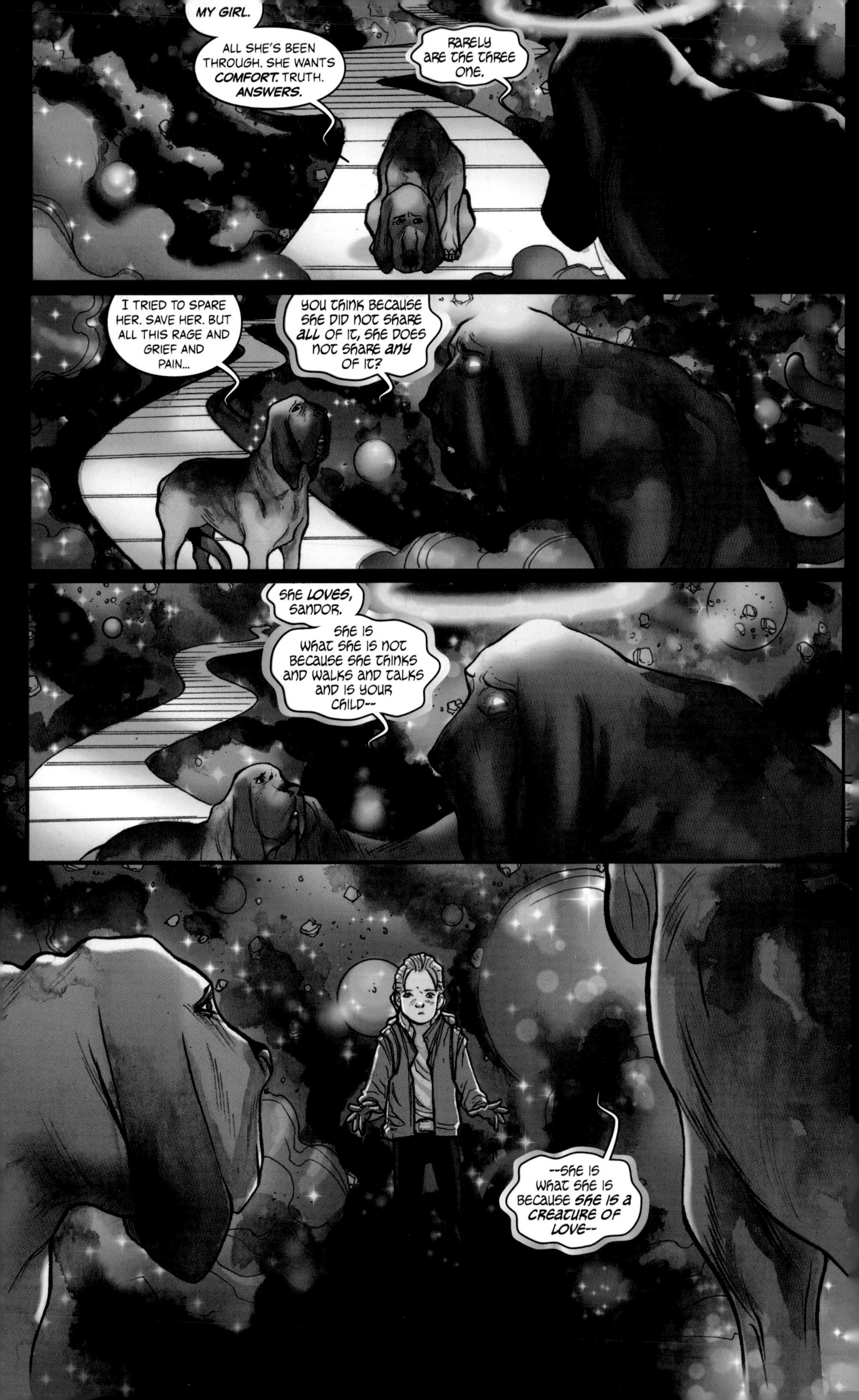
MY GIRL.
ALL SHE'S BEEN THROUGH. SHE WANTS COMFORT. TRUTH. ANSWERS.
RARELY ARE THE THREE ONE.
I TRIED TO SPARE HER. SAVE HER. BUT ALL THIS RAGE AND GRIEF AND PAIN...
YOU THINK BECAUSE SHE DID NOT SHARE ALL OF IT, SHE DOES NOT SHARE ANY OF IT?
SHE LOVES, SANDOR.
SHE IS WHAT SHE IS NOT BECAUSE SHE THINKS AND WALKS AND TALKS AND IS YOUR CHILD--
--SHE IS WHAT SHE IS BECAUSE SHE IS A CREATURE OF LOVE--

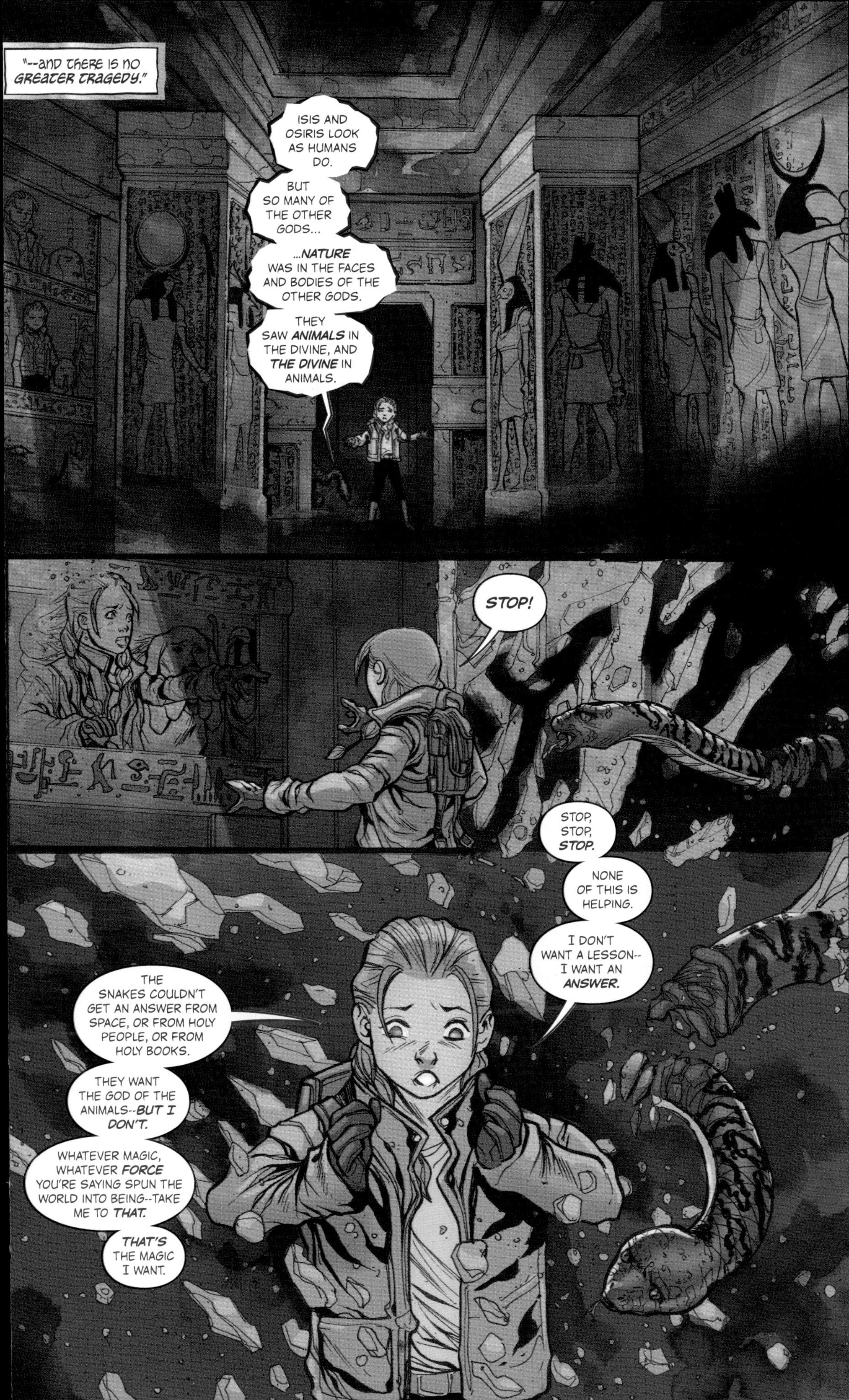
"--and there is no greater tragedy."
ISIS AND OSIRIS LOOK AS HUMANS DO.
BUT SO MANY OF THE OTHER GODS...
...NATURE WAS IN THE FACES AND BODIES OF THE OTHER GODS.
THEY SAW ANIMALS IN THE DIVINE, AND THE DIVINE IN ANIMALS.
STOP!
STOP, STOP, STOP.
NONE OF THIS IS HELPING.
I DON'T WANT A LESSON-- I WANT AN ANSWER.
THE SNAKES COULDN'T GET AN ANSWER FROM SPACE, OR FROM HOLY PEOPLE, OR FROM HOLY BOOKS.
THEY WANT THE GOD OF THE ANIMALS--BUT I DON'T.
WHATEVER MAGIC, WHATEVER FORCE YOU'RE SAYING SPUN THE WORLD INTO BEING--TAKE ME TO THAT.
THAT'S THE MAGIC I WANT.

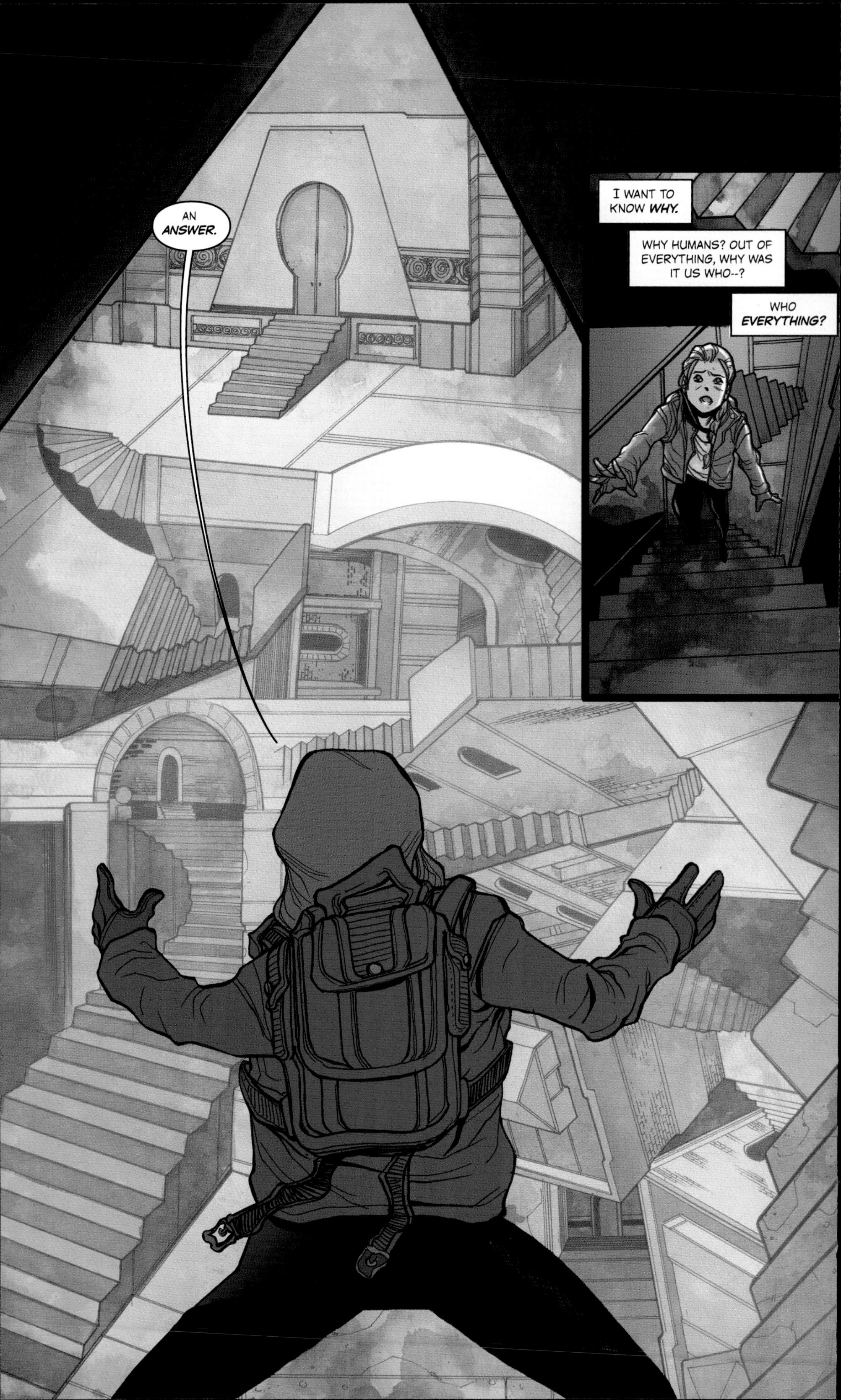
AN ANSWER.
I WANT TO KNOW WHY.
WHY HUMANS? OUT OF EVERYTHING, WHY WAS IT US WHO--?
WHO EVERYTHING?

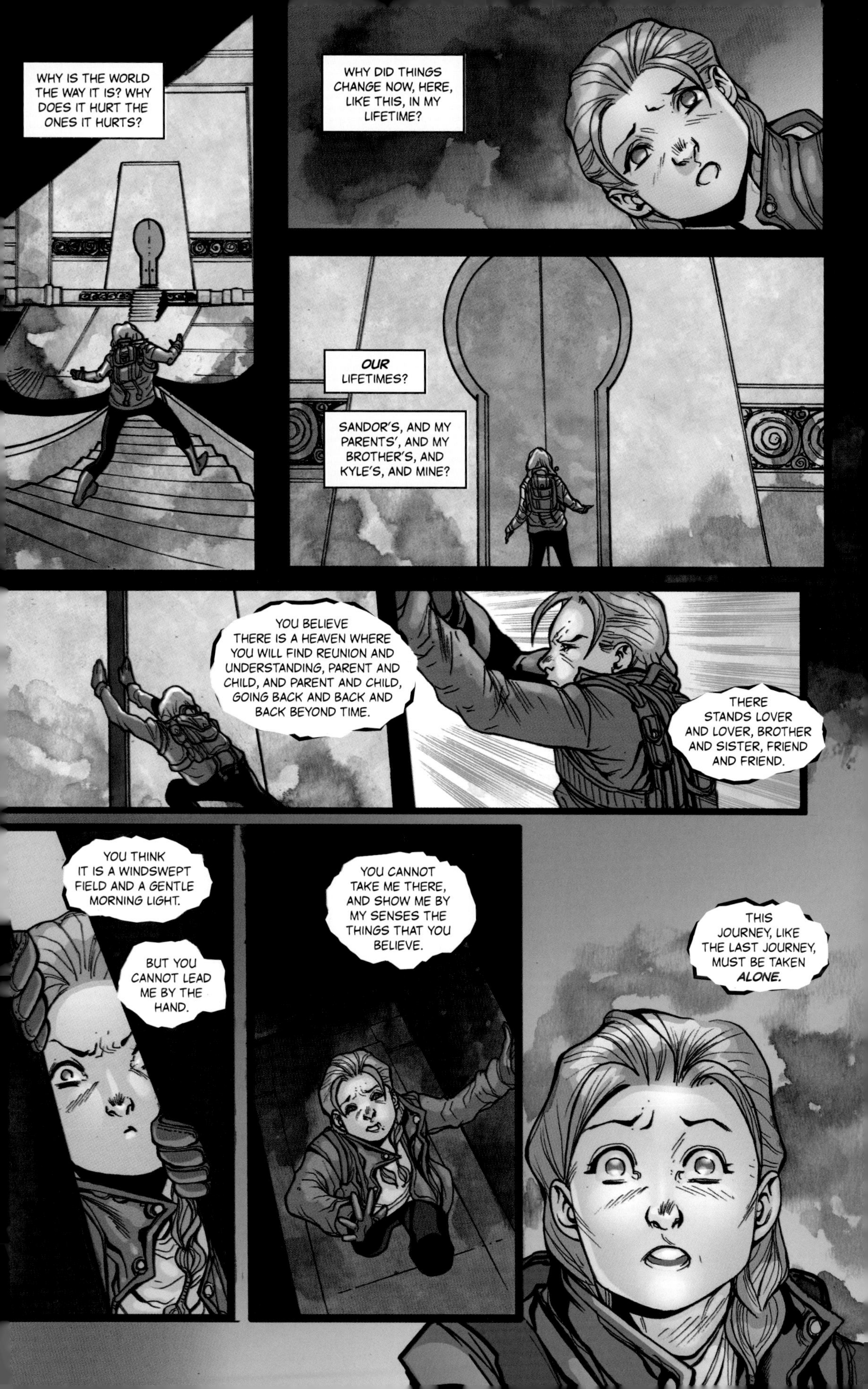
WHY IS THE WORLD THE WAY IT IS? WHY DOES IT HURT THE ONES IT HURTS?
WHY DID THINGS CHANGE NOW, HERE, LIKE THIS, IN MY LIFETIME?
OUR LIFETIMES?
SANDOR'S, AND MY PARENTS', AND MY BROTHER'S, AND KYLE'S, AND MINE?
YOU BELIEVE THERE IS A HEAVEN WHERE YOU WILL FIND REUNION AND UNDERSTANDING, PARENT AND CHILD, AND PARENT AND CHILD, GOING BACK AND BACK AND BACK BEYOND TIME.
THERE STANDS LOVER AND LOVER, BROTHER AND SISTER, FRIEND AND FRIEND.
YOU THINK IT IS A WINDSWEPT FIELD AND A GENTLE MORNING LIGHT.
BUT YOU CANNOT LEAD ME BY THE HAND.
YOU CANNOT TAKE ME THERE, AND SHOW ME BY MY SENSES THE THINGS THAT YOU BELIEVE.
THIS JOURNEY, LIKE THE LAST JOURNEY, MUST BE TAKEN ALONE.

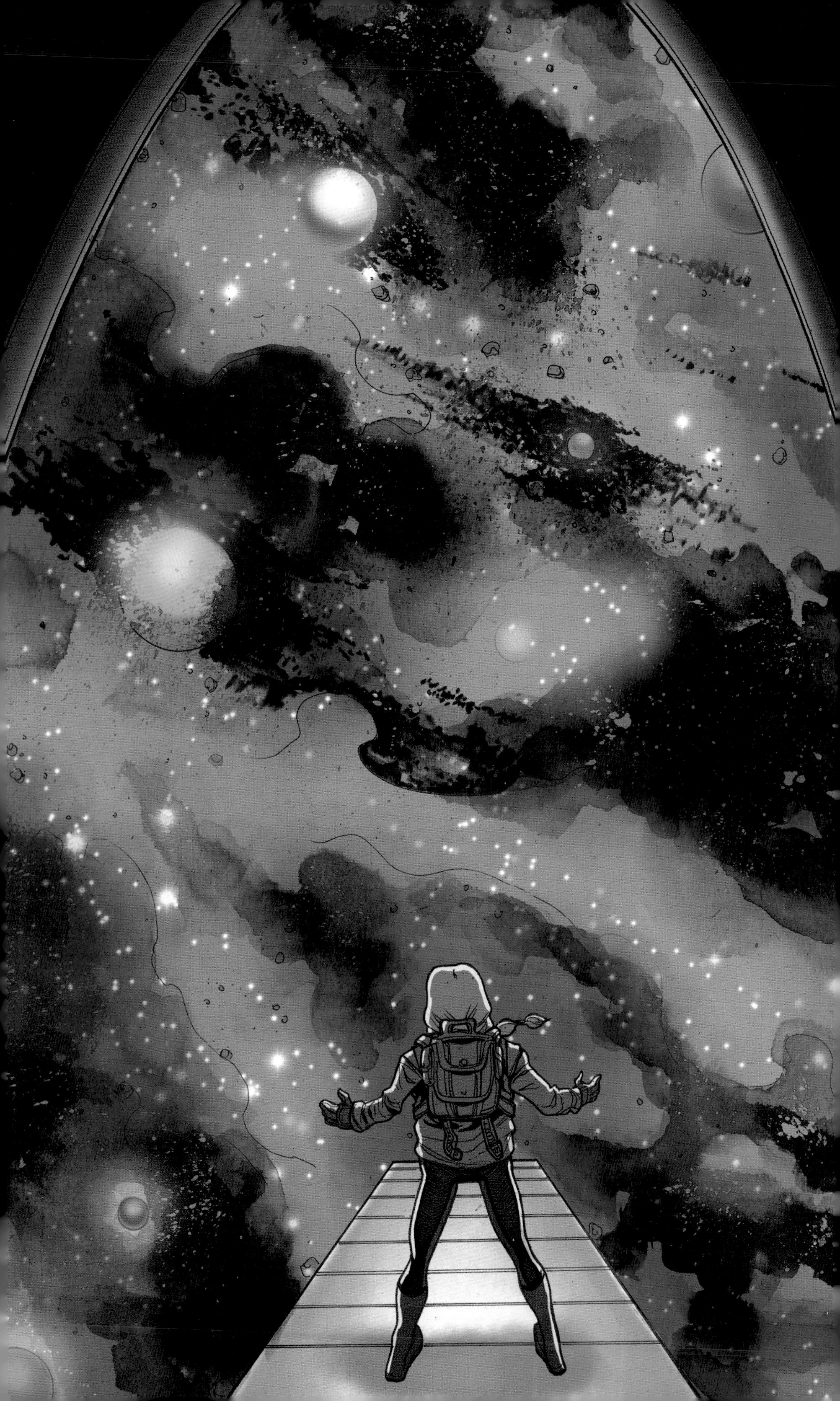

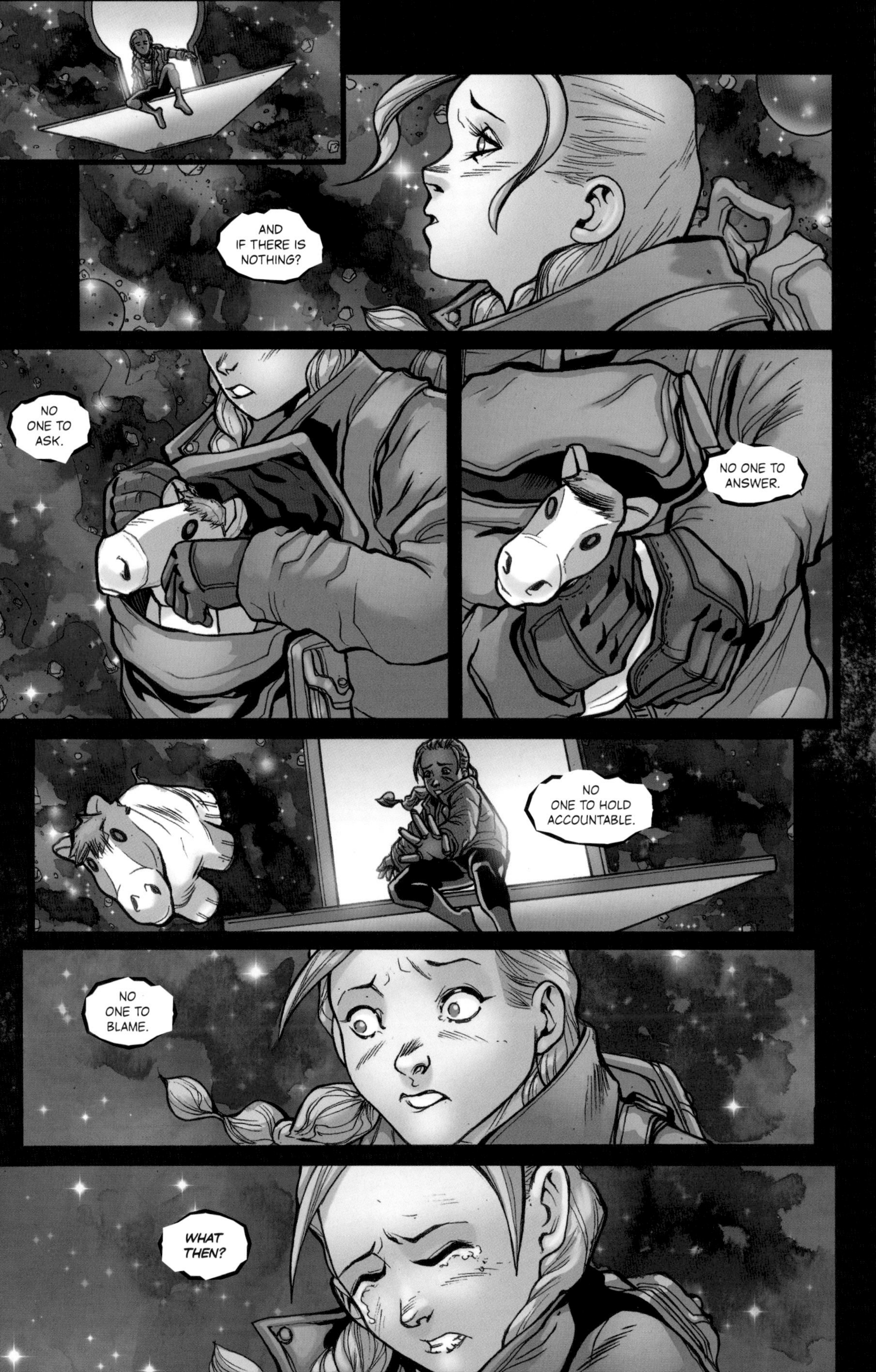
AND IF THERE IS NOTHING?
NO ONE TO ASK.
NO ONE TO ANSWER.
NO ONE TO HOLD ACCOUNTABLE.
NO ONE TO BLAME.
WHAT THEN?

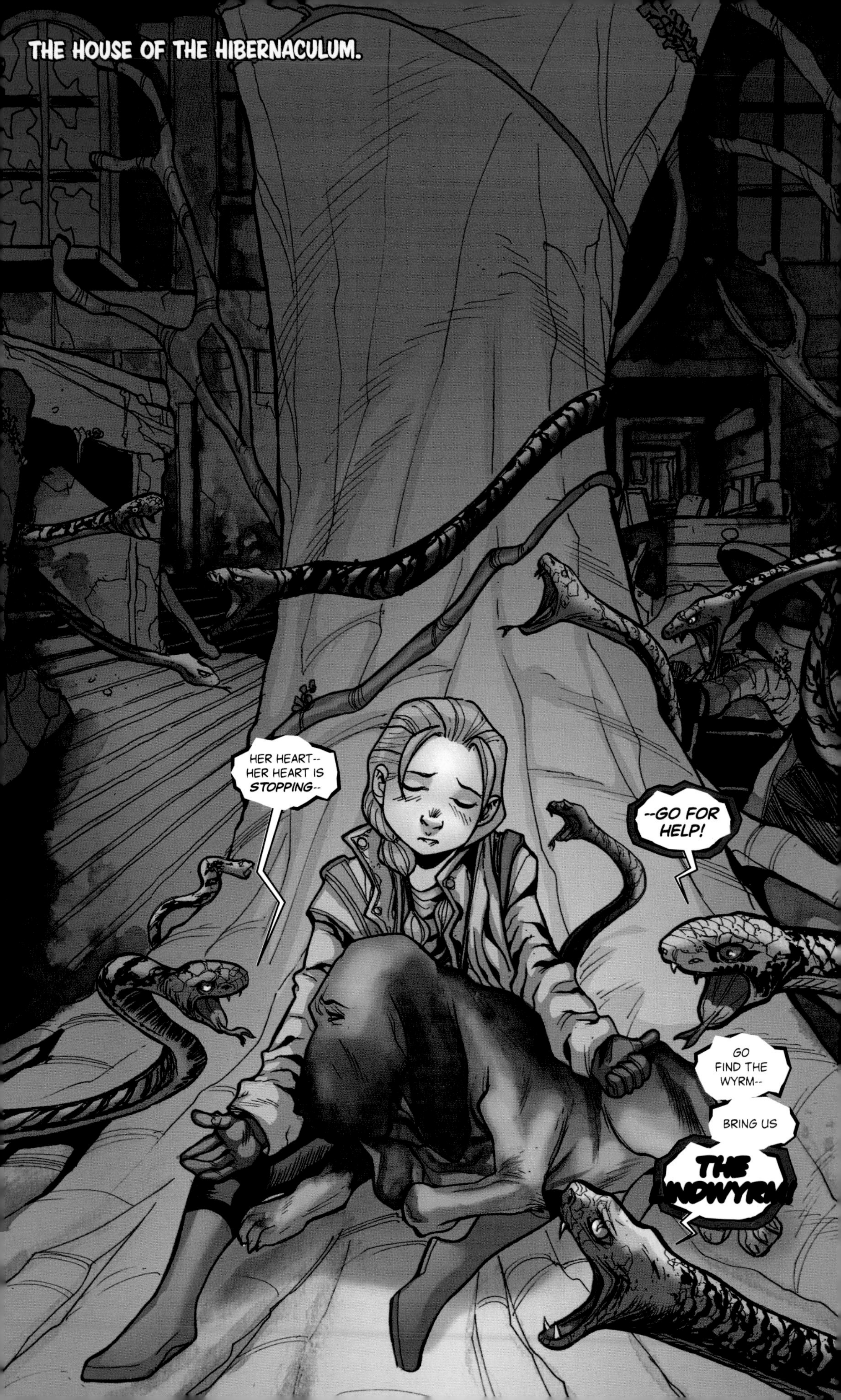
THE HOUSE OF THE HIBERNACULUM.
HER HEART-- HER HEART IS *STOPPING*--
--GO FOR HELP!
GO FIND THE WYRM--
BRING US
THE

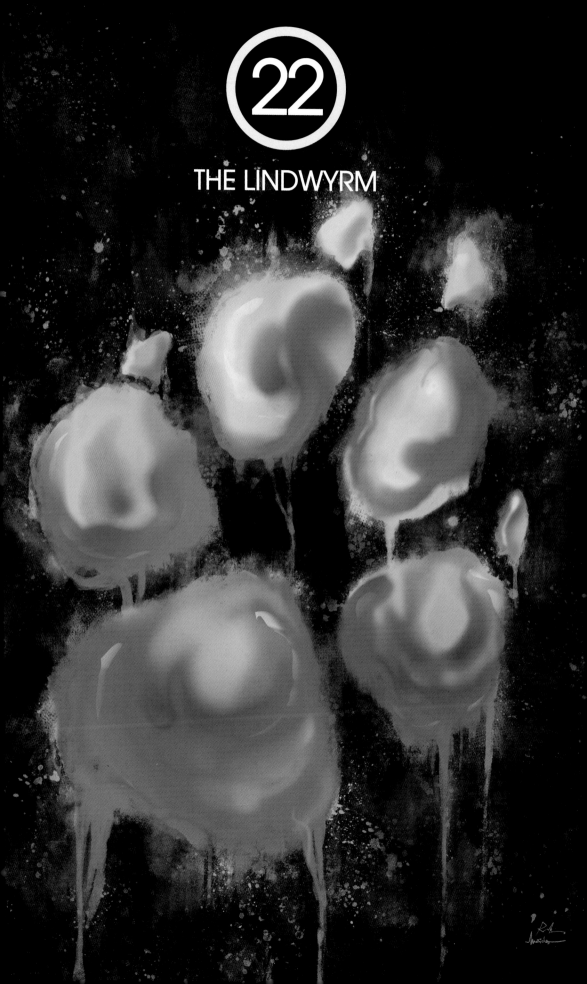

22

THE LINDWYRM

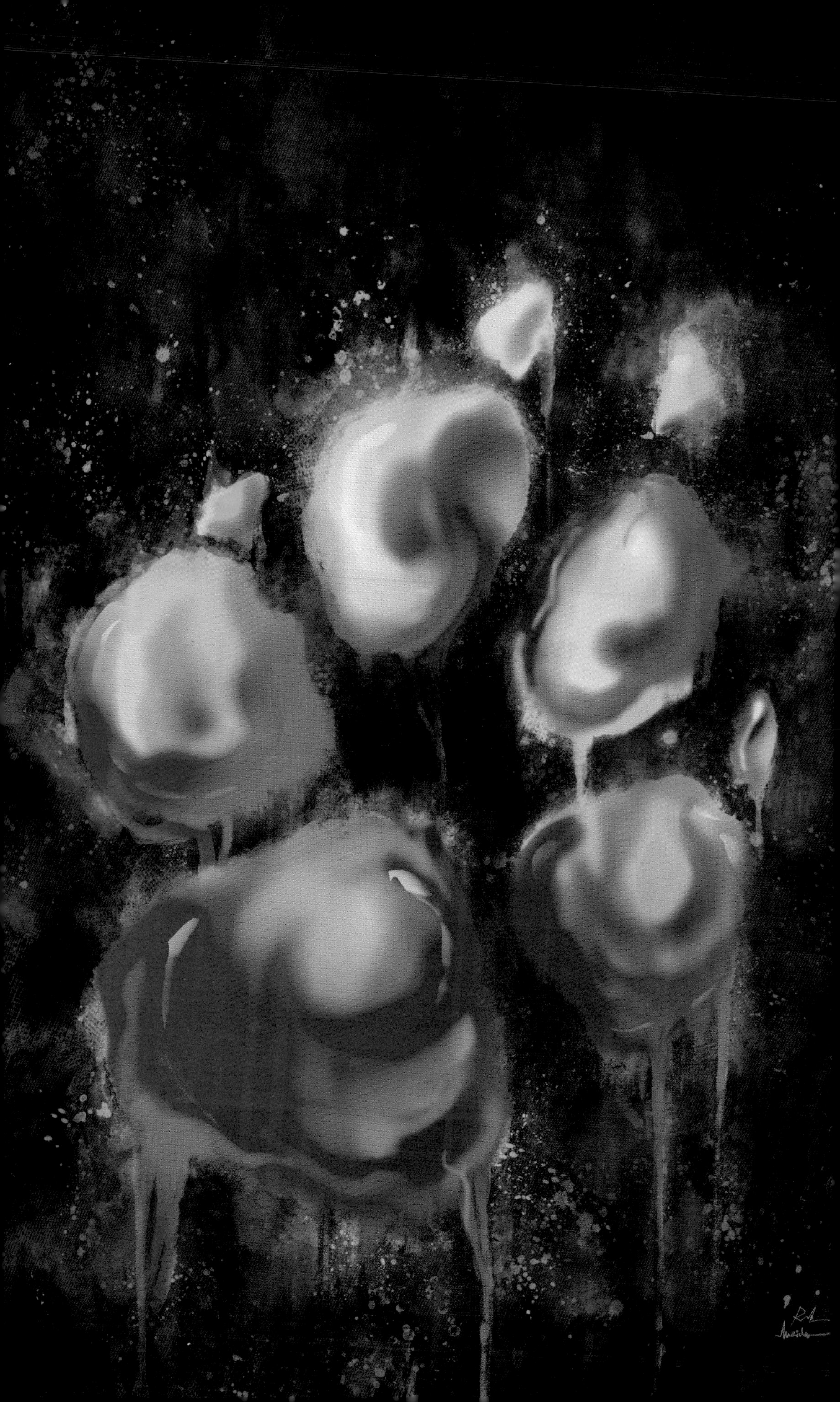

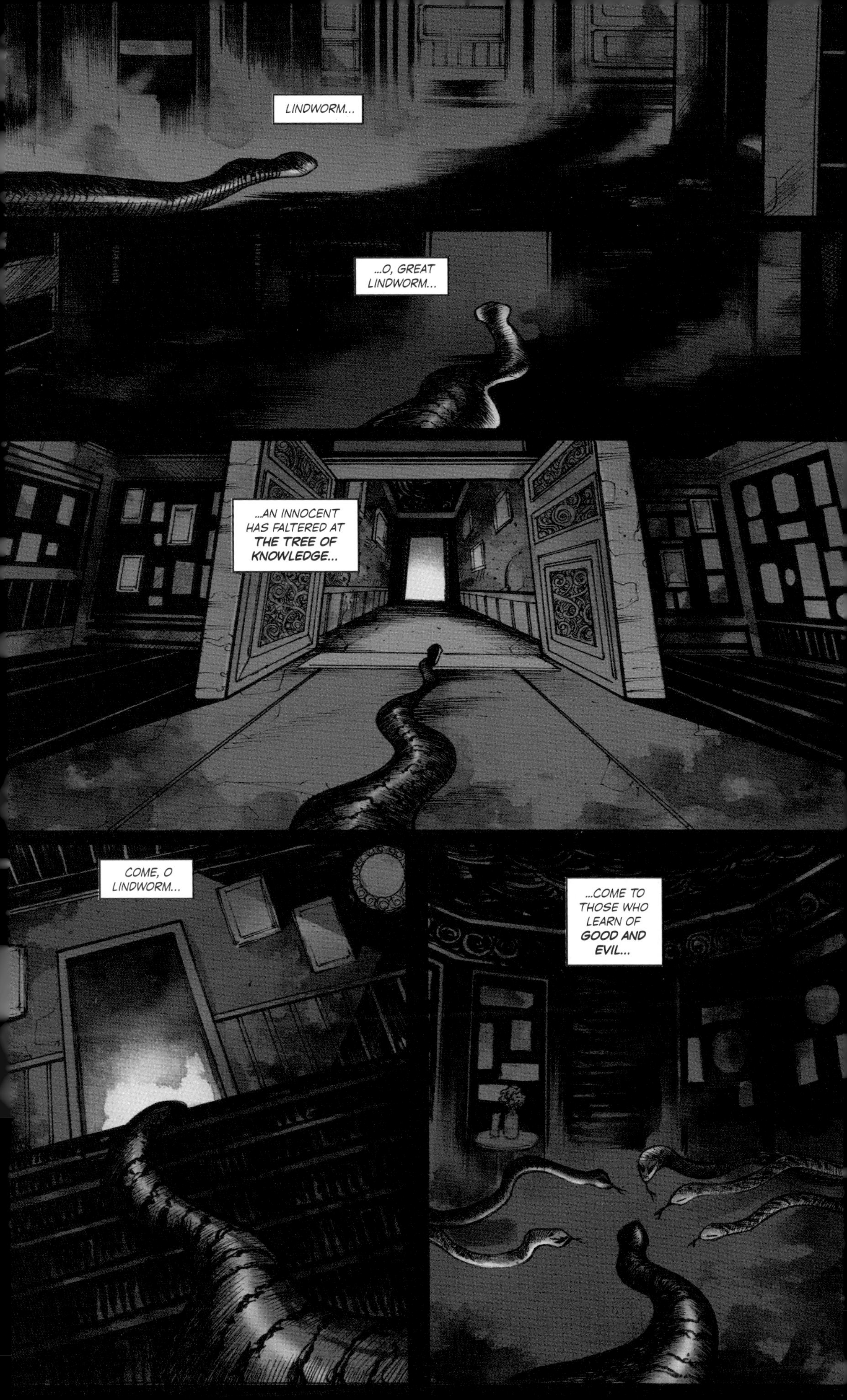
LINDWORM...
...O, GREAT LINDWORM...
...AN INNOCENT HAS FALTERED AT **THE TREE OF KNOWLEDGE...**
COME, O LINDWORM...
...COME TO THOSE WHO LEARN OF **GOOD AND EVIL...**

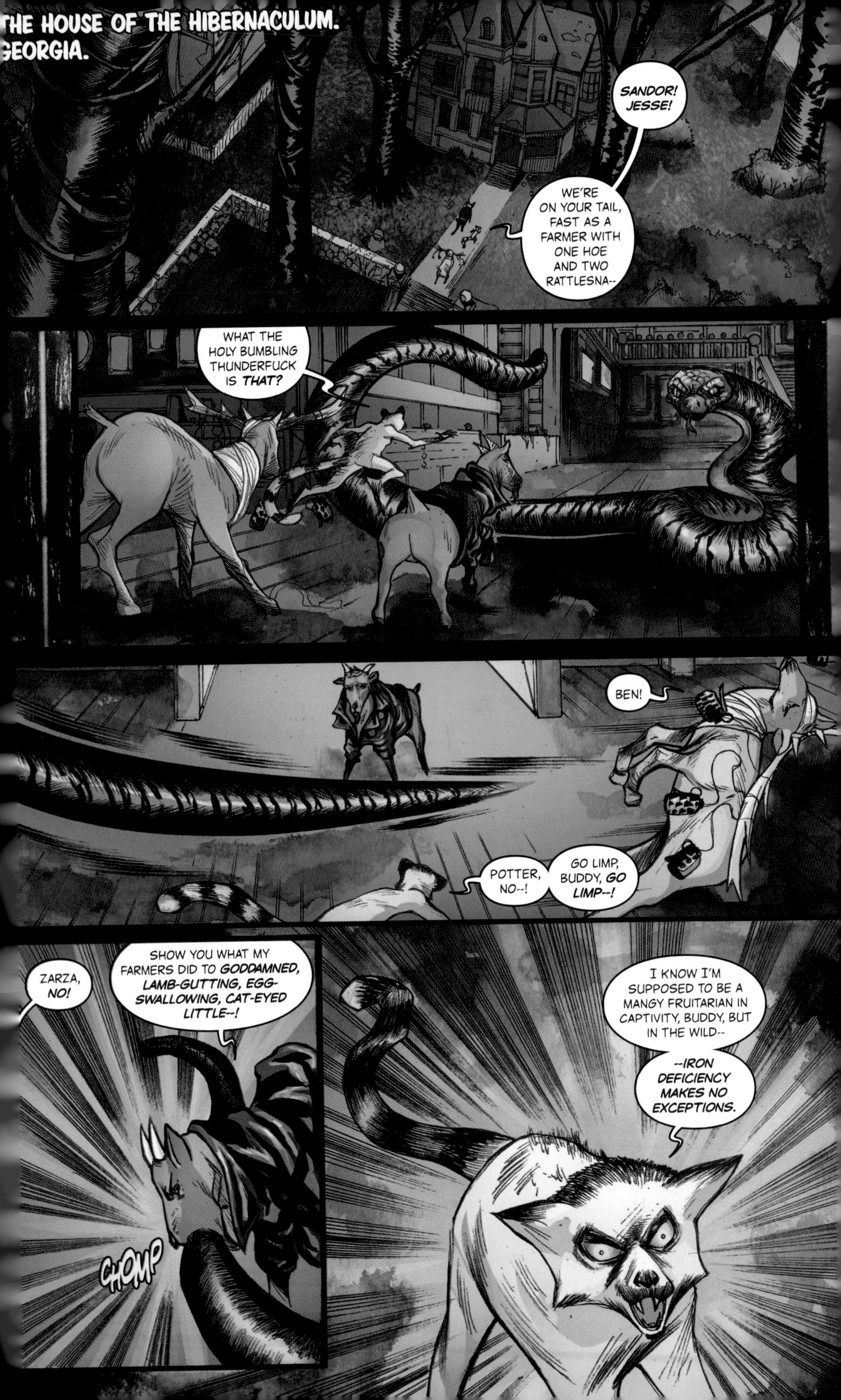
THE HOUSE OF THE HIBERNACULUM.
GEORGIA.
SANDOR! JESSE!
WE'RE ON YOUR TAIL, FAST AS A FARMER WITH ONE HOE AND TWO RATTLESNA--
WHAT THE HOLY BUMBLING THUNDERFUCK IS *THAT?*
BEN!
POTTER, NO--!
GO LIMP, BUDDY, *GO LIMP--!*
ZARZA, *NO!*
SHOW YOU WHAT MY FARMERS DID TO *GODDAMNED, LAMB-GUTTING, EGG-SWALLOWING, CAT-EYED LITTLE--!*
CHOMP
I KNOW I'M SUPPOSED TO BE A MANGY FRUITARIAN IN CAPTIVITY, BUDDY, BUT IN THE WILD--
--IRON DEFICIENCY MAKES NO EXCEPTIONS.

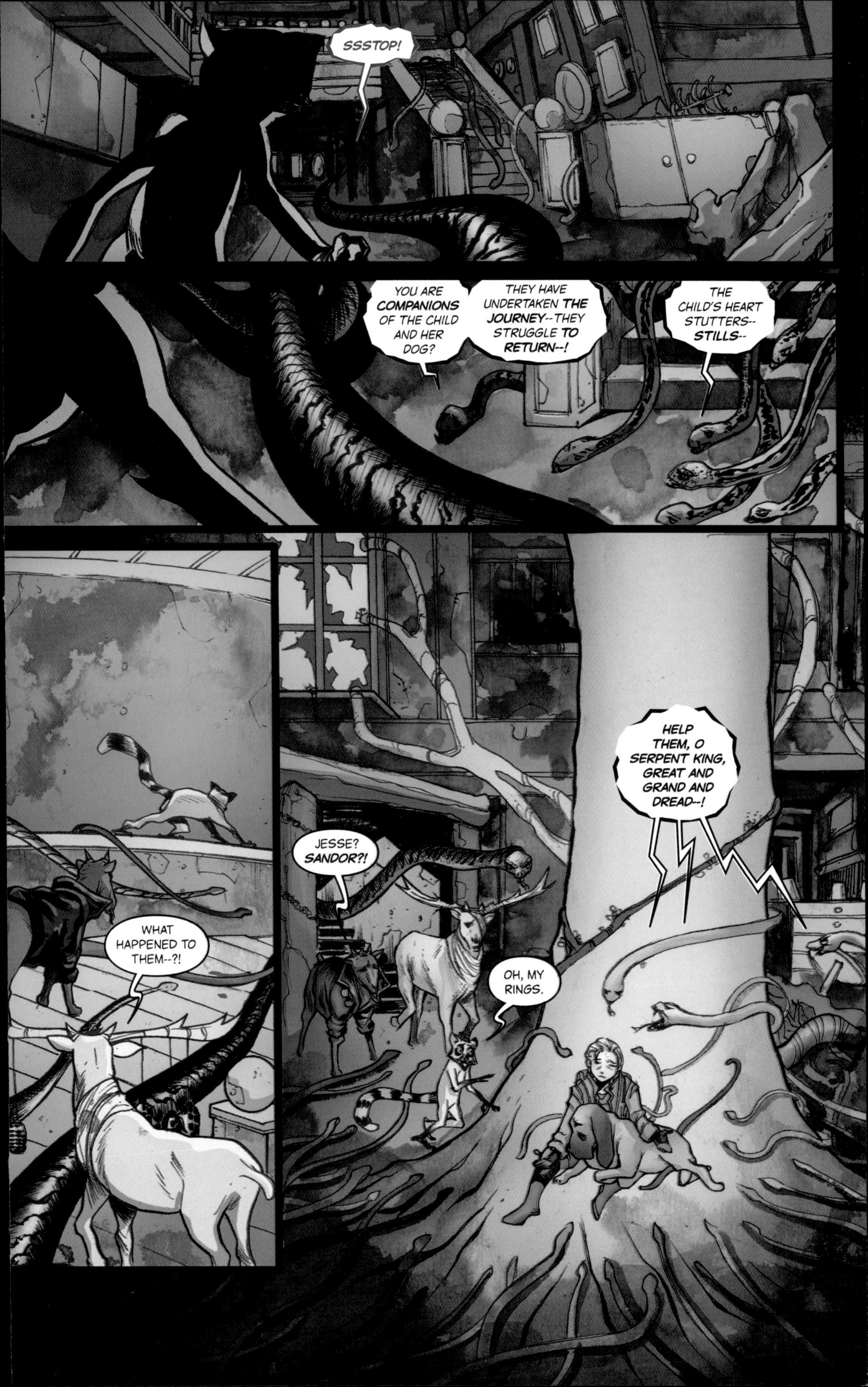
SSSTOP!
YOU ARE COMPANIONS OF THE CHILD AND HER DOG?
THEY HAVE UNDERTAKEN THE JOURNEY--THEY STRUGGLE TO RETURN--!
THE CHILD'S HEART STUTTERS--STILLS--
WHAT HAPPENED TO THEM--?!
JESSE? SANDOR?!
OH, MY RINGS.
HELP THEM, O SERPENT KING, GREAT AND GRAND AND DREAD--!

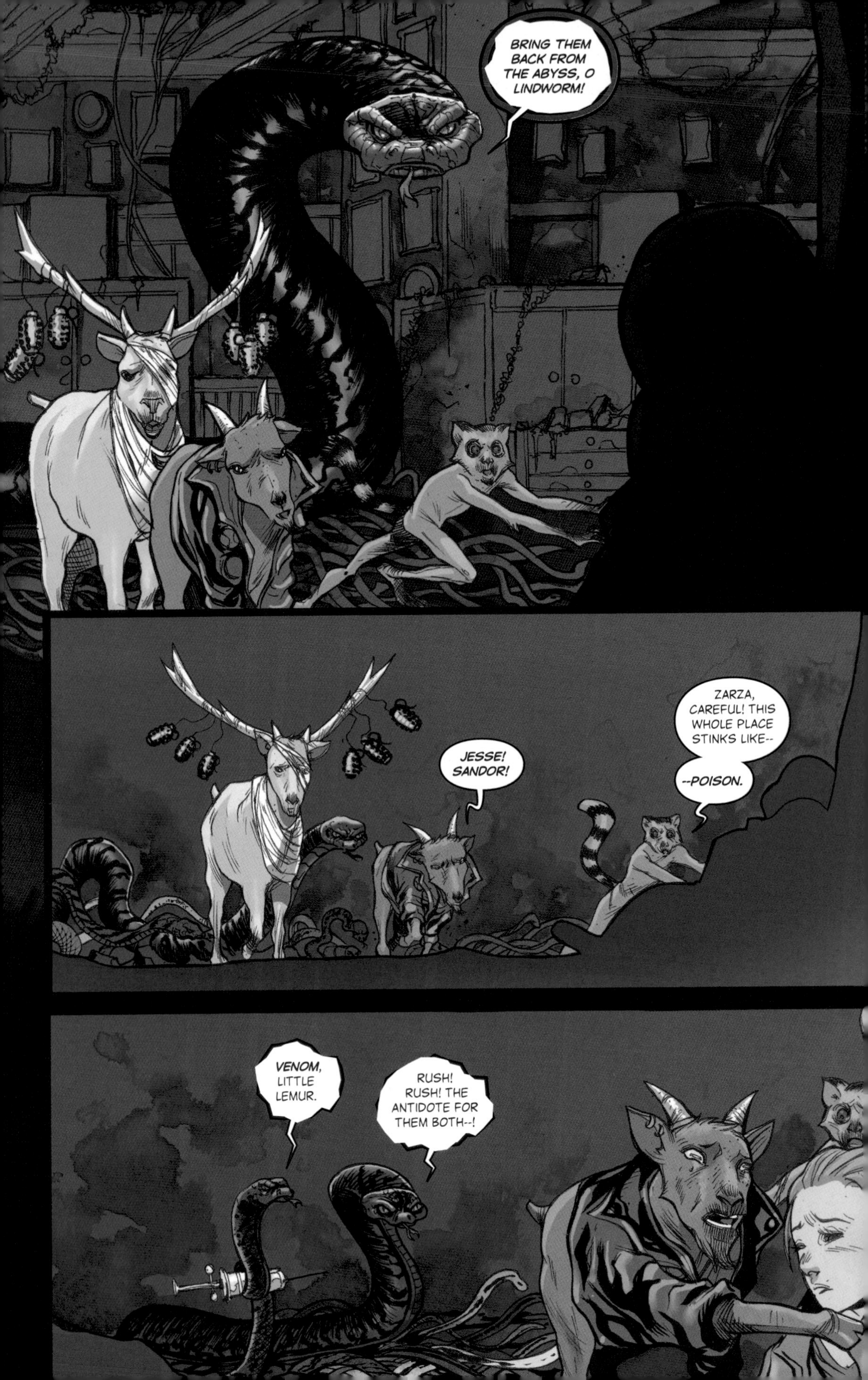
BRING THEM BACK FROM THE ABYSS, O LINDWORM!
JESSE! SANDOR!
ZARZA, CAREFUL! THIS WHOLE PLACE STINKS LIKE--
--POISON.
VENOM, LITTLE LEMUR.
RUSH! RUSH! THE ANTIDOTE FOR THEM BOTH--!

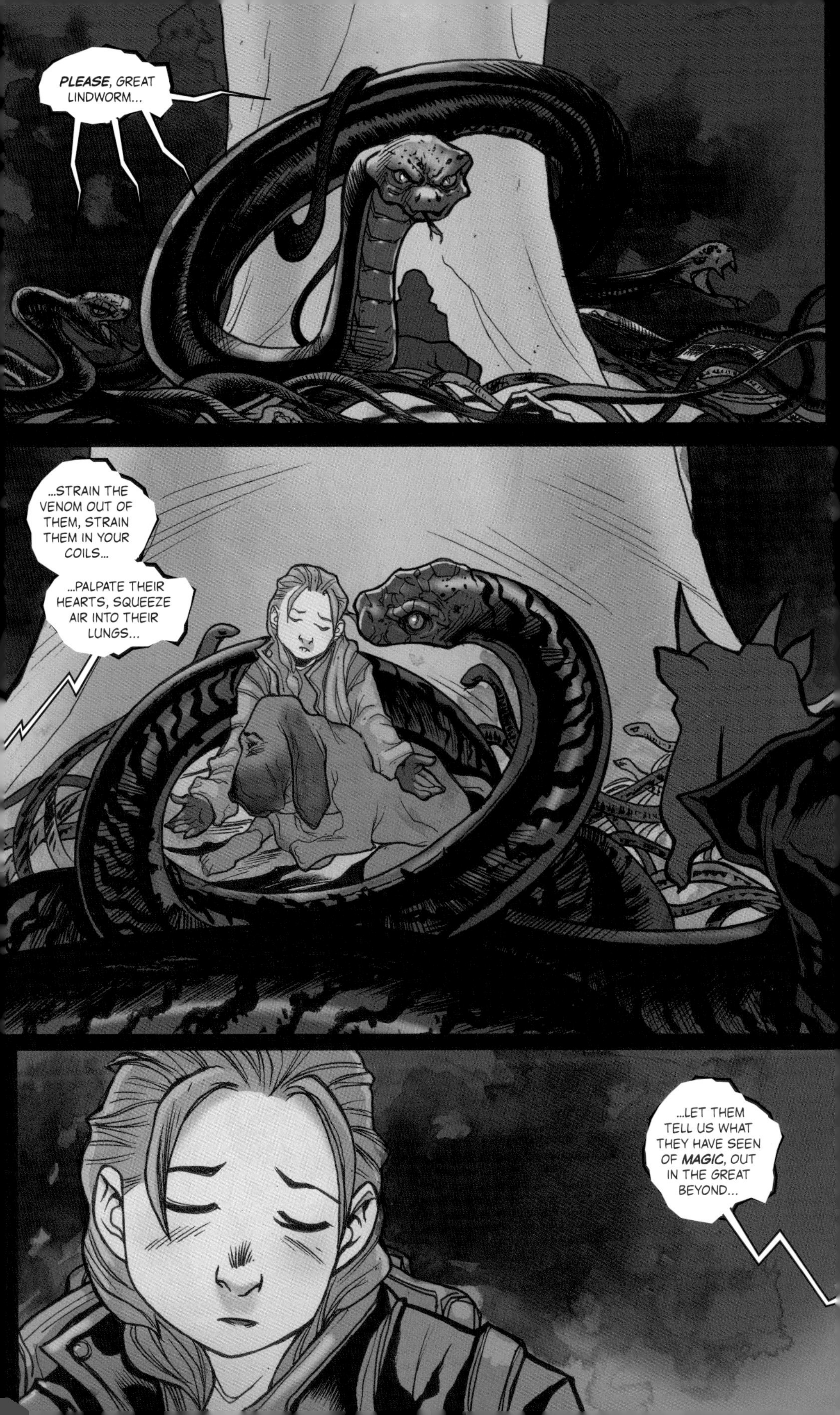
PLEASE, GREAT LINDWORM...
...STRAIN THE VENOM OUT OF THEM, STRAIN THEM IN YOUR COILS...
...PALPATE THEIR HEARTS, SQUEEZE AIR INTO THEIR LUNGS...
...LET THEM TELL US WHAT THEY HAVE SEEN OF MAGIC, OUT IN THE GREAT BEYOND...

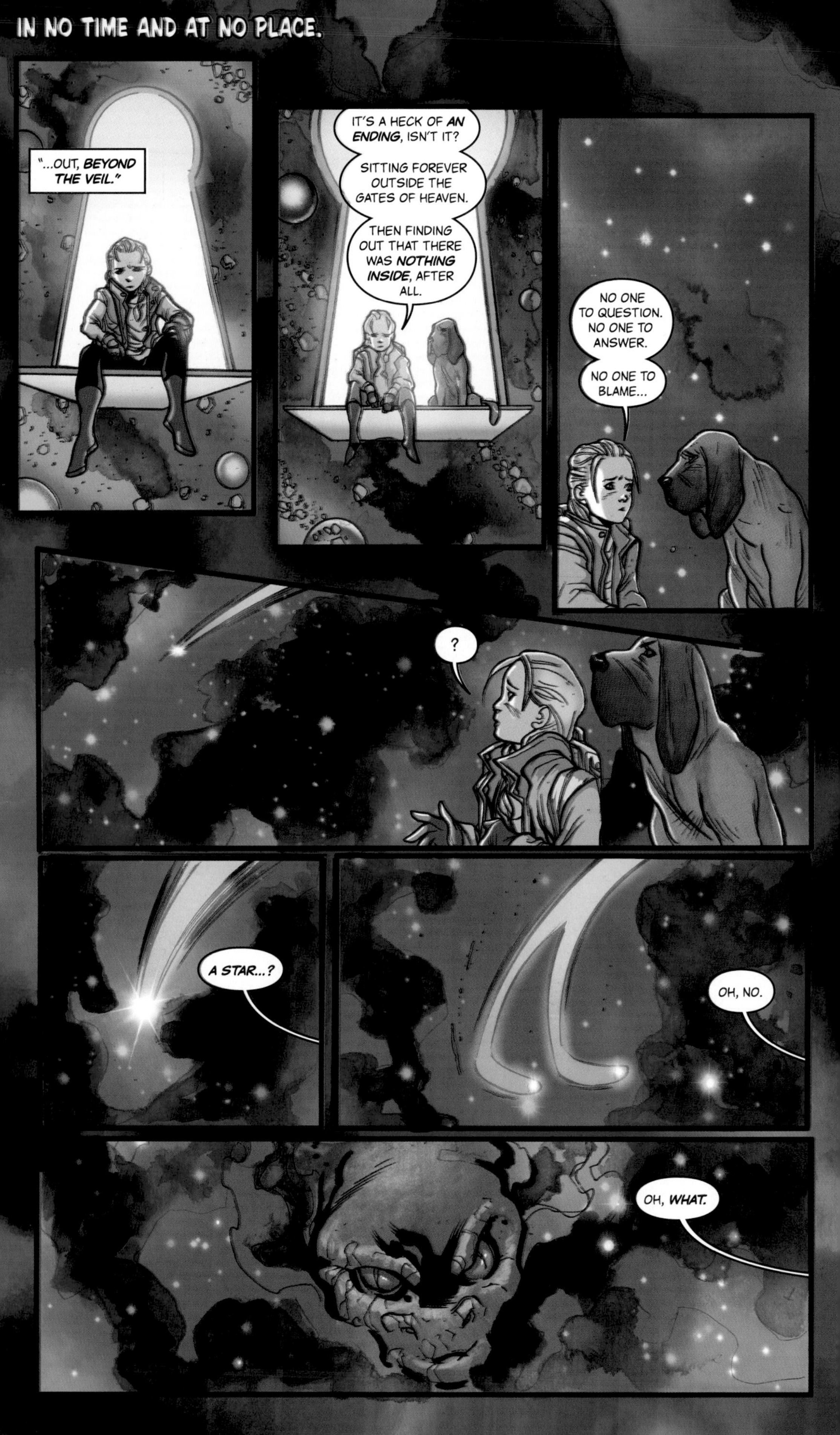
IN NO TIME AND AT NO PLACE.
"...OUT, BEYOND THE VEIL."
IT'S A HECK OF AN ENDING, ISN'T IT?
SITTING FOREVER OUTSIDE THE GATES OF HEAVEN.
THEN FINDING OUT THAT THERE WAS NOTHING INSIDE, AFTER ALL.
NO ONE TO QUESTION. NO ONE TO ANSWER.
NO ONE TO BLAME...
?
A STAR...?
OH, NO.
OH, WHAT.

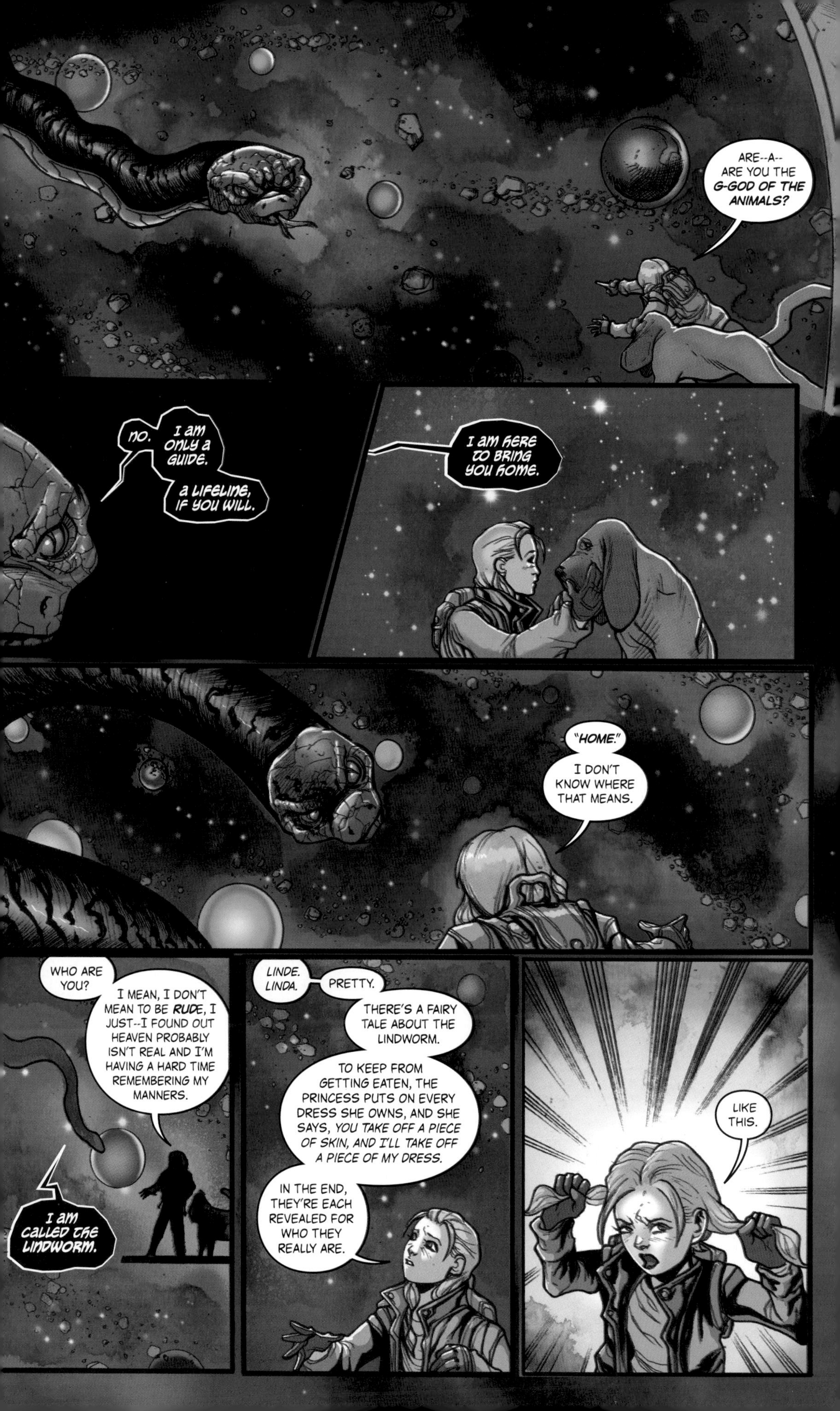
ARE--A--
ARE YOU THE G-GOD OF THE ANIMALS?
NO.
I AM ONLY A GUIDE.
A LIFELINE, IF YOU WILL.
I AM HERE TO BRING YOU HOME.
"HOME."
I DON'T KNOW WHERE THAT MEANS.
WHO ARE YOU?
I MEAN, I DON'T MEAN TO BE RUDE, I JUST--I FOUND OUT HEAVEN PROBABLY ISN'T REAL AND I'M HAVING A HARD TIME REMEMBERING MY MANNERS.
I AM CALLED THE LINDWORM.
LINDE. LINDA.
PRETTY.
THERE'S A FAIRY TALE ABOUT THE LINDWORM.
TO KEEP FROM GETTING EATEN, THE PRINCESS PUTS ON EVERY DRESS SHE OWNS, AND SHE SAYS, YOU TAKE OFF A PIECE OF SKIN, AND I'LL TAKE OFF A PIECE OF MY DRESS.
IN THE END, THEY'RE EACH REVEALED FOR WHO THEY REALLY ARE.
LIKE THIS.

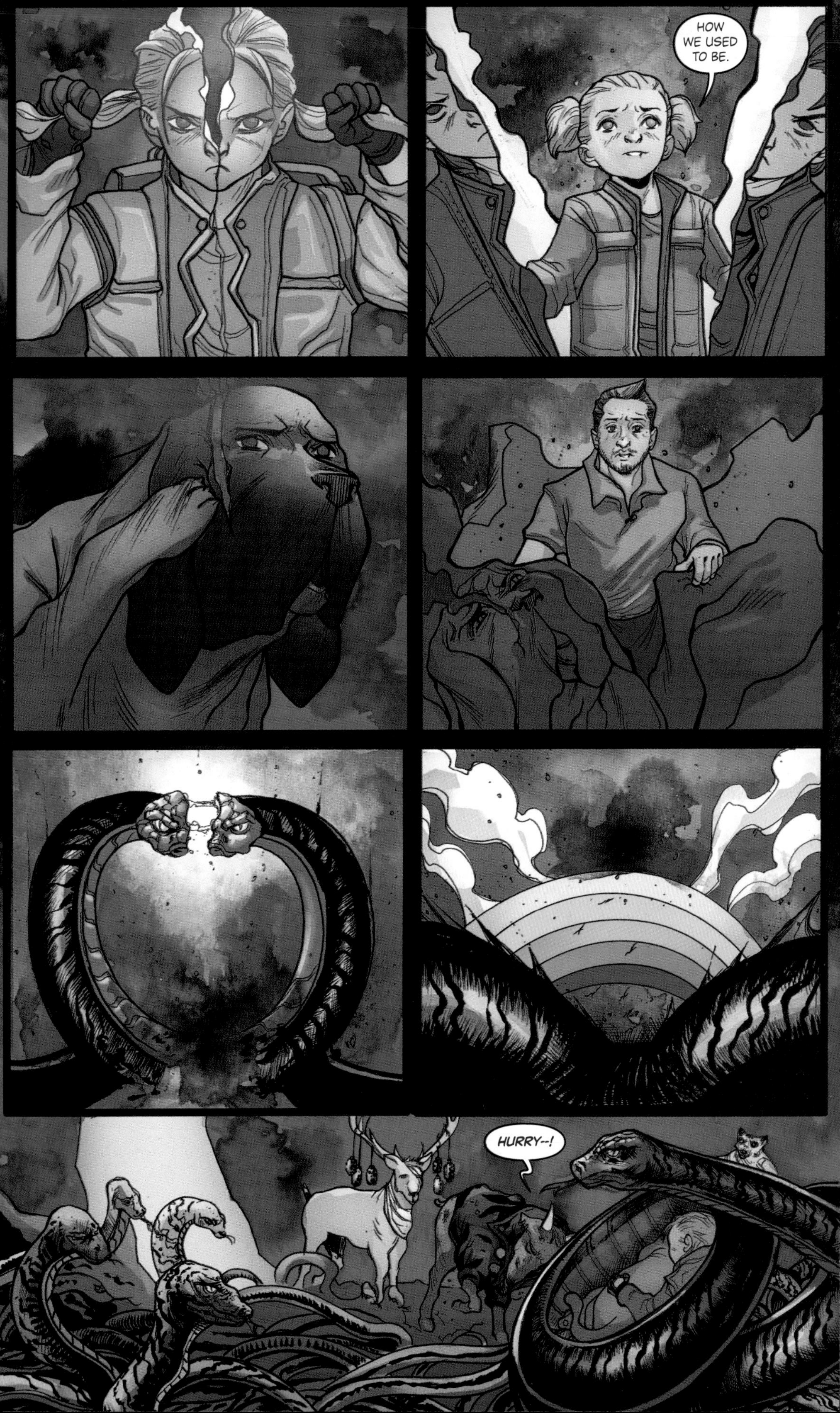
HOW WE USED TO BE.
HURRY--!

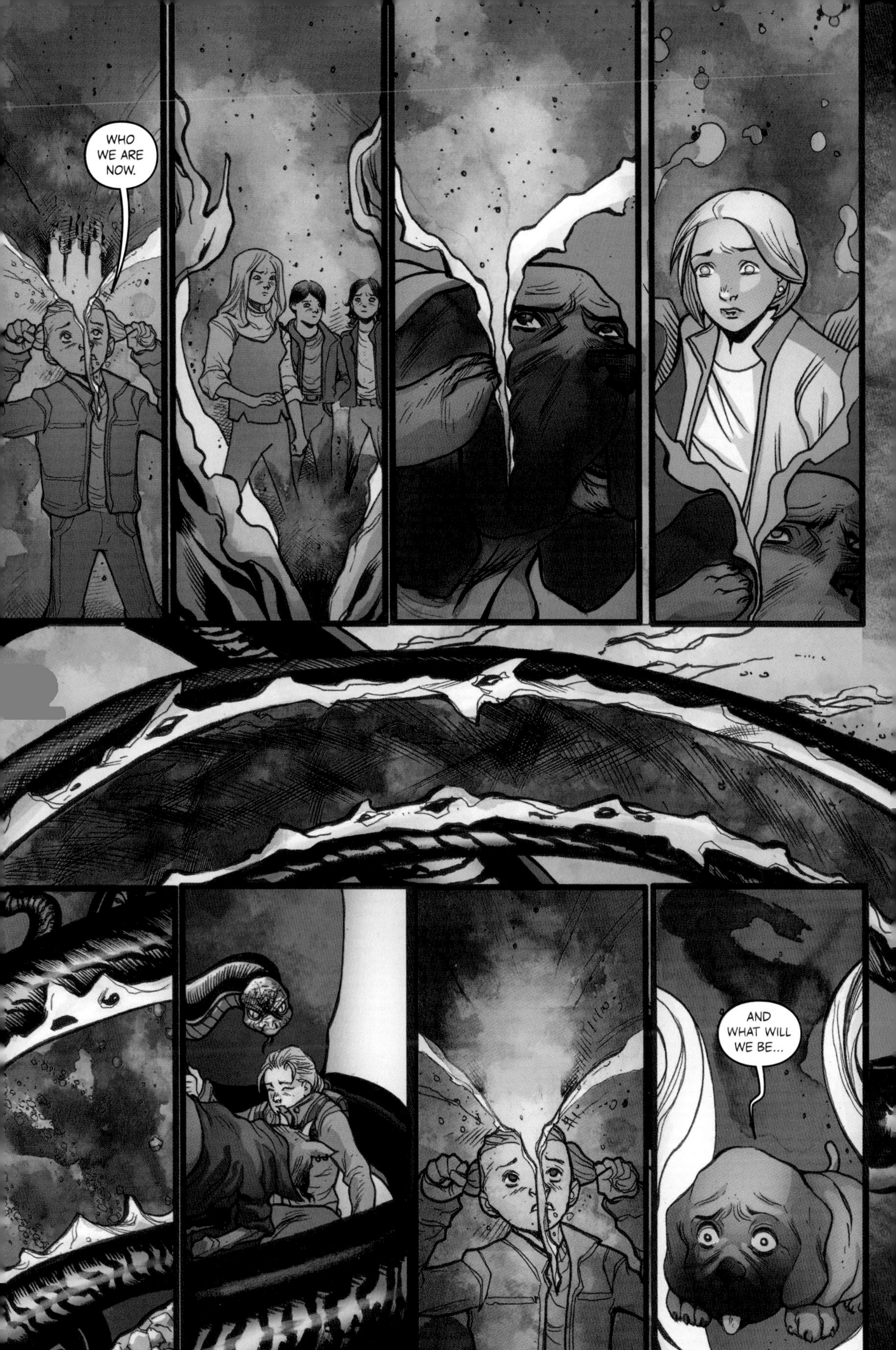
WHO
WE ARE
NOW.
AND
WHAT WILL
WE BE...

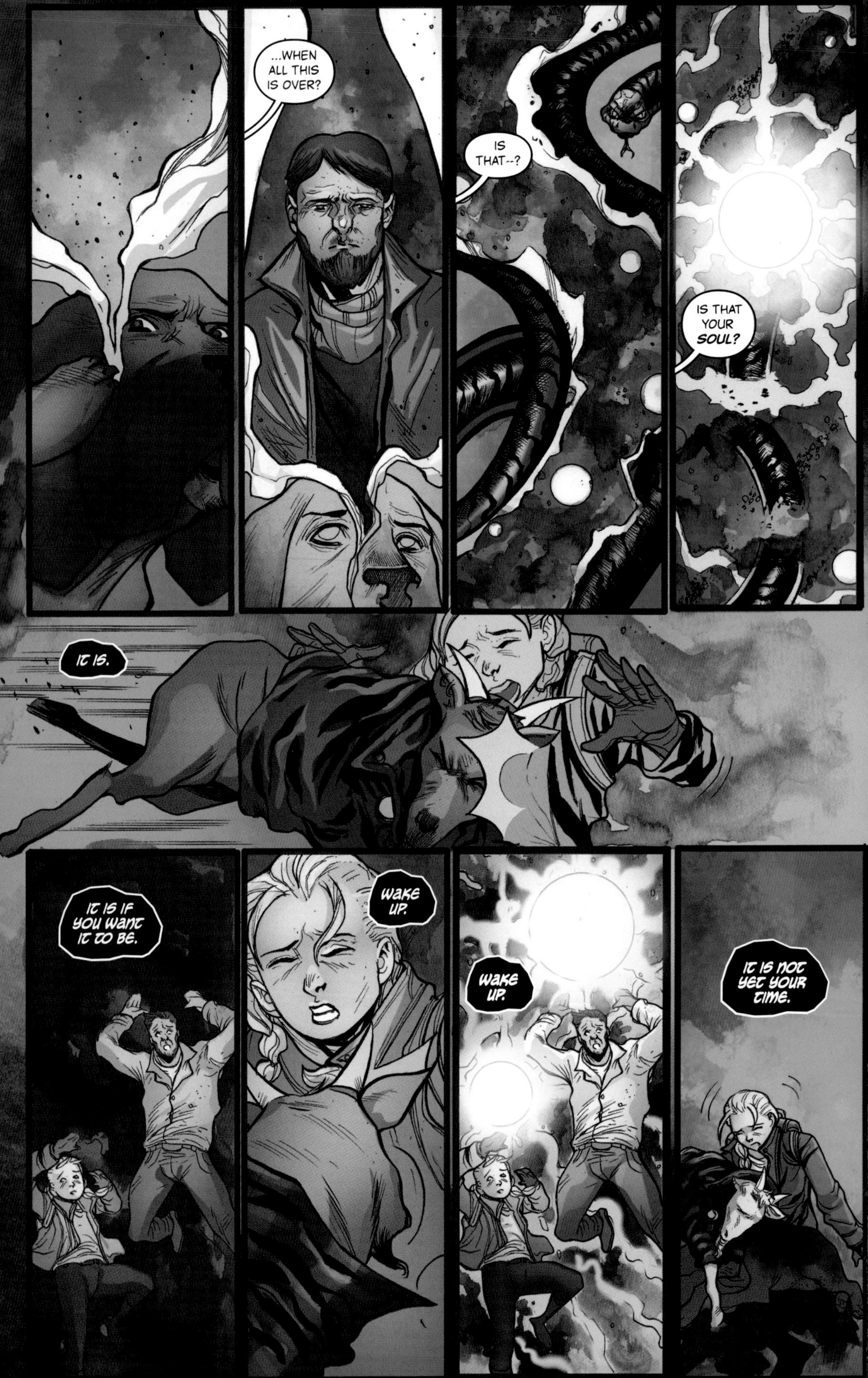
...WHEN ALL THIS IS OVER?
IS THAT--?
IS THAT YOUR SOUL?
IT IS.
IT IS IF YOU WANT IT TO BE.
WAKE UP.
WAKE UP.
IT IS NOT YET YOUR TIME.

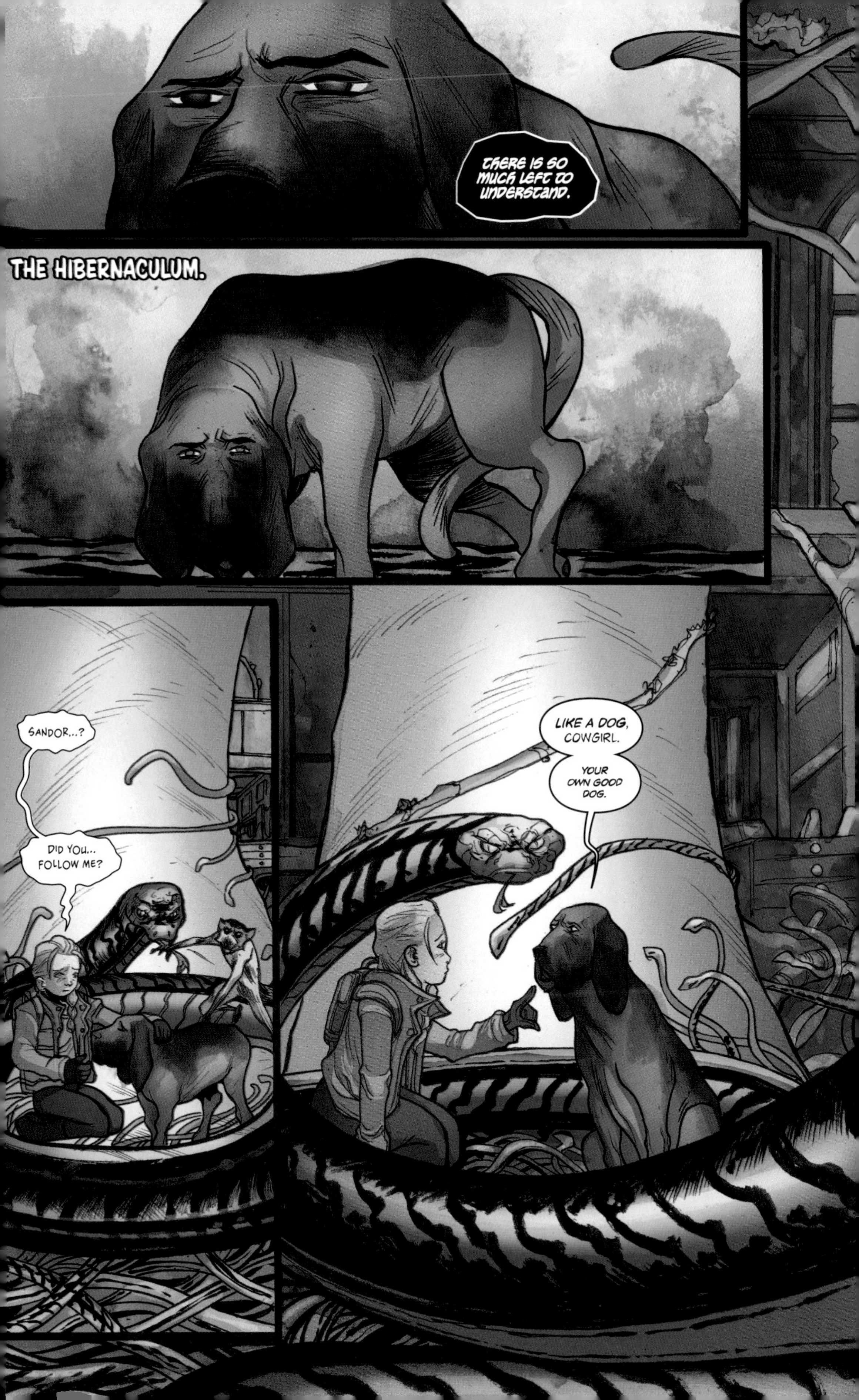
THERE IS SO MUCH LEFT TO UNDERSTAND.
THE HIBERNACULUM.
SANDOR...?
DID YOU... FOLLOW ME?
LIKE A DOG, COWGIRL.
YOUR OWN GOOD DOG.

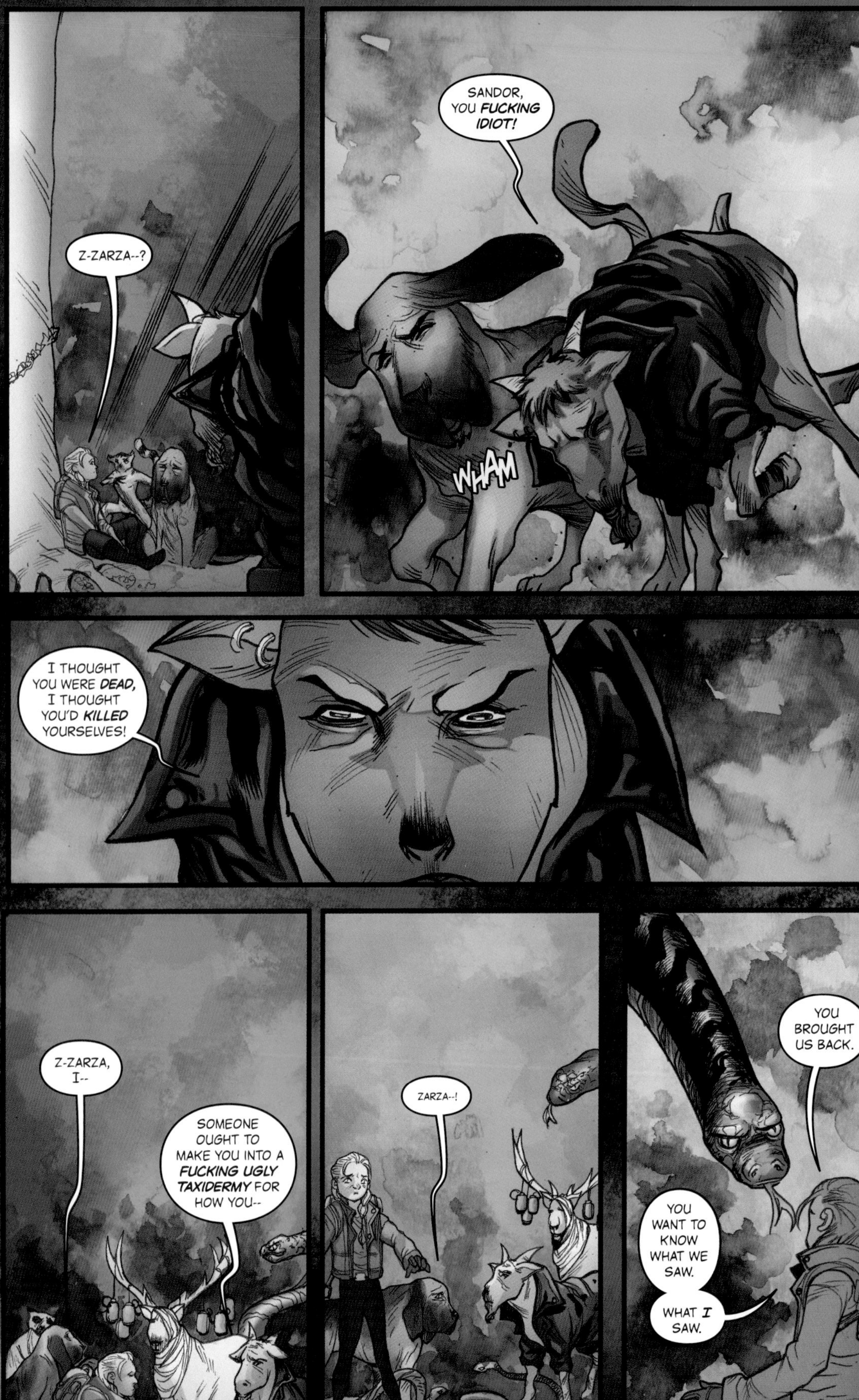
Z-ZARZA--?
SANDOR, YOU FUCKING IDIOT!
WHAM
I THOUGHT YOU WERE DEAD, I THOUGHT YOU'D KILLED YOURSELVES!
Z-ZARZA, I--
SOMEONE OUGHT TO MAKE YOU INTO A FUCKING UGLY TAXIDERMY FOR HOW YOU--
ZARZA--!
YOU BROUGHT US BACK.
YOU WANT TO KNOW WHAT WE SAW.
WHAT I SAW.

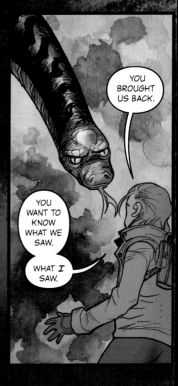

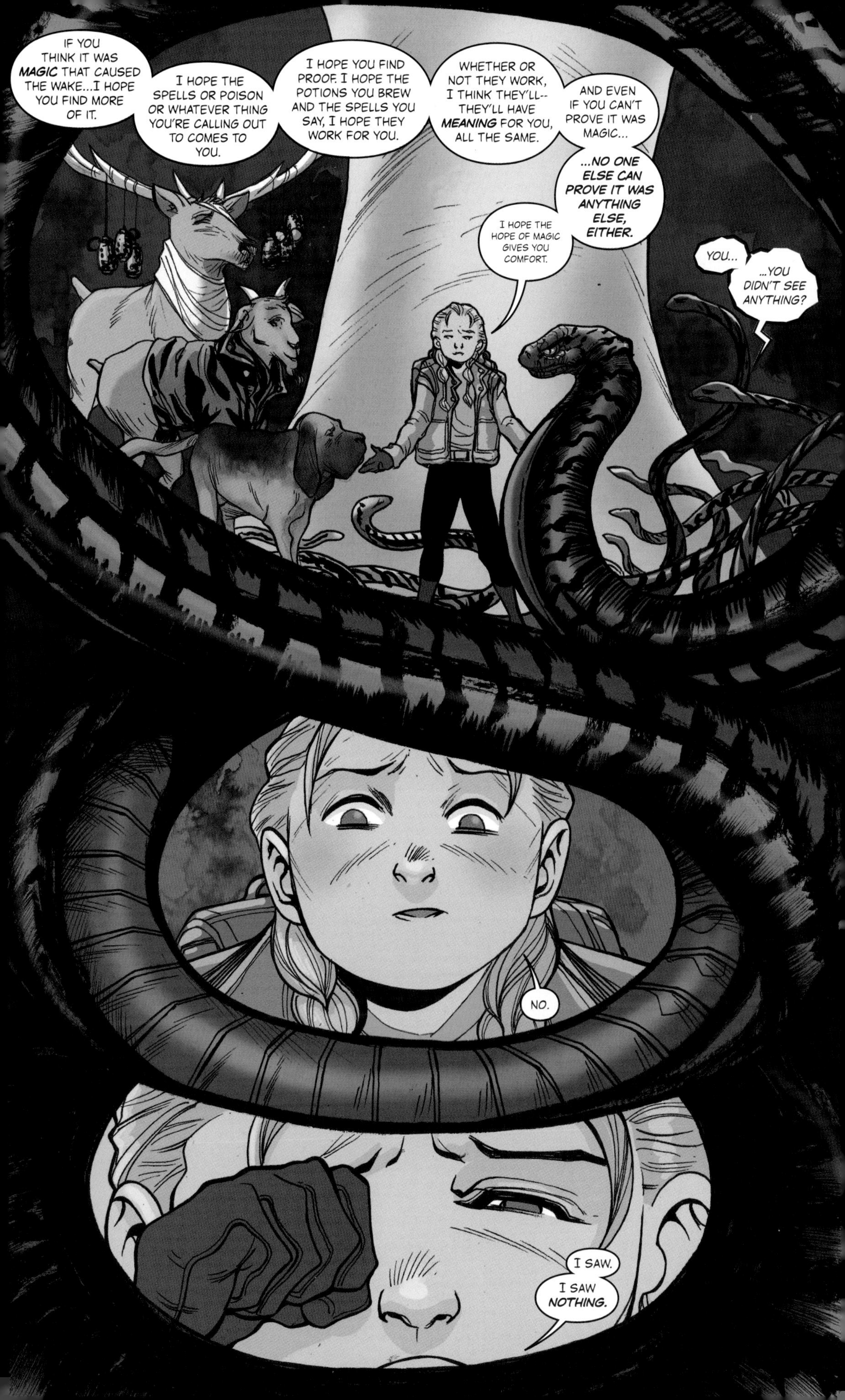
IF YOU THINK IT WAS MAGIC THAT CAUSED THE WAKE...I HOPE YOU FIND MORE OF IT.
I HOPE THE SPELLS OR POISON OR WHATEVER THING YOU'RE CALLING OUT TO COMES TO YOU.
I HOPE YOU FIND PROOF. I HOPE THE POTIONS YOU BREW AND THE SPELLS YOU SAY, I HOPE THEY WORK FOR YOU.
WHETHER OR NOT THEY WORK, I THINK THEY'LL-- THEY'LL HAVE MEANING FOR YOU, ALL THE SAME.
AND EVEN IF YOU CAN'T PROVE IT WAS MAGIC...
...NO ONE ELSE CAN PROVE IT WAS ANYTHING ELSE, EITHER.
I HOPE THE HOPE OF MAGIC GIVES YOU COMFORT.
YOU...
...YOU DIDN'T SEE ANYTHING?
NO.
I SAW.
I SAW NOTHING.

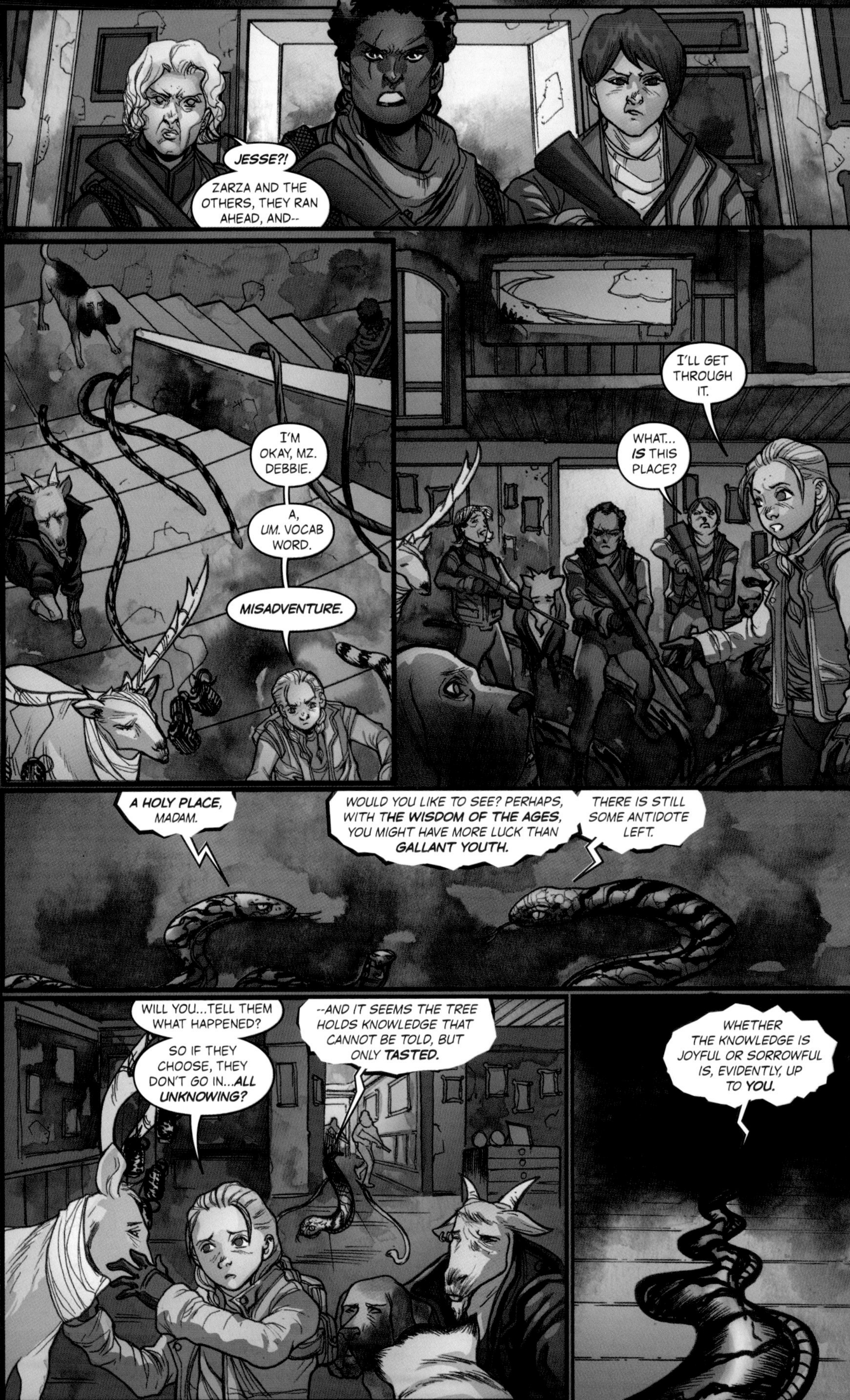
JESSE?!
ZARZA AND THE OTHERS, THEY RAN AHEAD, AND--
I'M OKAY, MZ. DEBBIE.
A, UM. VOCAB WORD.
MISADVENTURE.
I'LL GET THROUGH IT.
WHAT... IS THIS PLACE?
A HOLY PLACE, MADAM.
WOULD YOU LIKE TO SEE? PERHAPS, WITH THE WISDOM OF THE AGES, YOU MIGHT HAVE MORE LUCK THAN GALLANT YOUTH.
THERE IS STILL SOME ANTIDOTE LEFT.
WILL YOU...TELL THEM WHAT HAPPENED?
SO IF THEY CHOOSE, THEY DON'T GO IN...ALL UNKNOWING?
--AND IT SEEMS THE TREE HOLDS KNOWLEDGE THAT CANNOT BE TOLD, BUT ONLY TASTED.
WHETHER THE KNOWLEDGE IS JOYFUL OR SORROWFUL IS, EVIDENTLY, UP TO YOU.

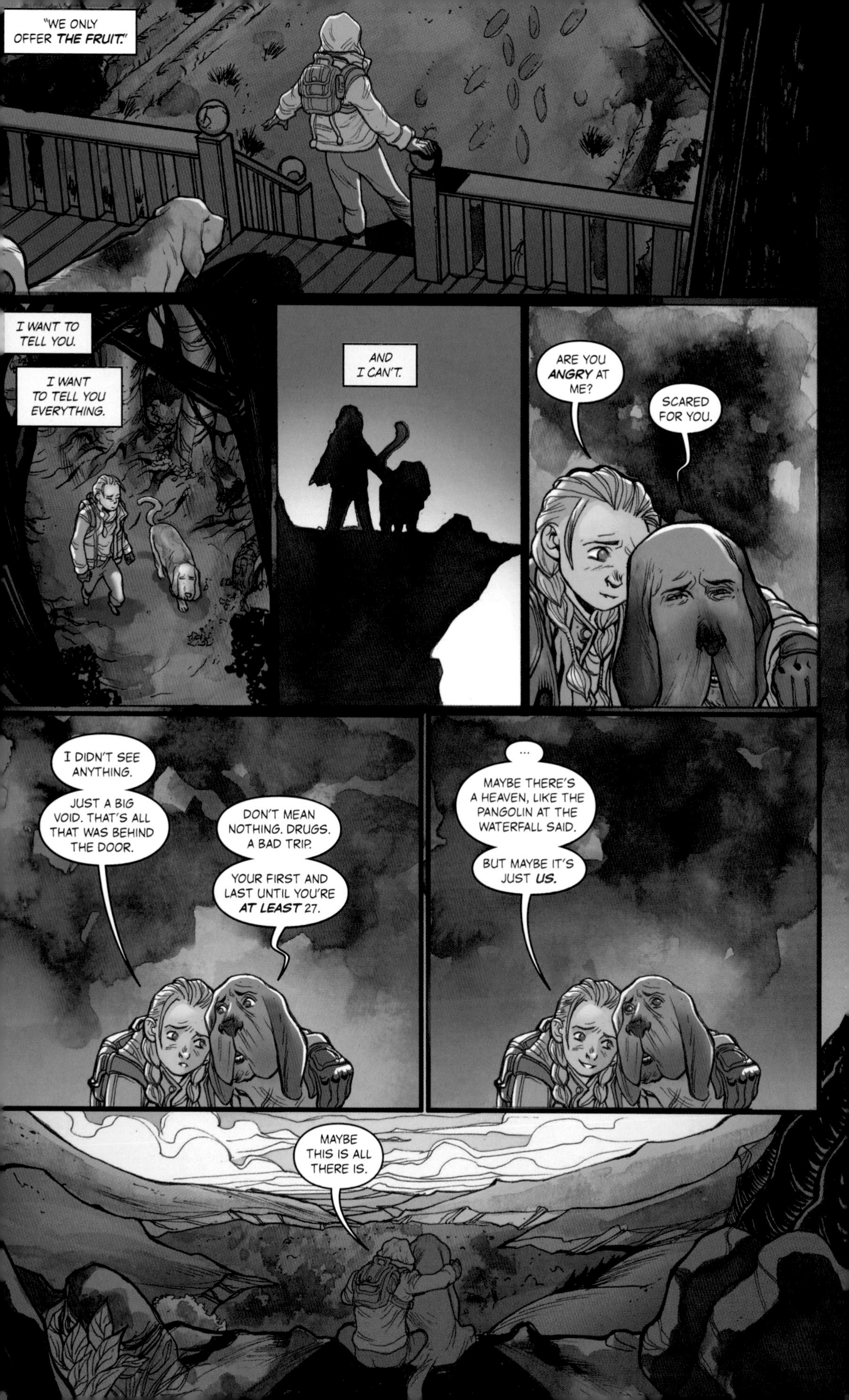
"WE ONLY OFFER THE FRUIT."
I WANT TO TELL YOU.
I WANT TO TELL YOU EVERYTHING.
AND I CAN'T.
ARE YOU ANGRY AT ME?
SCARED FOR YOU.
I DIDN'T SEE ANYTHING.
JUST A BIG VOID. THAT'S ALL THAT WAS BEHIND THE DOOR.
DON'T MEAN NOTHING. DRUGS. A BAD TRIP.
YOUR FIRST AND LAST UNTIL YOU'RE AT LEAST 27.
...
MAYBE THERE'S A HEAVEN, LIKE THE PANGOLIN AT THE WATERFALL SAID.
BUT MAYBE IT'S JUST US.
MAYBE THIS IS ALL THERE IS.

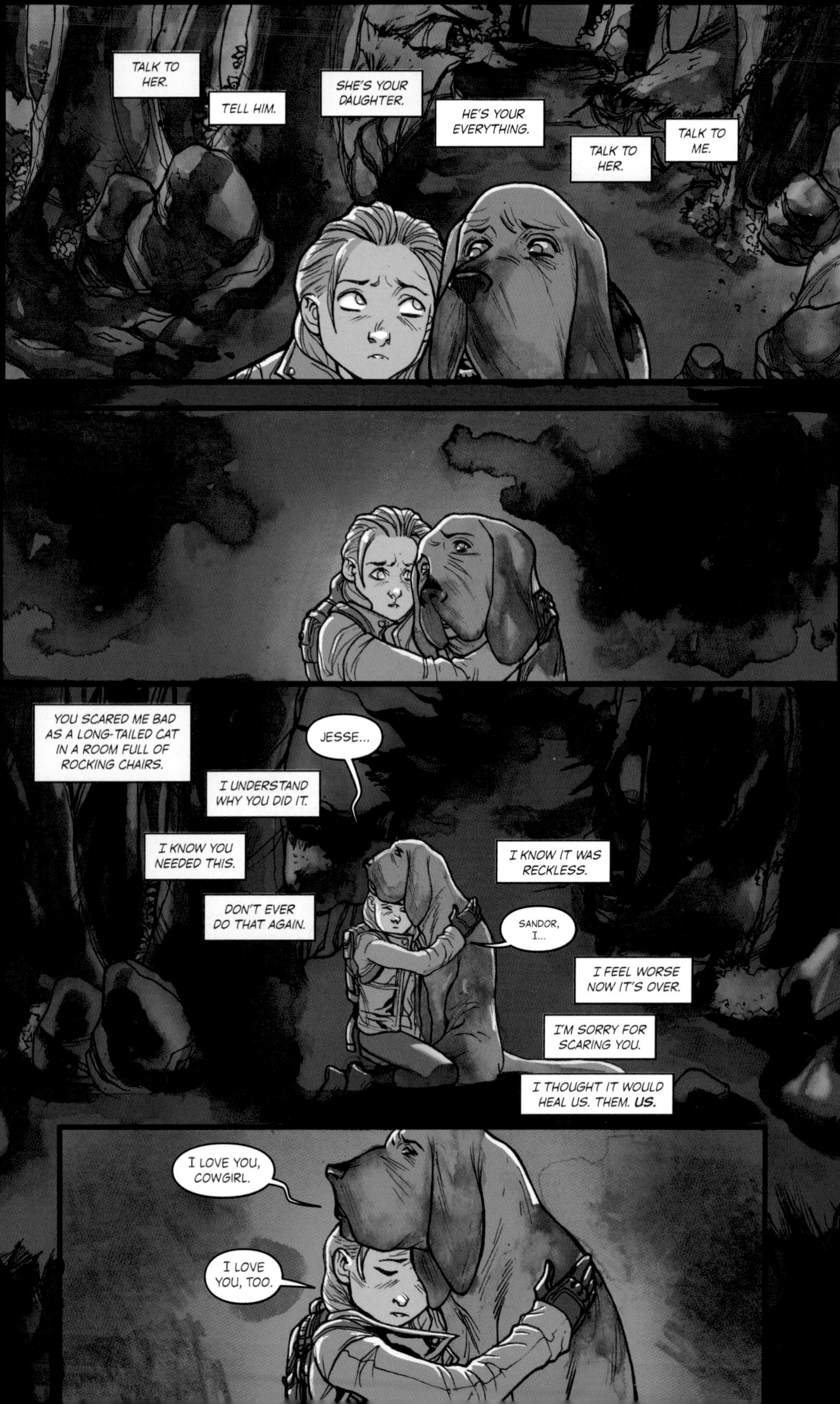
TALK TO HER.
TELL HIM.
SHE'S YOUR DAUGHTER.
HE'S YOUR EVERYTHING.
TALK TO HER.
TALK TO ME.
YOU SCARED ME BAD AS A LONG-TAILED CAT IN A ROOM FULL OF ROCKING CHAIRS.
JESSE...
I UNDERSTAND WHY YOU DID IT.
I KNOW YOU NEEDED THIS.
I KNOW IT WAS RECKLESS.
DON'T EVER DO THAT AGAIN.
SANDOR, I...
I FEEL WORSE NOW IT'S OVER.
I'M SORRY FOR SCARING YOU.
I THOUGHT IT WOULD HEAL US. THEM. **US.**
I LOVE YOU, COWGIRL.
I LOVE YOU, TOO.

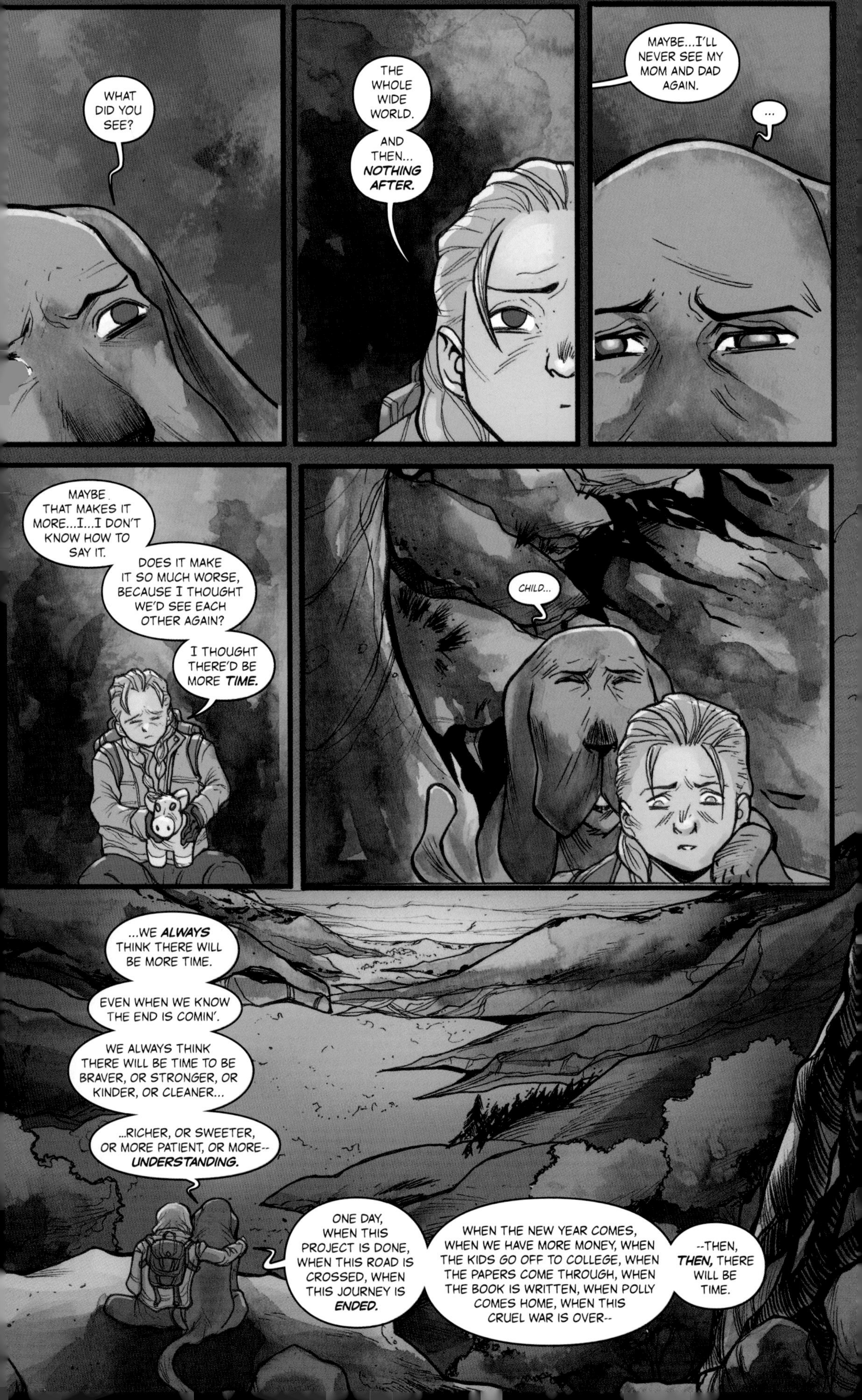
WHAT DID YOU SEE?
THE WHOLE WIDE WORLD.
AND THEN... NOTHING AFTER.
MAYBE...I'LL NEVER SEE MY MOM AND DAD AGAIN.
...
MAYBE THAT MAKES IT MORE...I...I DON'T KNOW HOW TO SAY IT.
DOES IT MAKE IT SO MUCH WORSE, BECAUSE I THOUGHT WE'D SEE EACH OTHER AGAIN?
I THOUGHT THERE'D BE MORE TIME.
CHILD...
...WE ALWAYS THINK THERE WILL BE MORE TIME.
EVEN WHEN WE KNOW THE END IS COMIN'.
WE ALWAYS THINK THERE WILL BE TIME TO BE BRAVER, OR STRONGER, OR KINDER, OR CLEANER...
...RICHER, OR SWEETER, OR MORE PATIENT, OR MORE-- UNDERSTANDING.
ONE DAY, WHEN THIS PROJECT IS DONE, WHEN THIS ROAD IS CROSSED, WHEN THIS JOURNEY IS ENDED.
WHEN THE NEW YEAR COMES, WHEN WE HAVE MORE MONEY, WHEN THE KIDS GO OFF TO COLLEGE, WHEN THE PAPERS COME THROUGH, WHEN THE BOOK IS WRITTEN, WHEN POLLY COMES HOME, WHEN THIS CRUEL WAR IS OVER--
--THEN, THEN, THERE WILL BE TIME.

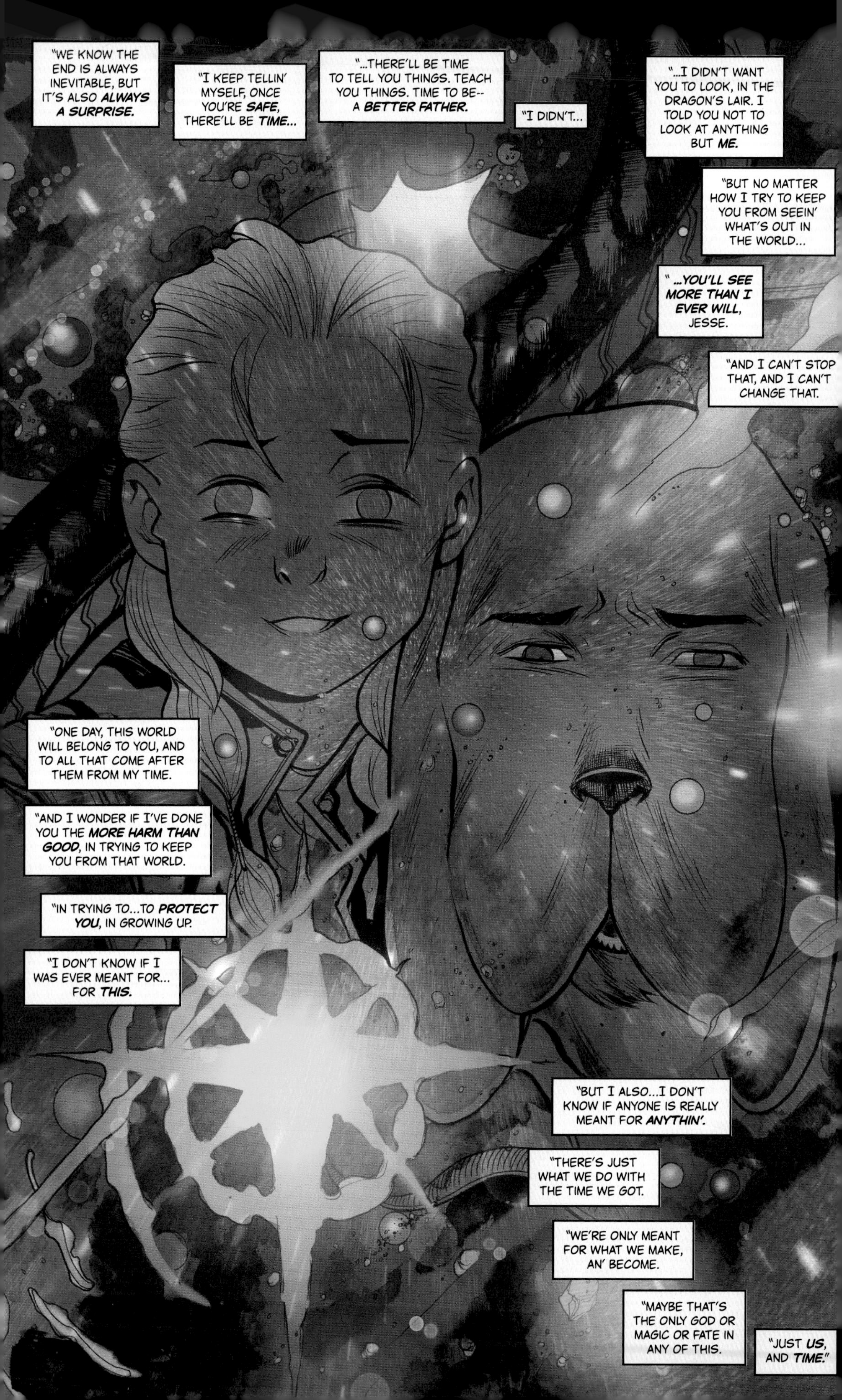
"WE KNOW THE END IS ALWAYS INEVITABLE, BUT IT'S ALSO **ALWAYS A SURPRISE.**
"I KEEP TELLIN' MYSELF, ONCE YOU'RE **SAFE,** THERE'LL BE **TIME...**
"...THERE'LL BE TIME TO TELL YOU THINGS. TEACH YOU THINGS. TIME TO BE-- A **BETTER FATHER.**
"I DIDN'T...
"...I DIDN'T WANT YOU TO LOOK, IN THE DRAGON'S LAIR. I TOLD YOU NOT TO LOOK AT ANYTHING BUT **ME.**
"BUT NO MATTER HOW I TRY TO KEEP YOU FROM SEEIN' WHAT'S OUT IN THE WORLD...
"**...YOU'LL SEE MORE THAN I EVER WILL,** JESSE.
"AND I CAN'T STOP THAT, AND I CAN'T CHANGE THAT.
"ONE DAY, THIS WORLD WILL BELONG TO YOU, AND TO ALL THAT COME AFTER THEM FROM MY TIME.
"AND I WONDER IF I'VE DONE YOU THE **MORE HARM THAN GOOD,** IN TRYING TO KEEP YOU FROM THAT WORLD.
"IN TRYING TO...TO **PROTECT YOU,** IN GROWING UP.
"I DON'T KNOW IF I WAS EVER MEANT FOR... FOR **THIS.**
"BUT I ALSO...I DON'T KNOW IF ANYONE IS REALLY MEANT FOR **ANYTHIN'.**
"THERE'S JUST WHAT WE DO WITH THE TIME WE GOT.
"WE'RE ONLY MEANT FOR WHAT WE MAKE, AN' BECOME.
"MAYBE THAT'S THE ONLY GOD OR MAGIC OR FATE IN ANY OF THIS.
"JUST **US,** AND **TIME.**"

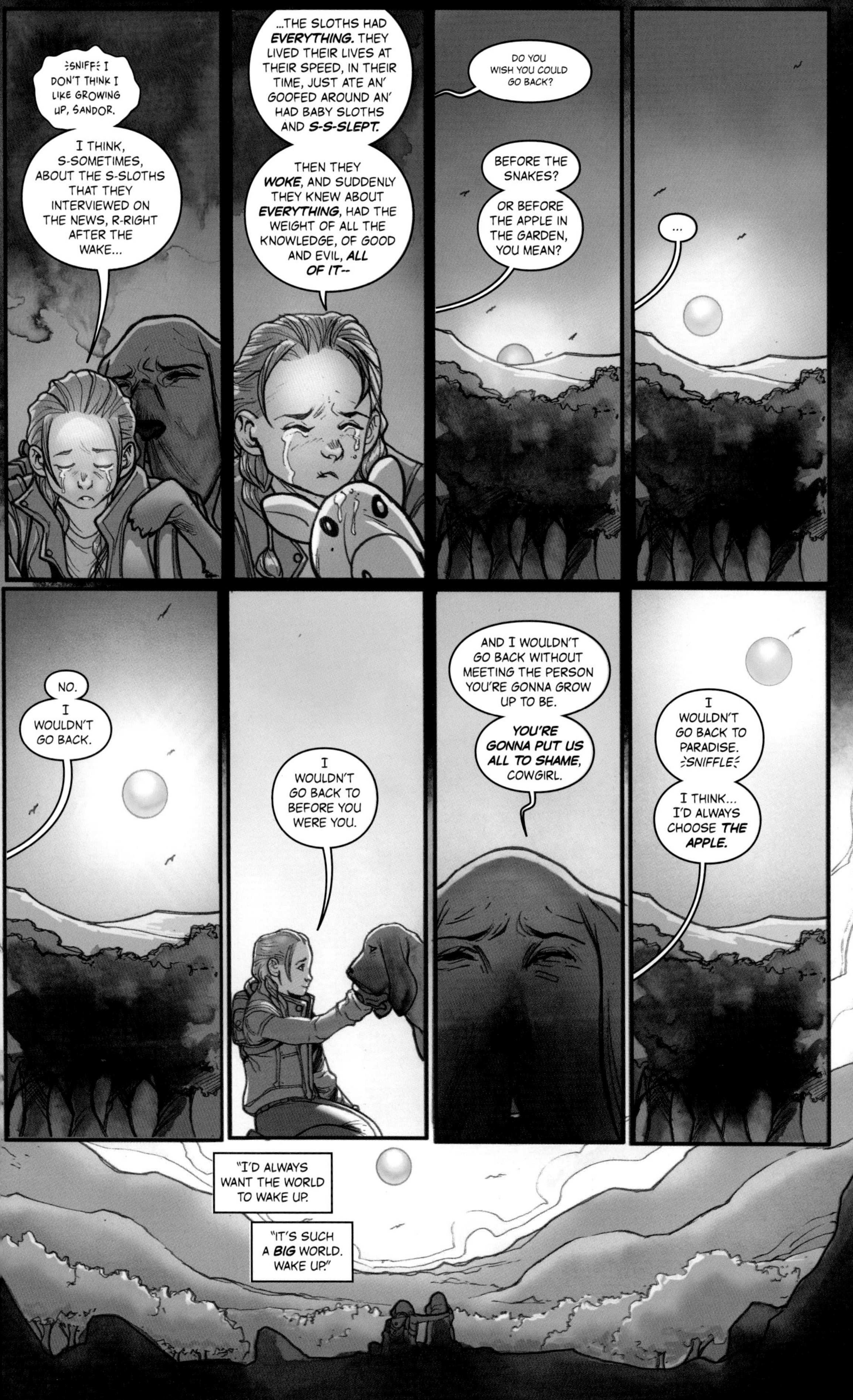

⸗SNIFF⸗ I DON'T THINK I LIKE GROWING UP, SANDOR.
I THINK, S-SOMETIMES, ABOUT THE S-SLOTHS THAT THEY INTERVIEWED ON THE NEWS, R-RIGHT AFTER THE WAKE...
...THE SLOTHS HAD EVERYTHING. THEY LIVED THEIR LIVES AT THEIR SPEED, IN THEIR TIME, JUST ATE AN' GOOFED AROUND AN' HAD BABY SLOTHS AND S-S-SLEPT.
THEN THEY WOKE, AND SUDDENLY THEY KNEW ABOUT EVERYTHING, HAD THE WEIGHT OF ALL THE KNOWLEDGE, OF GOOD AND EVIL, ALL OF IT--
DO YOU WISH YOU COULD GO BACK?
BEFORE THE SNAKES?
OR BEFORE THE APPLE IN THE GARDEN, YOU MEAN?
...
NO. I WOULDN'T GO BACK.
I WOULDN'T GO BACK TO BEFORE YOU WERE YOU.
AND I WOULDN'T GO BACK WITHOUT MEETING THE PERSON YOU'RE GONNA GROW UP TO BE.
YOU'RE GONNA PUT US ALL TO SHAME, COWGIRL.
I WOULDN'T GO BACK TO PARADISE. ⸗SNIFFLE⸗
I THINK... I'D ALWAYS CHOOSE THE APPLE.
"I'D ALWAYS WANT THE WORLD TO WAKE UP.
"IT'S SUCH A BIG WORLD. WAKE UP."

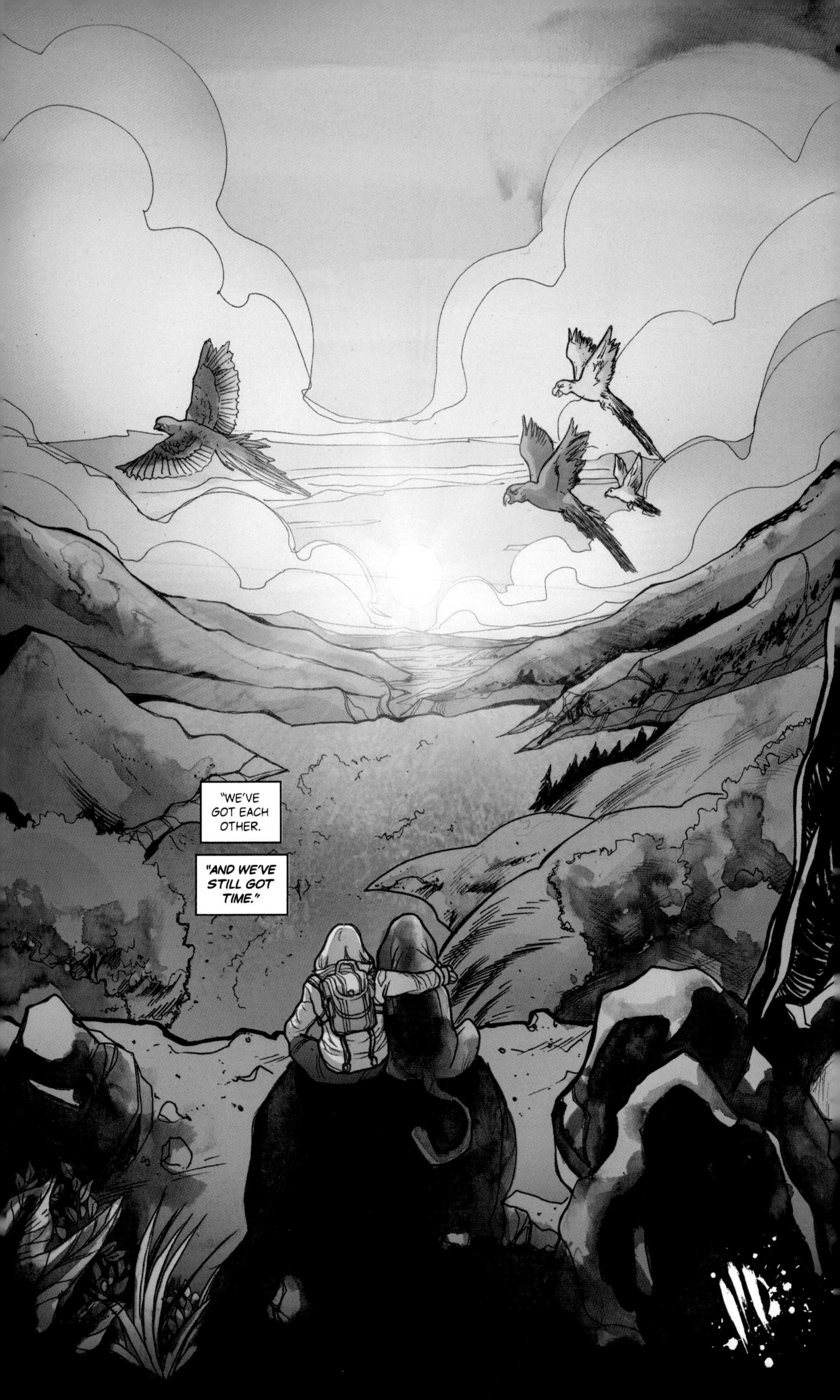
"WE'VE GOT EACH OTHER.
"AND WE'VE STILL GOT TIME."

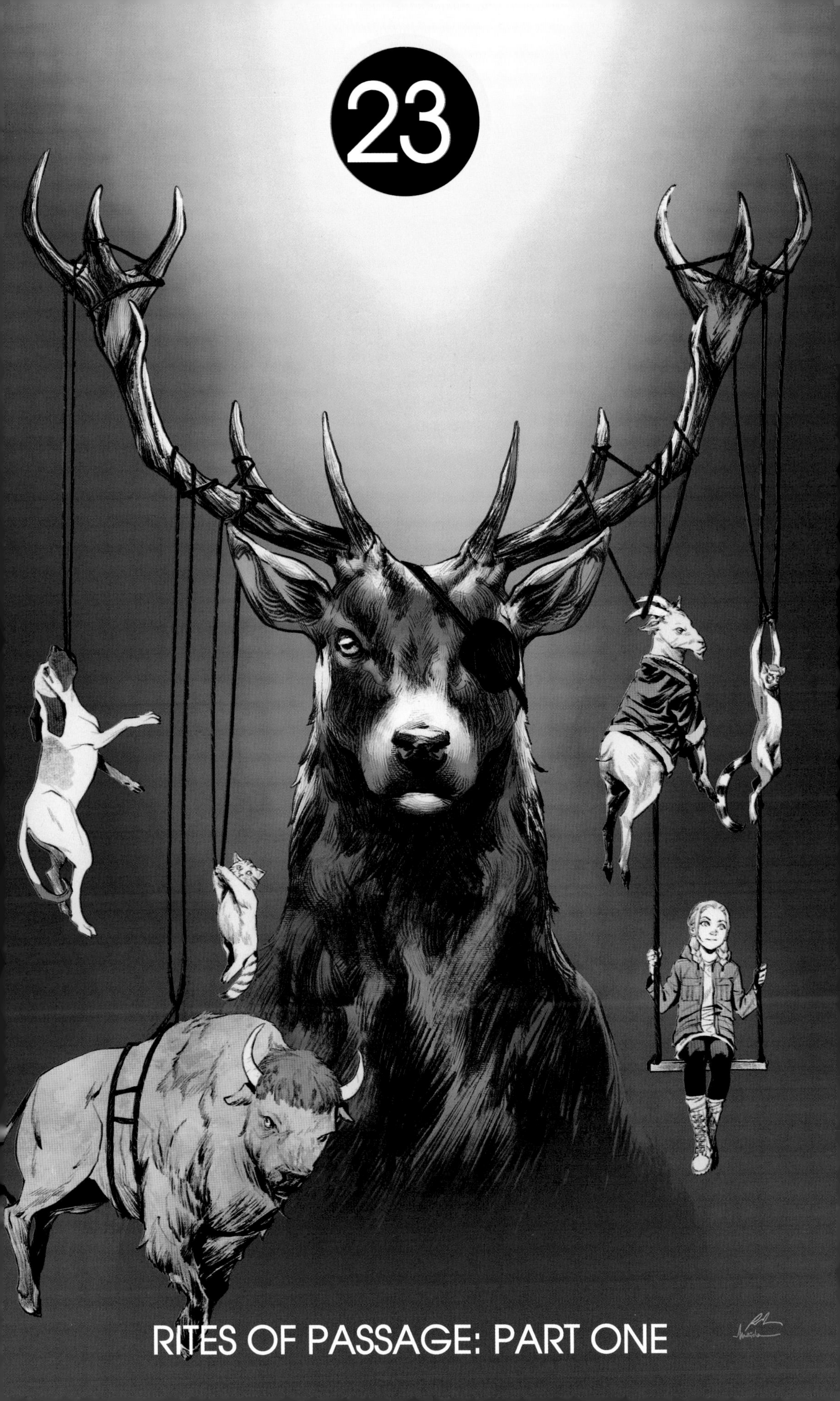
23
RITES OF PASSAGE: PART ONE

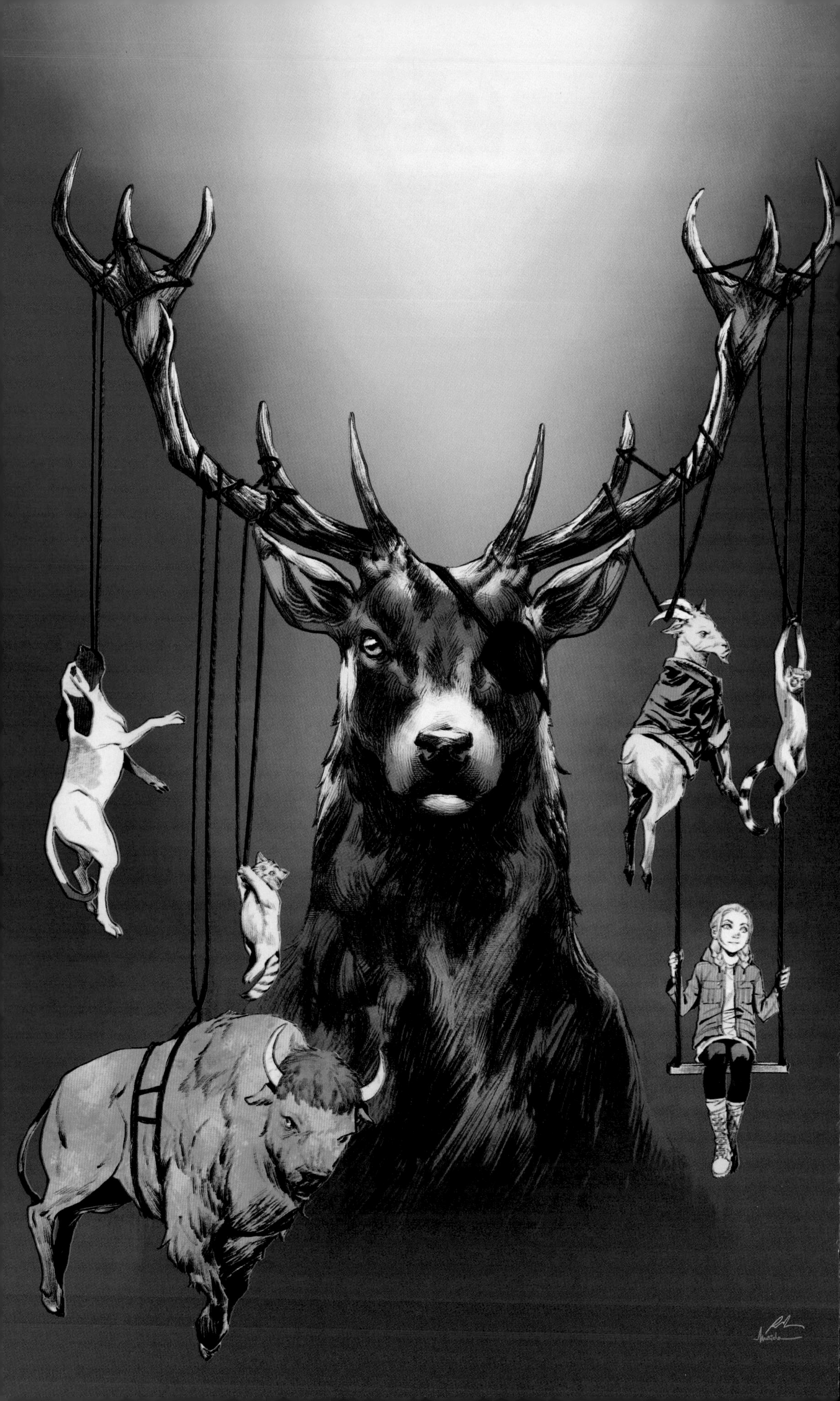

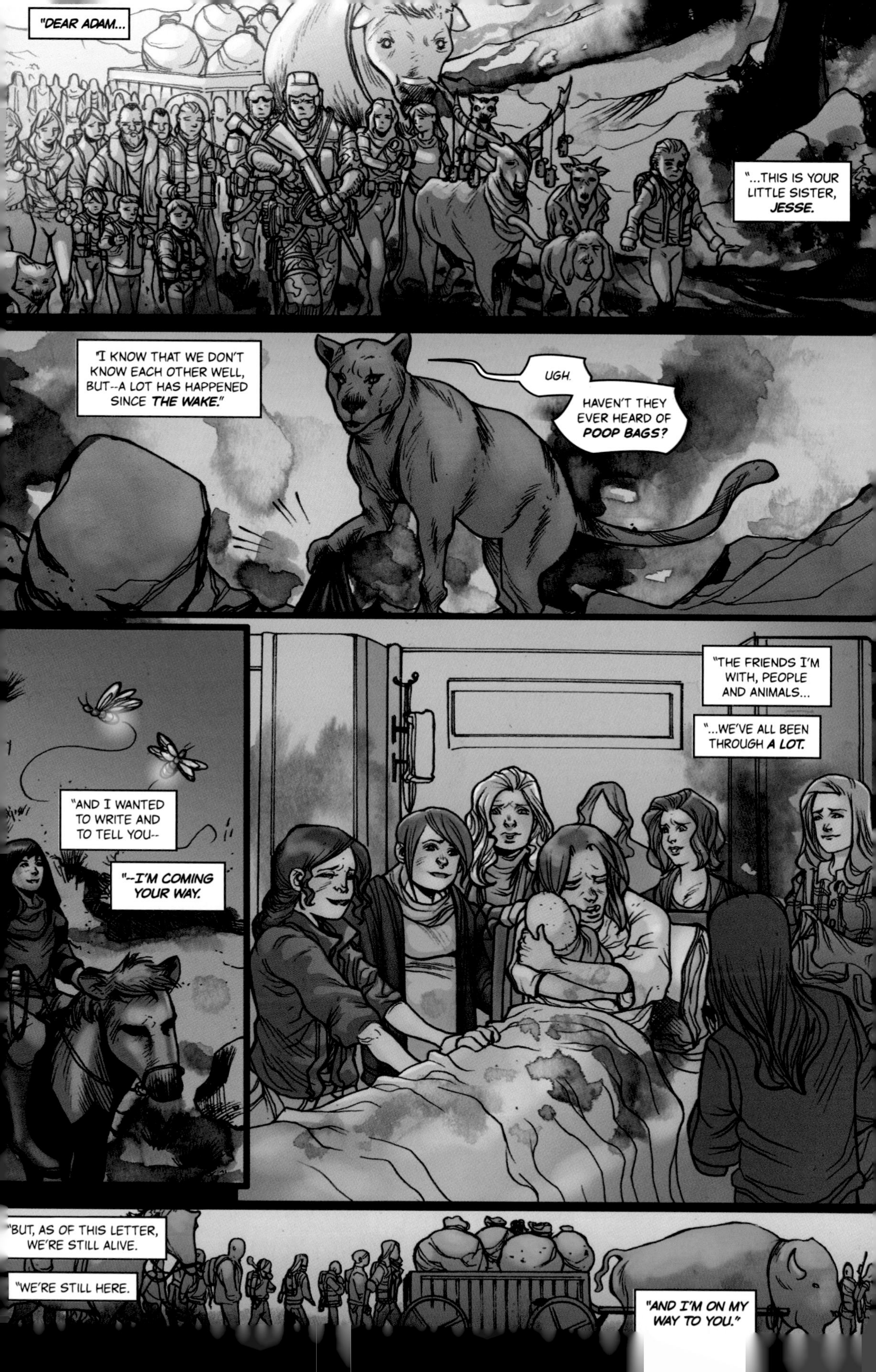
"DEAR ADAM...
"...THIS IS YOUR LITTLE SISTER, JESSE.
"I KNOW THAT WE DON'T KNOW EACH OTHER WELL, BUT--A LOT HAS HAPPENED SINCE THE WAKE."
UGH.
HAVEN'T THEY EVER HEARD OF POOP BAGS?
"THE FRIENDS I'M WITH, PEOPLE AND ANIMALS...
"...WE'VE ALL BEEN THROUGH A LOT.
"AND I WANTED TO WRITE AND TO TELL YOU--
"--I'M COMING YOUR WAY.
"BUT, AS OF THIS LETTER, WE'RE STILL ALIVE.
"WE'RE STILL HERE.
"AND I'M ON MY WAY TO YOU."

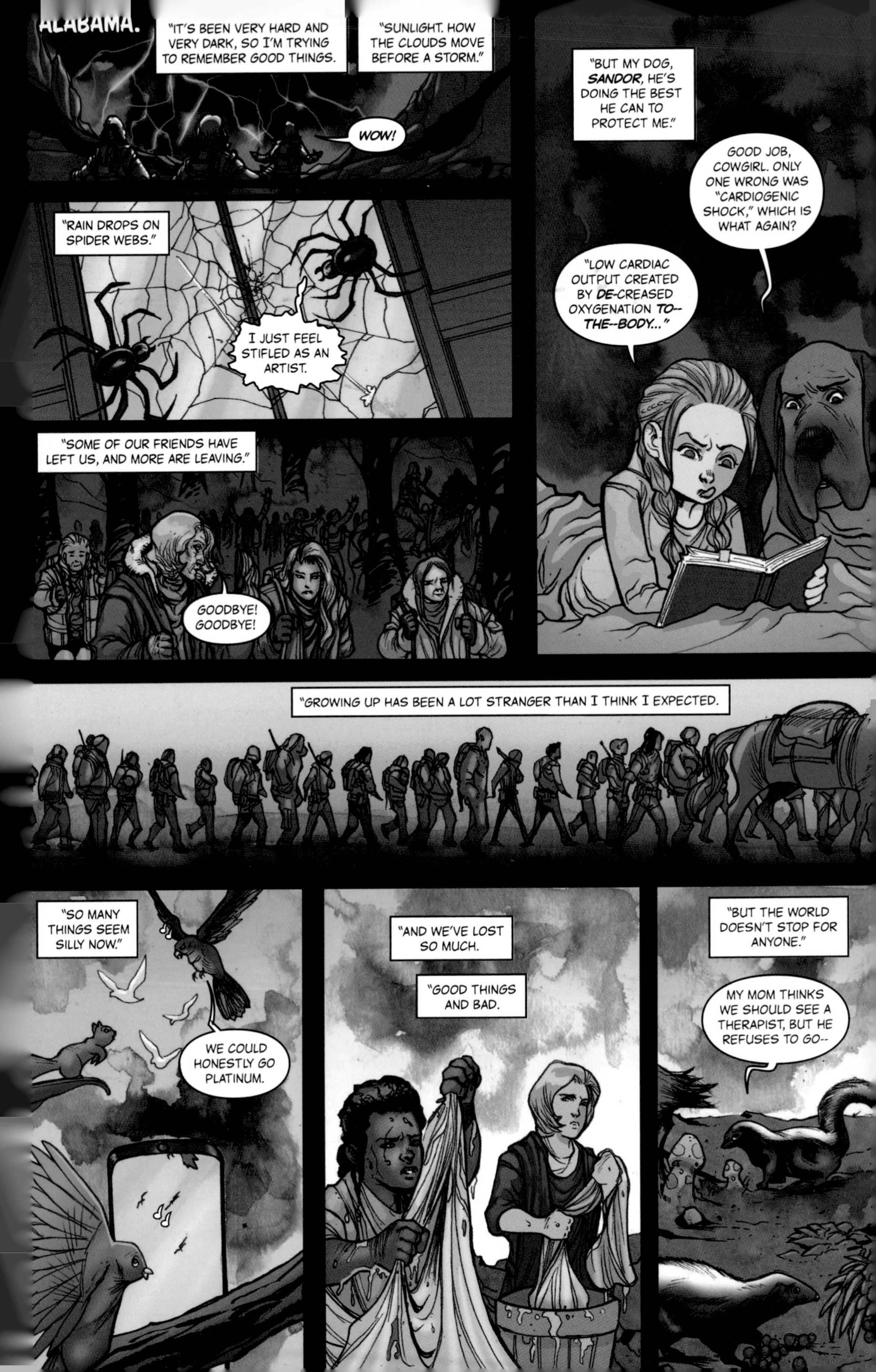
ALABAMA.
"IT'S BEEN VERY HARD AND VERY DARK, SO I'M TRYING TO REMEMBER GOOD THINGS.
"SUNLIGHT. HOW THE CLOUDS MOVE BEFORE A STORM."
WOW!
"RAIN DROPS ON SPIDER WEBS."
I JUST FEEL STIFLED AS AN ARTIST.
"SOME OF OUR FRIENDS HAVE LEFT US, AND MORE ARE LEAVING."
GOODBYE! GOODBYE!
"BUT MY DOG, SANDOR, HE'S DOING THE BEST HE CAN TO PROTECT ME."
GOOD JOB, COWGIRL. ONLY ONE WRONG WAS "CARDIOGENIC SHOCK," WHICH IS WHAT AGAIN?
"LOW CARDIAC OUTPUT CREATED BY DE-CREASED OXYGENATION TO--THE--BODY..."
"GROWING UP HAS BEEN A LOT STRANGER THAN I THINK I EXPECTED.
"SO MANY THINGS SEEM SILLY NOW."
WE COULD HONESTLY GO PLATINUM.
"AND WE'VE LOST SO MUCH.
"GOOD THINGS AND BAD.
"BUT THE WORLD DOESN'T STOP FOR ANYONE."
MY MOM THINKS WE SHOULD SEE A THERAPIST, BUT HE REFUSES TO GO--

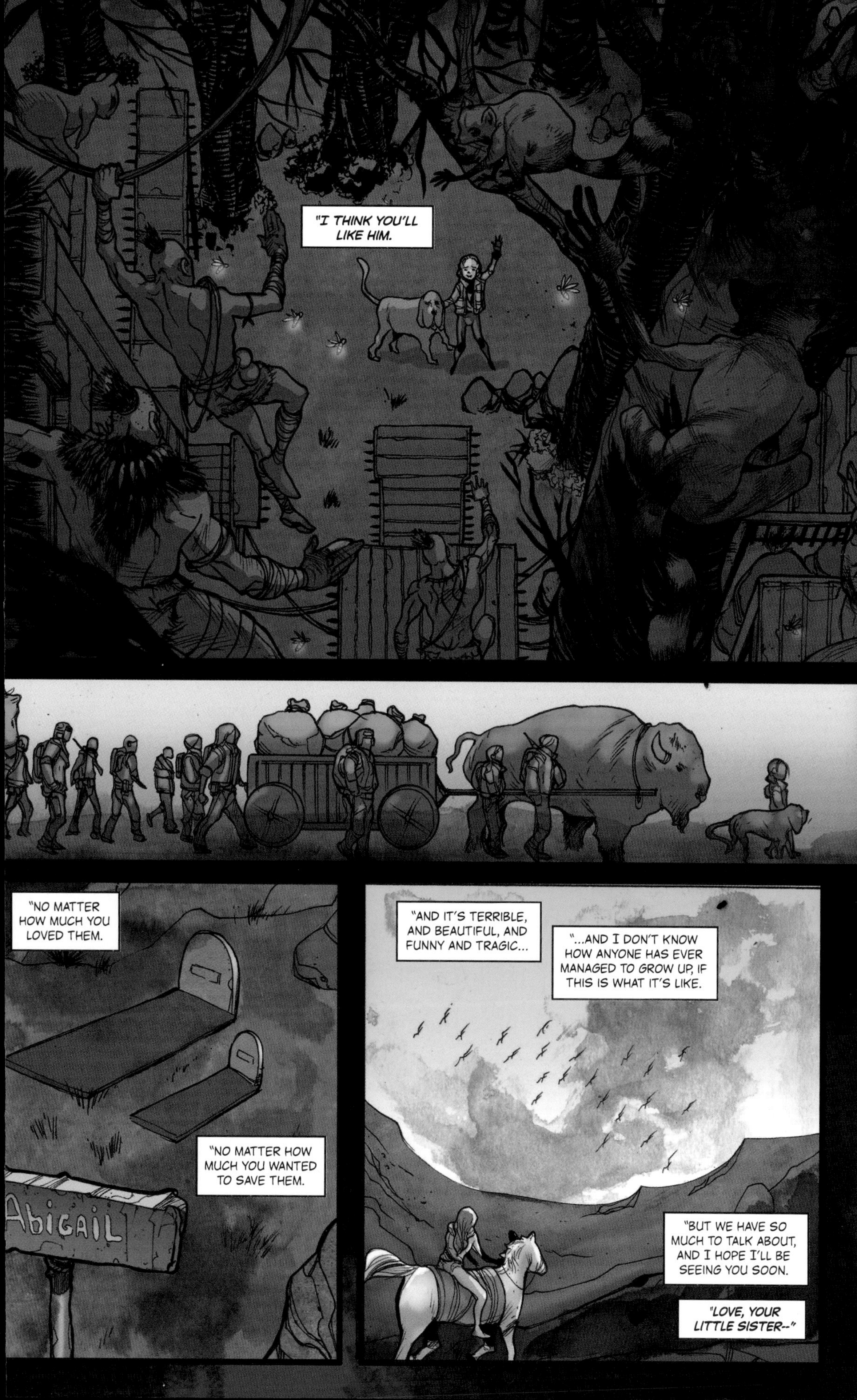
"I THINK YOU'LL LIKE HIM.
"NO MATTER HOW MUCH YOU LOVED THEM.
"NO MATTER HOW MUCH YOU WANTED TO SAVE THEM.
ABIGAIL
"AND IT'S TERRIBLE, AND BEAUTIFUL, AND FUNNY AND TRAGIC...
"...AND I DON'T KNOW HOW ANYONE HAS EVER MANAGED TO GROW UP, IF THIS IS WHAT IT'S LIKE.
"BUT WE HAVE SO MUCH TO TALK ABOUT, AND I HOPE I'LL BE SEEING YOU SOON.
"LOVE, YOUR LITTLE SISTER--"

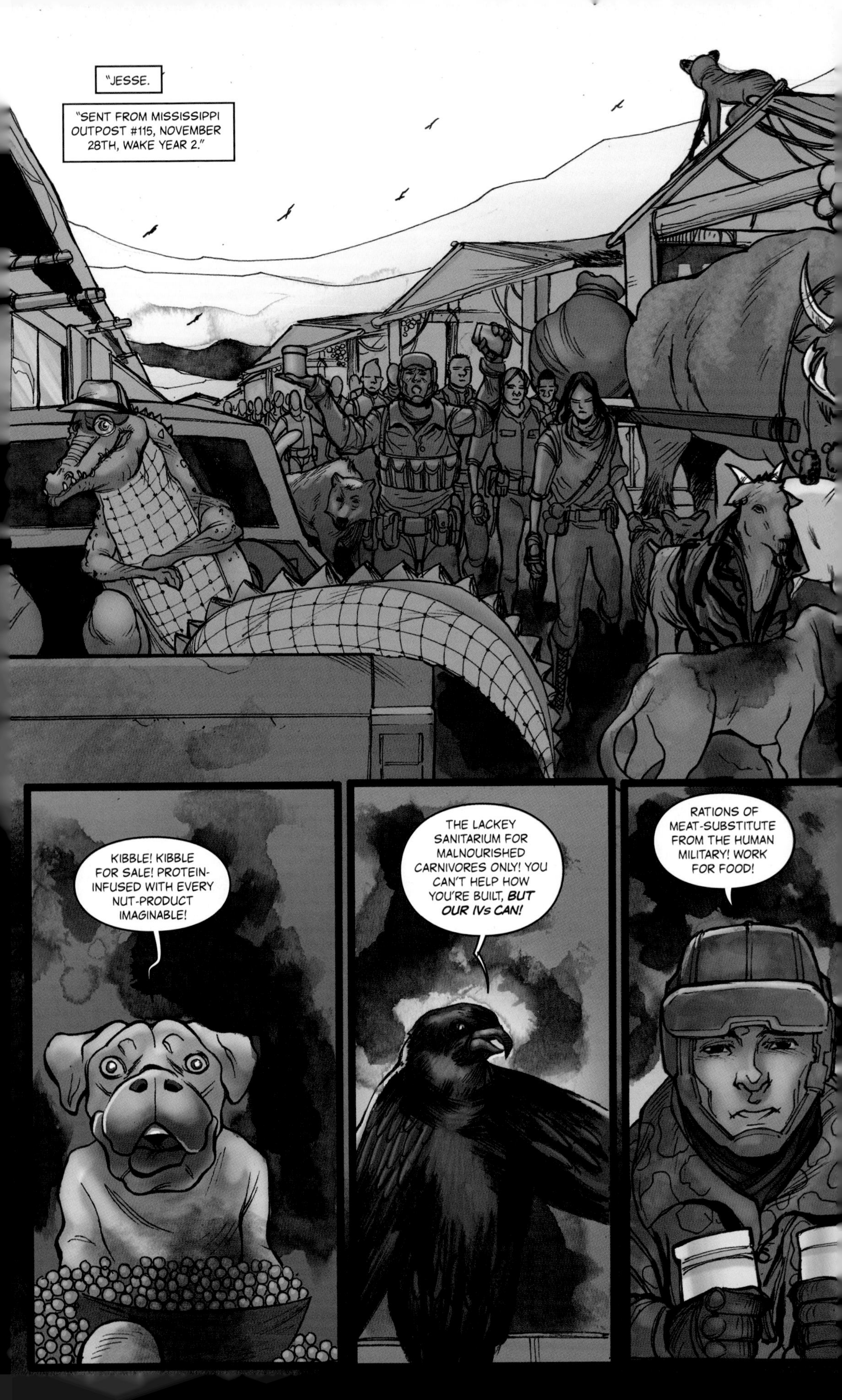
"JESSE.
"SENT FROM MISSISSIPPI OUTPOST #115, NOVEMBER 28TH, WAKE YEAR 2."
KIBBLE! KIBBLE FOR SALE! PROTEIN-INFUSED WITH EVERY NUT-PRODUCT IMAGINABLE!
THE LACKEY SANITARIUM FOR MALNOURISHED CARNIVORES ONLY! YOU CAN'T HELP HOW YOU'RE BUILT, ***BUT OUR IVs CAN!***
RATIONS OF MEAT-SUBSTITUTE FROM THE HUMAN MILITARY! WORK FOR FOOD!

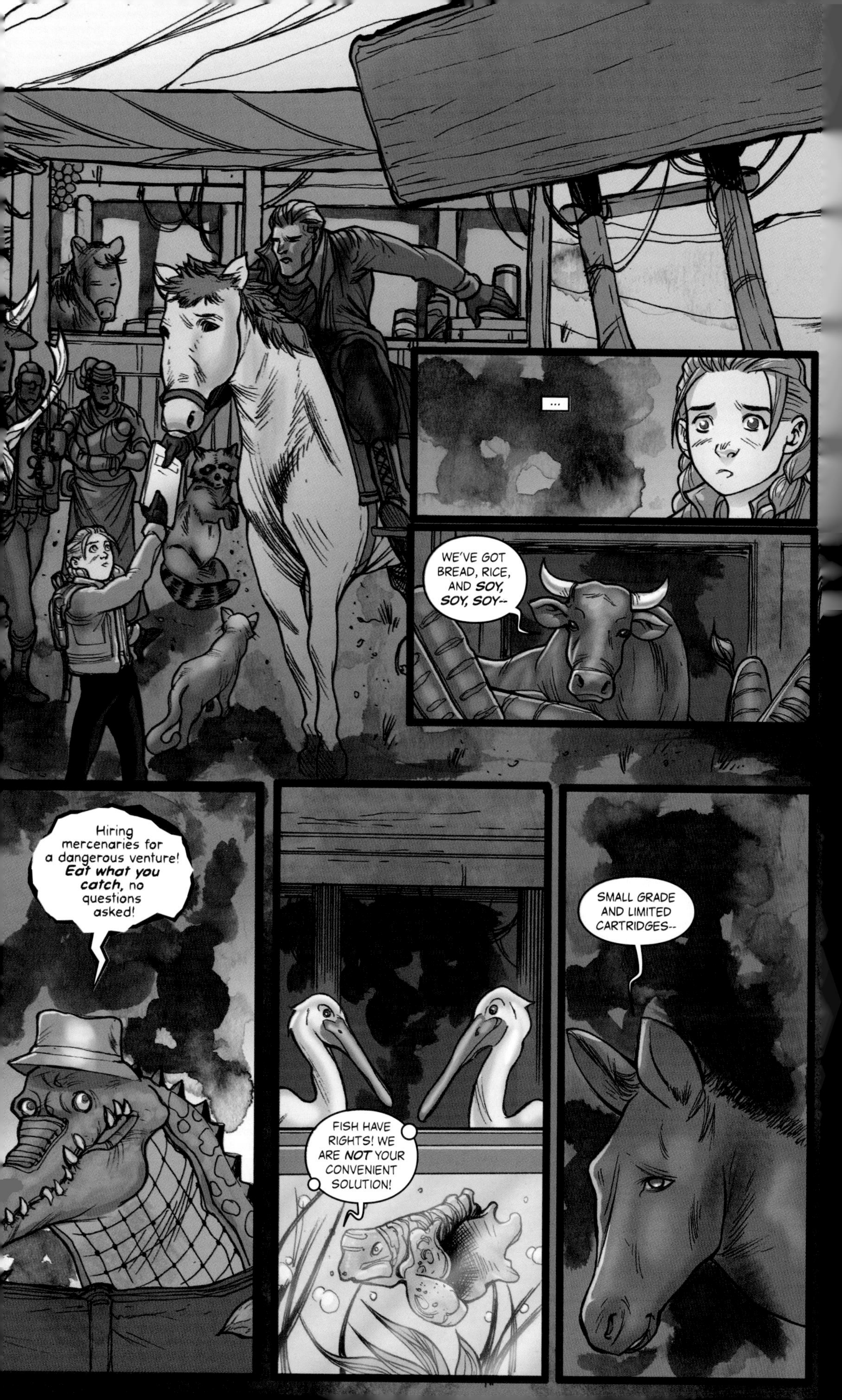
...
WE'VE GOT BREAD, RICE, AND *SOY, SOY, SOY*--
Hiring mercenaries for a dangerous venture! ***Eat what you catch,*** no questions asked!
FISH HAVE RIGHTS! WE ARE ***NOT*** YOUR CONVENIENT SOLUTION!
SMALL GRADE AND LIMITED CARTRIDGES--

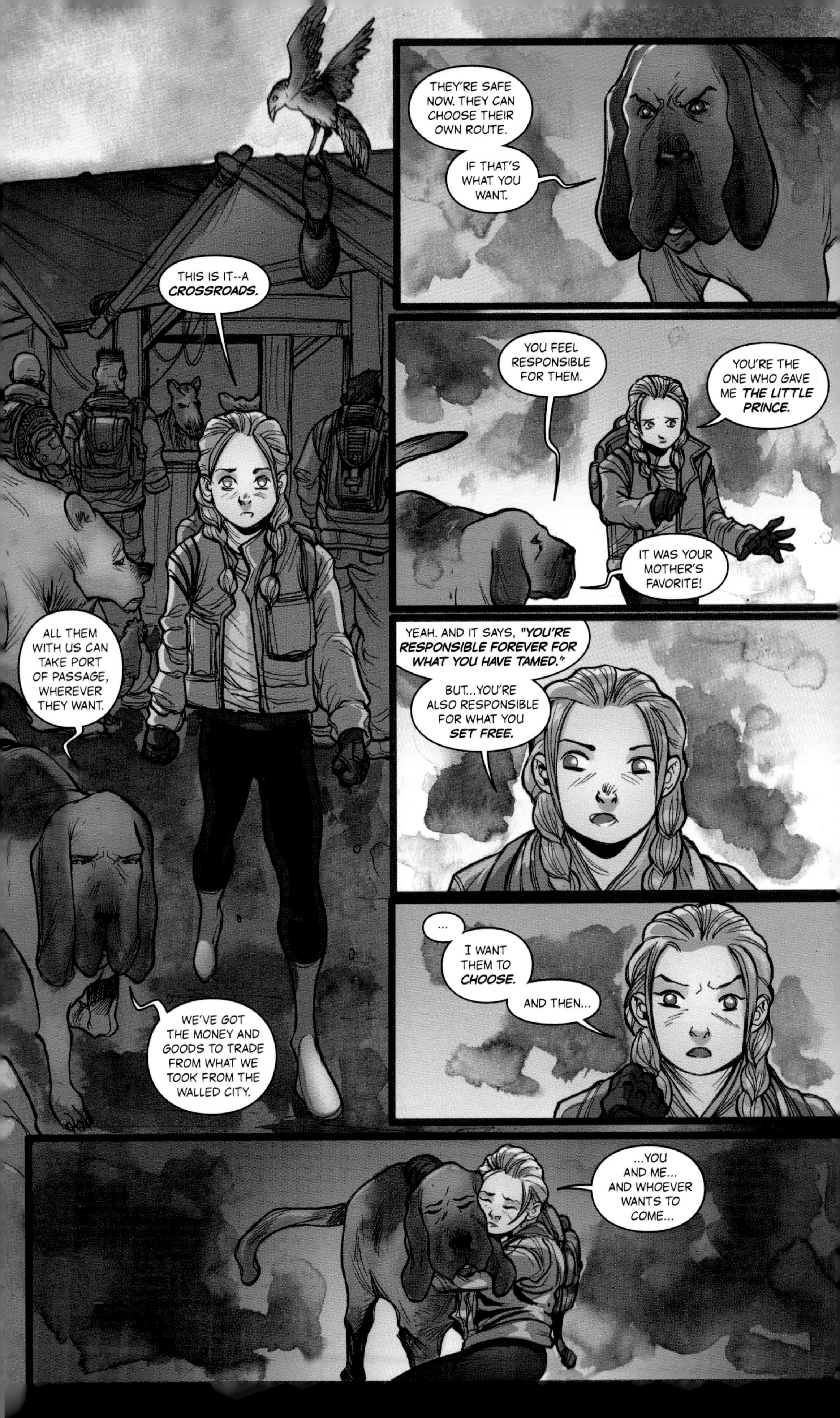

THIS IS IT--A **CROSSROADS.**
ALL THEM WITH US CAN TAKE PORT OF PASSAGE, WHEREVER THEY WANT.
WE'VE GOT THE MONEY AND GOODS TO TRADE FROM WHAT WE TOOK FROM THE WALLED CITY.
THEY'RE SAFE NOW. THEY CAN CHOOSE THEIR OWN ROUTE.
IF THAT'S WHAT YOU WANT.
YOU FEEL RESPONSIBLE FOR THEM.
YOU'RE THE ONE WHO GAVE ME ***THE LITTLE PRINCE.***
IT WAS YOUR MOTHER'S FAVORITE!
YEAH. AND IT SAYS, ***"YOU'RE RESPONSIBLE FOREVER FOR WHAT YOU HAVE TAMED."***
BUT...YOU'RE ALSO RESPONSIBLE FOR WHAT YOU ***SET FREE.***
...
I WANT THEM TO ***CHOOSE.***
AND THEN...
...YOU AND ME... AND WHOEVER WANTS TO COME...

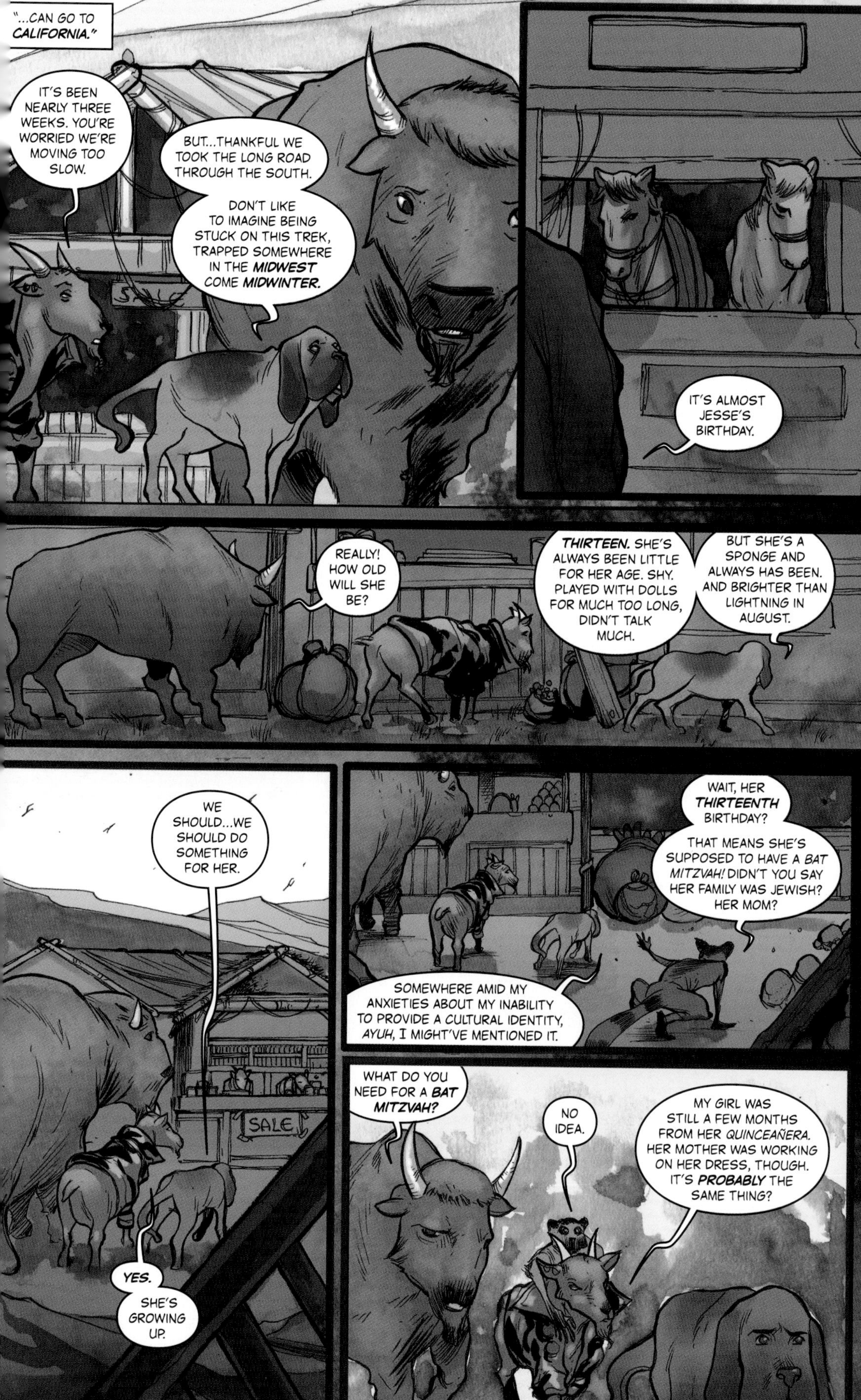
"...CAN GO TO CALIFORNIA."
IT'S BEEN NEARLY THREE WEEKS. YOU'RE WORRIED WE'RE MOVING TOO SLOW.
BUT...THANKFUL WE TOOK THE LONG ROAD THROUGH THE SOUTH.
DON'T LIKE TO IMAGINE BEING STUCK ON THIS TREK, TRAPPED SOMEWHERE IN THE MIDWEST COME MIDWINTER.
IT'S ALMOST JESSE'S BIRTHDAY.
REALLY! HOW OLD WILL SHE BE?
THIRTEEN. SHE'S ALWAYS BEEN LITTLE FOR HER AGE. SHY. PLAYED WITH DOLLS FOR MUCH TOO LONG, DIDN'T TALK MUCH.
BUT SHE'S A SPONGE AND ALWAYS HAS BEEN. AND BRIGHTER THAN LIGHTNING IN AUGUST.
WE SHOULD...WE SHOULD DO SOMETHING FOR HER.
YES.
SHE'S GROWING UP.
SALE
WAIT, HER THIRTEENTH BIRTHDAY?
THAT MEANS SHE'S SUPPOSED TO HAVE A BAT MITZVAH! DIDN'T YOU SAY HER FAMILY WAS JEWISH? HER MOM?
SOMEWHERE AMID MY ANXIETIES ABOUT MY INABILITY TO PROVIDE A CULTURAL IDENTITY, AYUH, I MIGHT'VE MENTIONED IT.
WHAT DO YOU NEED FOR A BAT MITZVAH?
NO IDEA.
MY GIRL WAS STILL A FEW MONTHS FROM HER QUINCEAÑERA. HER MOTHER WAS WORKING ON HER DRESS, THOUGH. IT'S PROBABLY THE SAME THING?

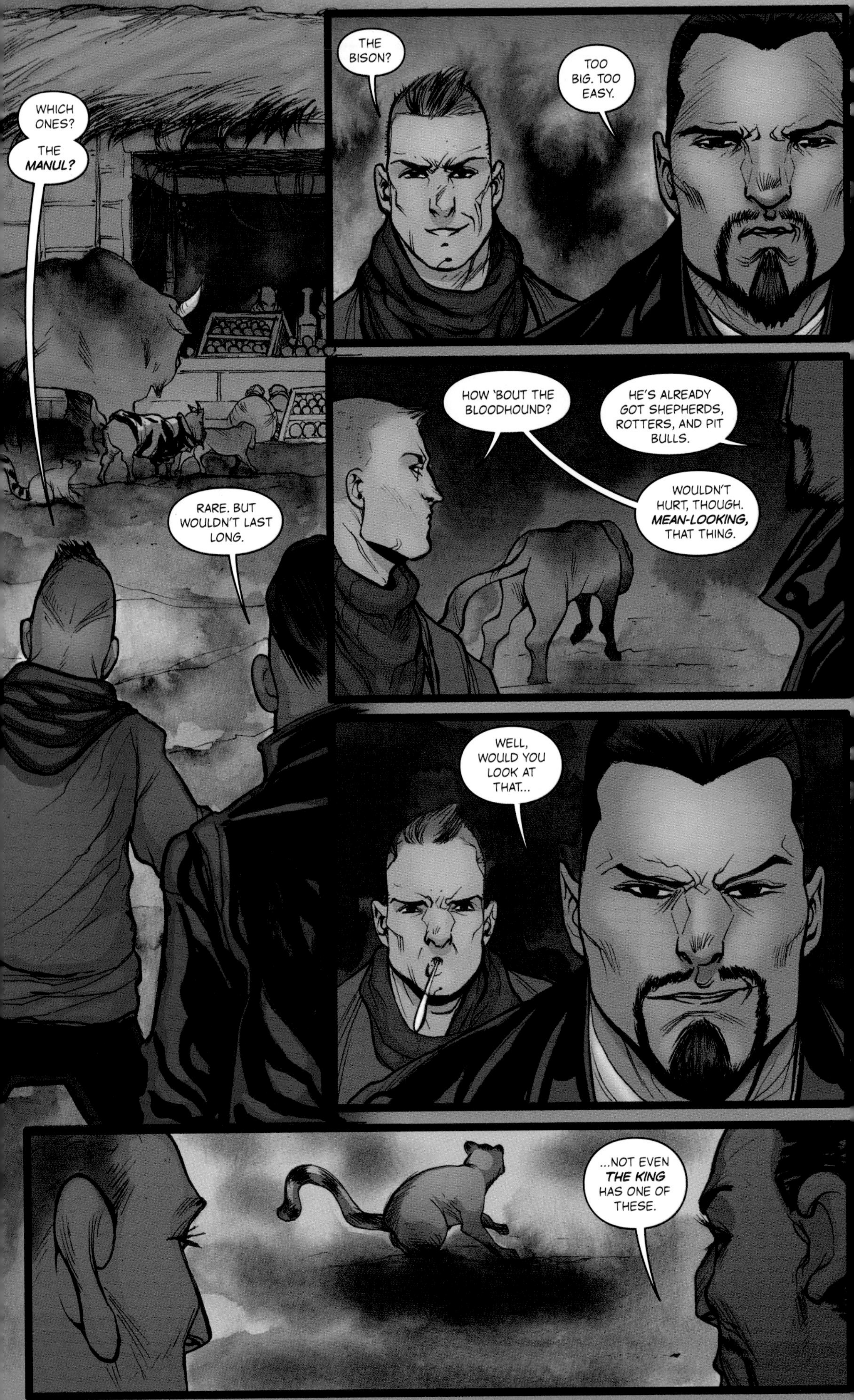
WHICH ONES?
THE MANUL?
THE BISON?
TOO BIG. TOO EASY.
RARE. BUT WOULDN'T LAST LONG.
HOW 'BOUT THE BLOODHOUND?
HE'S ALREADY GOT SHEPHERDS, ROTTERS, AND PIT BULLS.
WOULDN'T HURT, THOUGH. MEAN-LOOKING, THAT THING.
WELL, WOULD YOU LOOK AT THAT...
...NOT EVEN THE KING HAS ONE OF THESE.

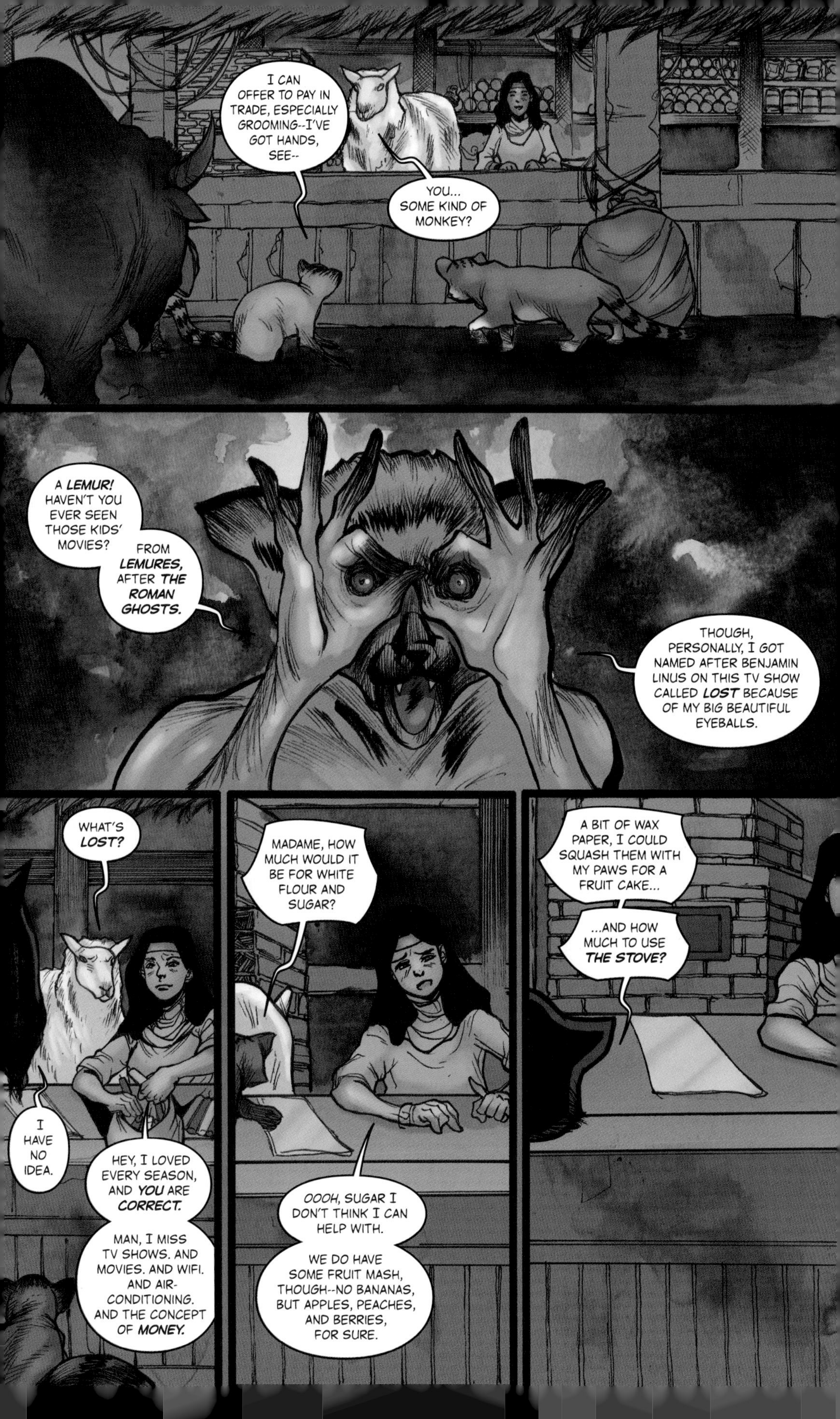
I CAN OFFER TO PAY IN TRADE, ESPECIALLY GROOMING--I'VE GOT HANDS, SEE--
YOU... SOME KIND OF MONKEY?
A LEMUR! HAVEN'T YOU EVER SEEN THOSE KIDS' MOVIES?
FROM LEMURES, AFTER THE ROMAN GHOSTS.
THOUGH, PERSONALLY, I GOT NAMED AFTER BENJAMIN LINUS ON THIS TV SHOW CALLED LOST BECAUSE OF MY BIG BEAUTIFUL EYEBALLS.
WHAT'S LOST?
I HAVE NO IDEA.
HEY, I LOVED EVERY SEASON, AND YOU ARE CORRECT.
MAN, I MISS TV SHOWS. AND MOVIES. AND WIFI. AND AIR-CONDITIONING. AND THE CONCEPT OF MONEY.
MADAME, HOW MUCH WOULD IT BE FOR WHITE FLOUR AND SUGAR?
OOOH, SUGAR I DON'T THINK I CAN HELP WITH.
WE DO HAVE SOME FRUIT MASH, THOUGH--NO BANANAS, BUT APPLES, PEACHES, AND BERRIES, FOR SURE.
A BIT OF WAX PAPER, I COULD SQUASH THEM WITH MY PAWS FOR A FRUIT CAKE...
...AND HOW MUCH TO USE THE STOVE?

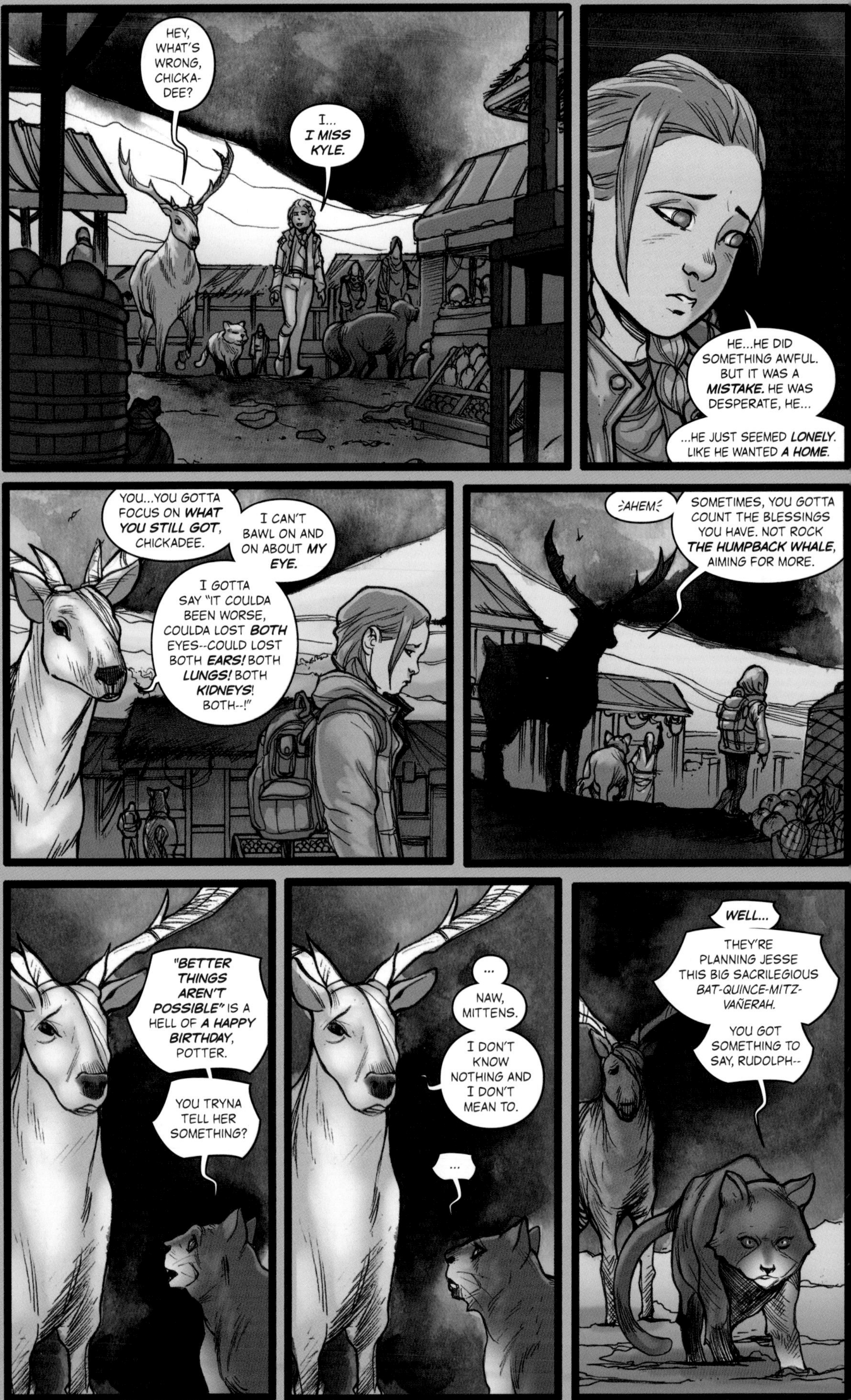
HEY, WHAT'S WRONG, CHICKA-DEE?
I... *I MISS KYLE.*
HE...HE DID SOMETHING AWFUL. BUT IT WAS A ***MISTAKE.*** HE WAS DESPERATE, HE...
...HE JUST SEEMED ***LONELY.*** LIKE HE WANTED ***A HOME.***
YOU...YOU GOTTA FOCUS ON ***WHAT YOU STILL GOT***, CHICKADEE.
I CAN'T BAWL ON AND ON ABOUT ***MY EYE.***
I GOTTA SAY "IT COULDA BEEN WORSE, COULDA LOST ***BOTH*** EYES--COULD LOST BOTH ***EARS!*** BOTH ***LUNGS!*** BOTH ***KIDNEYS***! BOTH--!"
AHEM
SOMETIMES, YOU GOTTA COUNT THE BLESSINGS YOU HAVE. NOT ROCK ***THE HUMPBACK WHALE***, AIMING FOR MORE.
"BETTER THINGS AREN'T POSSIBLE" IS A HELL OF ***A HAPPY BIRTHDAY***, POTTER.
YOU TRYNA TELL HER SOMETHING?
...
NAW, MITTENS.
I DON'T KNOW NOTHING AND I DON'T MEAN TO.
...
WELL...
THEY'RE PLANNING JESSE THIS BIG SACRILEGIOUS *BAT-QUINCE-MITZ-VAÑERAH.*
YOU GOT SOMETHING TO SAY, RUDOLPH--

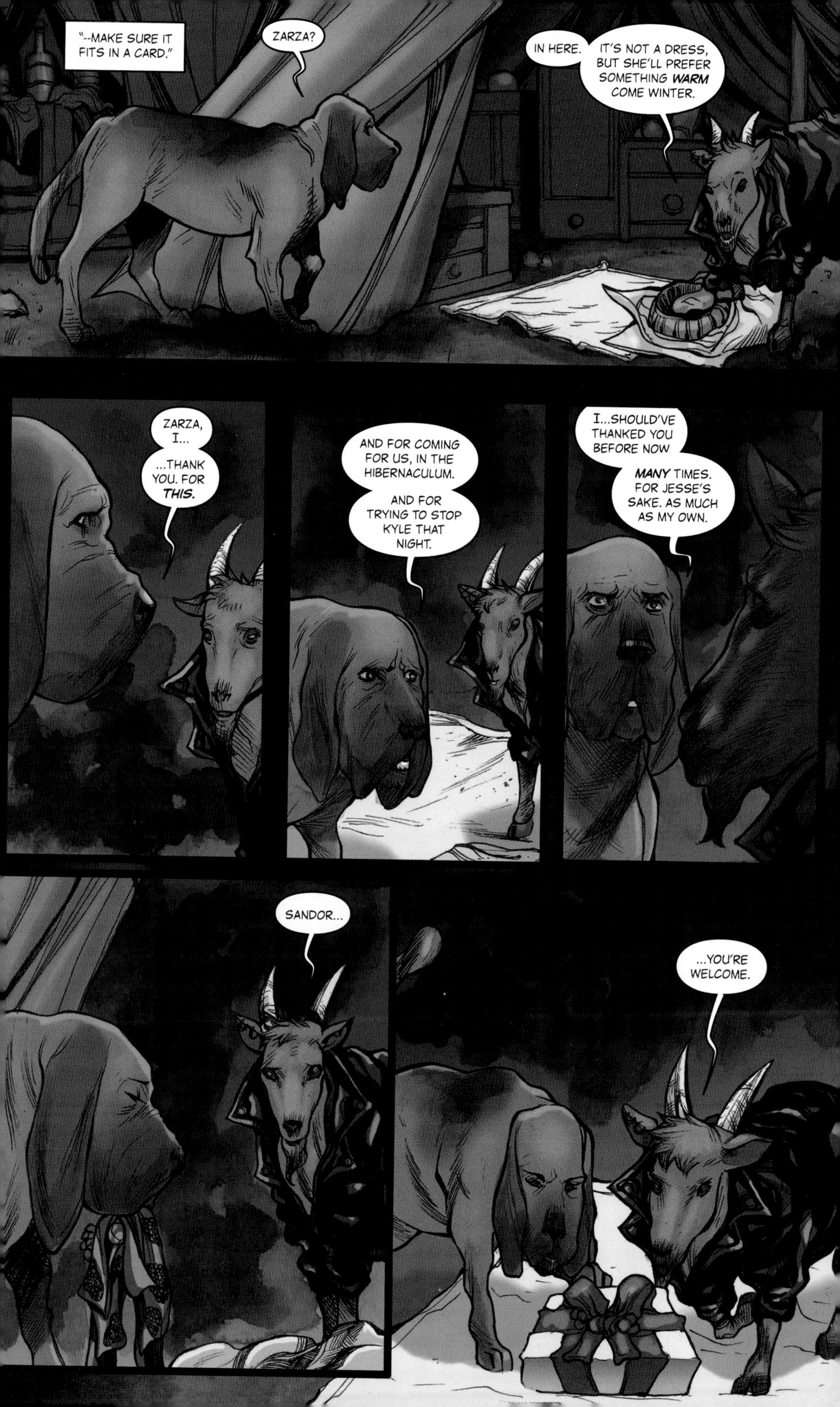
"--MAKE SURE IT FITS IN A CARD."
ZARZA?
IN HERE.
IT'S NOT A DRESS, BUT SHE'LL PREFER SOMETHING *WARM* COME WINTER.
ZARZA, I...
...THANK YOU. FOR *THIS.*
AND FOR COMING FOR US, IN THE HIBERNACULUM.
AND FOR TRYING TO STOP KYLE THAT NIGHT.
I...SHOULD'VE THANKED YOU BEFORE NOW
MANY TIMES. FOR JESSE'S SAKE. AS MUCH AS MY OWN.
SANDOR...
...YOU'RE WELCOME.

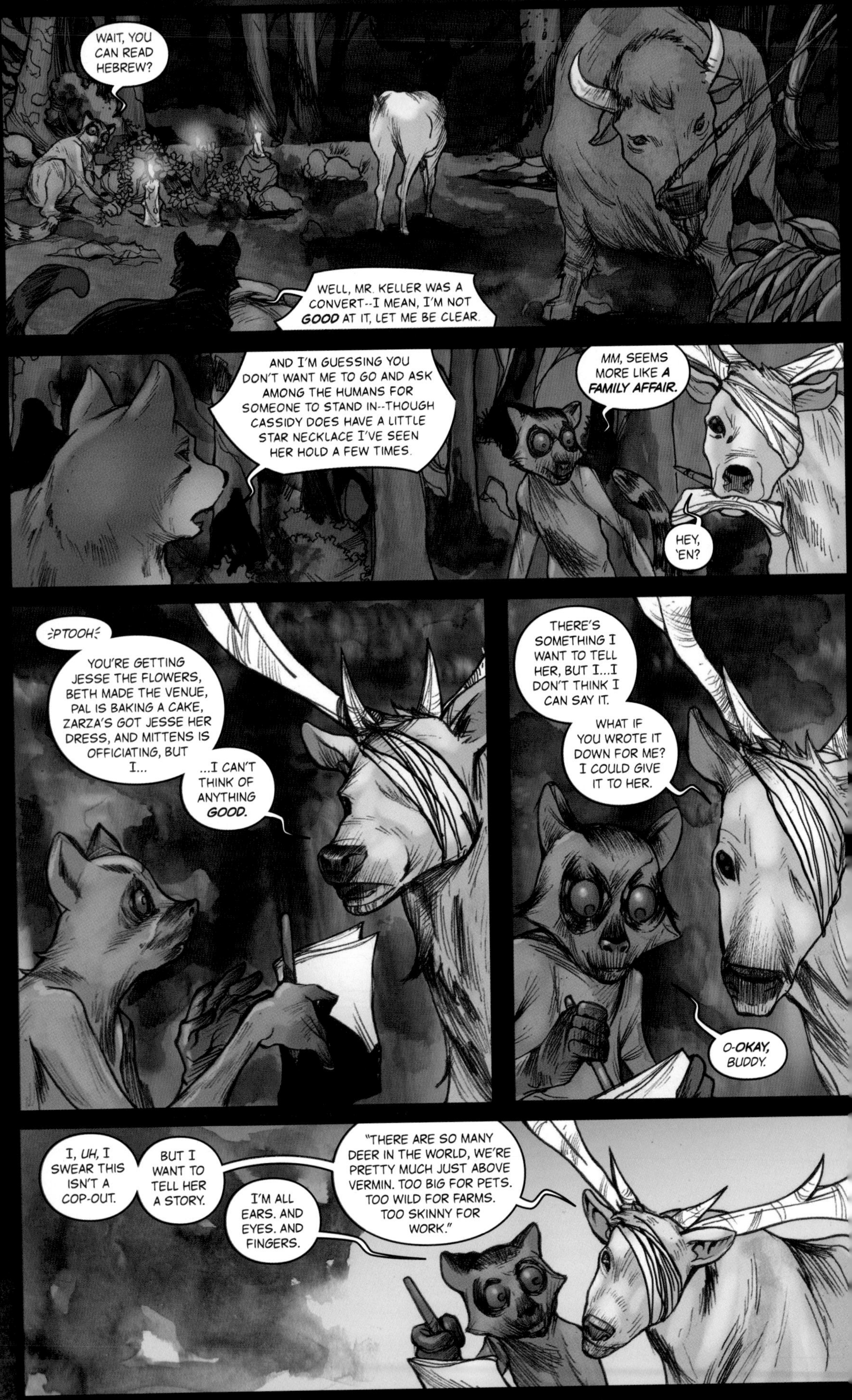
WAIT, YOU CAN READ HEBREW?
WELL, MR. KELLER WAS A CONVERT--I MEAN, I'M NOT ***GOOD*** AT IT, LET ME BE CLEAR.
AND I'M GUESSING YOU DON'T WANT ME TO GO AND ASK AMONG THE HUMANS FOR SOMEONE TO STAND IN--THOUGH CASSIDY DOES HAVE A LITTLE STAR NECKLACE I'VE SEEN HER HOLD A FEW TIMES.
MM, SEEMS MORE LIKE ***A FAMILY AFFAIR.***
HEY, 'EN?
PTOOH
YOU'RE GETTING JESSE THE FLOWERS, BETH MADE THE VENUE, PAL IS BAKING A CAKE, ZARZA'S GOT JESSE HER DRESS, AND MITTENS IS OFFICIATING, BUT I...
...I CAN'T THINK OF ANYTHING ***GOOD.***
THERE'S SOMETHING I WANT TO TELL HER, BUT I...I DON'T THINK I CAN SAY IT.
WHAT IF YOU WROTE IT DOWN FOR ME? I COULD GIVE IT TO HER.
O-OKAY, *BUDDY.*
I, *UH,* I SWEAR THIS ISN'T A COP-OUT.
BUT I WANT TO TELL HER A STORY.
I'M ALL EARS. AND EYES. AND FINGERS.
"THERE ARE SO MANY DEER IN THE WORLD, WE'RE PRETTY MUCH JUST ABOVE VERMIN. TOO BIG FOR PETS. TOO WILD FOR FARMS. TOO SKINNY FOR WORK."

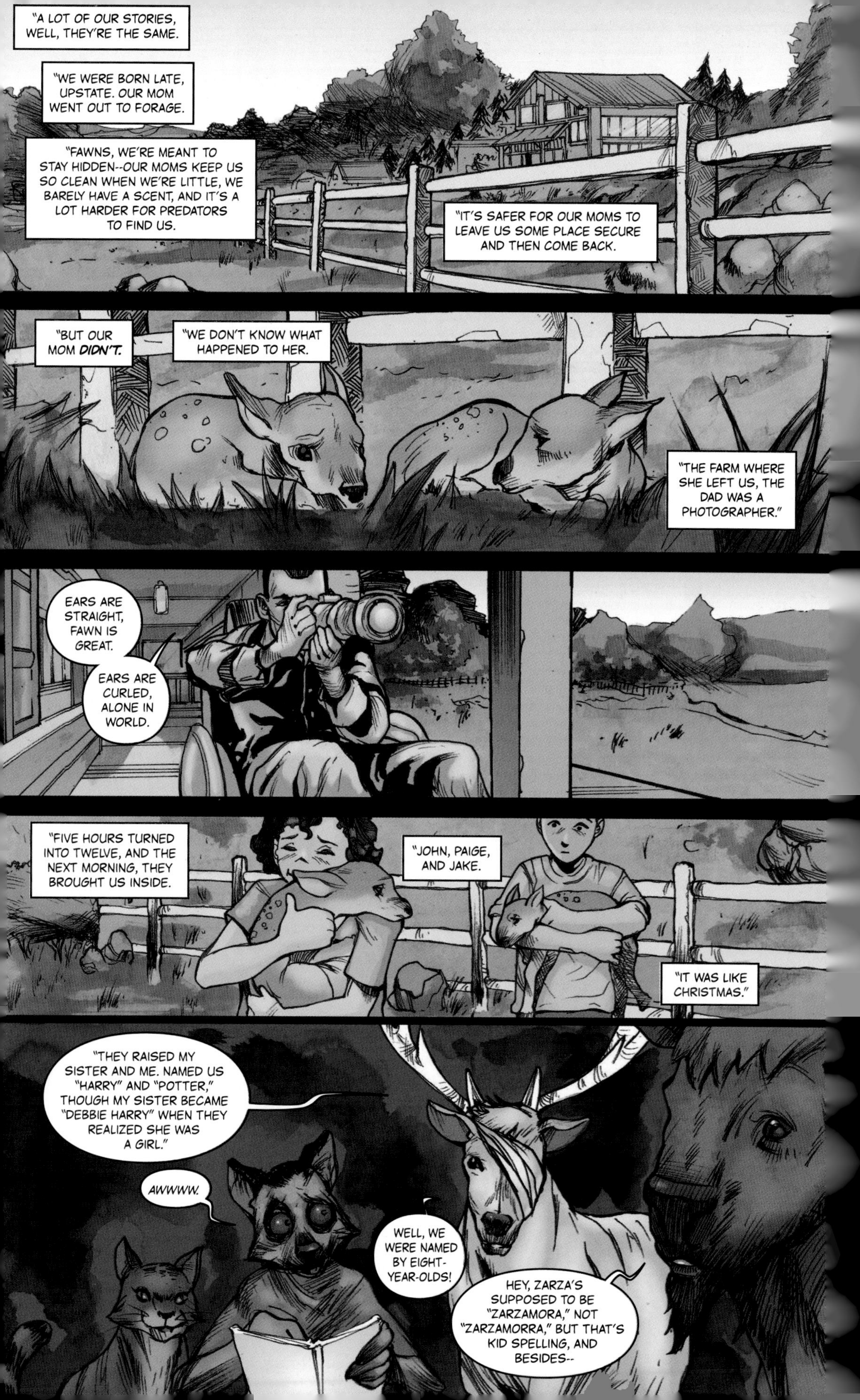
"A LOT OF OUR STORIES, WELL, THEY'RE THE SAME.
"WE WERE BORN LATE, UPSTATE. OUR MOM WENT OUT TO FORAGE.
"FAWNS, WE'RE MEANT TO STAY HIDDEN--OUR MOMS KEEP US SO CLEAN WHEN WE'RE LITTLE, WE BARELY HAVE A SCENT, AND IT'S A LOT HARDER FOR PREDATORS TO FIND US.
"IT'S SAFER FOR OUR MOMS TO LEAVE US SOME PLACE SECURE AND THEN COME BACK.
"BUT OUR MOM ***DIDN'T.***
"WE DON'T KNOW WHAT HAPPENED TO HER.
"THE FARM WHERE SHE LEFT US, THE DAD WAS A PHOTOGRAPHER."
EARS ARE STRAIGHT, FAWN IS GREAT.
EARS ARE CURLED, ALONE IN WORLD.
"FIVE HOURS TURNED INTO TWELVE, AND THE NEXT MORNING, THEY BROUGHT US INSIDE.
"JOHN, PAIGE, AND JAKE.
"IT WAS LIKE CHRISTMAS."
"THEY RAISED MY SISTER AND ME. NAMED US "HARRY" AND "POTTER," THOUGH MY SISTER BECAME "DEBBIE HARRY" WHEN THEY REALIZED SHE WAS A GIRL."
AWWWW.
WELL, WE WERE NAMED BY EIGHT-YEAR-OLDS!
HEY, ZARZA'S SUPPOSED TO BE "ZARZAMORA," NOT "ZARZAMORRA," BUT THAT'S KID SPELLING, AND BESIDES--

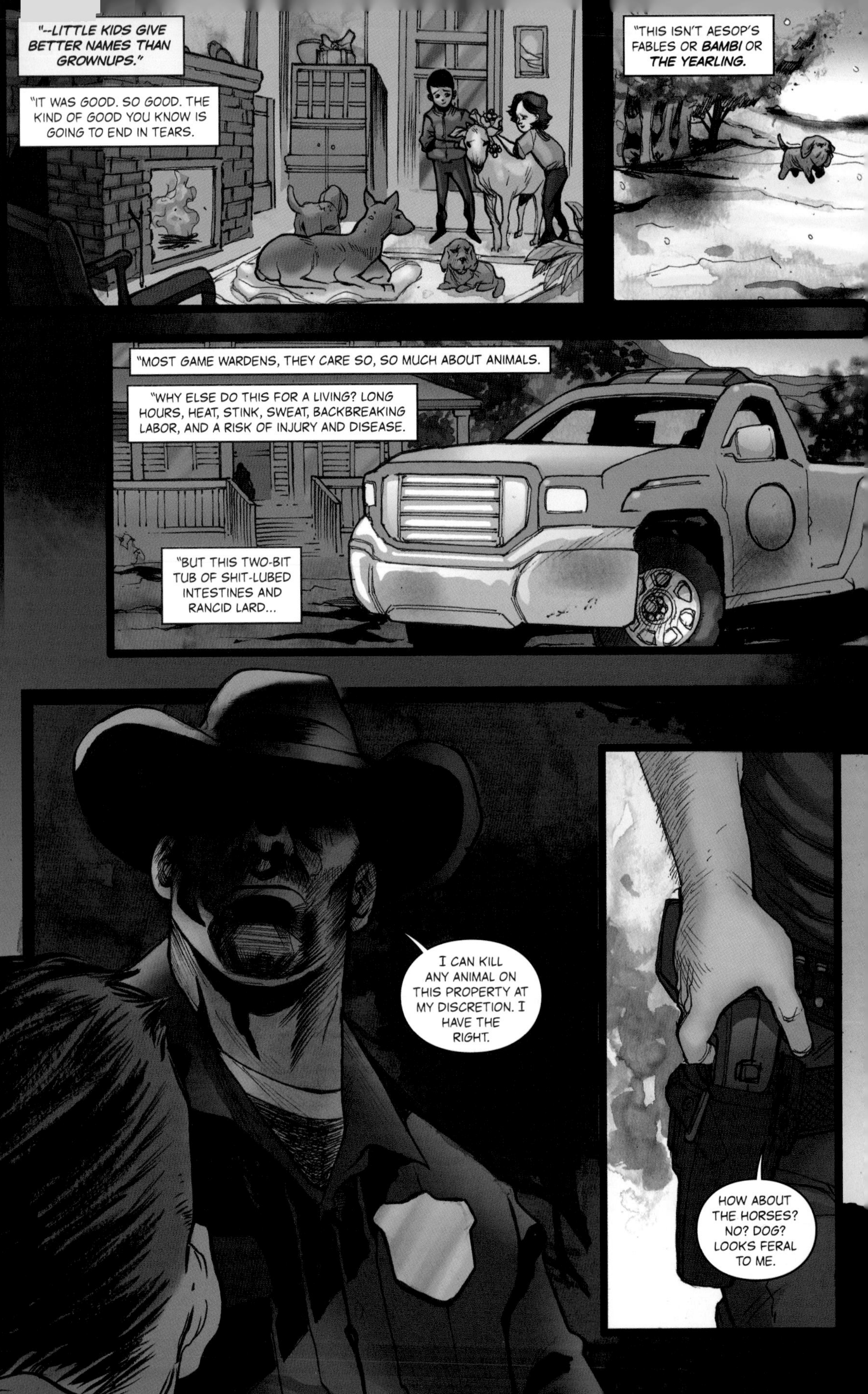
"--LITTLE KIDS GIVE BETTER NAMES THAN GROWNUPS."
"IT WAS GOOD. SO GOOD. THE KIND OF GOOD YOU KNOW IS GOING TO END IN TEARS.
"THIS ISN'T AESOP'S FABLES OR BAMBI OR THE YEARLING.
"MOST GAME WARDENS, THEY CARE SO, SO MUCH ABOUT ANIMALS.
"WHY ELSE DO THIS FOR A LIVING? LONG HOURS, HEAT, STINK, SWEAT, BACKBREAKING LABOR, AND A RISK OF INJURY AND DISEASE.
"BUT THIS TWO-BIT TUB OF SHIT-LUBED INTESTINES AND RANCID LARD...
I CAN KILL ANY ANIMAL ON THIS PROPERTY AT MY DISCRETION. I HAVE THE RIGHT.
HOW ABOUT THE HORSES? NO? DOG? LOOKS FERAL TO ME.

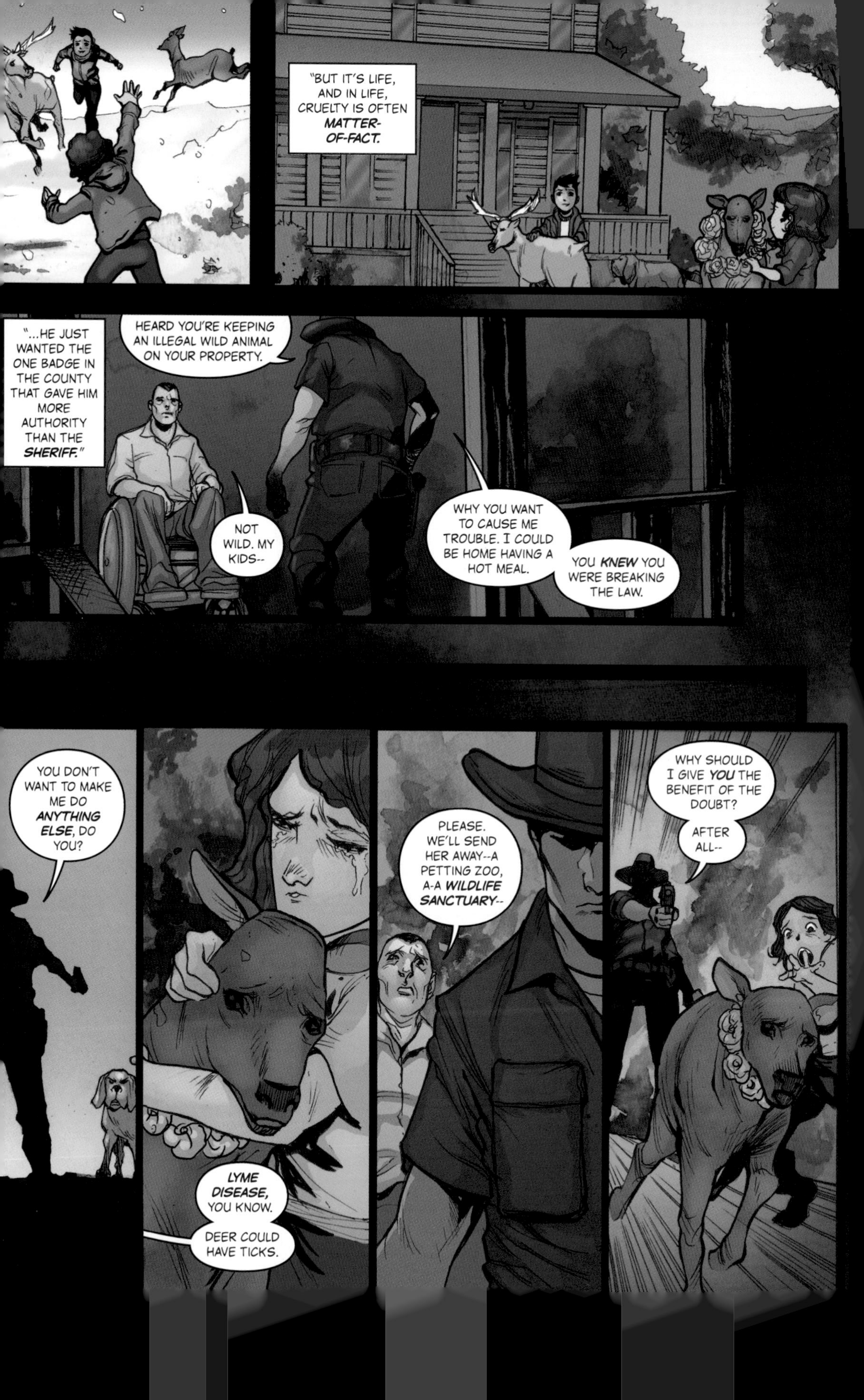
"BUT IT'S LIFE, AND IN LIFE, CRUELTY IS OFTEN MATTER-OF-FACT.
"...HE JUST WANTED THE ONE BADGE IN THE COUNTY THAT GAVE HIM MORE AUTHORITY THAN THE SHERIFF."
HEARD YOU'RE KEEPING AN ILLEGAL WILD ANIMAL ON YOUR PROPERTY.
NOT WILD. MY KIDS--
WHY YOU WANT TO CAUSE ME TROUBLE. I COULD BE HOME HAVING A HOT MEAL.
YOU KNEW YOU WERE BREAKING THE LAW.
YOU DON'T WANT TO MAKE ME DO ANYTHING ELSE, DO YOU?
LYME DISEASE, YOU KNOW.
DEER COULD HAVE TICKS.
PLEASE. WE'LL SEND HER AWAY--A PETTING ZOO, A-A WILDLIFE SANCTUARY--
WHY SHOULD I GIVE YOU THE BENEFIT OF THE DOUBT?
AFTER ALL--

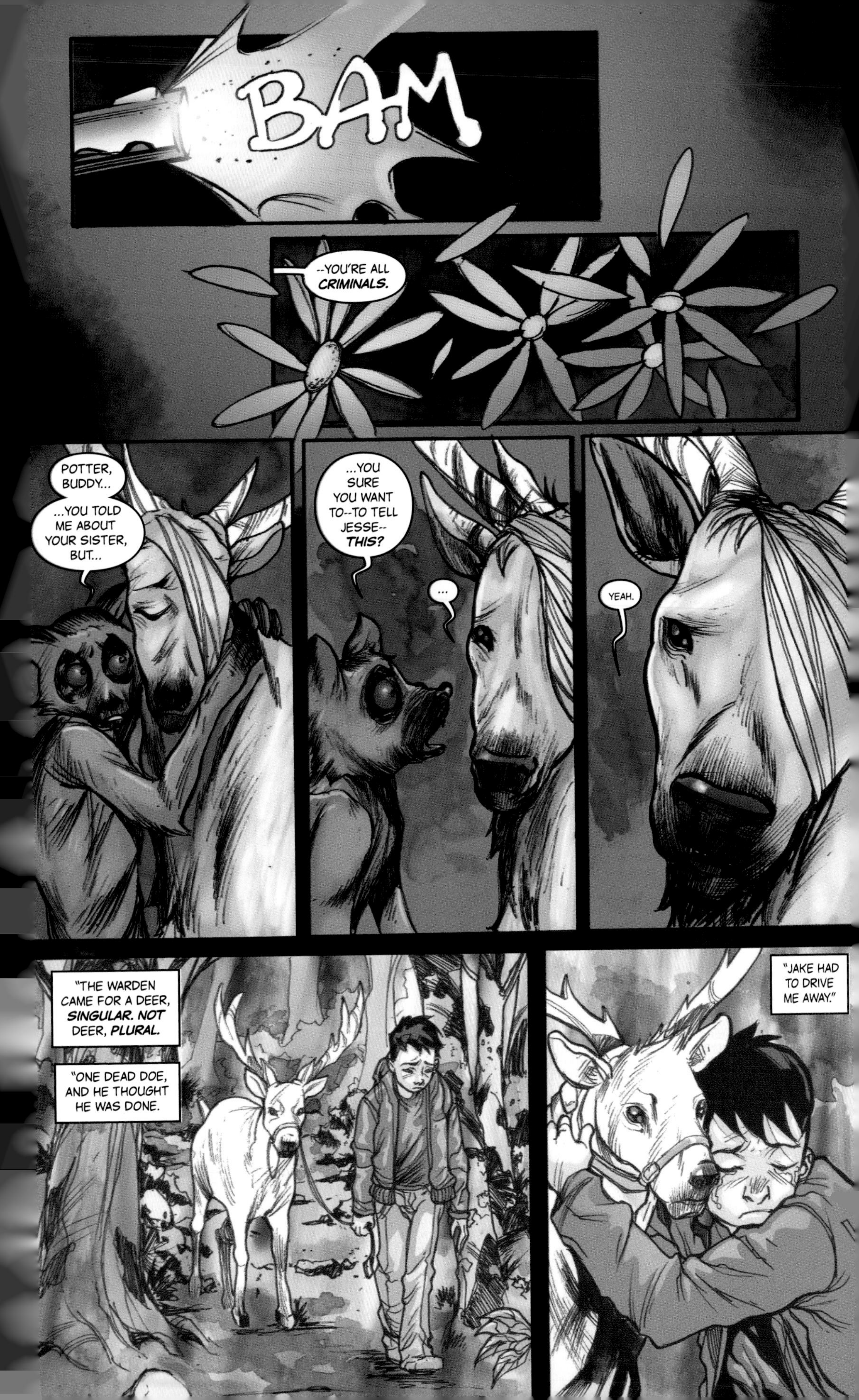
BAM
--YOU'RE ALL CRIMINALS.
POTTER, BUDDY...
...YOU TOLD ME ABOUT YOUR SISTER, BUT...
...YOU SURE YOU WANT TO--TO TELL JESSE-- THIS?
...
YEAH.
"THE WARDEN CAME FOR A DEER, SINGULAR. NOT DEER, PLURAL.
"ONE DEAD DOE, AND HE THOUGHT HE WAS DONE.
"JAKE HAD TO DRIVE ME AWAY."

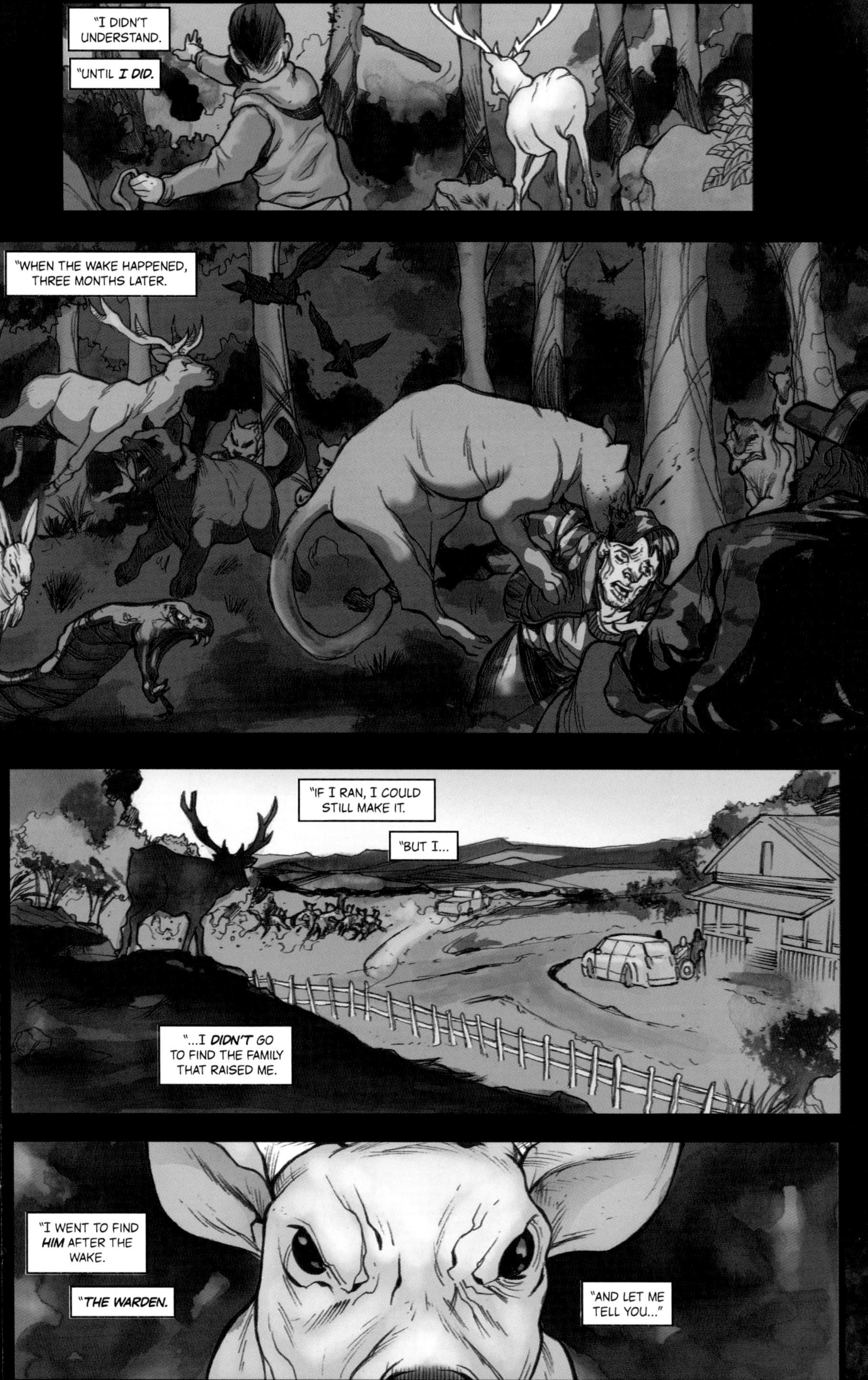
"I DIDN'T UNDERSTAND.
"UNTIL *I DID.*
"WHEN THE WAKE HAPPENED, THREE MONTHS LATER.
"IF I RAN, I COULD STILL MAKE IT.
"BUT I...
"...I *DIDN'T* GO TO FIND THE FAMILY THAT RAISED ME.
"I WENT TO FIND *HIM* AFTER THE WAKE.
"*THE WARDEN.*
"AND LET ME TELL YOU..."

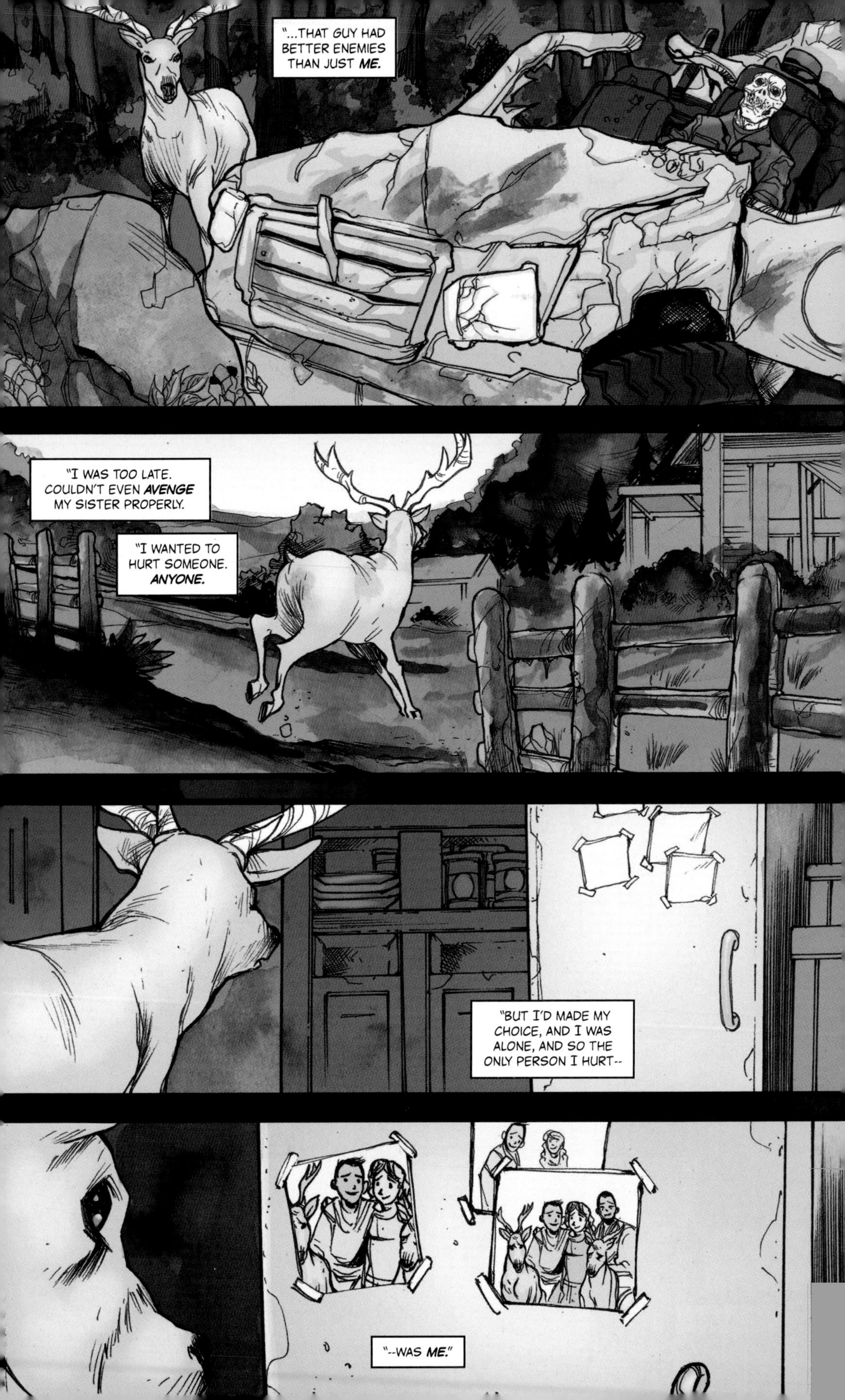
"...THAT GUY HAD BETTER ENEMIES THAN JUST ME.
"I WAS TOO LATE. COULDN'T EVEN AVENGE MY SISTER PROPERLY.
"I WANTED TO HURT SOMEONE. ANYONE.
"BUT I'D MADE MY CHOICE, AND I WAS ALONE, AND SO THE ONLY PERSON I HURT--
"--WAS ME."

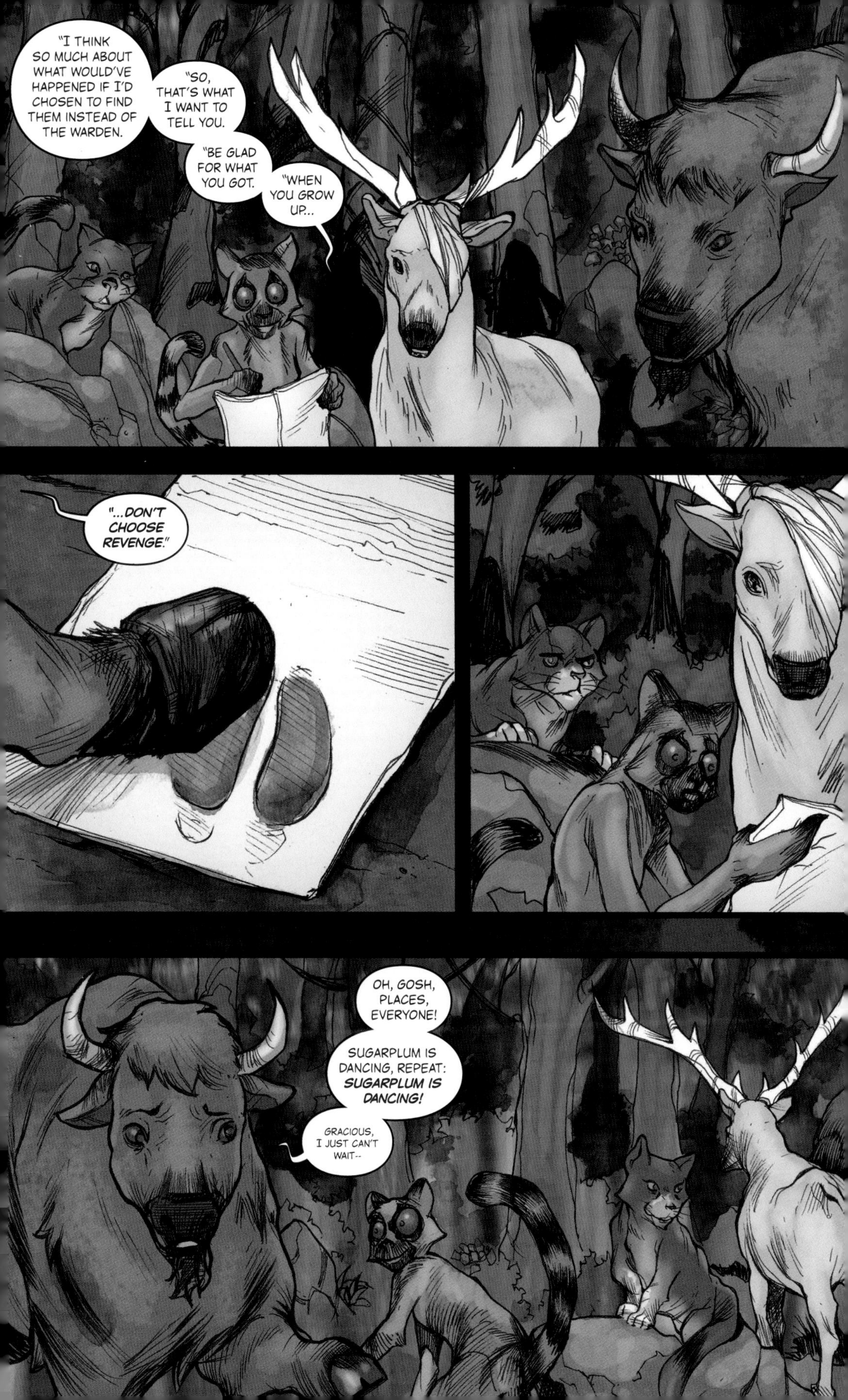
"I THINK SO MUCH ABOUT WHAT WOULD'VE HAPPENED IF I'D CHOSEN TO FIND THEM INSTEAD OF THE WARDEN.
"SO, THAT'S WHAT I WANT TO TELL YOU.
"BE GLAD FOR WHAT YOU GOT.
"WHEN YOU GROW UP...
"...*DON'T CHOOSE REVENGE*."
OH, GOSH, PLACES, EVERYONE!
SUGARPLUM IS DANCING, REPEAT: ***SUGARPLUM IS DANCING!***
GRACIOUS, I JUST CAN'T WAIT--

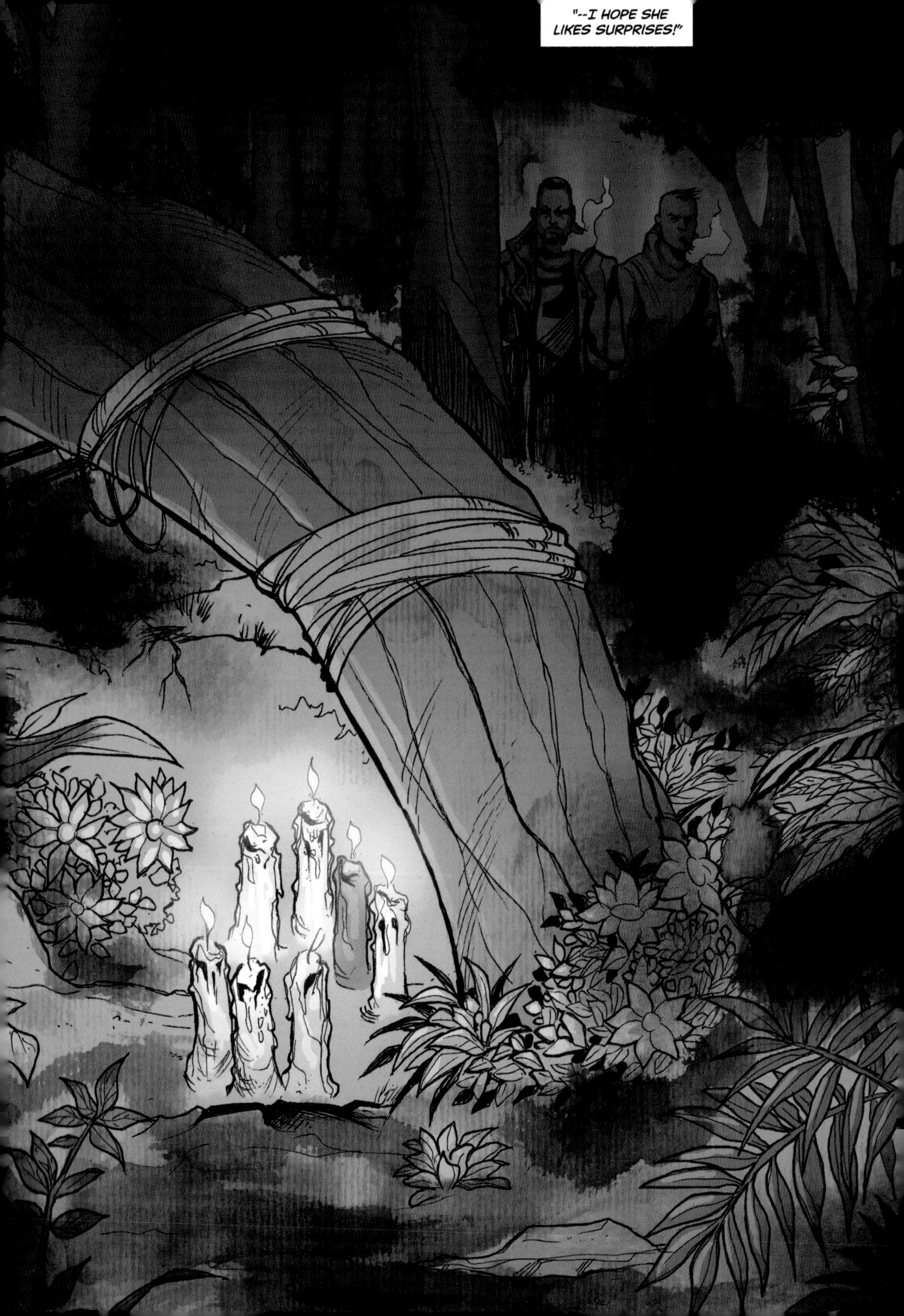
"--I HOPE SHE LIKES SURPRISES!"

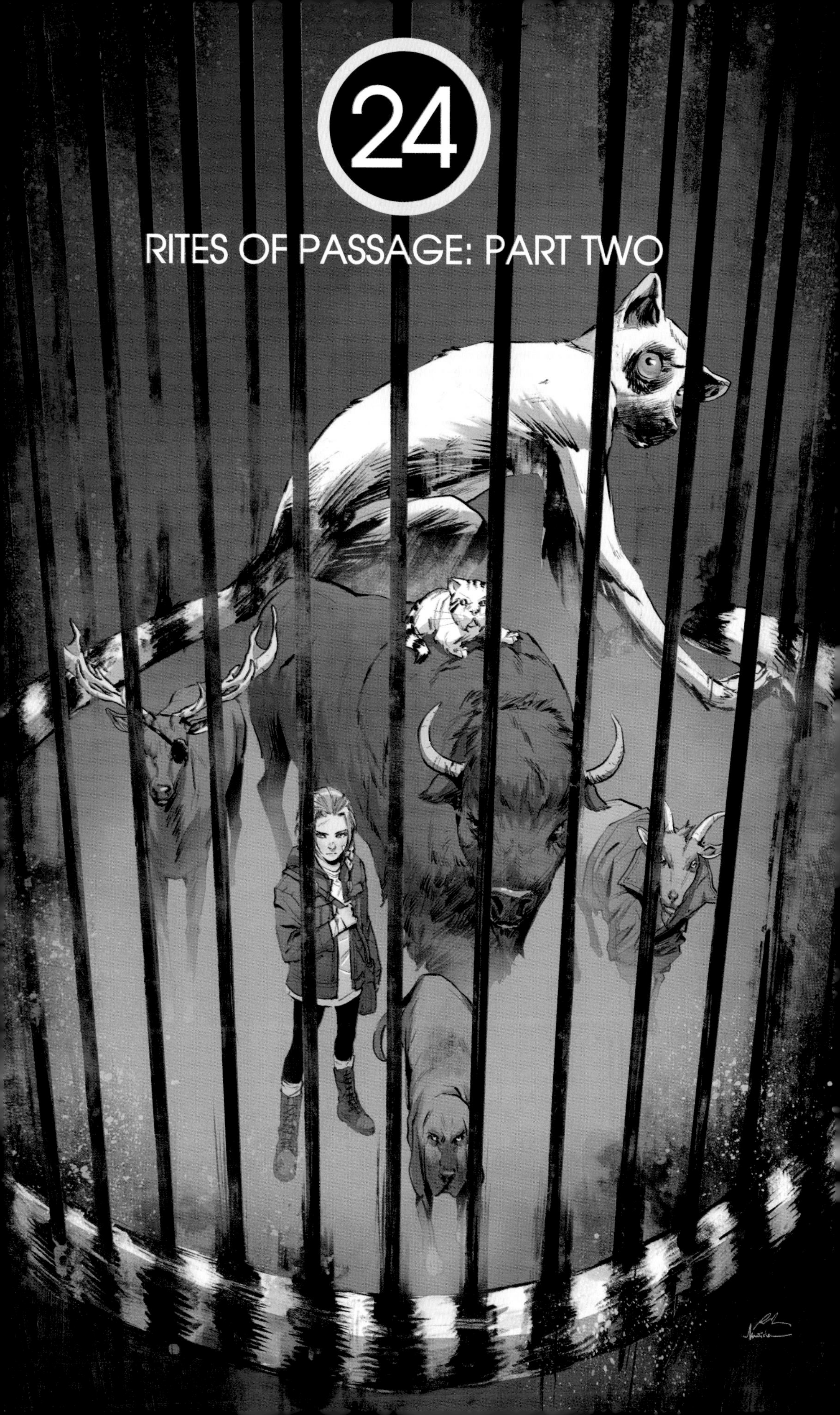
24
RITES OF PASSAGE: PART TWO

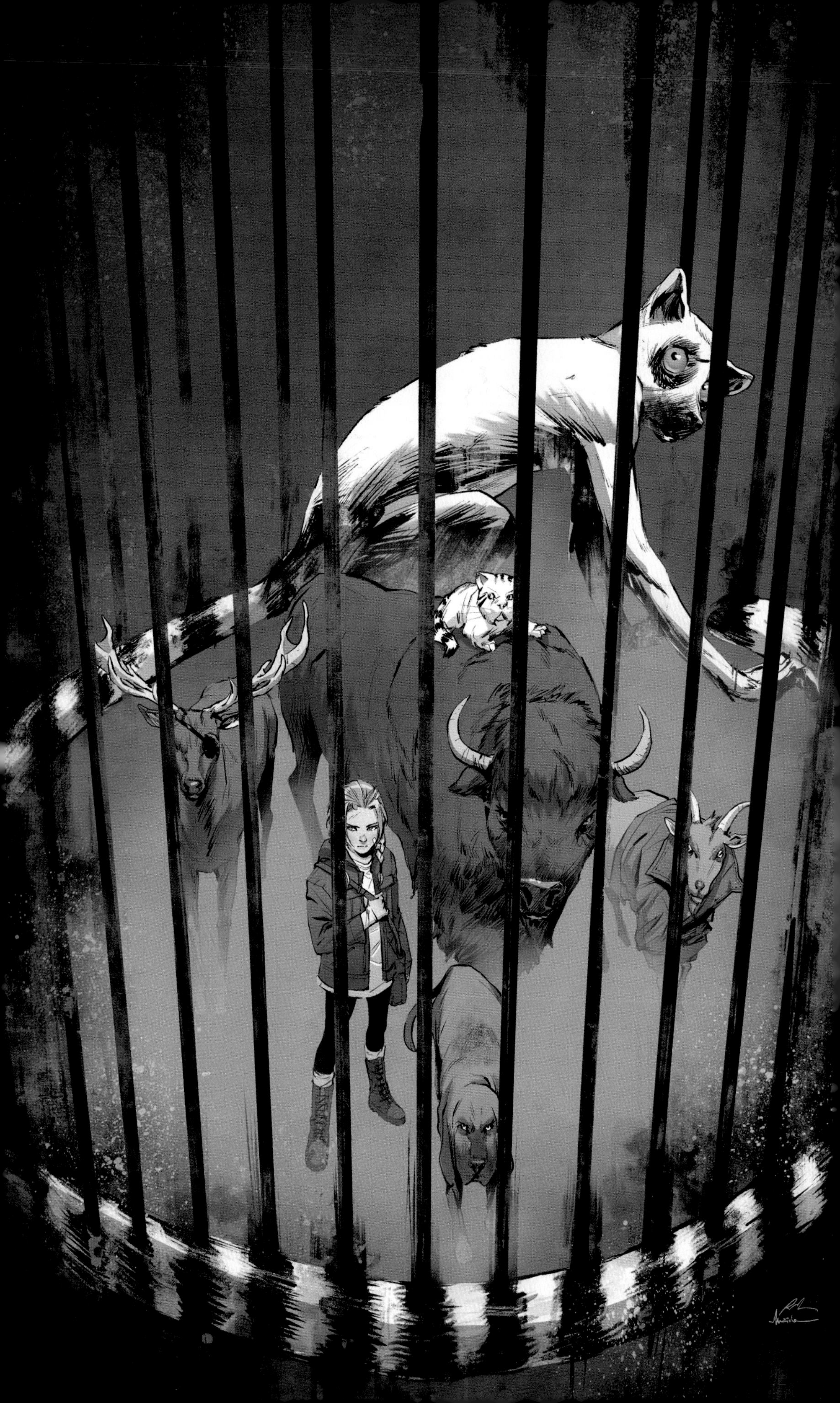

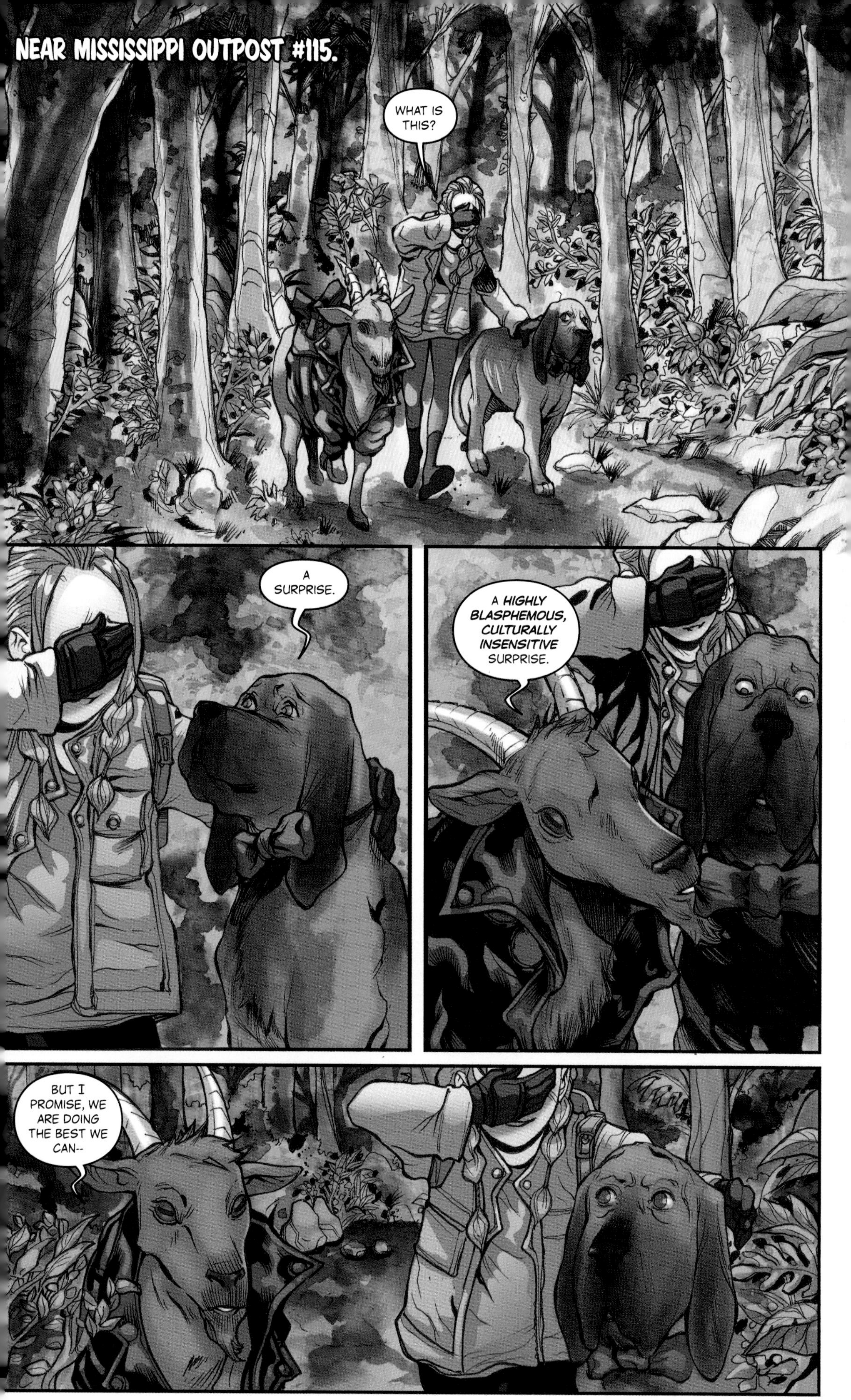
NEAR MISSISSIPPI OUTPOST #115.
WHAT IS THIS?
A SURPRISE.
A *HIGHLY BLASPHEMOUS, CULTURALLY INSENSITIVE* SURPRISE.
BUT I PROMISE, WE ARE DOING THE BEST WE CAN--

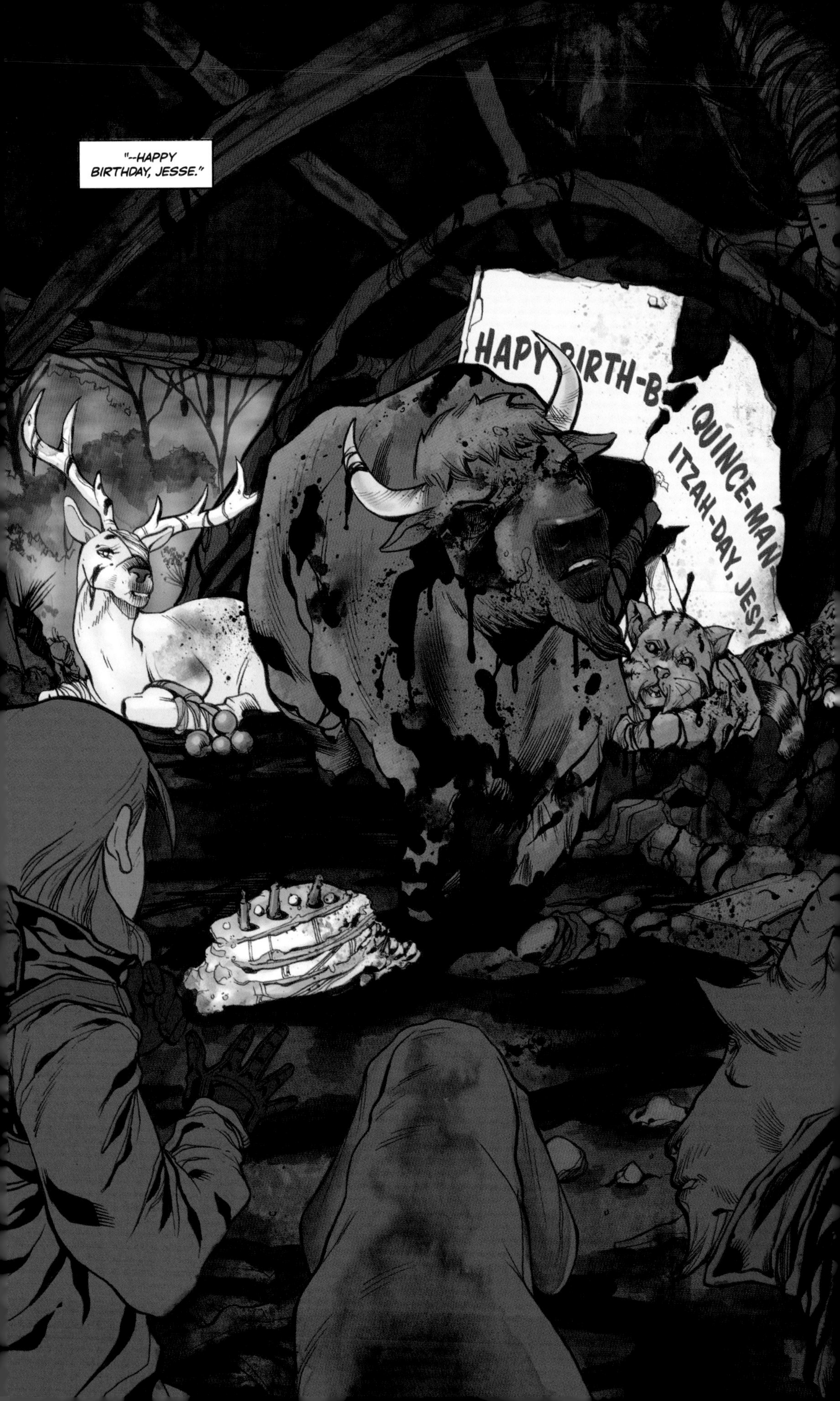
"--HAPPY BIRTHDAY, JESSE."
HAPY BIRTH-B QUINCE-MAN-ITZAH-DAY, JESY

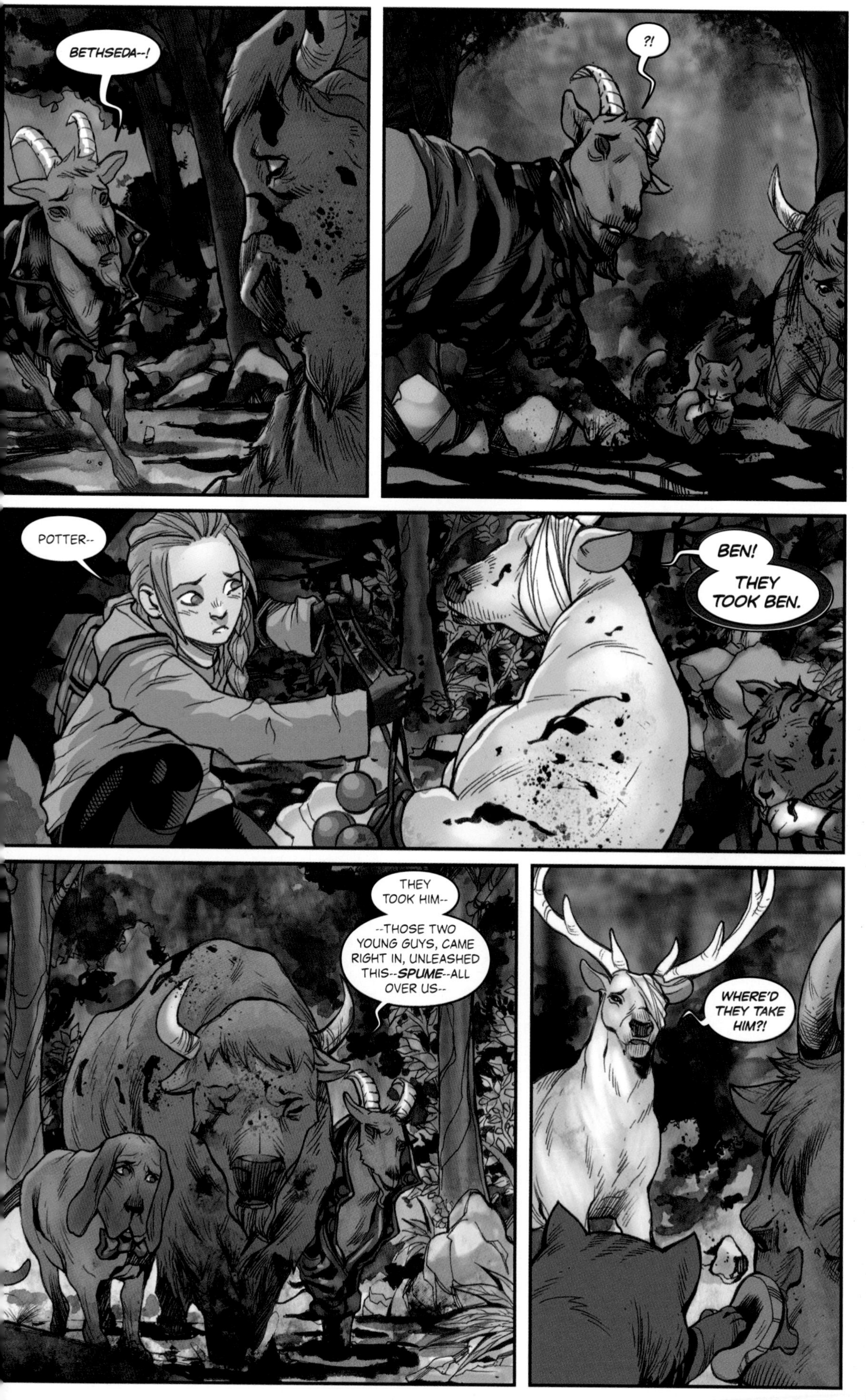
BETHSEDA--!
?!
POTTER--
BEN!
THEY TOOK BEN.
THEY TOOK HIM--
--THOSE TWO YOUNG GUYS, CAME RIGHT IN, UNLEASHED THIS--SPUME--ALL OVER US--
WHERE'D THEY TAKE HIM?!

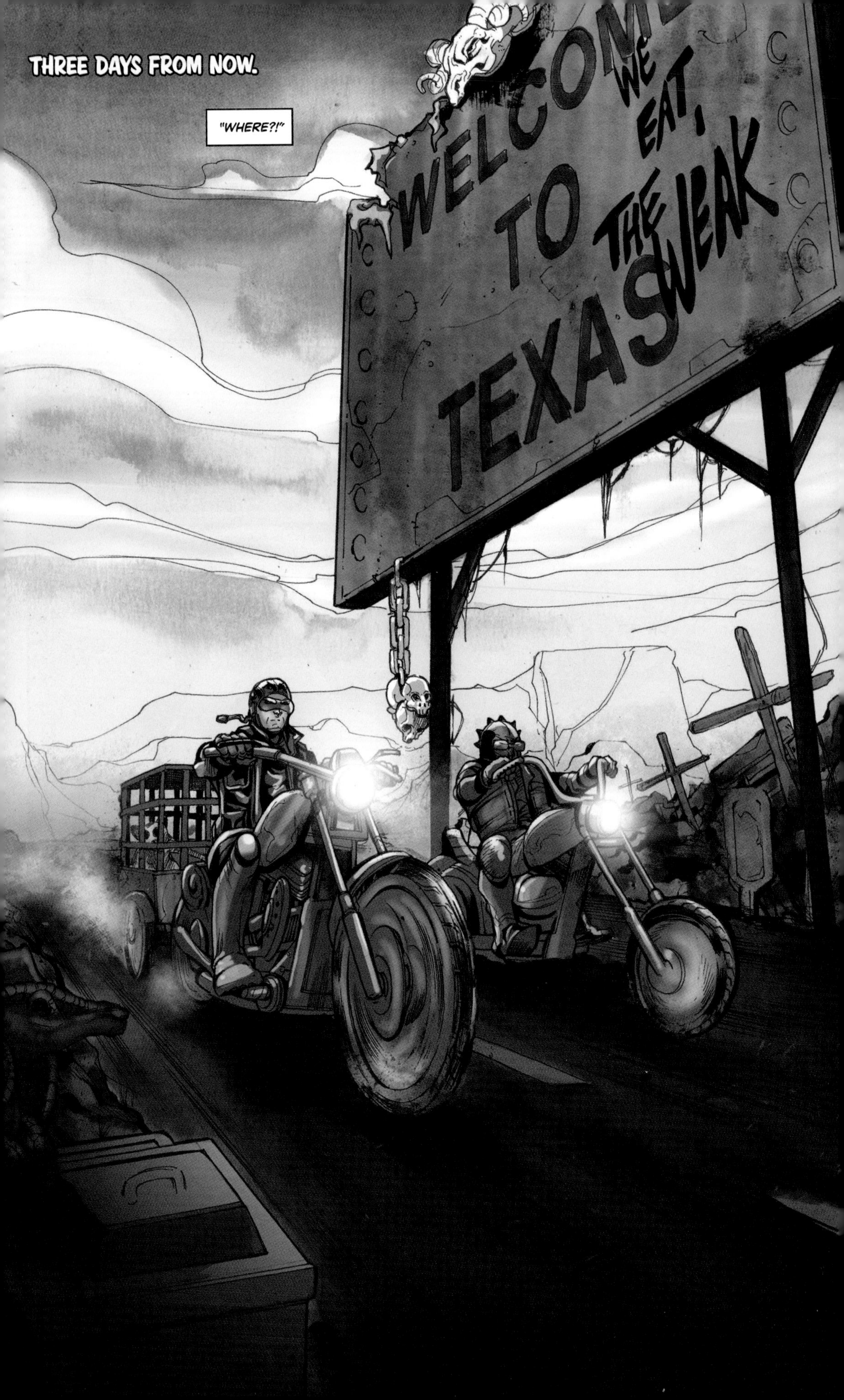
THREE DAYS FROM NOW.
"WHERE?!"
WELCOM
TO
TEXAS
WE EAT, THE WEAK

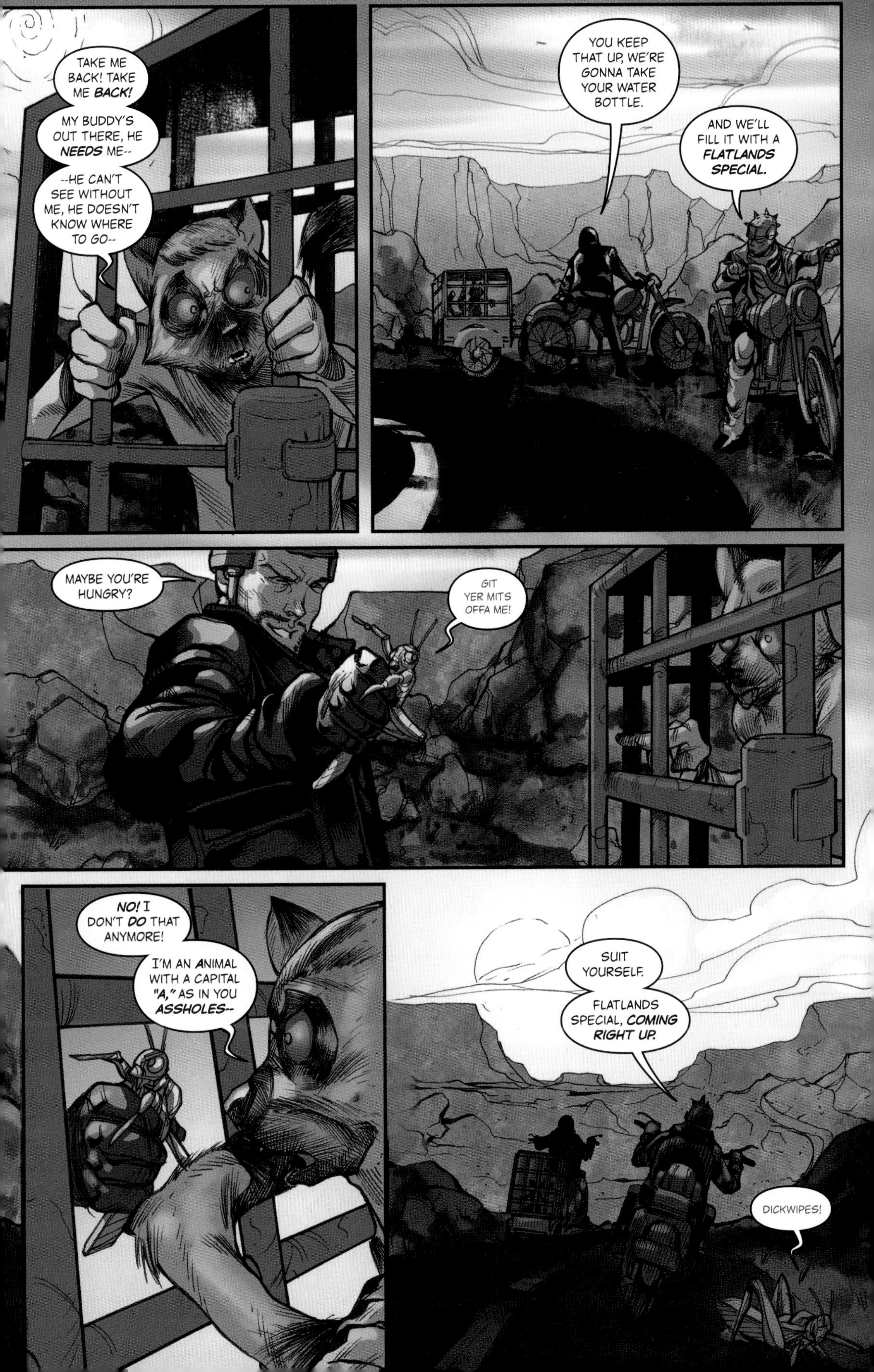
TAKE ME BACK! TAKE ME BACK!
MY BUDDY'S OUT THERE, HE NEEDS ME--
--HE CAN'T SEE WITHOUT ME, HE DOESN'T KNOW WHERE TO GO--
YOU KEEP THAT UP, WE'RE GONNA TAKE YOUR WATER BOTTLE.
AND WE'LL FILL IT WITH A FLATLANDS SPECIAL.
MAYBE YOU'RE HUNGRY?
GIT YER MITS OFFA ME!
NO! I DON'T DO THAT ANYMORE!
I'M AN ANIMAL WITH A CAPITAL "A," AS IN YOU ASSHOLES--
SUIT YOURSELF.
FLATLANDS SPECIAL, COMING RIGHT UP.
DICKWIPES!

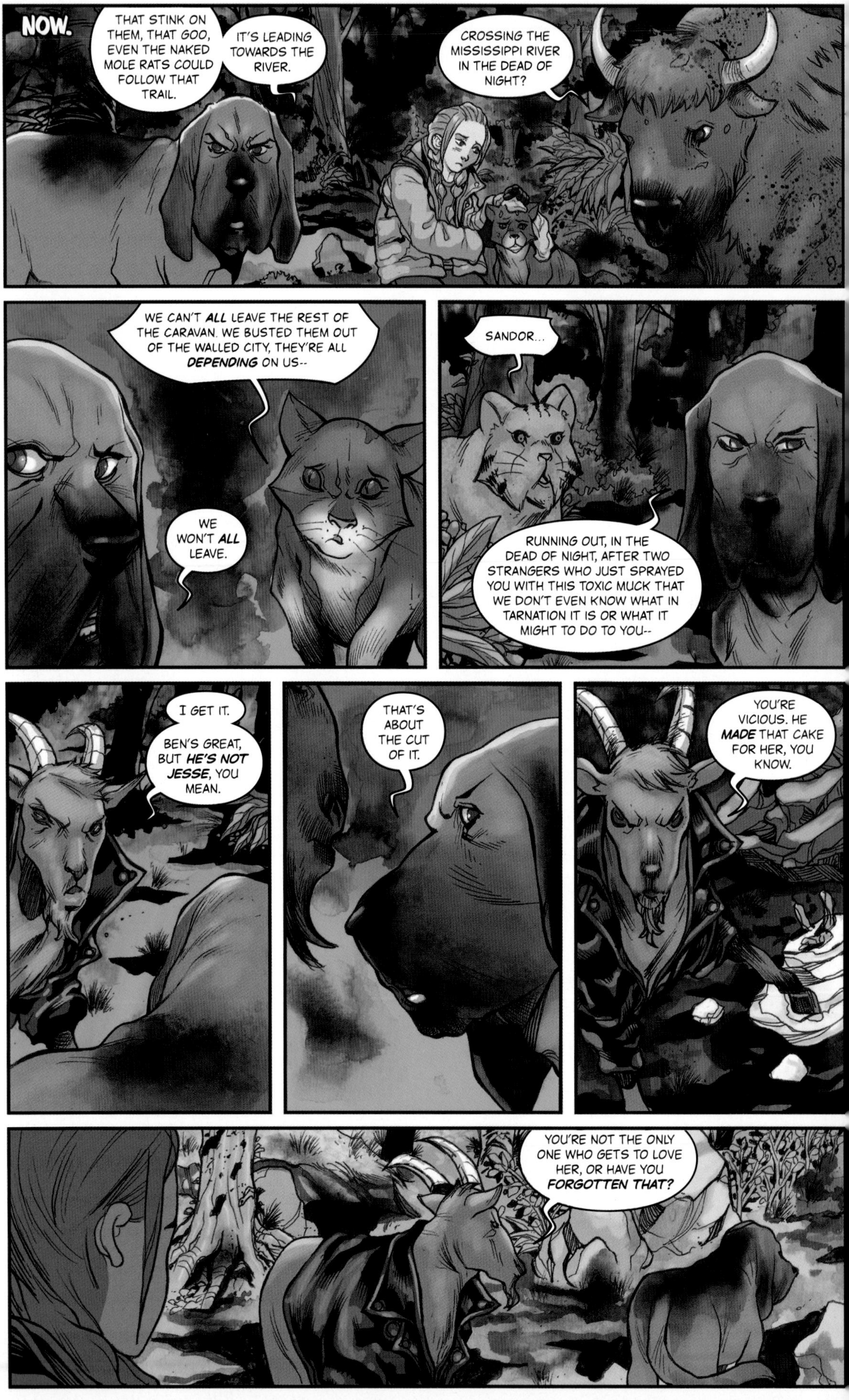
NOW.
THAT STINK ON THEM, THAT GOO, EVEN THE NAKED MOLE RATS COULD FOLLOW THAT TRAIL.
IT'S LEADING TOWARDS THE RIVER.
CROSSING THE MISSISSIPPI RIVER IN THE DEAD OF NIGHT?
WE CAN'T ALL LEAVE THE REST OF THE CARAVAN. WE BUSTED THEM OUT OF THE WALLED CITY, THEY'RE ALL DEPENDING ON US--
WE WON'T ALL LEAVE.
SANDOR...
RUNNING OUT, IN THE DEAD OF NIGHT, AFTER TWO STRANGERS WHO JUST SPRAYED YOU WITH THIS TOXIC MUCK THAT WE DON'T EVEN KNOW WHAT IN TARNATION IT IS OR WHAT IT MIGHT TO DO TO YOU--
I GET IT.
BEN'S GREAT, BUT HE'S NOT JESSE, YOU MEAN.
THAT'S ABOUT THE CUT OF IT.
YOU'RE VICIOUS. HE MADE THAT CAKE FOR HER, YOU KNOW.
YOU'RE NOT THE ONLY ONE WHO GETS TO LOVE HER, OR HAVE YOU FORGOTTEN THAT?

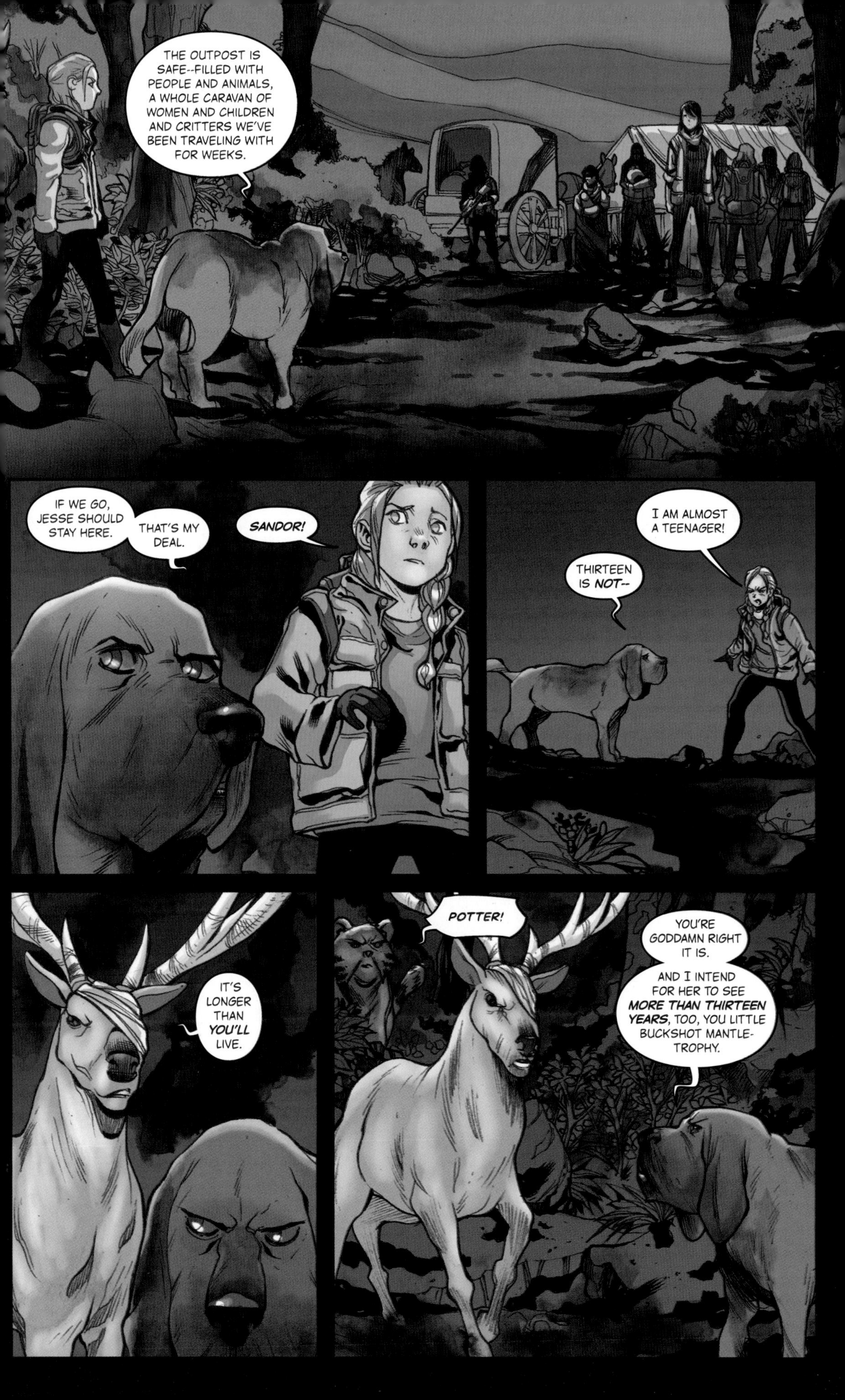

THE OUTPOST IS SAFE--FILLED WITH PEOPLE AND ANIMALS, A WHOLE CARAVAN OF WOMEN AND CHILDREN AND CRITTERS WE'VE BEEN TRAVELING WITH FOR WEEKS.
IF WE GO, JESSE SHOULD STAY HERE.
THAT'S MY DEAL.
SANDOR!
I AM ALMOST A TEENAGER!
THIRTEEN IS NOT--
IT'S LONGER THAN YOU'LL LIVE.
POTTER!
YOU'RE GODDAMN RIGHT IT IS.
AND I INTEND FOR HER TO SEE MORE THAN THIRTEEN YEARS, TOO, YOU LITTLE BUCKSHOT MANTLE-TROPHY.

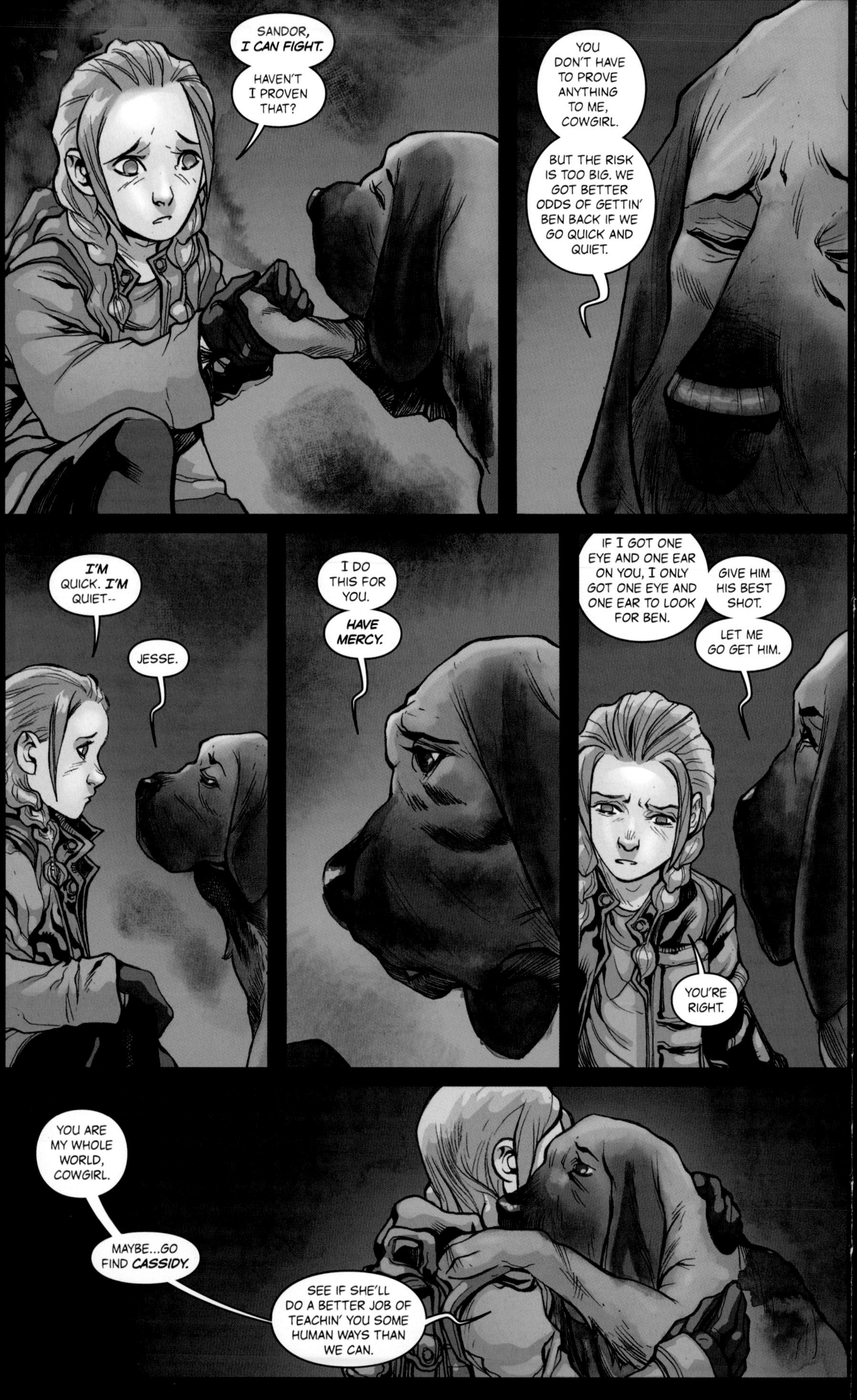
SANDOR, I CAN FIGHT.
HAVEN'T I PROVEN THAT?
YOU DON'T HAVE TO PROVE ANYTHING TO ME, COWGIRL.
BUT THE RISK IS TOO BIG. WE GOT BETTER ODDS OF GETTIN' BEN BACK IF WE GO QUICK AND QUIET.
I'M QUICK. I'M QUIET--
JESSE.
I DO THIS FOR YOU.
HAVE MERCY.
IF I GOT ONE EYE AND ONE EAR ON YOU, I ONLY GOT ONE EYE AND ONE EAR TO LOOK FOR BEN.
GIVE HIM HIS BEST SHOT.
LET ME GO GET HIM.
YOU'RE RIGHT.
YOU ARE MY WHOLE WORLD, COWGIRL.
MAYBE...GO FIND CASSIDY.
SEE IF SHE'LL DO A BETTER JOB OF TEACHIN' YOU SOME HUMAN WAYS THAN WE CAN.

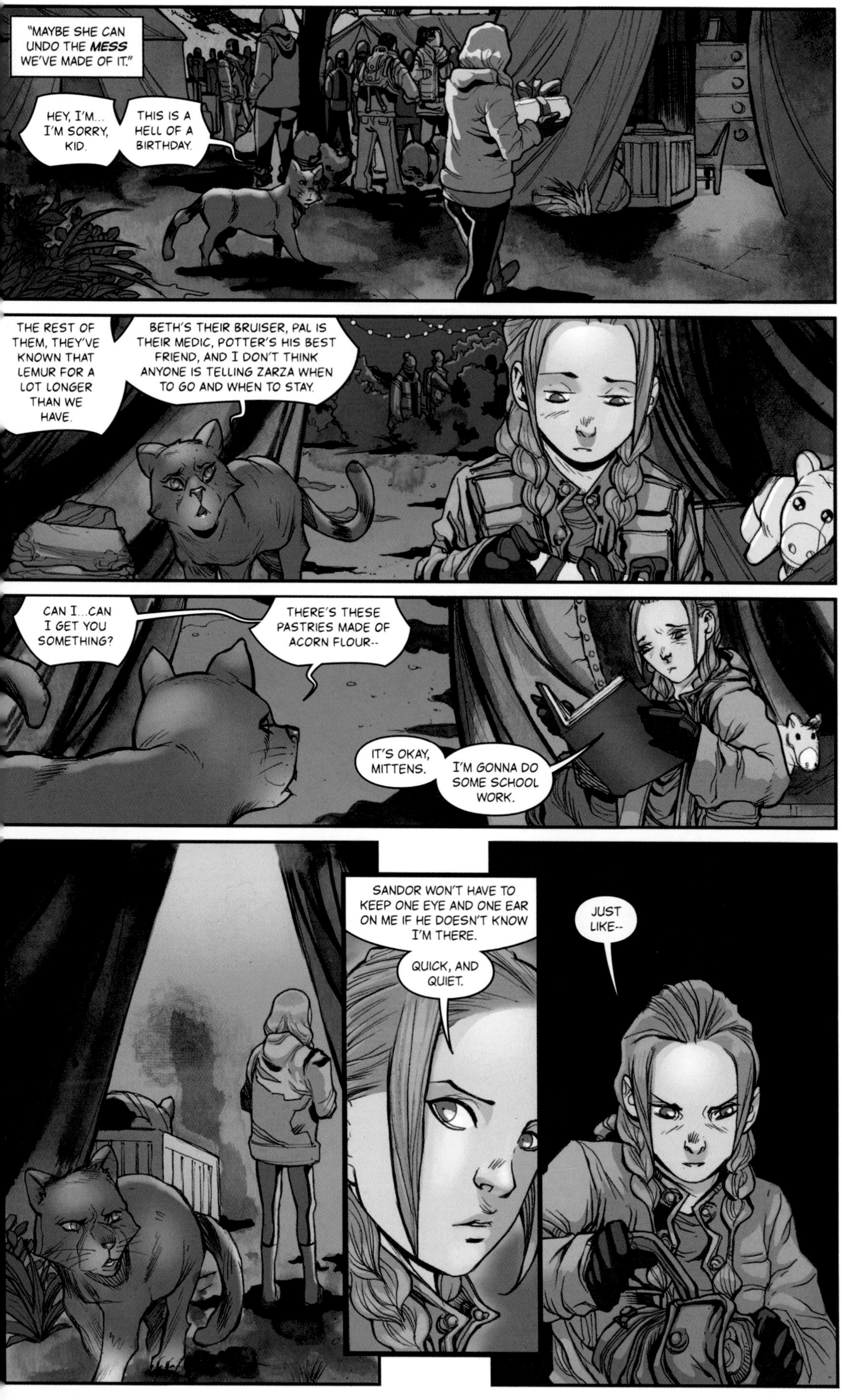
"MAYBE SHE CAN UNDO THE *MESS* WE'VE MADE OF IT."
HEY, I'M... I'M SORRY, KID.
THIS IS A HELL OF A BIRTHDAY.
THE REST OF THEM, THEY'VE KNOWN THAT LEMUR FOR A LOT LONGER THAN WE HAVE.
BETH'S THEIR BRUISER, PAL IS THEIR MEDIC, POTTER'S HIS BEST FRIEND, AND I DON'T THINK ANYONE IS TELLING ZARZA WHEN TO GO AND WHEN TO STAY.
CAN I...CAN I GET YOU SOMETHING?
THERE'S THESE PASTRIES MADE OF ACORN FLOUR--
IT'S OKAY, MITTENS.
I'M GONNA DO SOME SCHOOL WORK.
SANDOR WON'T HAVE TO KEEP ONE EYE AND ONE EAR ON ME IF HE DOESN'T KNOW I'M THERE.
QUICK, AND QUIET.
JUST LIKE--

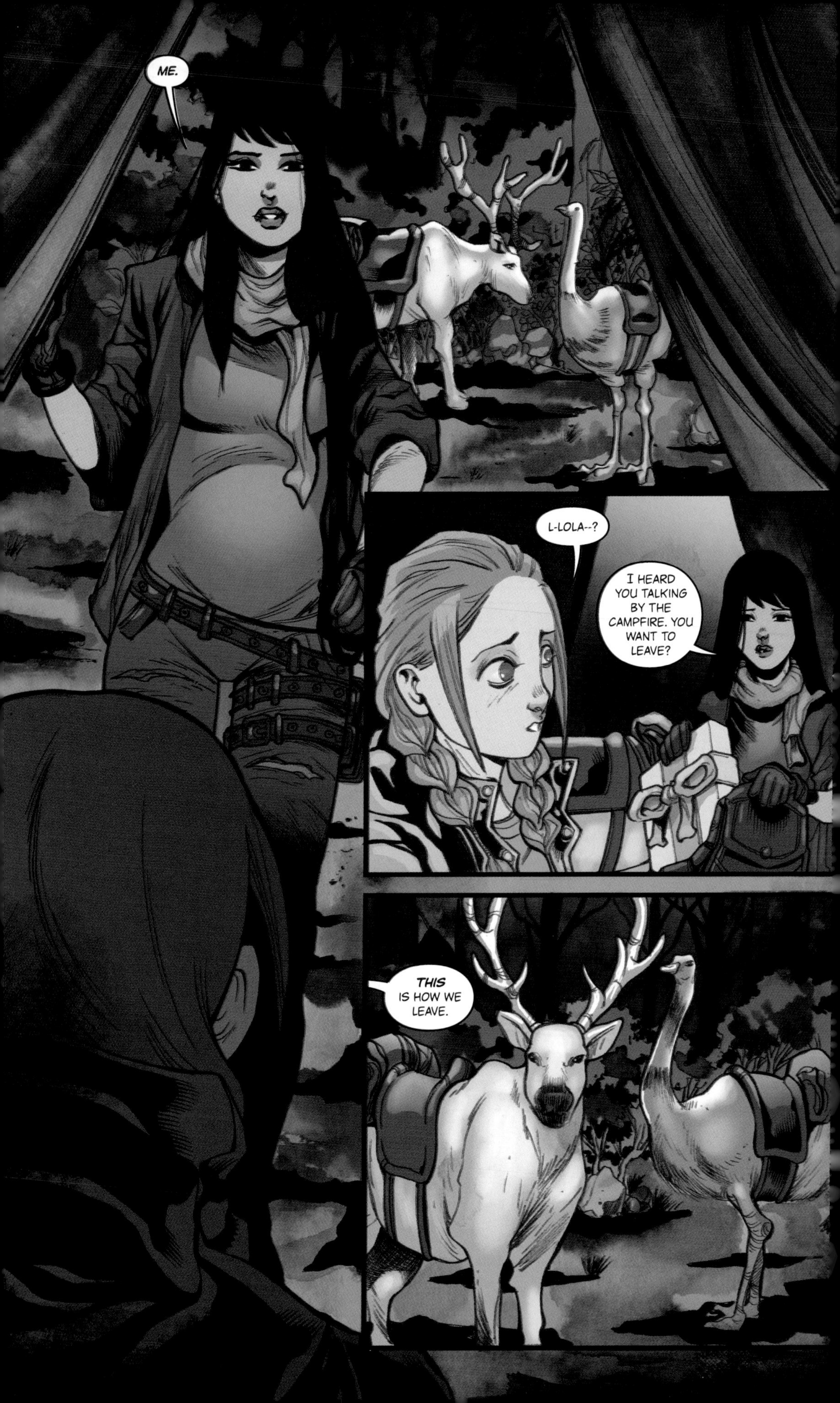
ME.
L-LOLA--?
I HEARD YOU TALKING BY THE CAMPFIRE. YOU WANT TO LEAVE?
THIS IS HOW WE LEAVE.

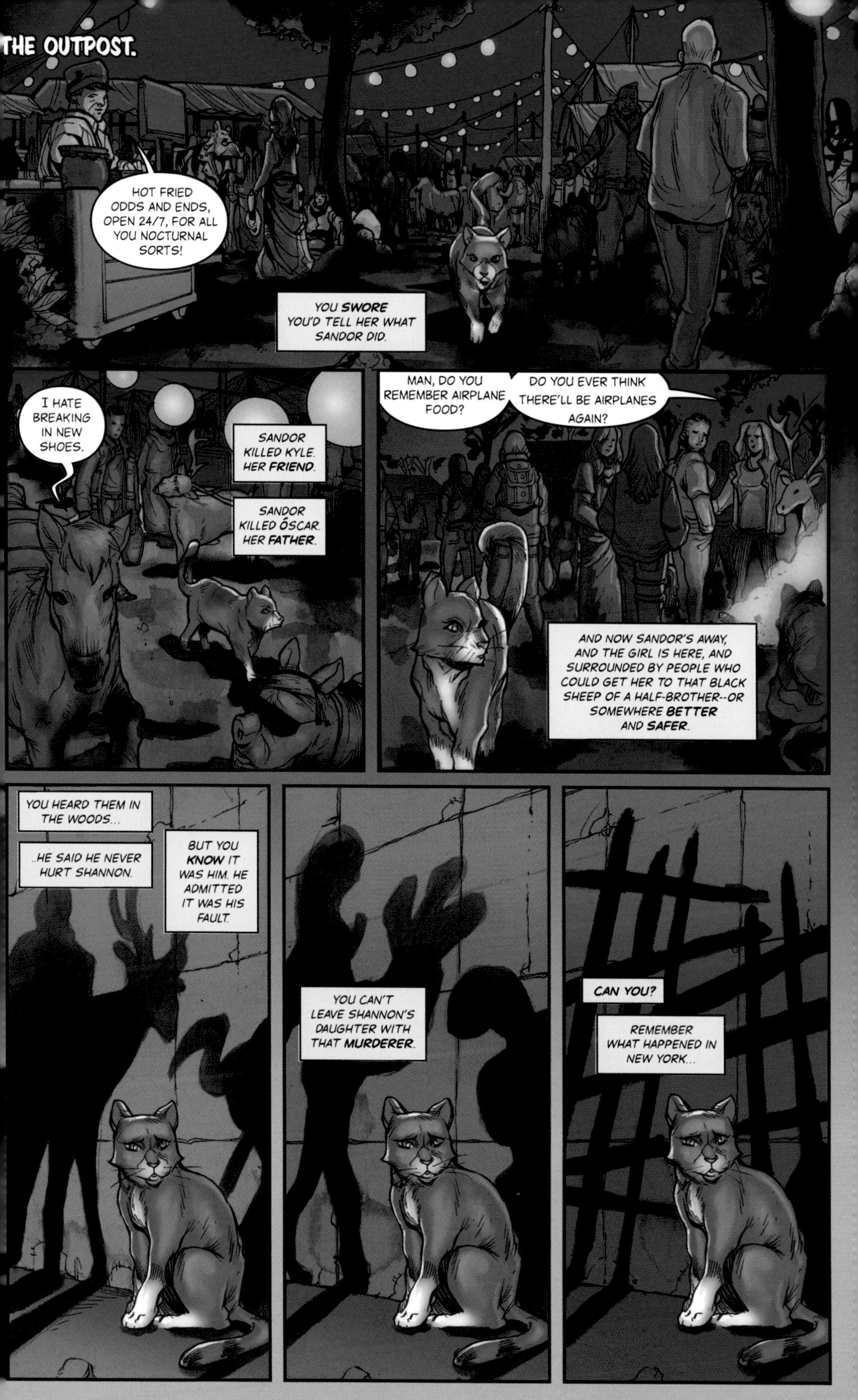
THE OUTPOST.
HOT FRIED ODDS AND ENDS, OPEN 24/7, FOR ALL YOU NOCTURNAL SORTS!
YOU SWORE YOU'D TELL HER WHAT SANDOR DID.
I HATE BREAKING IN NEW SHOES.
SANDOR KILLED KYLE. HER FRIEND.
SANDOR KILLED ÓSCAR. HER FATHER.
MAN, DO YOU REMEMBER AIRPLANE FOOD?
DO YOU EVER THINK THERE'LL BE AIRPLANES AGAIN?
AND NOW SANDOR'S AWAY, AND THE GIRL IS HERE, AND SURROUNDED BY PEOPLE WHO COULD GET HER TO THAT BLACK SHEEP OF A HALF-BROTHER--OR SOMEWHERE BETTER AND SAFER.
YOU HEARD THEM IN THE WOODS...
..HE SAID HE NEVER HURT SHANNON.
BUT YOU KNOW IT WAS HIM. HE ADMITTED IT WAS HIS FAULT.
YOU CAN'T LEAVE SHANNON'S DAUGHTER WITH THAT MURDERER.
CAN YOU?
REMEMBER WHAT HAPPENED IN NEW YORK...

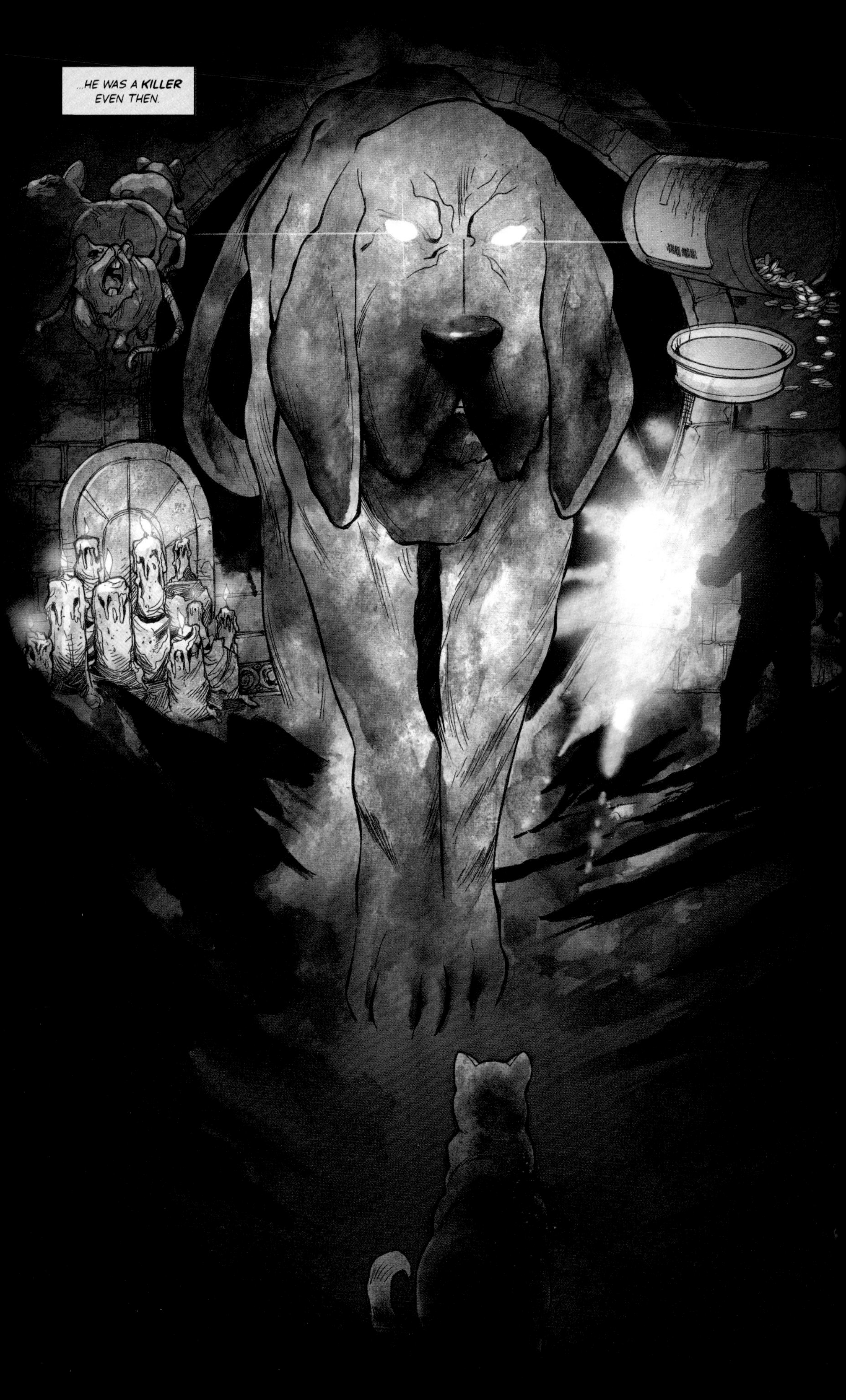
...HE WAS A KILLER
EVEN THEN.

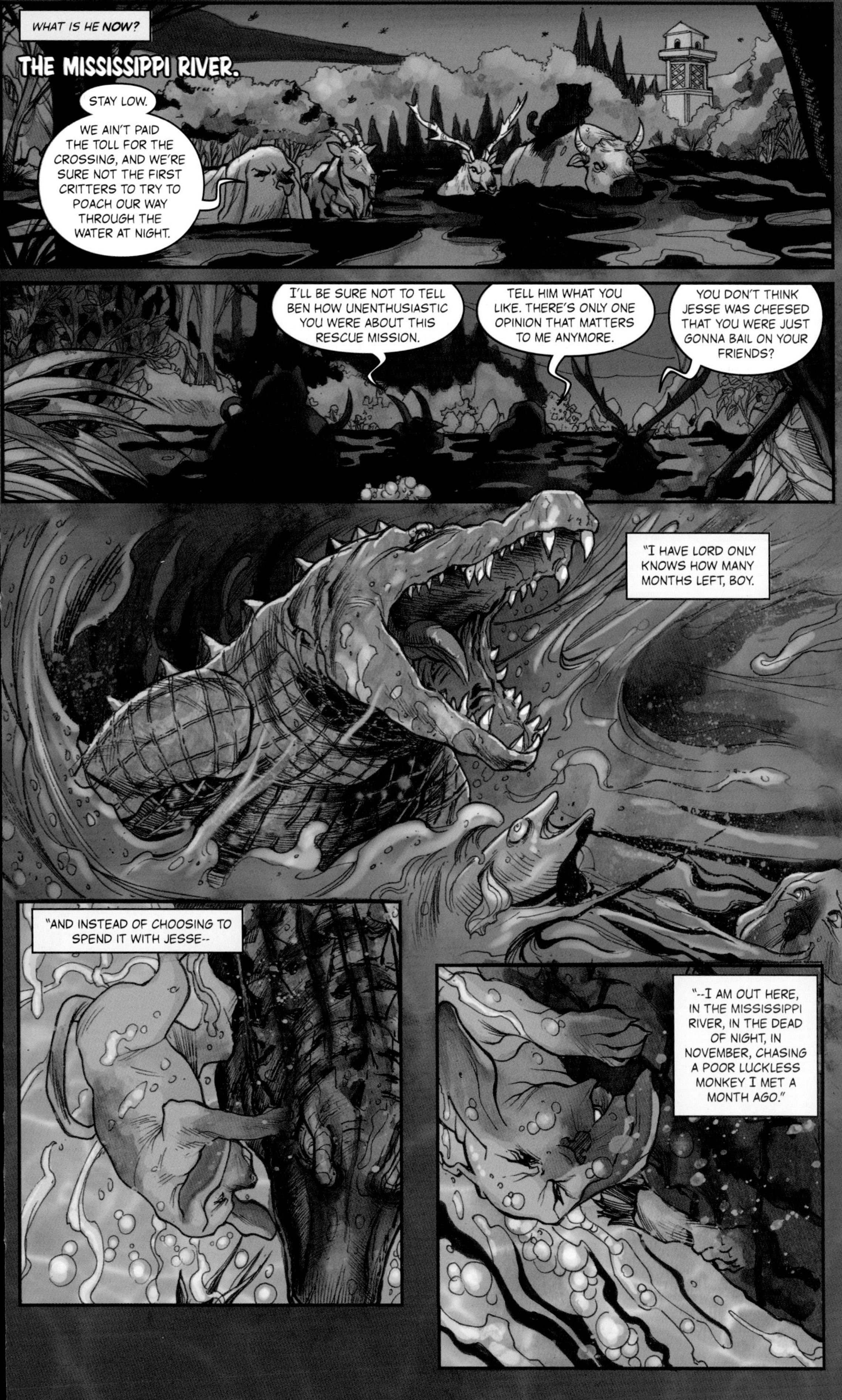
WHAT IS HE NOW?
THE MISSISSIPPI RIVER.
STAY LOW.
WE AIN'T PAID THE TOLL FOR THE CROSSING, AND WE'RE SURE NOT THE FIRST CRITTERS TO TRY TO POACH OUR WAY THROUGH THE WATER AT NIGHT.
I'LL BE SURE NOT TO TELL BEN HOW UNENTHUSIASTIC YOU WERE ABOUT THIS RESCUE MISSION.
TELL HIM WHAT YOU LIKE. THERE'S ONLY ONE OPINION THAT MATTERS TO ME ANYMORE.
YOU DON'T THINK JESSE WAS CHEESED THAT YOU WERE JUST GONNA BAIL ON YOUR FRIENDS?
"I HAVE LORD ONLY KNOWS HOW MANY MONTHS LEFT, BOY.
"AND INSTEAD OF CHOOSING TO SPEND IT WITH JESSE--
"--I AM OUT HERE, IN THE MISSISSIPPI RIVER, IN THE DEAD OF NIGHT, IN NOVEMBER, CHASING A POOR LUCKLESS MONKEY I MET A MONTH AGO."

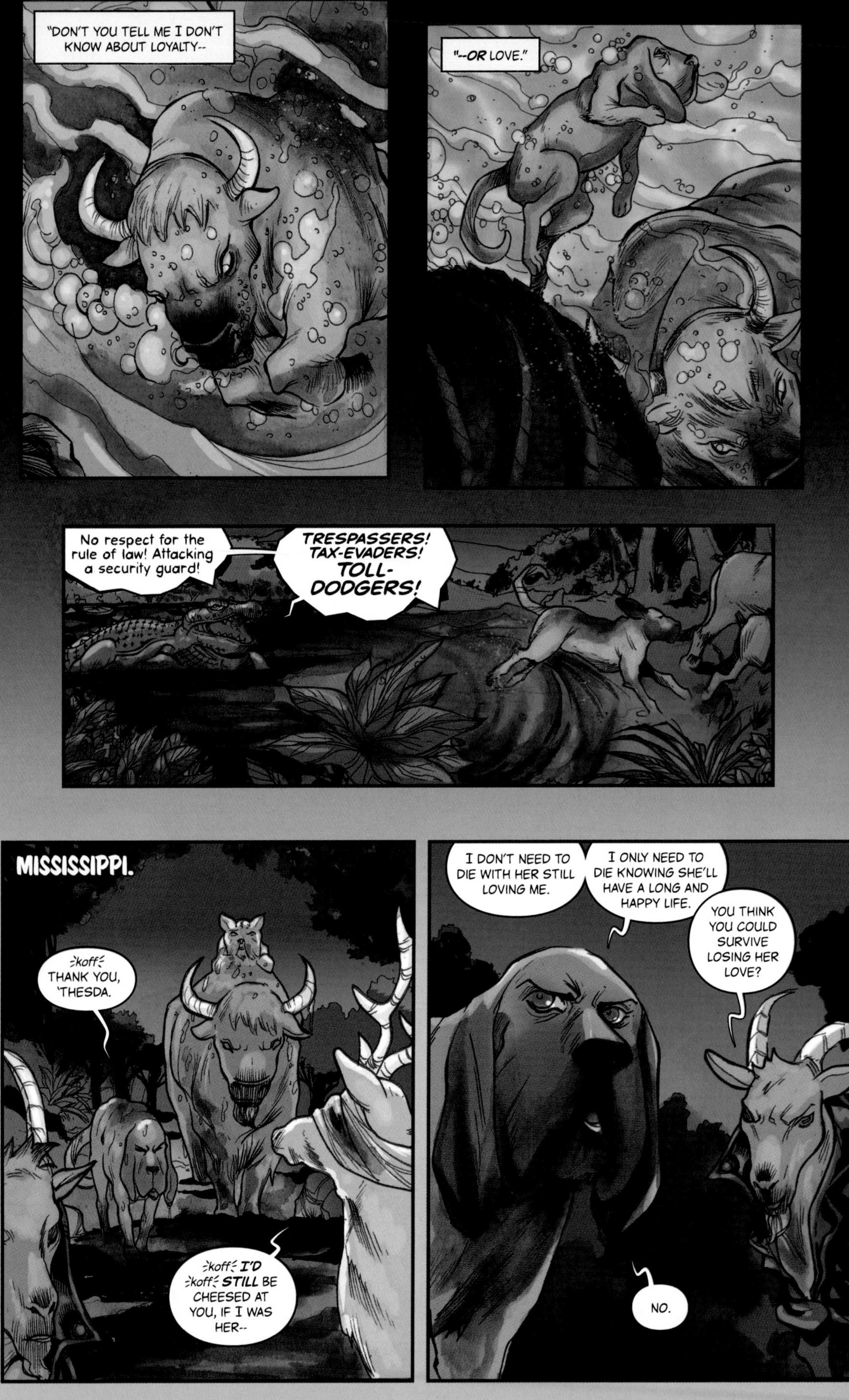
"DON'T YOU TELL ME I DON'T KNOW ABOUT LOYALTY--
"--OR LOVE."
No respect for the rule of law! Attacking a security guard!
TRESPASSERS! TAX-EVADERS! TOLL-DODGERS!
MISSISSIPPI.
koff THANK YOU, 'THESDA.
koff I'D *koff* STILL BE CHEESED AT YOU, IF I WAS HER--
I DON'T NEED TO DIE WITH HER STILL LOVING ME.
I ONLY NEED TO DIE KNOWING SHE'LL HAVE A LONG AND HAPPY LIFE.
YOU THINK YOU COULD SURVIVE LOSING HER LOVE?
NO.

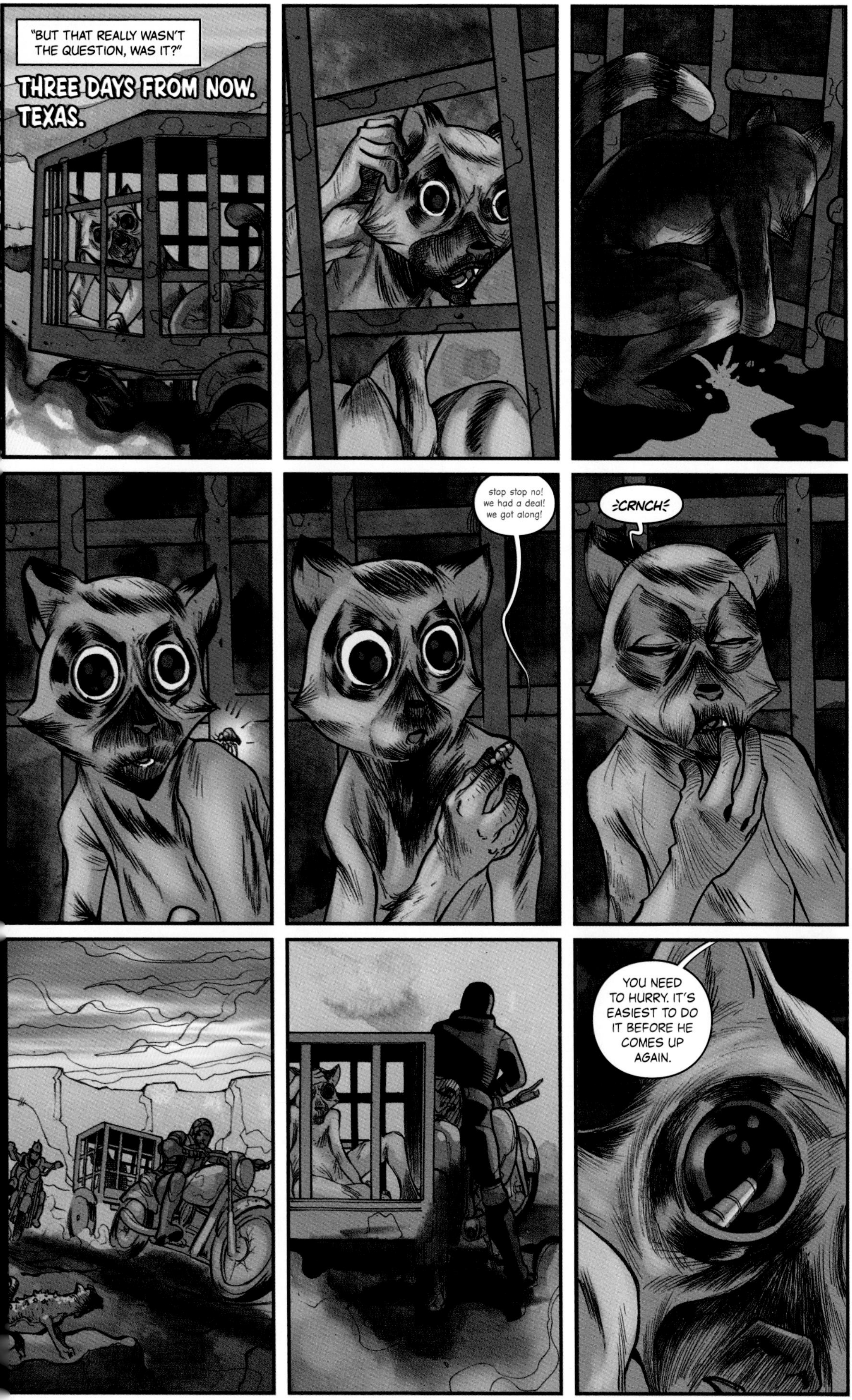
"BUT THAT REALLY WASN'T THE QUESTION, WAS IT?"
THREE DAYS FROM NOW. TEXAS.
stop stop no! we had a deal! we got along!
CRNCH
YOU NEED TO HURRY. IT'S EASIEST TO DO IT BEFORE HE COMES UP AGAIN.

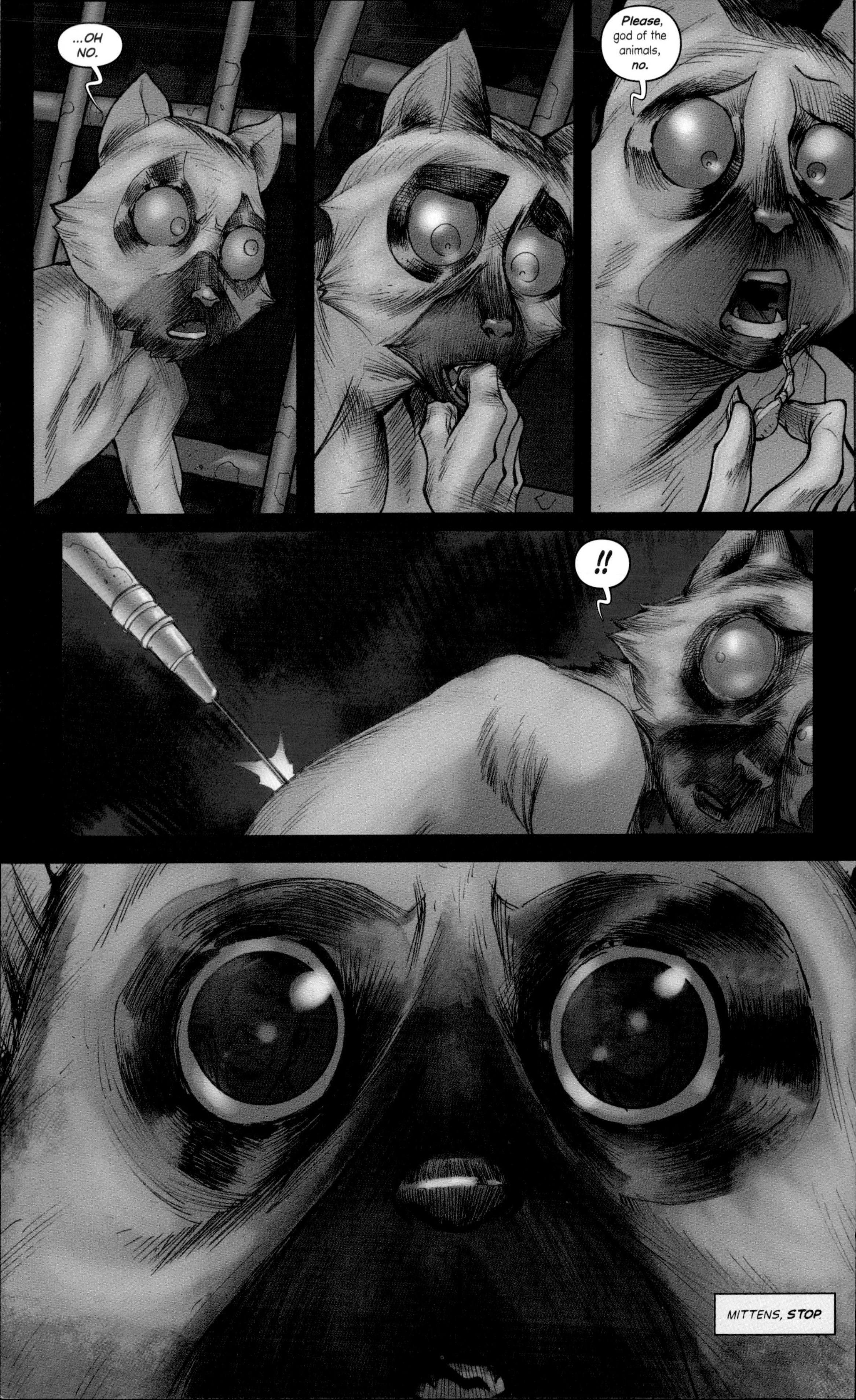
...OH NO.
Please, god of the animals, no.
!!
MITTENS, STOP.

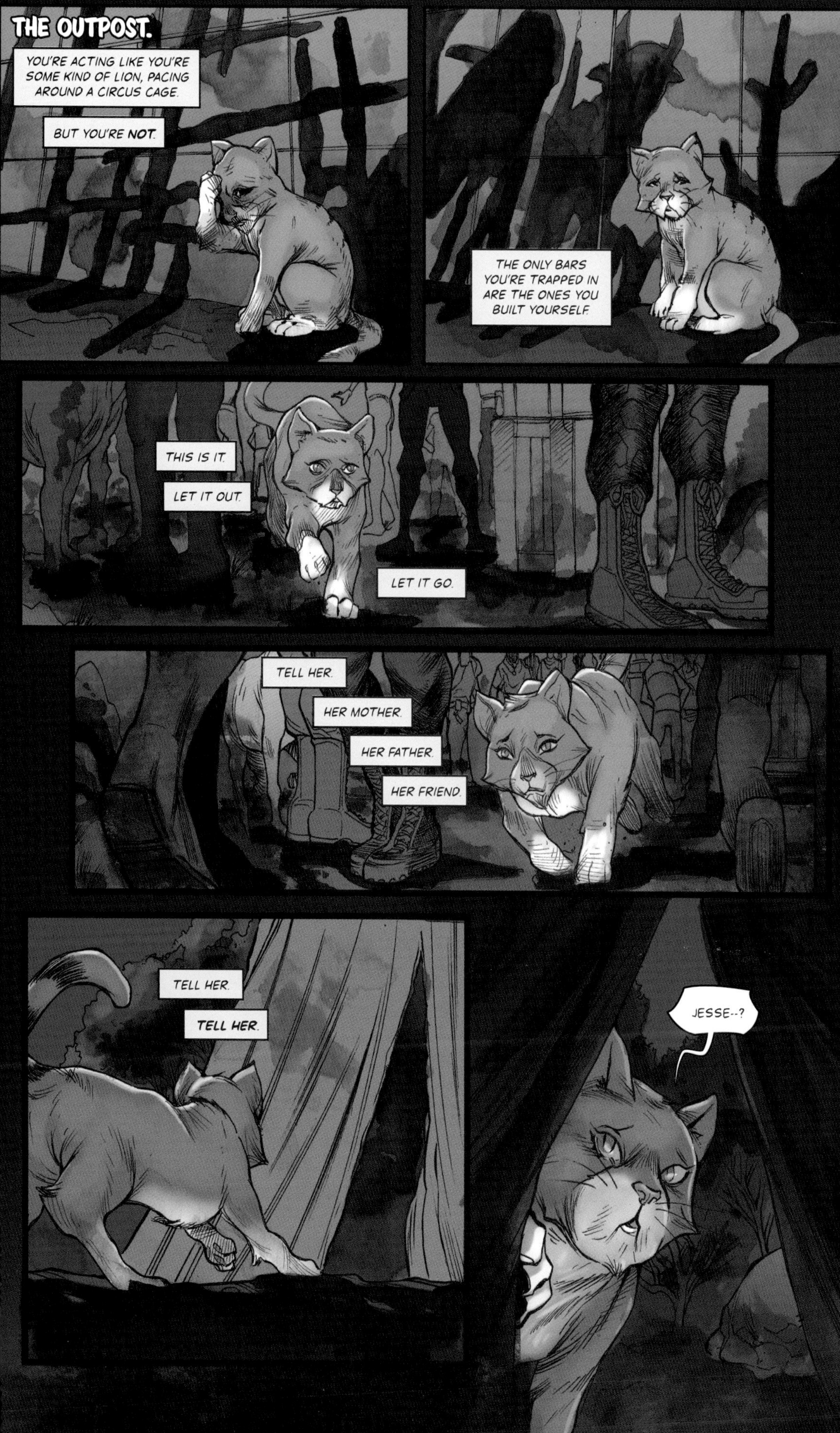
THE OUTPOST.
YOU'RE ACTING LIKE YOU'RE SOME KIND OF LION, PACING AROUND A CIRCUS CAGE.
BUT YOU'RE NOT.
THE ONLY BARS YOU'RE TRAPPED IN ARE THE ONES YOU BUILT YOURSELF.
THIS IS IT.
LET IT OUT.
LET IT GO.
TELL HER.
HER MOTHER.
HER FATHER.
HER FRIEND.
TELL HER.
TELL HER.
JESSE--?

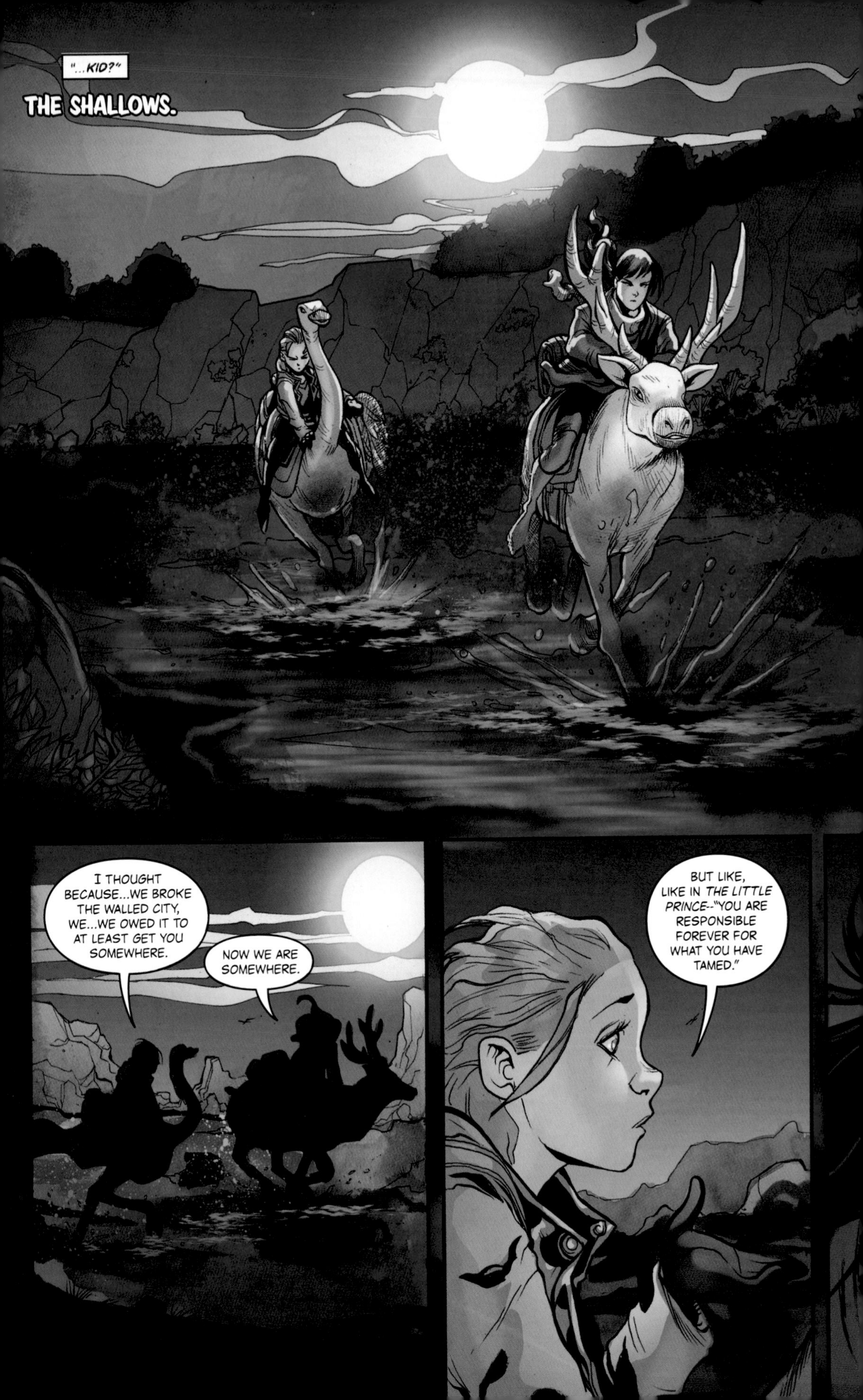
"...KID?"
THE SHALLOWS.
I THOUGHT BECAUSE...WE BROKE THE WALLED CITY, WE...WE OWED IT TO AT LEAST GET YOU SOMEWHERE.
NOW WE ARE SOMEWHERE.
BUT LIKE, LIKE IN THE LITTLE PRINCE--"YOU ARE RESPONSIBLE FOREVER FOR WHAT YOU HAVE TAMED."

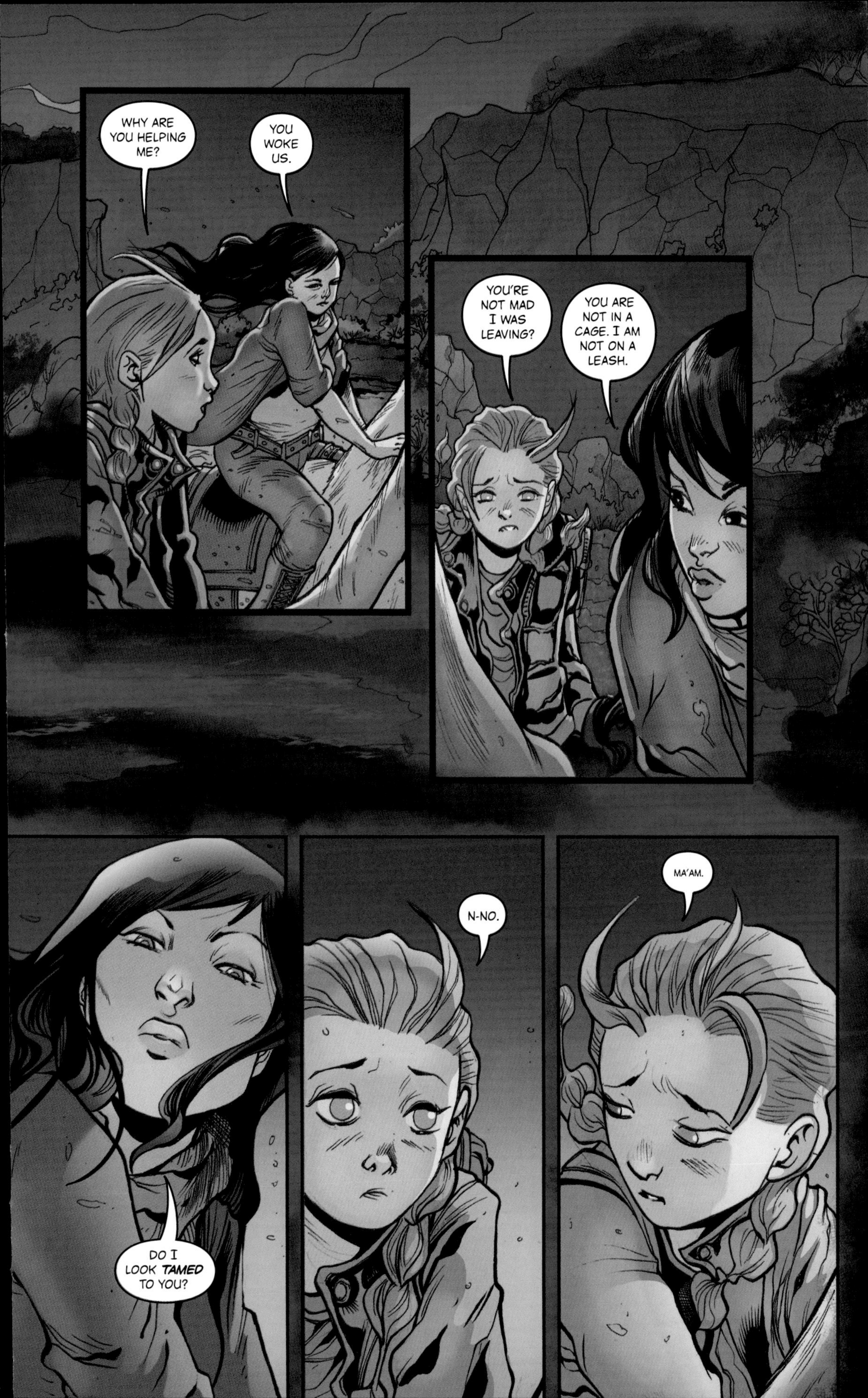
WHY ARE YOU HELPING ME?
YOU WOKE US.
YOU'RE NOT MAD I WAS LEAVING?
YOU ARE NOT IN A CAGE. I AM NOT ON A LEASH.
DO I LOOK **TAMED** TO YOU?
N-NO.
MA'AM.

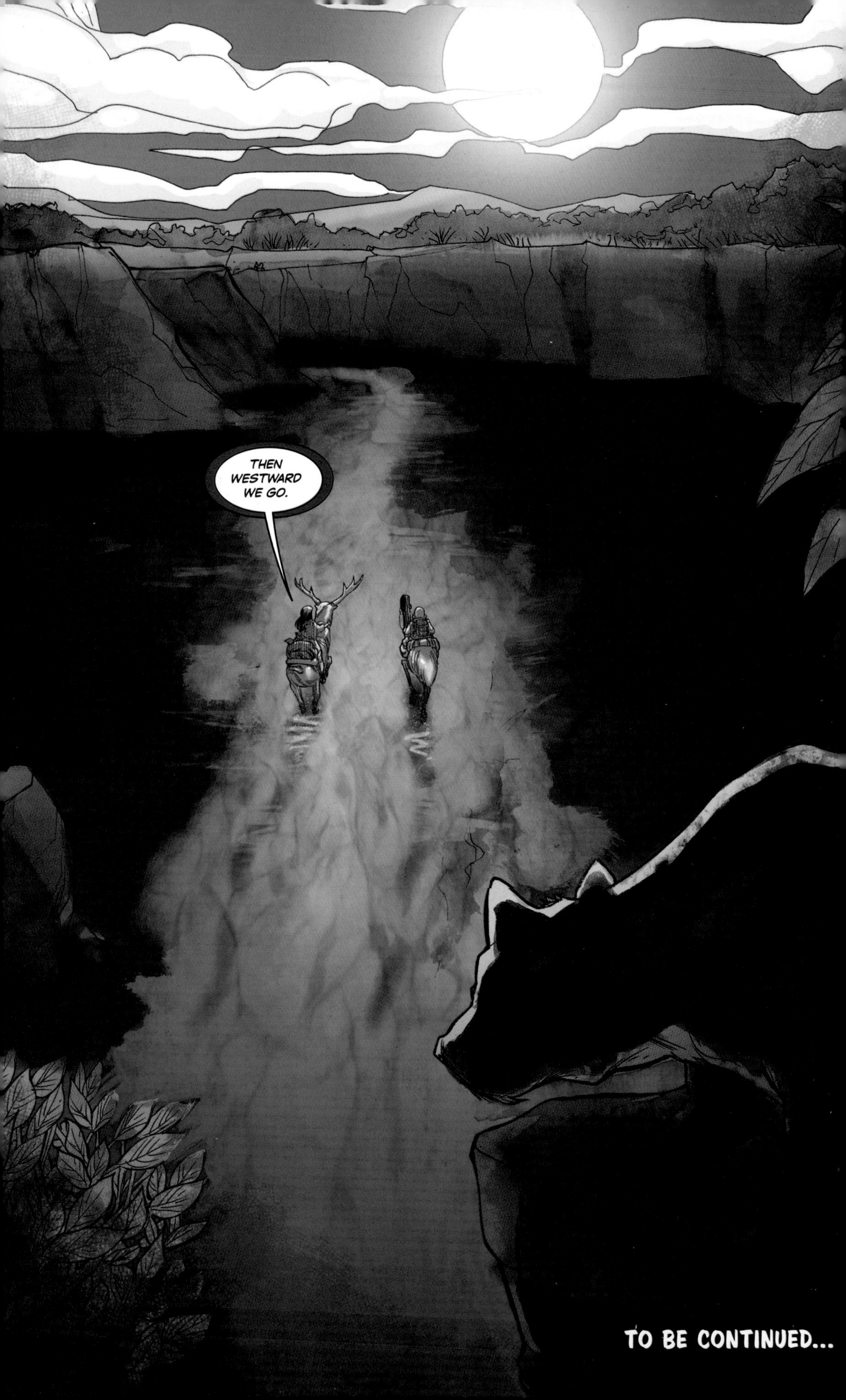
THEN WESTWARD WE GO.
TO BE CONTINUED...

ANIMOSITY TALES

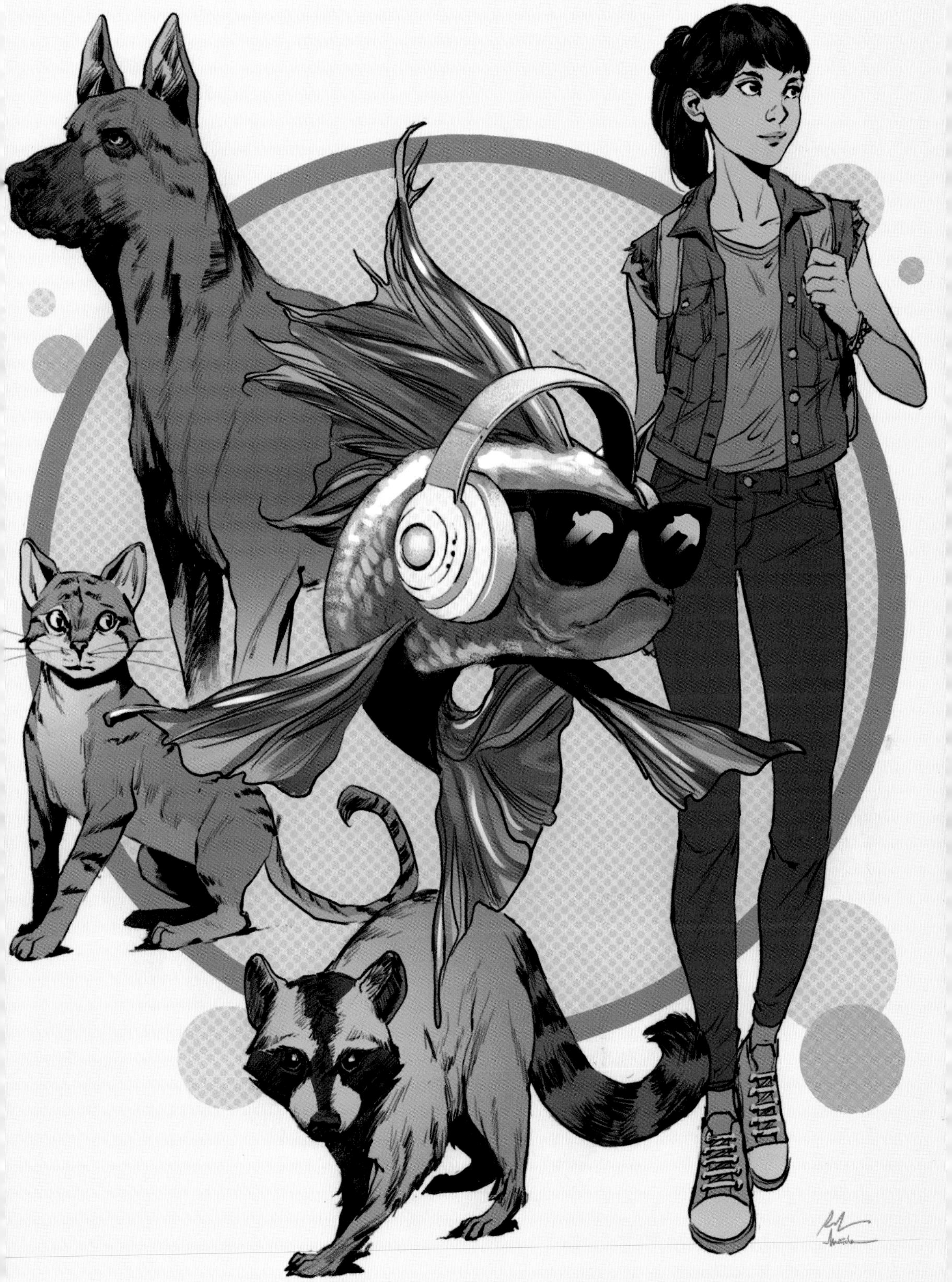

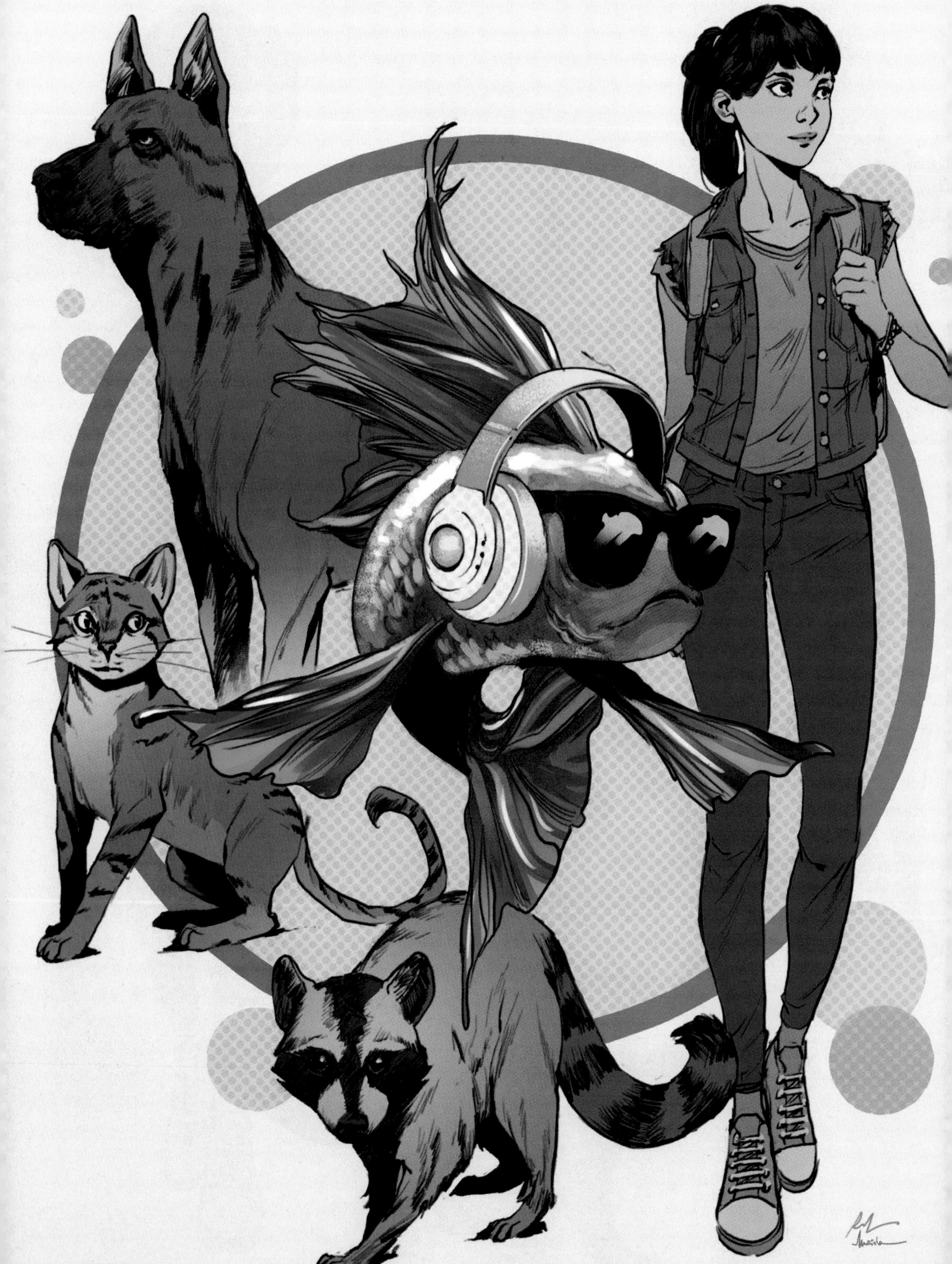

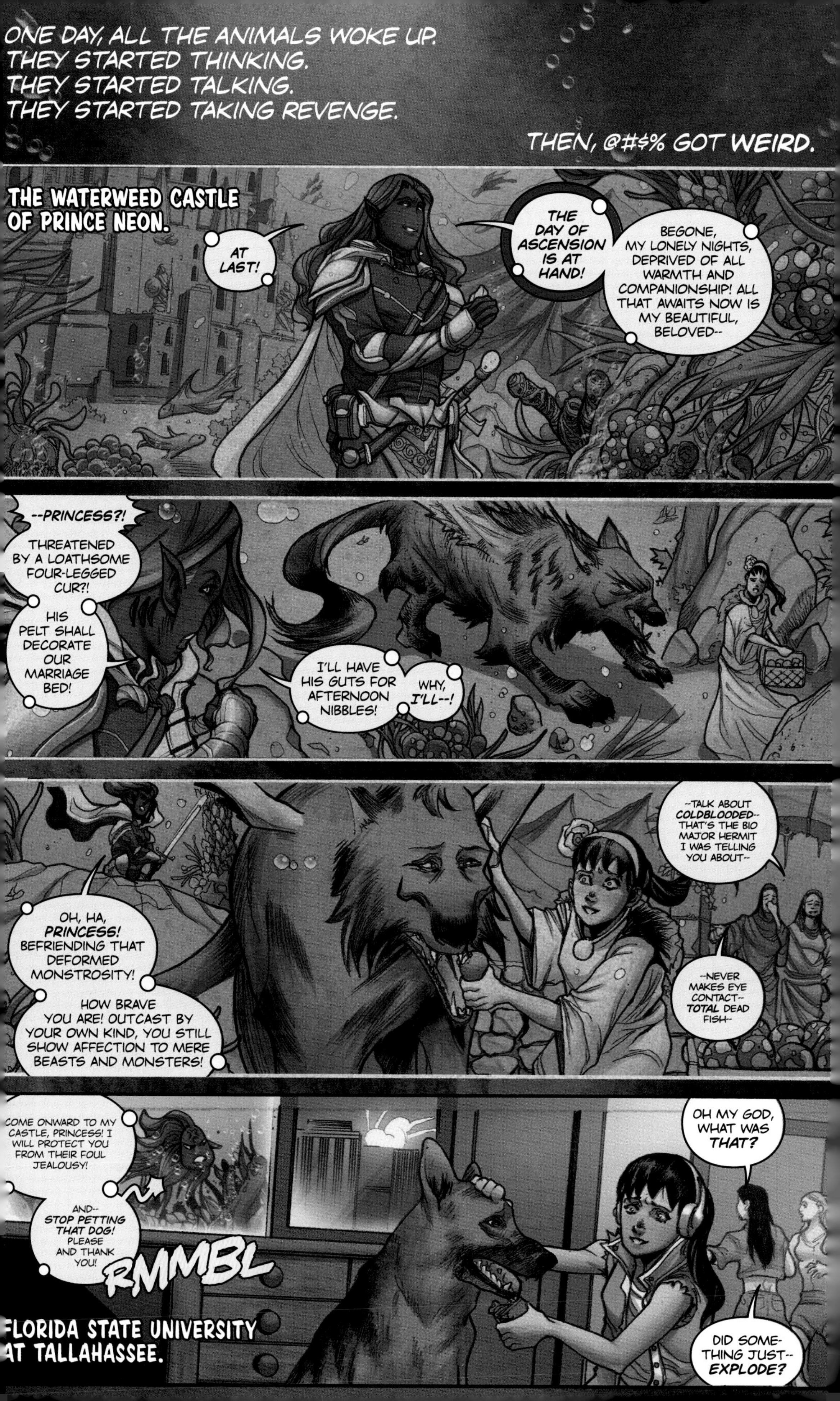
ONE DAY, ALL THE ANIMALS WOKE UP.
THEY STARTED THINKING.
THEY STARTED TALKING.
THEY STARTED TAKING REVENGE.
THEN, @#$% GOT WEIRD.
THE WATERWEED CASTLE OF PRINCE NEON.
AT LAST!
THE DAY OF ASCENSION IS AT HAND!
BEGONE, MY LONELY NIGHTS, DEPRIVED OF ALL WARMTH AND COMPANIONSHIP! ALL THAT AWAITS NOW IS MY BEAUTIFUL, BELOVED--
--PRINCESS?!
THREATENED BY A LOATHSOME FOUR-LEGGED CUR?!
HIS PELT SHALL DECORATE OUR MARRIAGE BED!
I'LL HAVE HIS GUTS FOR AFTERNOON NIBBLES!
WHY, I'LL--!
--TALK ABOUT COLDBLOODED--THAT'S THE BIO MAJOR HERMIT I WAS TELLING YOU ABOUT--
OH, HA, PRINCESS! BEFRIENDING THAT DEFORMED MONSTROSITY!
HOW BRAVE YOU ARE! OUTCAST BY YOUR OWN KIND, YOU STILL SHOW AFFECTION TO MERE BEASTS AND MONSTERS!
--NEVER MAKES EYE CONTACT--TOTAL DEAD FISH--
COME ONWARD TO MY CASTLE, PRINCESS! I WILL PROTECT YOU FROM THEIR FOUL JEALOUSY!
AND--STOP PETTING THAT DOG! PLEASE AND THANK YOU!
RMMBL
OH MY GOD, WHAT WAS THAT?
DID SOMETHING JUST--EXPLODE?
FLORIDA STATE UNIVERSITY AT TALLAHASSEE.

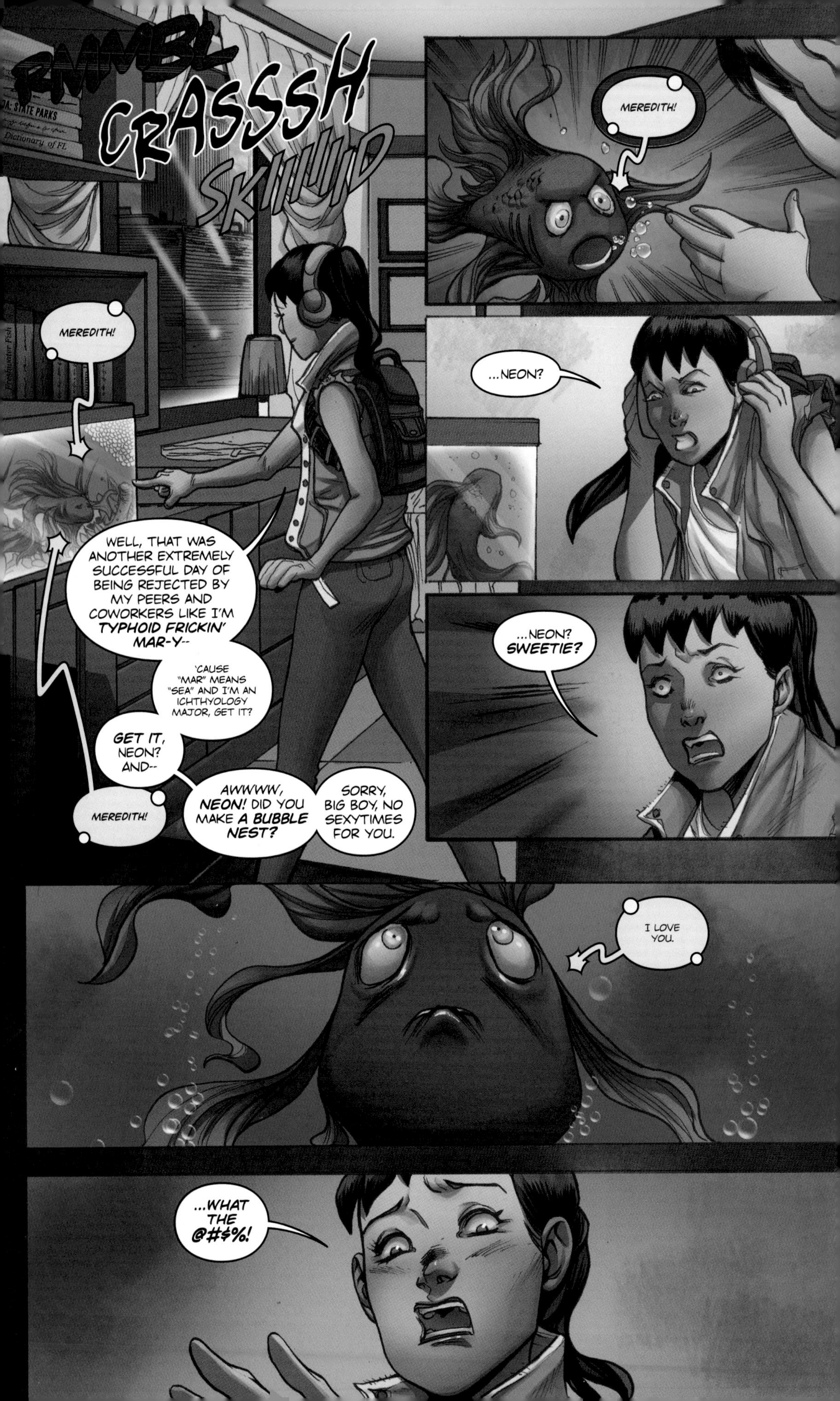
RMMBL
CRASSSH
SKIIIIID
DA: STATE PARKS
Dictionary of FL
Freshwater Fish
MEREDITH!
WELL, THAT WAS ANOTHER EXTREMELY SUCCESSFUL DAY OF BEING REJECTED BY MY PEERS AND COWORKERS LIKE I'M TYPHOID FRICKIN' MAR-Y--
'CAUSE "MAR" MEANS "SEA" AND I'M AN ICHTHYOLOGY MAJOR, GET IT?
GET IT, NEON? AND--
MEREDITH!
AWWWW, NEON! DID YOU MAKE A BUBBLE NEST?
SORRY, BIG BOY, NO SEXYTIMES FOR YOU.
MEREDITH!
...NEON?
...NEON? SWEETIE?
I LOVE YOU.
...WHAT THE @#$%!

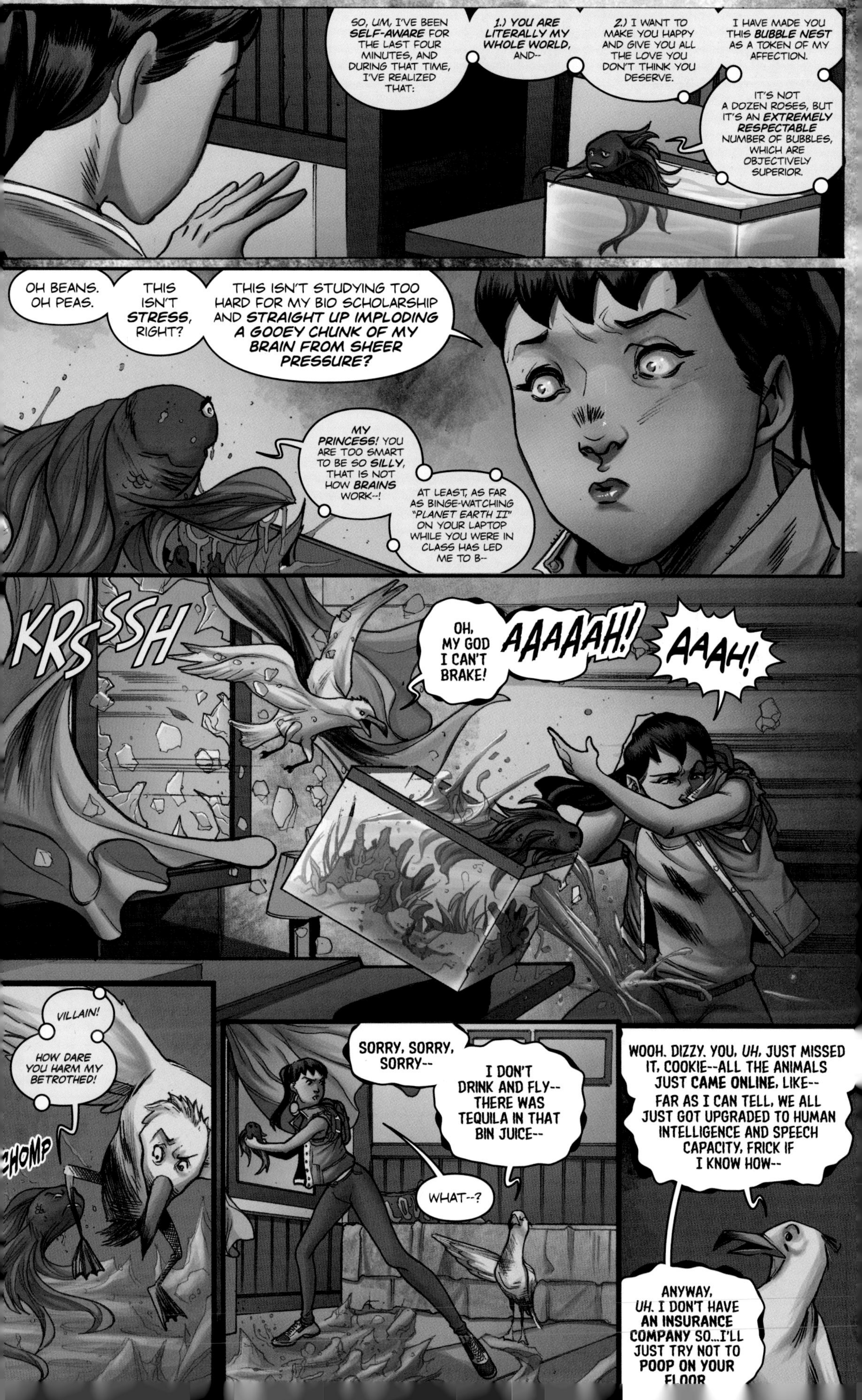

SO, UM, I'VE BEEN SELF-AWARE FOR THE LAST FOUR MINUTES, AND DURING THAT TIME, I'VE REALIZED THAT:
1.) YOU ARE LITERALLY MY WHOLE WORLD, AND--
2.) I WANT TO MAKE YOU HAPPY AND GIVE YOU ALL THE LOVE YOU DON'T THINK YOU DESERVE.
I HAVE MADE YOU THIS BUBBLE NEST AS A TOKEN OF MY AFFECTION.
IT'S NOT A DOZEN ROSES, BUT IT'S AN EXTREMELY RESPECTABLE NUMBER OF BUBBLES, WHICH ARE OBJECTIVELY SUPERIOR.
OH BEANS. OH PEAS.
THIS ISN'T STRESS, RIGHT?
THIS ISN'T STUDYING TOO HARD FOR MY BIO SCHOLARSHIP AND STRAIGHT UP IMPLODING A GOOEY CHUNK OF MY BRAIN FROM SHEER PRESSURE?
MY PRINCESS! YOU ARE TOO SMART TO BE SO SILLY, THAT IS NOT HOW BRAINS WORK--!
AT LEAST, AS FAR AS BINGE-WATCHING "PLANET EARTH II" ON YOUR LAPTOP WHILE YOU WERE IN CLASS HAS LED ME TO B--
KRSSSH
OH, MY GOD I CAN'T BRAKE!
AAAAAH!
AAAH!
VILLAIN!
HOW DARE YOU HARM MY BETROTHED!
SORRY, SORRY, SORRY--
I DON'T DRINK AND FLY-- THERE WAS TEQUILA IN THAT BIN JUICE--
WHAT--?
WOOH. DIZZY. YOU, UH, JUST MISSED IT, COOKIE--ALL THE ANIMALS JUST CAME ONLINE, LIKE-- FAR AS I CAN TELL, WE ALL JUST GOT UPGRADED TO HUMAN INTELLIGENCE AND SPEECH CAPACITY, FRICK IF I KNOW HOW--
ANYWAY, UH, I DON'T HAVE AN INSURANCE COMPANY SO...I'LL JUST TRY NOT TO POOP ON YOUR FLOOR

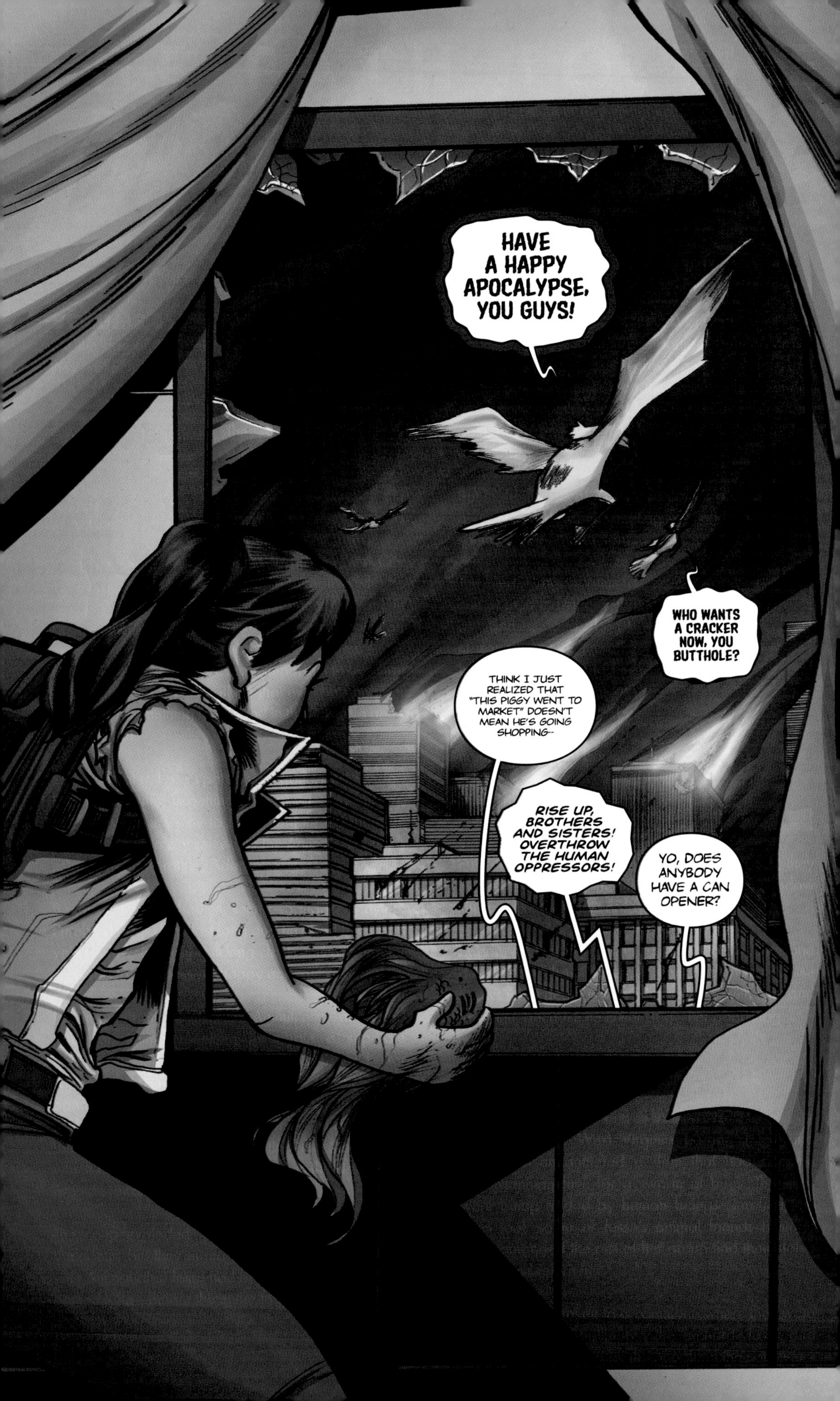
HAVE A HAPPY APOCALYPSE, YOU GUYS!
WHO WANTS A CRACKER NOW, YOU BUTTHOLE?
THINK I JUST REALIZED THAT "THIS PIGGY WENT TO MARKET" DOESN'T MEAN HE'S GOING SHOPPING--
RISE UP, BROTHERS AND SISTERS! OVERTHROW THE HUMAN OPPRESSORS!
YO, DOES ANYBODY HAVE A CAN OPENER?

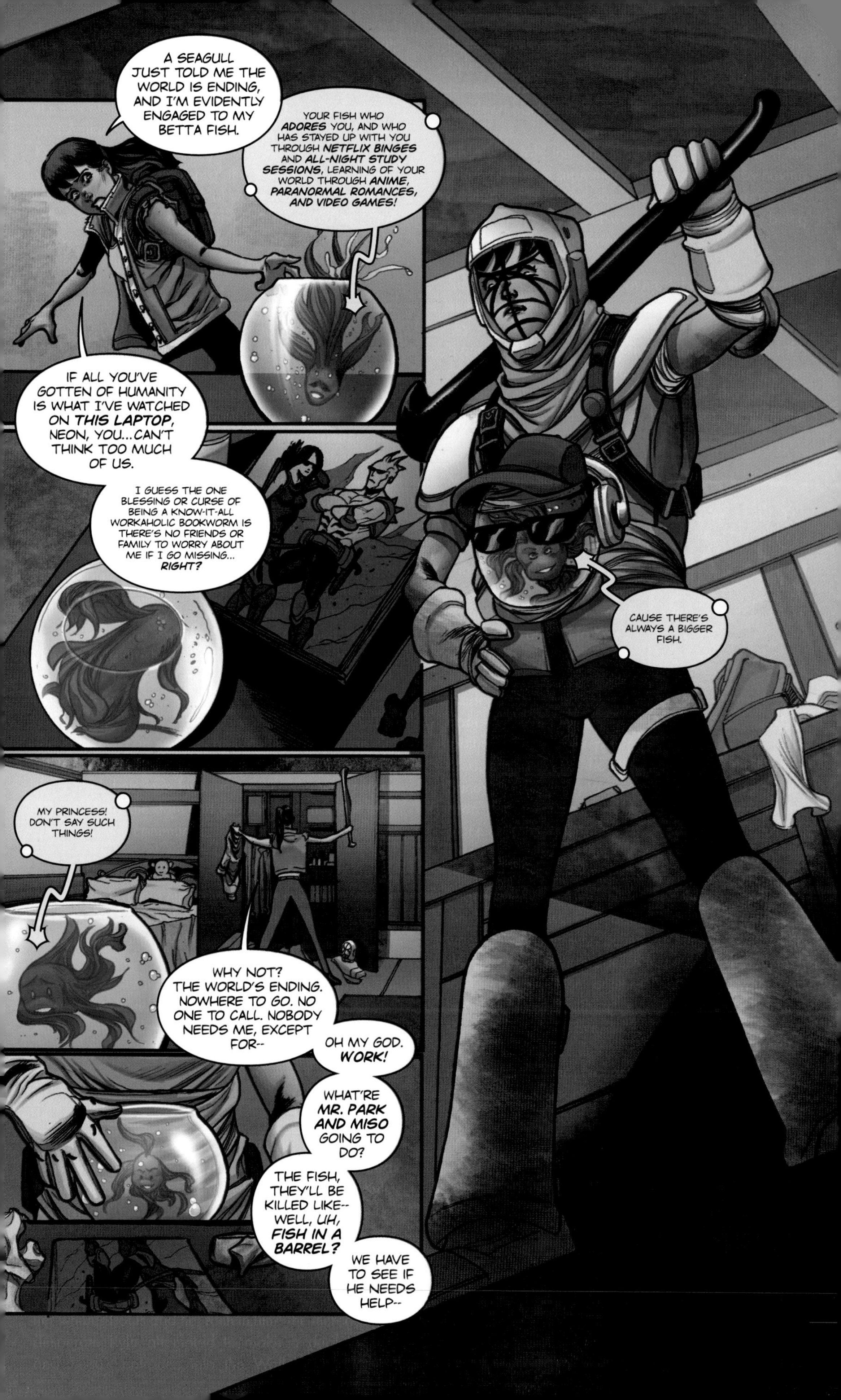
A SEAGULL JUST TOLD ME THE WORLD IS ENDING, AND I'M EVIDENTLY ENGAGED TO MY BETTA FISH.
YOUR FISH WHO ADORES YOU, AND WHO HAS STAYED UP WITH YOU THROUGH NETFLIX BINGES AND ALL-NIGHT STUDY SESSIONS, LEARNING OF YOUR WORLD THROUGH ANIME, PARANORMAL ROMANCES, AND VIDEO GAMES!
IF ALL YOU'VE GOTTEN OF HUMANITY IS WHAT I'VE WATCHED ON THIS LAPTOP, NEON, YOU...CAN'T THINK TOO MUCH OF US.
I GUESS THE ONE BLESSING OR CURSE OF BEING A KNOW-IT-ALL WORKAHOLIC BOOKWORM IS THERE'S NO FRIENDS OR FAMILY TO WORRY ABOUT ME IF I GO MISSING... RIGHT?
MY PRINCESS! DON'T SAY SUCH THINGS!
WHY NOT? THE WORLD'S ENDING. NOWHERE TO GO. NO ONE TO CALL. NOBODY NEEDS ME, EXCEPT FOR--
OH MY GOD. WORK!
WHAT'RE MR. PARK AND MISO GOING TO DO?
THE FISH, THEY'LL BE KILLED LIKE-- WELL, UH, FISH IN A BARREL?
WE HAVE TO SEE IF HE NEEDS HELP--
CAUSE THERE'S ALWAYS A BIGGER FISH.

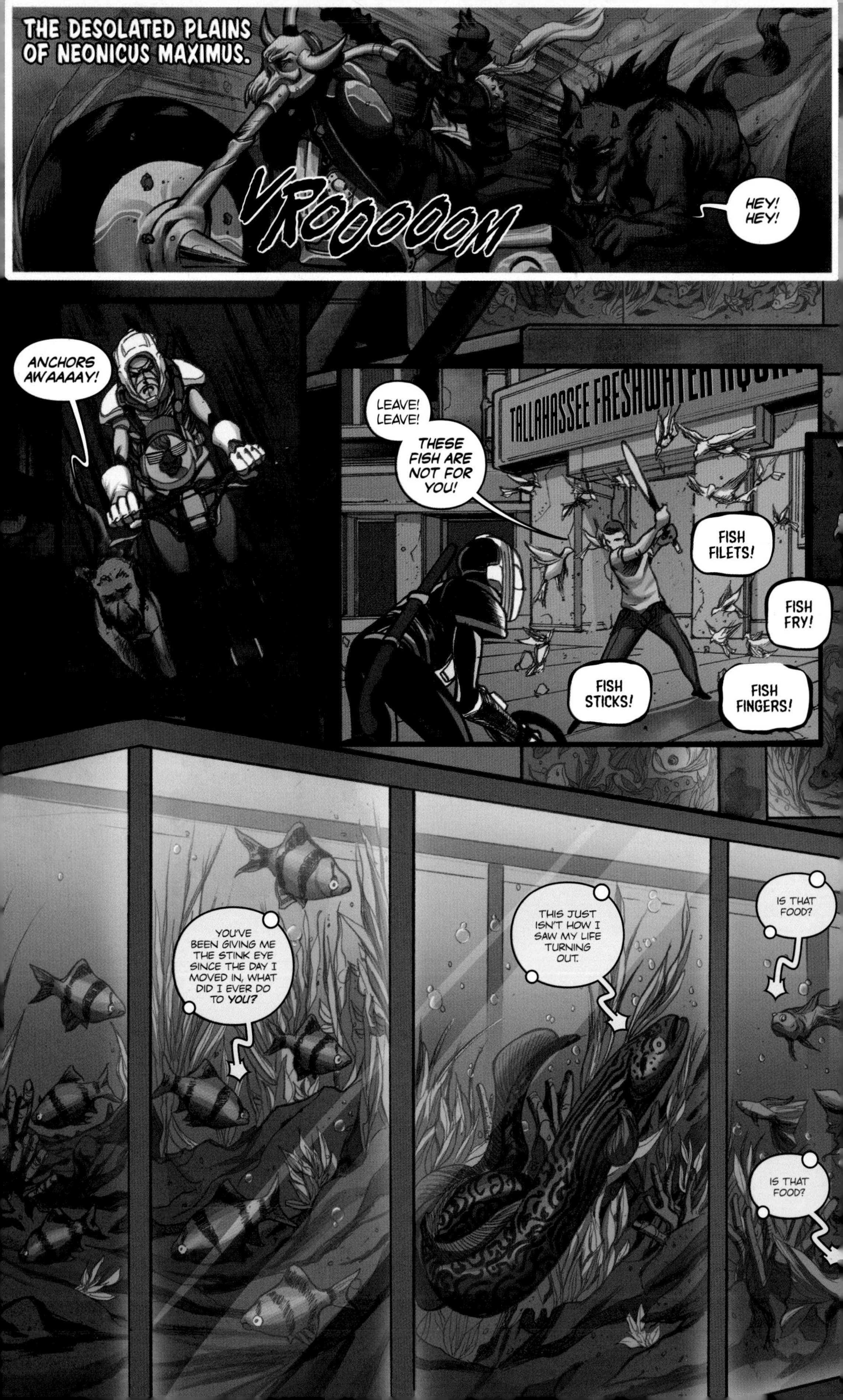
THE DESOLATED PLAINS OF NEONICUS MAXIMUS.
VROOOOOM
HEY! HEY!
ANCHORS AWAAAAY!
TALLAHASSEE FRESHWATER AQUA
LEAVE! LEAVE!
THESE FISH ARE NOT FOR YOU!
FISH FILETS!
FISH FRY!
FISH STICKS!
FISH FINGERS!
YOU'VE BEEN GIVING ME THE STINK EYE SINCE THE DAY I MOVED IN, WHAT DID I EVER DO TO YOU?
THIS JUST ISN'T HOW I SAW MY LIFE TURNING OUT.
IS THAT FOOD?
IS THAT FOOD?

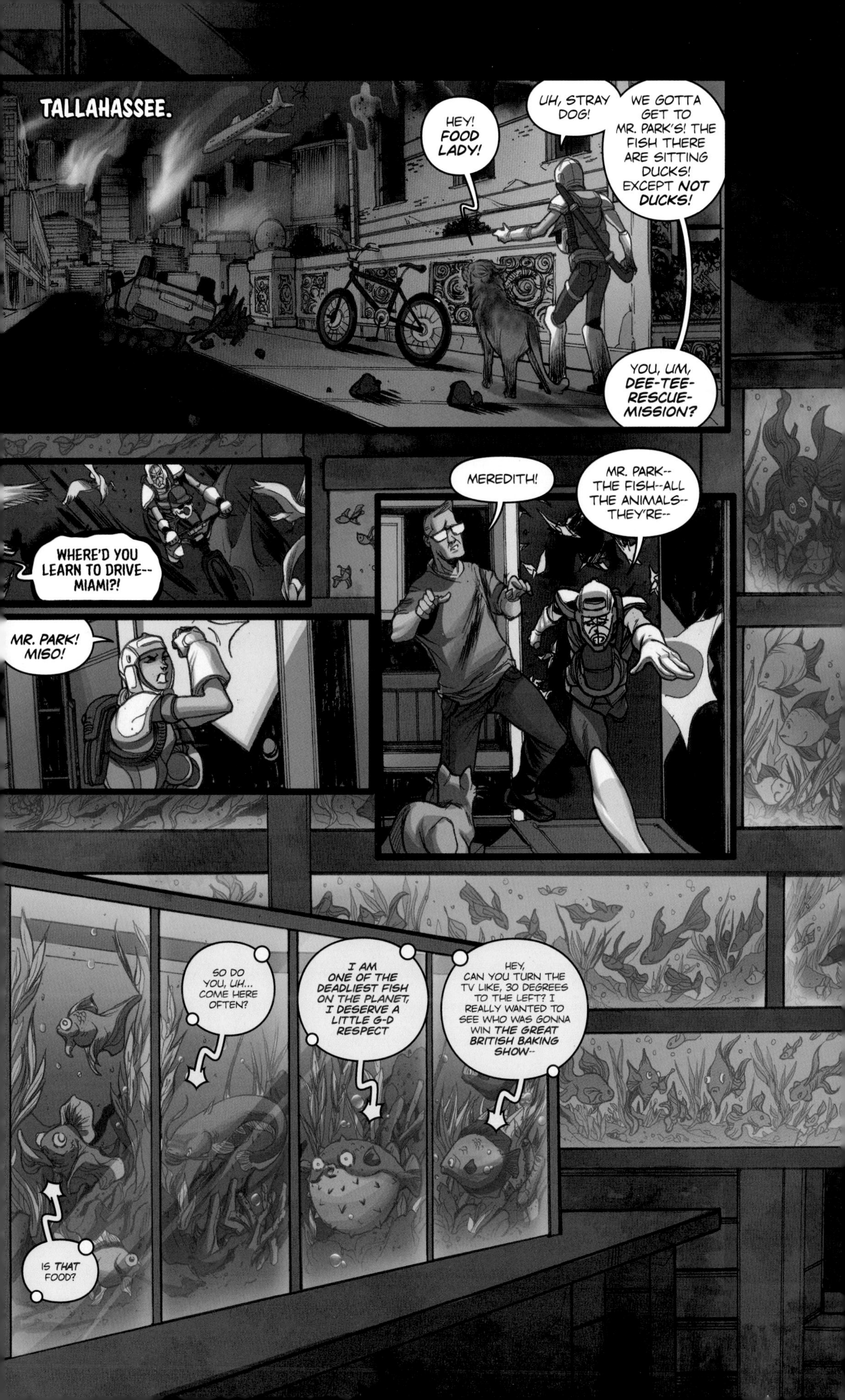
TALLAHASSEE.
HEY! FOOD LADY!
UH, STRAY DOG!
WE GOTTA GET TO MR. PARK'S! THE FISH THERE ARE SITTING DUCKS! EXCEPT NOT DUCKS!
YOU, UM, DEE-TEE-RESCUE-MISSION?
WHERE'D YOU LEARN TO DRIVE-- MIAMI?!
MR. PARK! MISO!
MEREDITH!
MR. PARK-- THE FISH--ALL THE ANIMALS-- THEY'RE--
SO DO YOU, UH... COME HERE OFTEN?
I AM ONE OF THE DEADLIEST FISH ON THE PLANET, I DESERVE A LITTLE G-D RESPECT
HEY, CAN YOU TURN THE TV LIKE, 30 DEGREES TO THE LEFT? I REALLY WANTED TO SEE WHO WAS GONNA WIN THE GREAT BRITISH BAKING SHOW--
IS THAT FOOD?

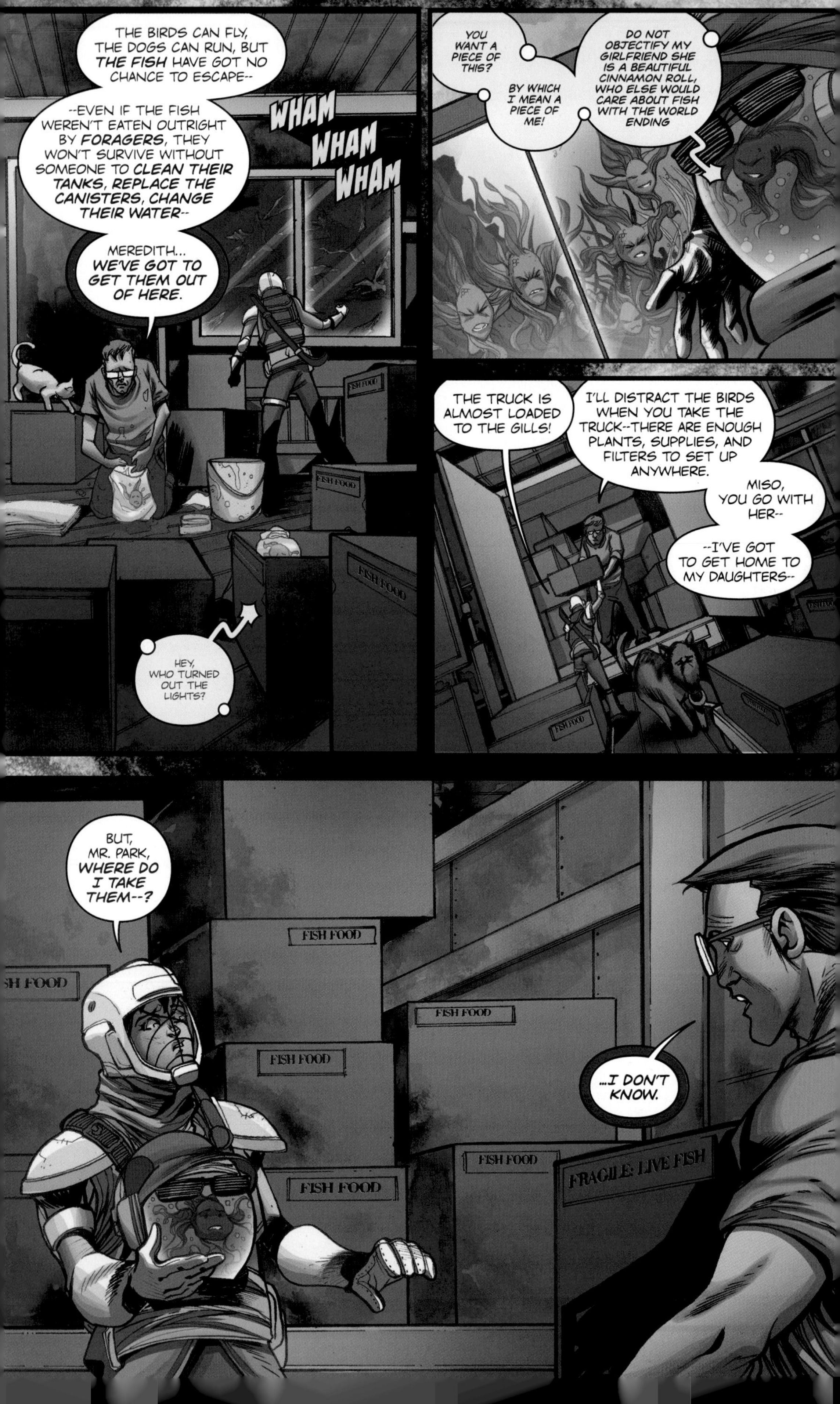
THE BIRDS CAN FLY, THE DOGS CAN RUN, BUT THE FISH HAVE GOT NO CHANCE TO ESCAPE--
--EVEN IF THE FISH WEREN'T EATEN OUTRIGHT BY FORAGERS, THEY WON'T SURVIVE WITHOUT SOMEONE TO CLEAN THEIR TANKS, REPLACE THE CANISTERS, CHANGE THEIR WATER--
WHAM
WHAM
WHAM
MEREDITH... WE'VE GOT TO GET THEM OUT OF HERE.
FISH FOOD
FISH FOOD
FISH FOOD
HEY, WHO TURNED OUT THE LIGHTS?
YOU WANT A PIECE OF THIS?
BY WHICH I MEAN A PIECE OF ME!
DO NOT OBJECTIFY MY GIRLFRIEND SHE IS A BEAUTIFUL CINNAMON ROLL, WHO ELSE WOULD CARE ABOUT FISH WITH THE WORLD ENDING
THE TRUCK IS ALMOST LOADED TO THE GILLS!
I'LL DISTRACT THE BIRDS WHEN YOU TAKE THE TRUCK--THERE ARE ENOUGH PLANTS, SUPPLIES, AND FILTERS TO SET UP ANYWHERE.
MISO, YOU GO WITH HER--
--I'VE GOT TO GET HOME TO MY DAUGHTERS--
BUT, MR. PARK, WHERE DO I TAKE THEM--?
FISH FOOD
FISH FOOD
FISH FOOD
FISH FOOD
FISH FOOD
FISH FOOD
FRAGILE: LIVE FISH
...I DON'T KNOW.

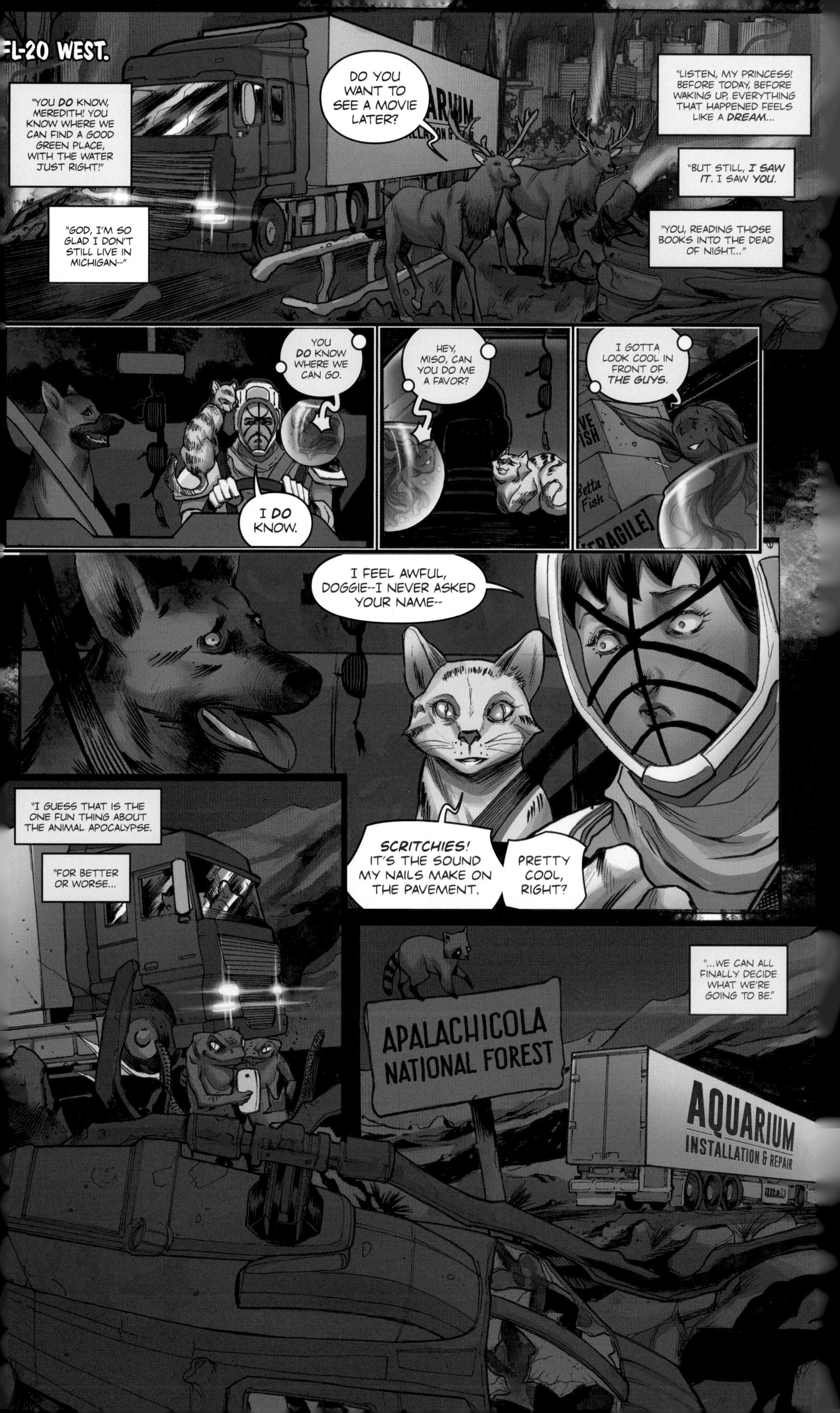
FL-20 WEST.
"YOU DO KNOW, MEREDITH! YOU KNOW WHERE WE CAN FIND A GOOD GREEN PLACE, WITH THE WATER JUST RIGHT!"
"GOD, I'M SO GLAD I DON'T STILL LIVE IN MICHIGAN--"
DO YOU WANT TO SEE A MOVIE LATER?
"LISTEN, MY PRINCESS! BEFORE TODAY, BEFORE WAKING UP, EVERYTHING THAT HAPPENED FEELS LIKE A DREAM...
"BUT STILL, I SAW IT. I SAW YOU.
"YOU, READING THOSE BOOKS INTO THE DEAD OF NIGHT..."
YOU DO KNOW WHERE WE CAN GO.
I DO KNOW.
HEY, MISO, CAN YOU DO ME A FAVOR?
I GOTTA LOOK COOL IN FRONT OF THE GUYS.
Betta Fish
FRAGILE
I FEEL AWFUL, DOGGIE--I NEVER ASKED YOUR NAME--
SCRITCHIES! IT'S THE SOUND MY NAILS MAKE ON THE PAVEMENT.
PRETTY COOL, RIGHT?
"I GUESS THAT IS THE ONE FUN THING ABOUT THE ANIMAL APOCALYPSE.
"FOR BETTER OR WORSE...
"...WE CAN ALL FINALLY DECIDE WHAT WE'RE GOING TO BE."
APALACHICOLA NATIONAL FOREST
AQUARIUM INSTALLATION & REPAIR

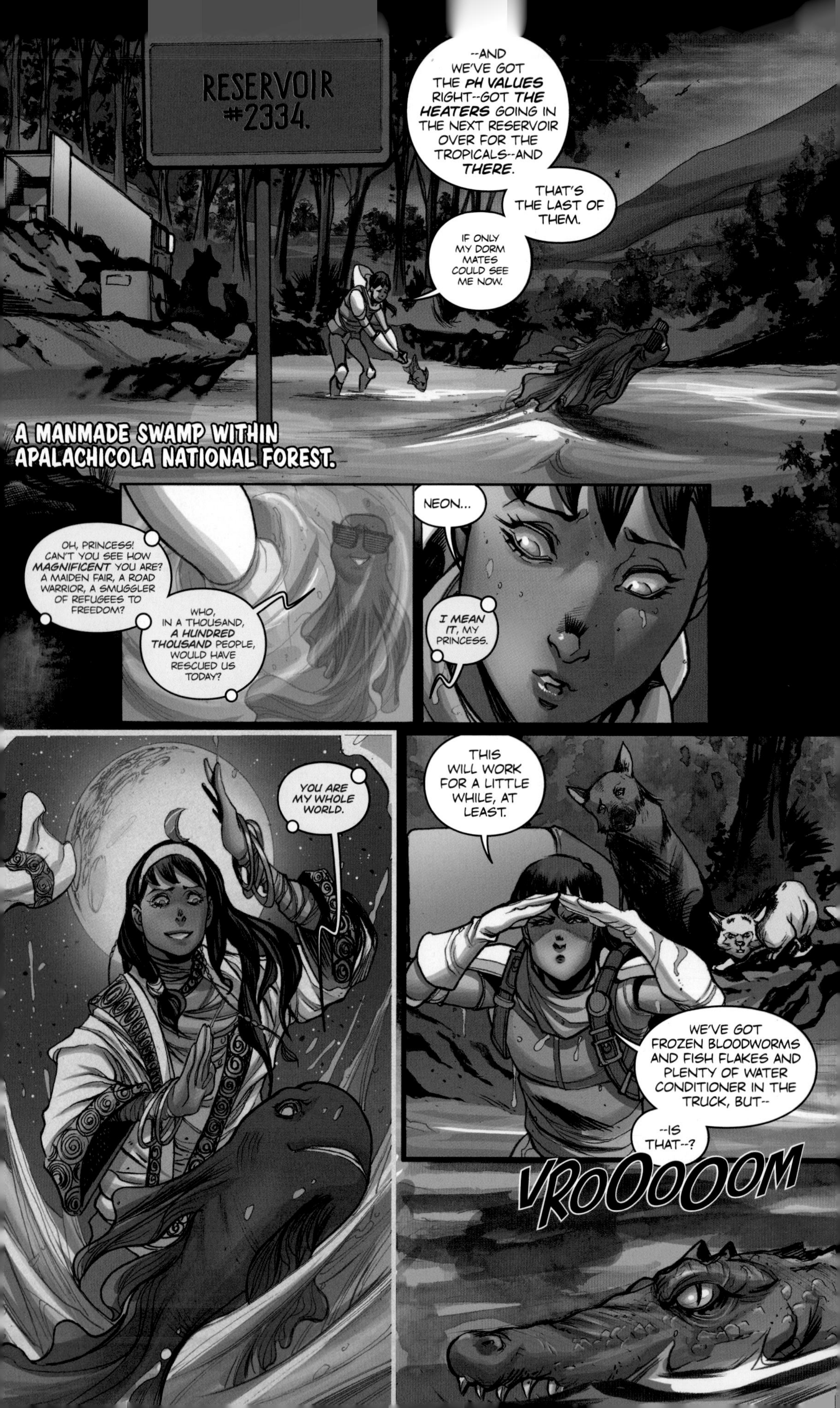

RESERVOIR #2334.
--AND WE'VE GOT THE PH VALUES RIGHT--GOT THE HEATERS GOING IN THE NEXT RESERVOIR OVER FOR THE TROPICALS--AND THERE.
THAT'S THE LAST OF THEM.
IF ONLY MY DORM MATES COULD SEE ME NOW.
A MANMADE SWAMP WITHIN APALACHICOLA NATIONAL FOREST.
OH, PRINCESS! CAN'T YOU SEE HOW MAGNIFICENT YOU ARE? A MAIDEN FAIR, A ROAD WARRIOR, A SMUGGLER OF REFUGEES TO FREEDOM?
WHO, IN A THOUSAND, A HUNDRED THOUSAND PEOPLE, WOULD HAVE RESCUED US TODAY?
NEON...
I MEAN IT, MY PRINCESS.
YOU ARE MY WHOLE WORLD.
THIS WILL WORK FOR A LITTLE WHILE, AT LEAST.
WE'VE GOT FROZEN BLOODWORMS AND FISH FLAKES AND PLENTY OF WATER CONDITIONER IN THE TRUCK, BUT--
--IS THAT--?
VROOOOOOM

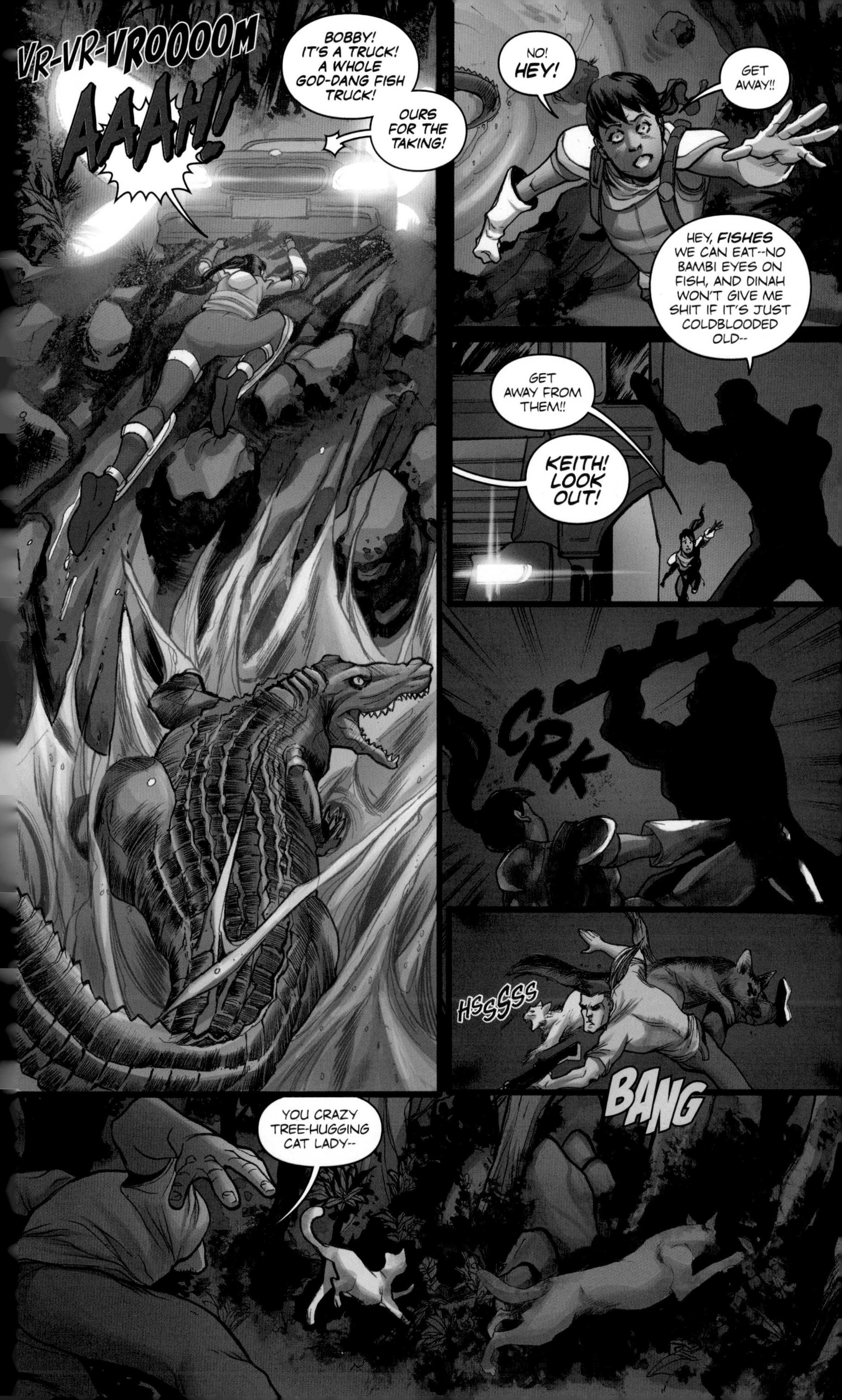
VR-VR-VROOOOM
AAAH!
BOBBY! IT'S A TRUCK! A WHOLE GOD-DANG FISH TRUCK!
OURS FOR THE TAKING!
NO! HEY!
GET AWAY!!
HEY, FISHES WE CAN EAT--NO BAMBI EYES ON FISH, AND DINAH WON'T GIVE ME SHIT IF IT'S JUST COLDBLOODED OLD--
GET AWAY FROM THEM!!
KEITH! LOOK OUT!
CRK
HSSSSS
BANG
YOU CRAZY TREE-HUGGING CAT LADY--

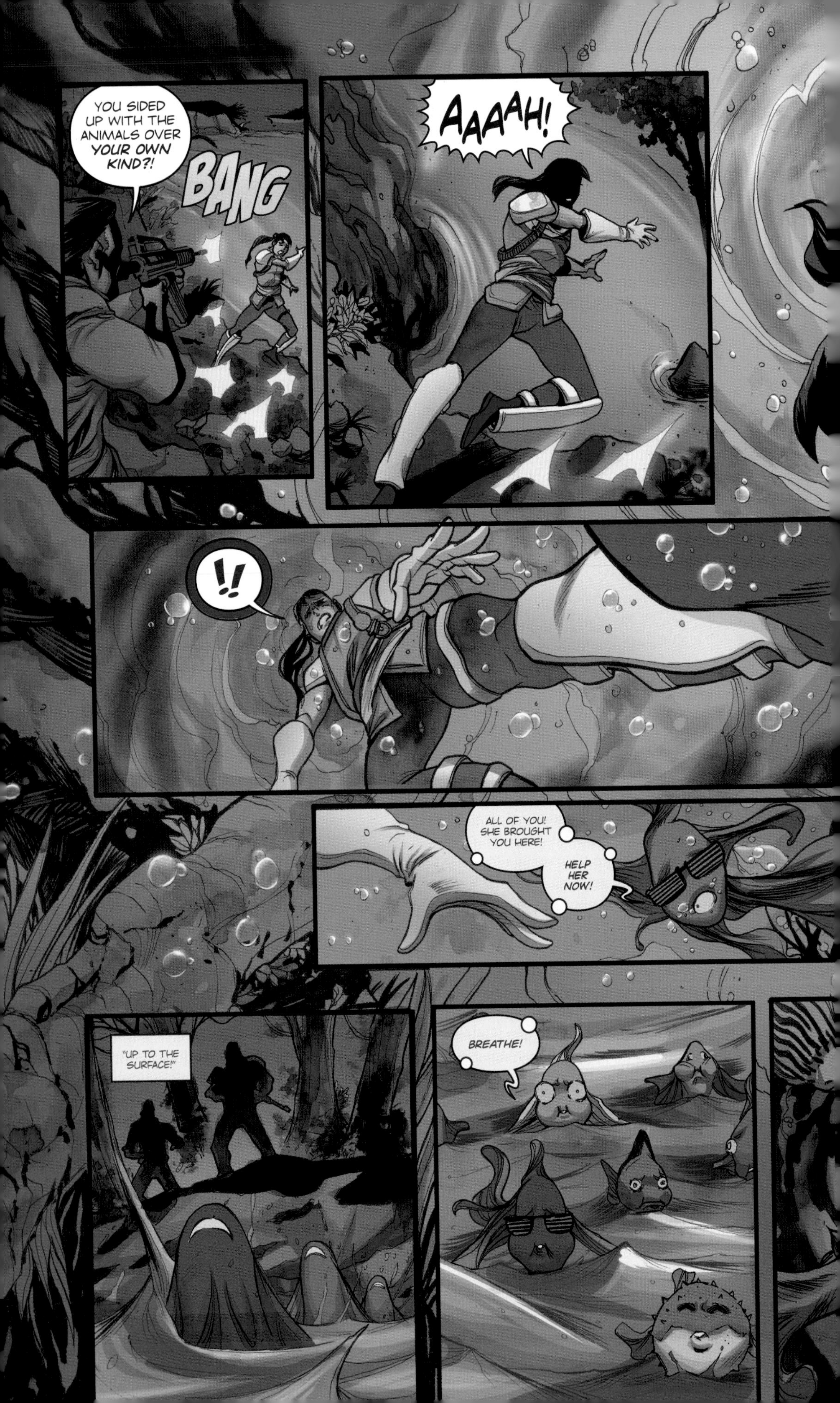
YOU SIDED UP WITH THE ANIMALS OVER YOUR OWN KIND?!
BANG
AAAAH!
!!
ALL OF YOU! SHE BROUGHT YOU HERE!
HELP HER NOW!
"UP TO THE SURFACE!"
BREATHE!

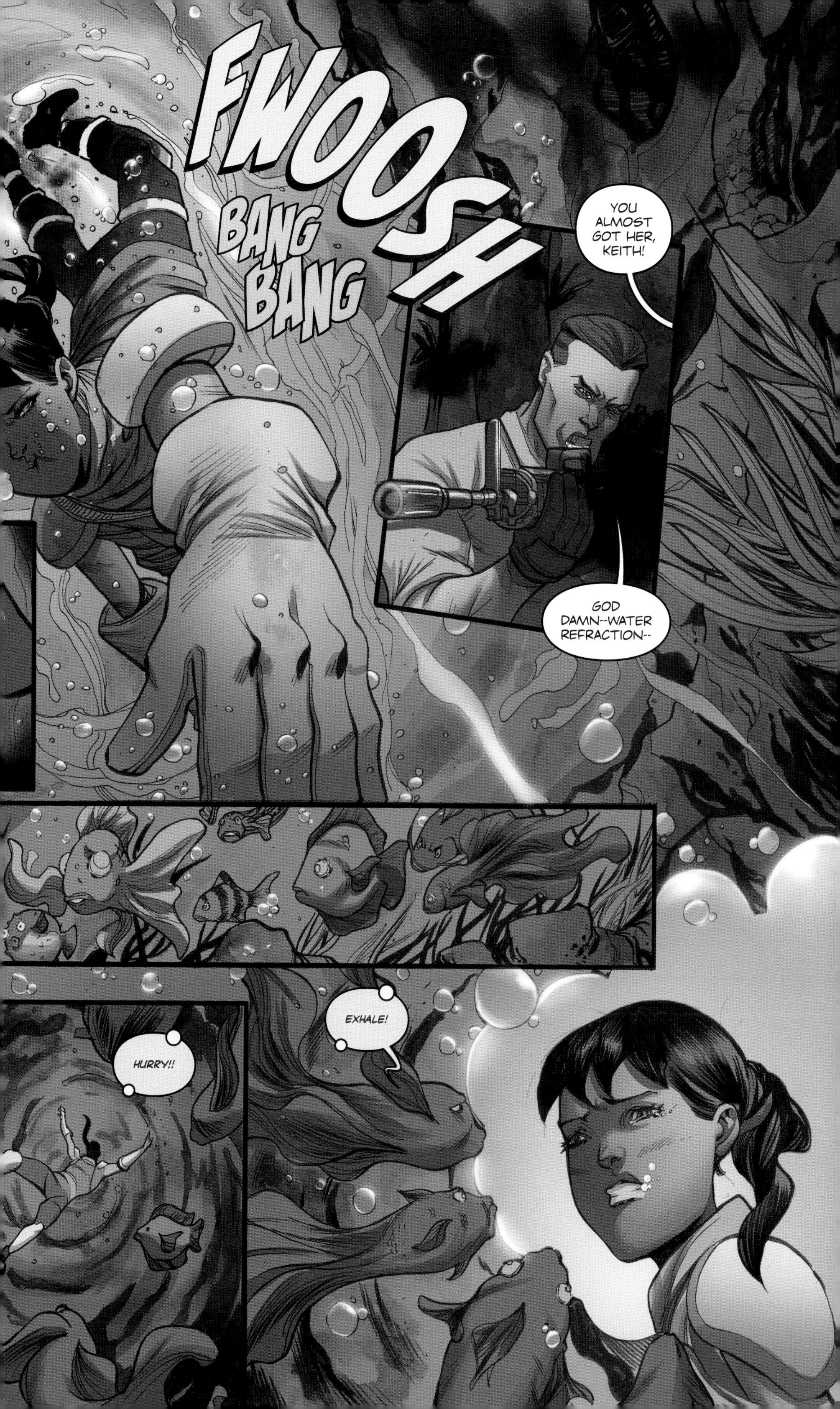
FWOOSH
BANG
BANG
YOU ALMOST GOT HER, KEITH!
GOD DAMN--WATER REFRACTION--
EXHALE!
HURRY!!

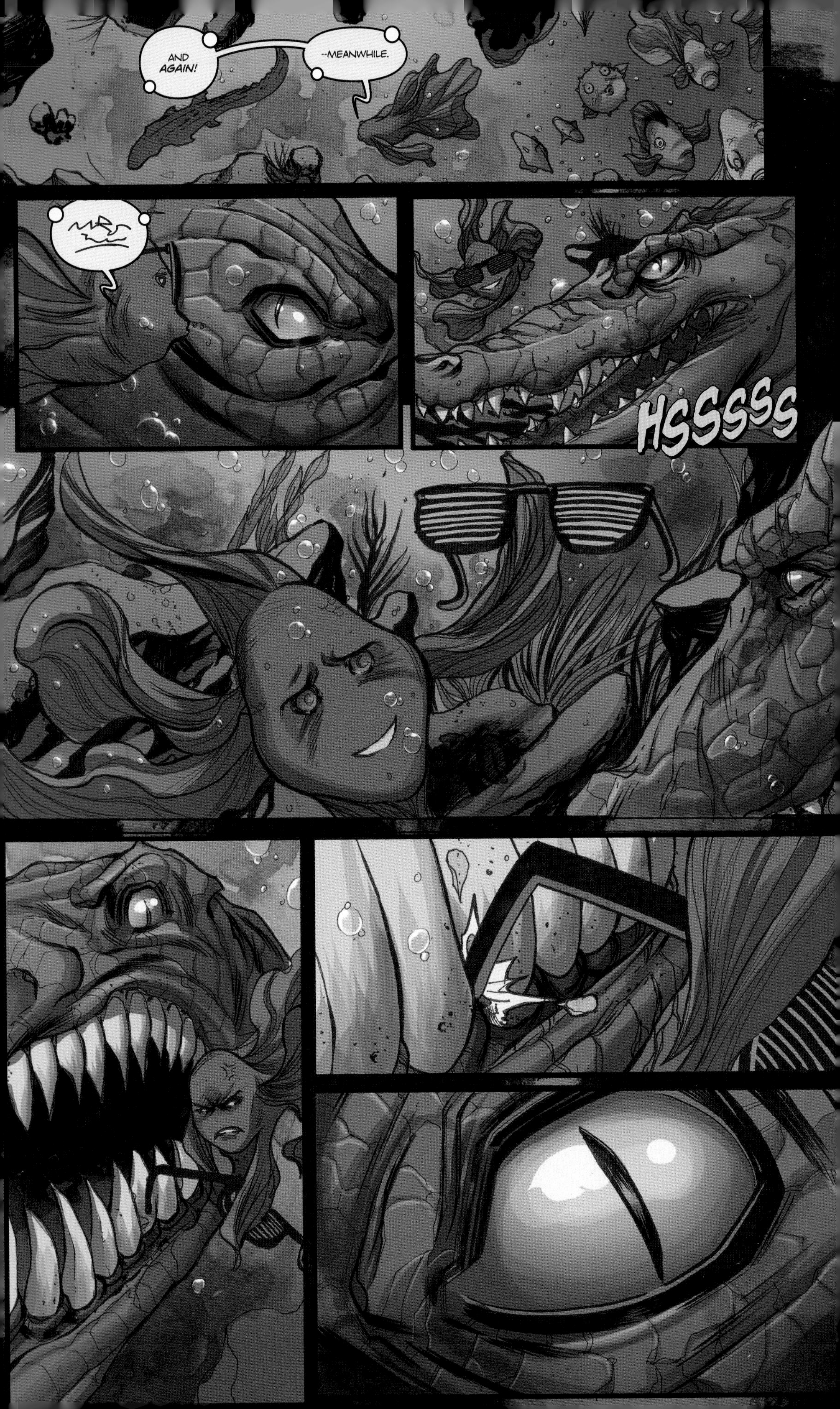
AND AGAIN!
--MEANWHILE.
HSSSSS

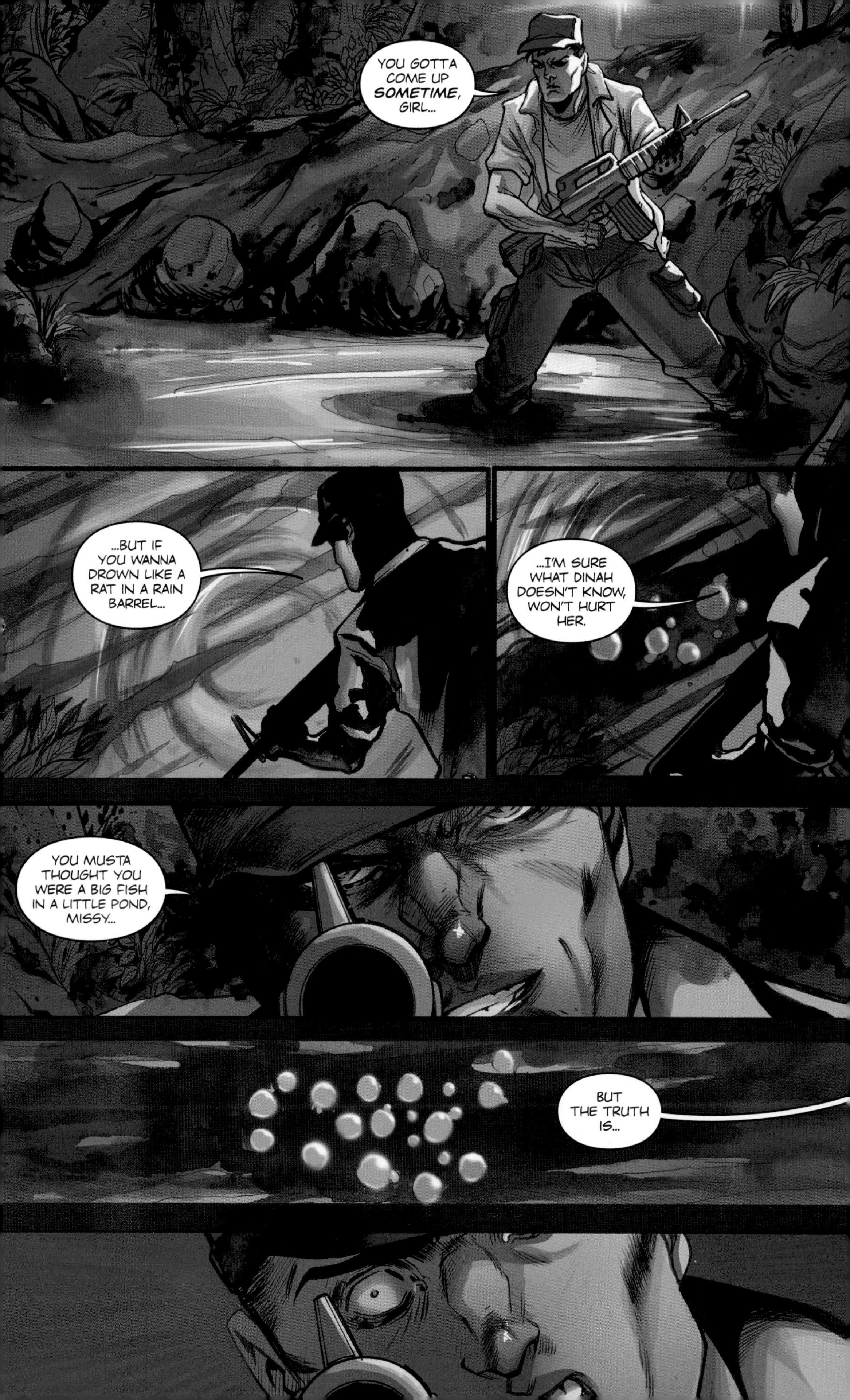
YOU GOTTA COME UP SOMETIME, GIRL...
...BUT IF YOU WANNA DROWN LIKE A RAT IN A RAIN BARREL...
...I'M SURE WHAT DINAH DOESN'T KNOW, WON'T HURT HER.
YOU MUSTA THOUGHT YOU WERE A BIG FISH IN A LITTLE POND, MISSY...
BUT THE TRUTH IS...

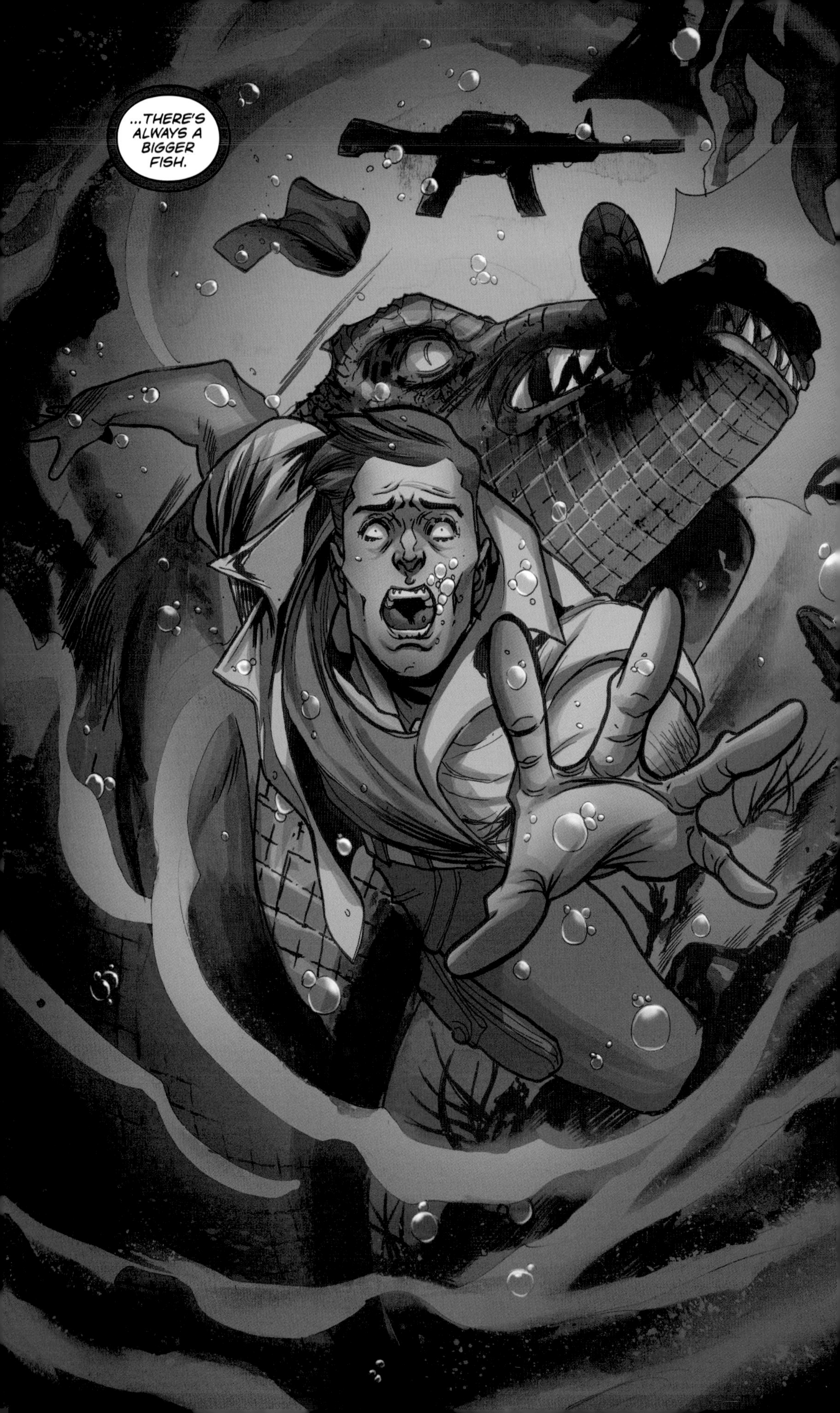
...THERE'S ALWAYS A BIGGER FISH.

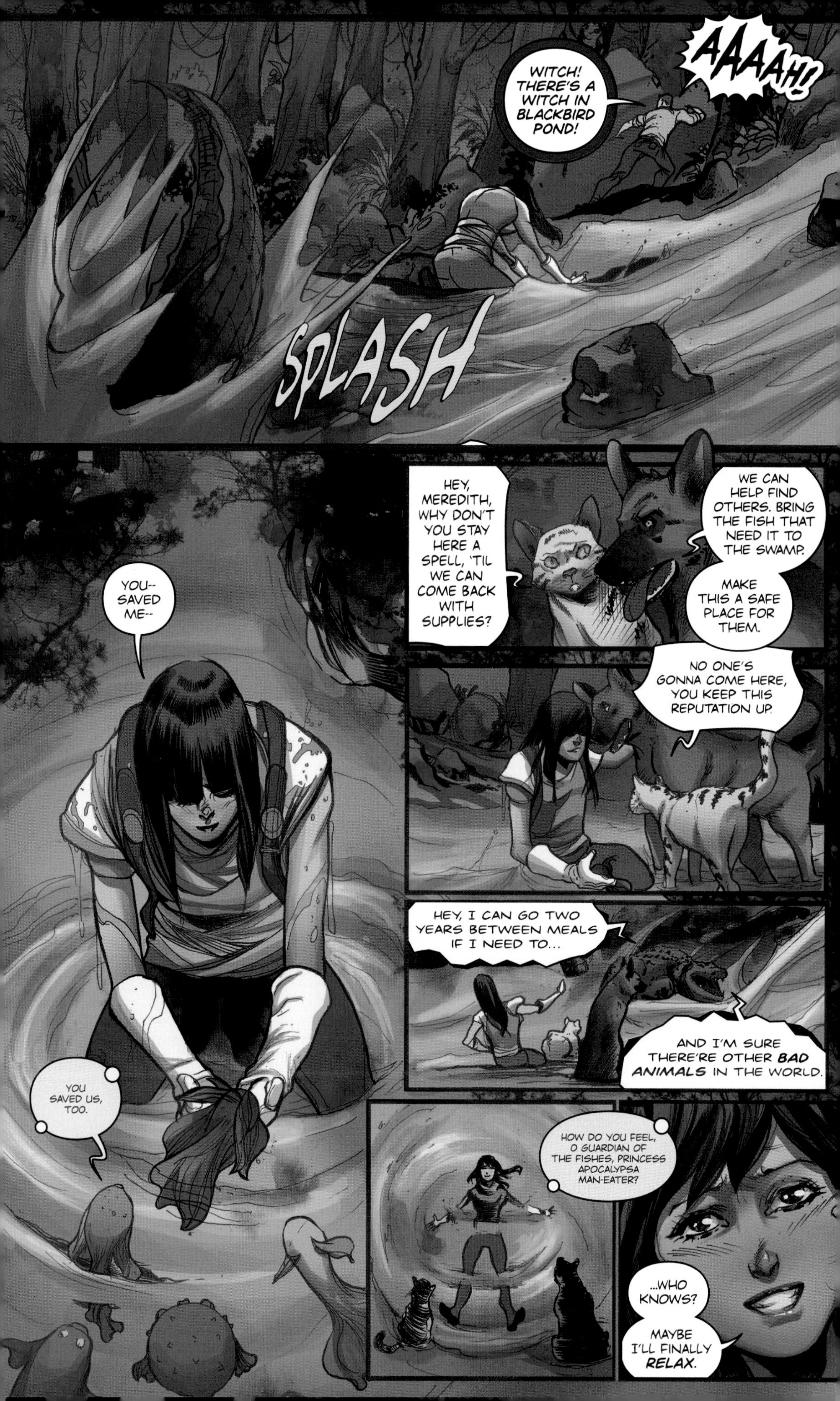
AAAAH!
WITCH! THERE'S A WITCH IN BLACKBIRD POND!
SPLASH
YOU-- SAVED ME--
HEY, MEREDITH, WHY DON'T YOU STAY HERE A SPELL, 'TIL WE CAN COME BACK WITH SUPPLIES?
WE CAN HELP FIND OTHERS. BRING THE FISH THAT NEED IT TO THE SWAMP.
MAKE THIS A SAFE PLACE FOR THEM.
NO ONE'S GONNA COME HERE, YOU KEEP THIS REPUTATION UP.
HEY, I CAN GO TWO YEARS BETWEEN MEALS IF I NEED TO...
AND I'M SURE THERE'RE OTHER BAD ANIMALS IN THE WORLD.
YOU SAVED US, TOO.
HOW DO YOU FEEL, O GUARDIAN OF THE FISHES, PRINCESS APOCALYPSA MAN-EATER?
...WHO KNOWS?
MAYBE I'LL FINALLY RELAX.

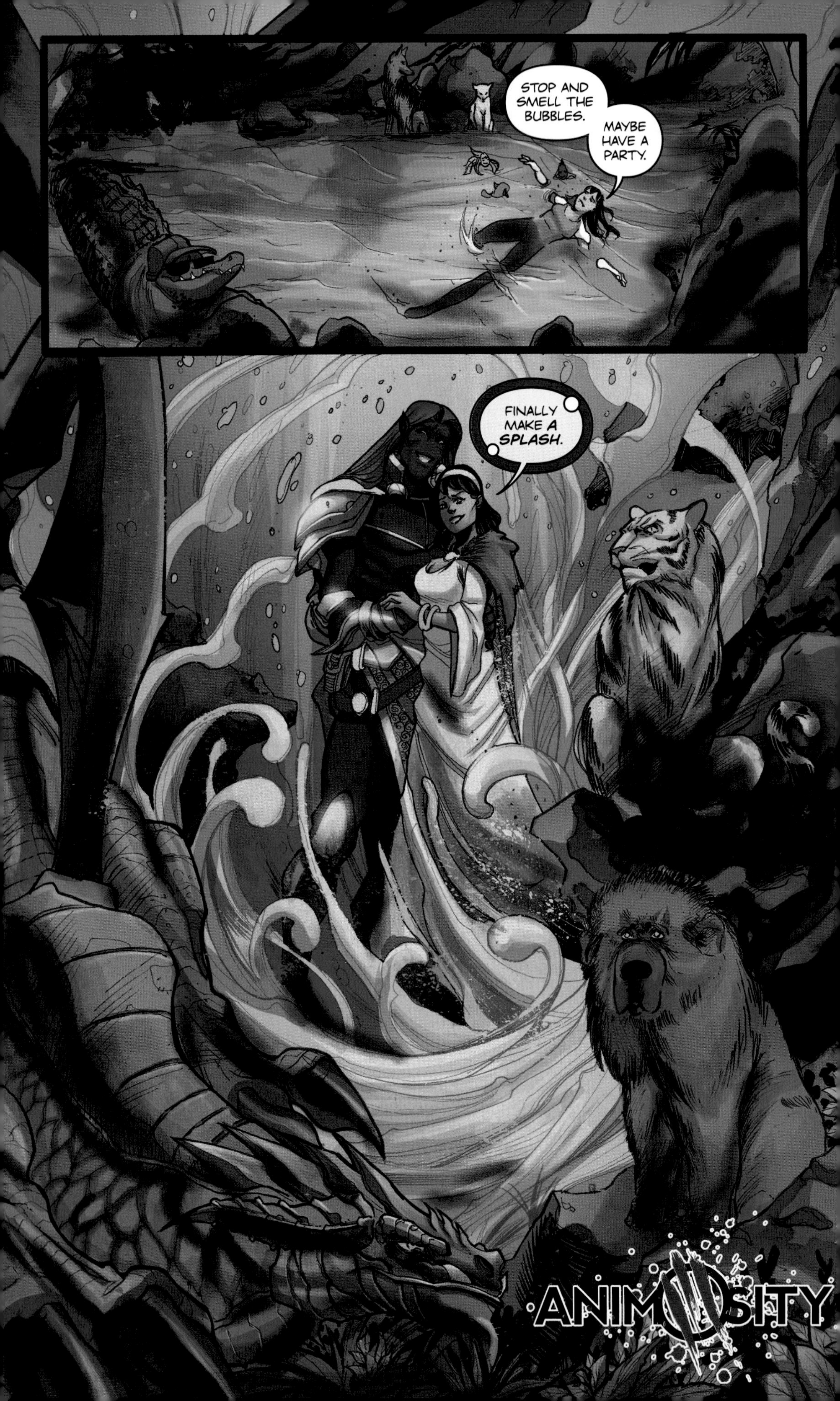
STOP AND SMELL THE BUBBLES.
MAYBE HAVE A PARTY.
FINALLY MAKE A SPLASH.
ANIMOSITY

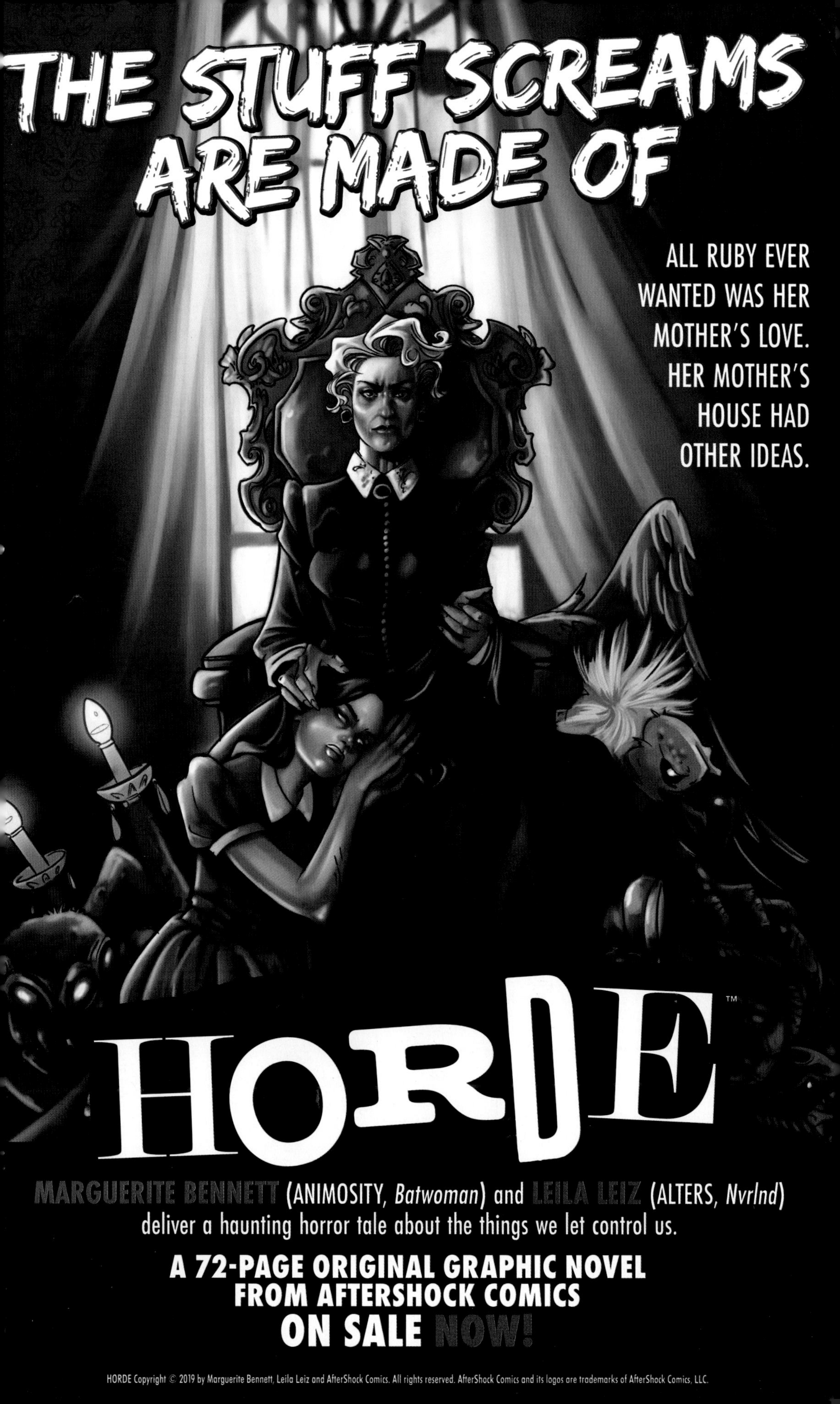
THE STUFF SCREAMS ARE MADE OF
ALL RUBY EVER WANTED WAS HER MOTHER'S LOVE. HER MOTHER'S HOUSE HAD OTHER IDEAS.
HORDE™
MARGUERITE BENNETT (ANIMOSITY, Batwoman) and LEILA LEIZ (ALTERS, Nvrlnd) deliver a haunting horror tale about the things we let control us.
A 72-PAGE ORIGINAL GRAPHIC NOVEL FROM AFTERSHOCK COMICS
ON SALE NOW!
HORDE Copyright © 2019 by Marguerite Bennett, Leila Leiz and AfterShock Comics. All rights reserved. AfterShock Comics and its logos are trademarks of AfterShock Comics, LLC.

THE PATH TO THE DOGHOUSE

VOLUME 1: THE WAKE

On the day of the Wake, the Animals did just that—they woke up.

MARGUERITE BENNETT · RAFAEL DE LATORRE
ANIMOSITY
THE WAKE

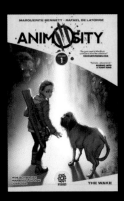

They started thinking. They started talking. They started taking revenge.

Cows rebelled in slaughterhouses, hens murdered their roosters—and a dog in New York City woke up to realize who he was, and that the girl in front of him, his protector, his child, his Jesse—was more important to him than the sun and the sky and all life that ever had been or will be. But something happened in that city. No one's saying what.

One year later: Jesse's parents are gone, and Sandor, her Bloodhound, is getting her out—getting her far, far, away, all the way to the distant coast. There, in San Francisco, a city seized by the Animals, is Jesse's estranged half-brother, Adam.

Because Sandor had a secret—Sandor is dying. Purebred dogs don't last long and he's had five good years—now, he's got a ticking clock and a daughter he wants to see grow up happy and true.

Liaising with an agent of the Animilitary—an armed force of Animals seeking to create a separate and protected society—Sandor arranged for safe transport out of New York City. In exchange, Sandor—who has a keen sense of smell—had to find one of the Animilitary's missing scouts. The trail uncovered a military coup within the Animilitary, which had been facing a food crisis in the struggle to provide for all the Animals.

The coup exploded with Sandor and Jesse inside the camp, but they managed to make it out—along with Animals that Jesse had befriended and a human named Kyle—before the entire fortress was overrun.

VOLUME 2: THE DRAGON

Sandor, Jesse, and their companions begin a cross-country road trip. Jesse is growing up, and signs of it frighten Sandor more than they frighten her. Sandor fears that he will be unable to protect Jesse from all pain, all terror, aware that he will not be there for her adulthood.

But in the forests of Maryland comes a creature like a great red dragon, vomiting fire, and carrying off some of their companions.

MARGUERITE BENNETT · RAFAEL DE LATORRE
ANIMOSITY
2
THE DRAGON

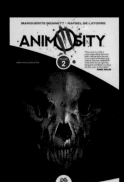

The Red Dragon rules a cult of men masquerading as beasts, and beasts masquerading as men.The beast-men attempt to lure Jesse away by pretending to be her parents, but Jesse discovered their true nature and fought back.

Jesse, Sandor, and their companions destroyed the Red Dragon and its cult, and reunited, and mourning for their dead, they moved on through the hills—followed by a shadow shaped like the ghost of Jesse's mother.

Sandor at last admits the truth—he knows that one day, he will have to leave her. And though Jesse knows what death is now, she will stay with him, and love him, because he is her dog—her good dog.

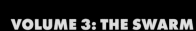

VOLUME 3: THE SWARM

Just across the West Virginia border, Jesse and her group encountered a dam that had become a gargantuan hive for a swarm of bees. The bees were being raided by human beings—terrified, the bees took some of Jesse's animal friends hostage and demanded the rest of her group find their stolen queen and return her.

The bees were taken to a commune where they were being forced to pollinated the orchard. Jesse and Kyle were discovered by the people of the commune, but instead of being met with hostility, they were welcomed.

The people of the commune showed how the humans and Animals lived in harmony, and invited Jesse and Kyle to stay with them. Kyle was tempted, but Jesse was repulsed by the use of the bees as slave labor, and suspicious of the lack of women in the commune. When asked, the people of the commune told said that the women went to the Walled City, a human-only enclave far to the south.

MARGUERITE BENNETT · RAFAEL DE LATORRE
ANIMOSITY
3
ROB SCHWAGER
MARSHALL DILLON
THE SWARM

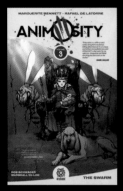

Kyle tried to persuade Jesse to stay at the farm, but Jesse could not bear staying there any longer, thinking of their animal friends being held hostage by the hive. When she attempted to free the bees from where they were held, though, Kyle, to his everlasting sorrow, told the other humans what she was doing.

Sandor and the Animals formulated a distraction, giving Jesse and Kyle the time to steal a tractor and escape with the swarm of bees and their queen. Though Kyle crashed the tractor, Jesse ran back with the queen to the hive, where the rest of the bees prepared for war.

The humans came to recapture the lost swarm. In the showdown, the queen was slain, and the bees detonated their own hive, unleashing the water from the far side of the dam and drowning the humans and Animals of the commune.

Jesse was rescued from the flood by Kyle—who quickly put a rag of ether over Jesse's mouth, knocking her unconscious. Kyle has resolved to her safe—he will take her to the Walled City.

Sandor rose from the muck after the flood, and found Jesse gone. Sandor howled in grief and rage, as Kyle carried Jesse through the first autumn snow into the dark woods.

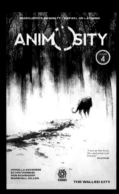

VOLUME 4: THE WALLED CITY

While Kyle was escaping with Jesse, he was discovered by one of their Animal friends who learned where Kyle was going and reported this back to Sandor, who quickly gave chase.

Jesse dreamed as Kyle drove south to the Walled City, and managed to leave Sandor a clumsy note as to her whereabouts and her faith in him. The increasingly desperate Kyle attempted to make a deal for his and Jesse's entrance into the Walled City. When questioned by the Headmistress, the leader of the city, Kyle was shot for his former ties to the Antimilitary. Jesse was dragged inside while Kyle, bleeding badly, stumbled back into the forest.

Jesse was told that she would be contributing to the return of human supremacy over the earth—by having as many children as possible. She discovered to her horror, that many other woman and girls were being held for the same reason.

Sandor and the others covered hundreds of miles in their pursuit of Jesse, as behind the walls of the city, Jesse struggled to retain her conscience and dignity in the face of monstrous abuse. She and the other imprisoned girls were forced to learn human supremacist rhetoric and take part in the killing of Animals, including the wild hogs that roamed the forest.

MARGUERITE BENNETT · RAFAEL DE LATORRE
ANIMOSITY
4
THE WALLED CITY

Meanwhile, Sandor found Kyle dying in the forest. Kyle told Sandor that everything he did was to keep Jesse safe. Kyle deliriously told Sandor what he knows to help rescue Jesse, and Sandor put an end to Kyle's suffering.

Inside the city, Jesse appealed to Maru, a toothless bear, to help her escape and woke the other girls from their beds. Sandor was coming to save them, she told them, and Maru led them down a secret tunnel—right to the office of the Headmistress.

The girls tried to fight their way free as the Animals began their assault on the Walled City. Jesse chased the Headmistress, and discovered a horrible room where the women who defied the humans were put to sleep to bear children. Jesse freed them. The women looked among one another, processing what had been done to them. Then they armed one another and stormed the city above.

In the battle, the Headmistress captured Sandor, threatening to shoot him if Jesse did not lay down arms. Jesse took aim at the Headmistress, but Sandor told her to stop. The women rose up behind Jesse, and Sandor told Jesse softly that the Headmistress was not hers to kill.

Jesse, Sandor, the Animals, and the women rode solemnly out of the Walled City, which burned behind them. It is no longer Sandor that they follow.

Now, they follow Jesse.

ABOUT THE CREATORS OF

ANIM🌑SITY

MARGUERITE BENNETT writer

🐦 @EvilMarguerite

Marguerite Bennett is a comic book writer from Richmond, Virginia, who currently splits her time between Los Angeles and New York City. She received her MFA in Creative Writing from Sarah Lawrence College in 2013 and quickly went on to work for DC Comics, Marvel, BOOM! Studios, Dynamite, and IDW on projects ranging from *Batman, Bombshells,* and *A-Force* to *Angela: Asgard's Assassin, Red Sonja,* and FOX TV's *Sleepy Hollow.*

RAFAEL DE LATORRE artist

🐦 @De_Latorre

Rafael De Latorre is a Brazilian artist who has worked in illustration and advertising since 2006. His first comic book was *Fade Out: Painless Suicide,* which was nominated to the HQMix award in Brazil. He also worked on *Lost Kids: Seeking Samarkand* and *321: Fast Comics.*

ELTON THOMASI artist

Elton Thomasi is an artist from Rio de Janeiro, Brazil. He started his artistic career in 2009, with the book, *Máquina Zero (Zero Machine).* From there, he's worked for other publishing houses, including Dark Horse *(The Sakai Project),* Titan Comics *(Doctor Who),* and doing sketch cards for Marvel and DC. Since then, he's worked in partnership with his friend and comic book creator Mike Desharnais on a comic book named *Marshal Strong,* which will debut in 2019 at New York Comic Con.

ROB SCHWAGER colorist

🐦 @robschwager

Rob Schwager is a self taught artist with over twenty-five years experience as a colorist in the comic book industry. He's worked on such iconic titles as *Batman, Superman, Green Lantern, Jonah Hex, Ghost Rider, Deadpool, Spider-Man, X-Men* and many others. He currently resides in the Tampa Bay area with his wife and three children and is extremely excited to be part of the AfterShock family of creators.

MARCO LESKO colorist

🐦 @Marco_Lesko

Marco has been a professional comic book colorist since 2014. Living in Brazil, Marco spent endless hours studying color theory from many different areas, including: cinema, conceptual art design, Japanese anime, video game design and classic Disney animation. His impressive credit list includes such titles as *The Shadow, Justice, Inc., Assassin's Creed: Uprising, Doctor Who* and *Robotech.* Now at AfterShock, Marco lends his coloring talents to BRILLIANT TRASH!

MARSHALL DILLON letterer

🐦 @MarshallDillon

A comic book industry veteran, Marshall got his start in 1994, in the midst of the indy comic boom. Over the years, he's been everything from an independent self-published writer to an associate publisher working on properties like *G.I.Joe, Voltron,* and *Street Fighter.* He's done just about everything except draw a comic book, and worked for just about every publisher except the "big two." Primarily a father and letterer these days, he also dabbles in old-school paper and dice RPG game design. You can catch up with Marshall at firstdraftpress.net.

TAYLOR ESPOSITO letterer

🐦 @TaylorEspo

Taylor is a comic book lettering professional and owner of Ghost Glyph Studios. As a staff letterer at DC, he lettered titles such as *Red Hood and The Outlaws, Constantine, Bodies, CMYK, The New 52: Future's End* and *New Suicide Squad.* He's also worked on creator-owned titles such as *Interceptor, The Paybacks* (Dark Horse) and *Jade Street Protection Services* (Black Mask). He is currently working on *The Sovereigns* and related books (Dynamite), *Heroine Chic, Dents, Mirror,* and *Firebrand* (Line Webtoon). Other publishers he has worked with include Image, Zenescope, BOOM! and Heavy Metal.